# SCHOOL SOCIAL WORK

# SCHOOL SOCIAL WORK

*National Perspectives on Practice in Schools*

*Edited by*

*Leticia Villarreal Sosa*

*Tory Cox*

AND

*Michelle Alvarez*

OXFORD
UNIVERSITY PRESS

# OXFORD

UNIVERSITY PRESS

Oxford University Press is a department of the University of Oxford. It furthers
the University's objective of excellence in research, scholarship, and education
by publishing worldwide. Oxford is a registered trade mark of Oxford University
Press in the UK and certain other countries.

Published in the United States of America by Oxford University Press
198 Madison Avenue, New York, NY 10016, United States of America.

Library of Congress Cataloging-in-Publication Data
Names: Villarreal, Leticia, editor.
Title: School social work : national perspectives on practice in schools
edited by Leticia Villarreal Sosa, Tory Cox, Michelle Alvarez.
Description: Oxford; New York: Oxford University Press, 2016. | Includes index.
Identifiers: LCCN 2016017239 | ISBN 9780190273842 (alk. paper)
Subjects: LCSH: School social work.
Classification: LCC LB3013.4 .S363 2016 | DDC 371.7—dc23
LC record available at https://lccn.loc.gov/2016017239

# CONTENTS

[†]Gary Lee Shaffer deceased on 04-09-2009.

# ABOUT THE EDITORS

**Michelle Alvarez, MSW, EdD,** is Associate Dean of Social Sciences at Southern New Hampshire University. She served as President of the School Social Work Association of America (SSWAA). She was a school social worker in Florida and supervised school social workers in Indiana. She is committed to the betterment of the field of school social work and has published books and articles on the topic.

**Tory Cox, MSW, LCSW,** Clinical Associate Professor, is Assistant Director of Field Education for the University of Southern California (USC) School of Social Work and the field coordinator for the Social Work & Business in a Global Society Concentration. Since 2010, he has been an academic advisor and field liaison for Foundation and Concentration Year MSW students and taught Integrative Seminar and Leadership courses. In these positions, he has helped train a new generation of social workers dedicated to the ethics and principles of professional social work. Previously, he was a school social worker for 13 years with the Long Beach Unified School District (LBUSD), serving as a field instructor for MSW student interns, among other duties. During this time, he helped train new school social workers as field faculty, adjunct lecturer, and field instructor for students at the USC School of Social Work, as well as at California State Long Beach, the University of California at Los Angeles, and California State Dominiguez Hills social work programs. As the Lead School Social Worker for LBUSD from 2006 to 2010, he helped lead a team dedicated to prevention and intervention across the district through federally funded grant programs, community collaborations, attendance initiatives, and site-based direct practice. His current work on nonprofit boards includes Standards & Practice Chair for the SSWAA; President of the California Association of School Social Workers; and Board Member/CEU Coordinator for End Abuse, Long Beach (EALB), a child abuse and domestic violence prevention council. He is the current Trends & Resources editor for the journal *Children & Schools* and is a contributing author to journals specializing in school-based social work. In 2013, he received the Abuse Prevention Award from EALB and commendations from local, state, and federal legislators for his work in training future social workers. In 2010, he received the "Social Worker of the Year" award from NASW-CA's Region I, Long Beach Unit, and "Most Inspirational Professor" for his work at the School of Social Work at California State University,

Long Beach. In his social work career, Mr. Cox has been a Licensed Clinical Social Worker specializing in private practice, Director of the Stevenson/YMCA Community School in Long Beach, and Foster Care Social Worker and Recreation Director for Ettie Lee Homes for Youth, a group home agency.

**Leticia Villarreal Sosa, AM, PhD, LCSW,** is Associate Professor at Dominican University's Graduate School of Social Work. She earned her PhD from The University of Chicago, SSA. Her research focuses on understanding issues of social identity among Latino youth and their educational experiences. Additional research interests include gender, migration, mental health, social identity, adolescent development, and violence. She has recently published articles on effective school teams and collaboration and the role of the school social worker in the state of Louisiana and also a chapter on Chicana feminisms and social work for a book titled *Globalization and Gender Oppression*. Her current research projects seek to explore social identity of Latino youth in suburban settings and suburban schools working toward equity and inclusion. Prior to her work at Dominican, she was a school social worker for 14 years in urban and suburban settings with multiple age groups and school settings.

# ABOUT THE CONTRIBUTORS

**Chris Ahlman, MSW, PhD,** Adjunct, Boise State University. After receiving her MSW from the University of Illinois at Chicago, in 1986, she began her school social work career at Rutland School District, contracting out to six school districts (nine schools). She became a member of the Illinois Association of School Social Workers and then SSWAA. In 1993, she earned her PhD in social work from the University of Illinois at Chicago. In 1996, she accepted a position at Aurora University, where she was the school social work coordinator until 2004, when she relocated to Lewis–Clark State College in Idaho. She is a founding member of the Idaho School Social Work Organization and remains active there, as well as being on the board of the National Association of Social Workers (NASW) Idaho. She has continued to publish and present on issues related to working with parents and students. Currently, she is working part time and teaching for Capella University.

**Sachiko Bamba, MSSW, PhD,** is Associate Professor at Tokyo Gakukgei University. She received her PhD from the University of Illinois, Urbana–Champaign, School of Social Work. She received her Master of Science in Social Administration from Case Western Reserve University and Master of Sociology from Kwansei Gakuin University. She received a research grant from the Japan Society of Promotion of Science (2013–2016) for the study titled "A Research Project Toward the Development of Standards for School Social Work Services in Japan." She is author of chapters in three school social work textbooks published in Japan. She is coauthor of *Child Welfare and Development: A Japanese Case Study* (Cambridge University Press, 2011). She has also published a number of articles in Japanese and English, including in *Children and Youth Services Review* and *Social Work*.

**Stefan Battle, MSW, EdD,** is Assistant Professor at Rhode Island College School of Social BSW Program. For 25 years as a social worker, he has worked with children and their families in various organizations (community-based, public health, and city government). He has held the position of School Social Worker/Guidance Counselor in various school districts, both urban and suburban. Working with children and their families, he focused his practice on children and families of color, specifically Black families. His research interest involves examining the social and racial construct of White teachers and their teacher-student relationship with Black boys in the classroom. He has presented on this topic at national conferences.

**Andrew Brake**, MSW, PhD, is Assistant Professor in the Department of Social Work at Northeastern Illinois University. He received his doctorate from the University of Chicago, School of Social Service Administration, where he worked as a research assistant and lecturer in the school social work program of study. His research broadly examines social and academic supports in urban, public high schools, with a particular interest on the role of trust and trust-building in teacher and social work practice. His dissertation examined the development and impact of ninth grade teacher–student relationships in one neighborhood public high school in Chicago. Combining his research and practice experiences in youth development, school social work, and teacher and social worker training, his scholarship highlights the potential of social workers to lead in the alignment of academic, social–emotional, and culturally responsive practices in urban public high schools.

**Janet B. Cherry**, MSW, LCSW, has extensive experience working with exceptional children in various day-treatment, partial hospitalization, and therapeutic programs. She is approved as an Instructor for Youth Mental Health First Aid USA, Non-Violent Crisis Prevention Intervention and System of Care: Child and Family Team in North Carolina. She has a keen interest in promoting mental health wellness and awareness, program development and implementation.

**Nic T. Dibble**, MSW, LSSW, CISC, is State Consultant for School Social Work for the Wisconsin Department of Public Instruction. His areas of responsibility include mental health, Positive Behavioral Interventions and Supports (PBIS), student records, child welfare and maltreatment, homebound instruction, school discipline, attendance and truancy, and teen parents. His work involves technical assistance, resource and professional development, and interagency collaboration. He worked 12 years as a school social worker before joining the Department of Public Instruction and also served as the Program Manager for the Families and Schools Together (FAST) program in Madison, Wisconsin. Other experiences include serving as president of his local school board and chair of the Wisconsin Children's Trust Fund Board.

**Randy A. Fisher**, MSW, LCSW, received his M.S.W. in 1973 from the University of Illinois at Chicago and began a 31 year career as a school social worker for Mannheim School District 83, in west suburban Chicago. He was active in the Illinois Association of School Social Workers and the Midwest Council of School Social Work. In 1994 he became the interim chair of the School Social Work Association of America (SSWAA). He then became the first President and later the first Executive Director of SSWAA. He retired in 2012 from the School of Social Work at Aurora University after 8 years. He was a frequent speaker on across the United States and in Japan, Korea, Singapore and Sweden. He authored a number of articles with a special interest in the history and the organization development of the state, regional and national school social work associations.

**Cynthia Franklin**, MSSW, PhD, LCSW, LMFT, is the Stiernberg/Spencer Family Professor in Mental Health and Associate Dean for Doctoral Education in the School of Social Work at the University of Texas at Austin. She also holds a faculty fellow appointment at the Meadows Center for Preventing Educational Risk in the Department of Special Education. During the past 25 years, she has worked as a therapist, consultant, trainer, and researcher for schools and mental health agencies. She is a clinical fellow of the American Association of Marriage and

Family Therapy. Her research includes a meta-analysis of randomized controlled trial studies on school mental health services; efficacy and effectiveness studies on solution-focused brief therapy (SFBT), and studies and systematic reviews of SFBT for the purposes of developing SFBT into an empirically supported treatment. Studies and systematic reviews have resulted in SFBT being recognized by federal agencies such as the Substance Abuse and Mental Health Services Administration's National Registry for Evidence-Based Programs and Practices (2013). Taking Charge, an intervention that she helped develop for Latina adolescents, was also recognized as a promising practice by the Office of Juvenile Justice and Delinquency Prevention and was added to the Crime Solutions model programs guide (2013). She has more than 150 publications in the professional literature and is a world-renowned scholar in school mental health. Her research examines the practice and effectiveness of solution-focused brief therapy with children and adolescents. She is Editor-in-Chief of the *Encyclopedia of Social Work* and is author of several books, including *The School Services Sourcebook: A Guide for School-Based Professionals* (Oxford University Press, 2012) and *Solution-Focused Brief Therapy: A Handbook of Evidence-Based Practice* (Oxford University Press, 2011).

**Andy J. Frey, MSW, PhD,** is Professor at the Kent School of Social Work at the Kent School of Social Work at the University of Louisville. He earned his MSW from the University of Michigan in 1994 and his PhD from the University of Denver in 2000. He was a school social worker and behavioral consultant in Douglas County Schools, Colorado, from 1995–2000. His research focuses on the development and evaluation of interventions for children with challenging behavior, as well as the mental health and social work service delivery systems that adopt and implement these interventions.

**Mary Beth Harris, MSW, PhD,** a licensed clinical social worker, teaches in the Families and Children concentration, as well as in the foundation year practice sequence. For more than 20 years, she was a clinical social worker with families and children in the border region of Mexico and West Texas. As a clinical administrator and family therapist, she worked with child sexual abuse and domestic violence victims, and she served as an assessment trainer in the family court systems of West Texas, New Mexico, and Oklahoma. Recently, she developed a school-based group intervention for adolescent mothers designed to support high school graduation and economic self-sufficiency. She has conducted several effectiveness studies of the program and coauthored the book, *Taking Charge: A School-Based Life Skills Program for Adolescent Mothers* (Oxford University Press, 2007), which includes the treatment manual for the program. Harris is also coeditor with Cynthia Franklin and Paula Allen-Meares of *School Services Sourcebook* (Oxford University Press, 2012), a comprehensive resource for school social workers and mental health practitioners.

**Laura Hopson, MSW, PhD,** is Associate Professor at the University of Alabama School of Social Work. Her research focuses on risk and protective factors associated with academic outcomes and behavior during adolescence. She also assists schools in assessing school climate and understanding its impact on students.

**Gunay Ismayilova, MSW,** is Head of Child, Family, and Youth Department of Azerbaijan Social Workers Public Union, Azerbaijan. She earned her first degree from Azerbaijan University of Languages in European Studies faculty in 2005. In 2012, she earned her master's degree from Columbia University School of Social Work in the concentration of Advanced Clinical Practice with special focus on children, youth, and families. At the same time, she obtained her minor in International Social Welfare. She works for the nonprofit agency United Aid for Azerbaijan, which is focused on child welfare and protection of children with disabilities and their families, as a project coordinator. Currently, she also works part-time for Save the Children Azerbaijan Country Office as a program coordinator in the Special Economic Action for the Blind program. In addition, she works part-time for Hilfswerk Austria International as Social Work Expert in the development of alternative services, such as small group homes and family counseling and training centers for children at risk and their families. She is a member of the board of directors of Azerbaijan Social Work Public Union, which is represented by the International Federation of Social Workers. She is an organizational development specialist at Chemonics, Inc., on the project "Building Local Capacity for Development." At Azerbaijan University (a private school), she taught courses titled "Social Work with Refugees and IDPs" and "Social Work with Children and Adolescents" during the 2012–2013 academic year.

**Kimberly Israel, MSW, MPH, LCSW,** is the Coordinator of Community Outreach for the Escondido Union School District in Escondido, California. In her current role, she is responsible for overseeing the operations of 23 family engagement centers staffed with family liaisons and providing linkage between the school district and community and governmental agencies in Escondido. She formally served as the Project Director of the CARE Youth Project, a multimillion dollar grant program that launched the develop of a multi-tiered system of support for students and families at all 23 EUSD school sites. She began her career as a middle school and high school teacher before receiving her Master's in Social Work and Public Health from the University of Michigan, and, in 2003, obtaining her License in Clinical Social Work. In her 16 year tenure with the Escondido Union School District, she has expanded the School Social Work Program from 1 full-time school social worker to 26 full-time school social workers and fifteen school social work interns, established a districtwide family engagement program, and she has been the district lead in the development of grant programs bringing in more than $6.5 million in student support services to district students, staff, and families. In addition to her role to expand school social work services in Escondido, she has led advocacy efforts on a countrywide and statewide level to increase social workers in California schools. This advocacy led to the development of school social work programs in multiple San Diego County school districts.

**Annette Johnson, MSW,** is a Clinical Associate Professor at the University of Illinois at Chicago, Jane Addams College of Social Work. Before joining the faculty at UIC, she was director of Social Work at the Chicago Public Schools, where she provided leadership for the one of the largest school social work departments in the country with a staff of over 400 master's level school social workers. She served on the Illinois Children Mental Health Partnership; as co-chair of the School Policy and Standards Committee, she was responsible for the development of the Illinois Social and Emotional Learning Standards which now serves as a model for other states. She has been recognized as School Social Worker of the Year by the Illinois Association of School Social Workers and the Midwest School Social Work Council. Her research interests are social and emotional learning and critical service learning. She has a keen interest in developing school-based clinical practices that focus on strengths and assets. She has trained and consulted school social workers and school districts extensively on social and emotional learning and other innovative approaches.

**Rebecca Kunkel, MSSW,** is School Social Worker and Adjunct Instructor at the University of Texas at Austin. She has a Master's in Social Work from the University of Texas at Austin and a bachelor's degree in psychology from Baylor University in Waco, Texas. She has more than 20 years of experience providing social work services in the school setting and is adjunct faculty at the University of Texas at Austin. In addition, she is a past board member of the SSWAA and is currently Associate Executive Director of SSWAA. She has particular interest in provision of services and program planning for at-risk youth; developing strong social, emotional, and behavioral supports for students; PBIS; social–emotional learning; service learning; peer mediation; tolerance education; student leadership development; and enhancing parental involvement in schools.

**Brenda Lindsey, MSW, EdD, LCSW,** is Clinical Associate Professor at the University of Illinois at Urbana–Champaign. Her educational background includes an EdD in Education Organization Leadership from the University of Illinois at Urbana–Champaign in 2005; an MSW from the University of Illinois at Urbana–Champaign School of Social Work in 1994; an MA in psychology from the University of Northern Colorado in 1984; and a BSW from Southern Illinois University–Carbondale in 1980. She is a former school social worker and also has professional experience in providing children's mental health services. She has an LCSW, a Type 73 School Social Work certificate, and a Type 75 Administrative certificate in Illinois. She is active in several professional social work organizations, including the National Association of Social Workers–Illinois Chapter, the Illinois Association of School Social Workers, and the SSWAA.

**Anne McInerney, LICSW,** has been a school social worker in St. Paul Public Schools for 18 years. For 9 years, she was the team lead of a Federal Setting IV Therapeutic School, and for 3 years she was the supervisor for the Homeless Education program under Title I. She has presented at numerous local and national conferences, held leadership positions within the Minnesota School Social Workers Association, and is President of the SSWAA.

**Cassandra McKay-Jackson, MSSW, PhD,** is Associate Professor at the University of Illinois at Chicago, Jane Addams College of Social Work. She received her BA from the University of Iowa, her MSSW from the University of Wisconsin–Madison, and her PhD in curriculum and education from the University of Illinois at Chicago. She has over 10 years of experience providing therapeutic services to youth and families in outpatient and school settings and supervising staff of mental health professionals and managing a statewide training department for child welfare agencies. Her research interests include the social construction of race, critical service learning, and youth activism. She is the principal investigator for three current studies.

**Y. Kafi Moragne-Patterson, MSW, PhD,** is Assistant Professor at the Graduate School of Social Work, Dominican University. She received her MSW from the University of Illinois, Urbana-Champaign, School of Social Work, and her PhD from the University of Chicago, School of Social Service Administration. Her research encompasses broad interdisciplinary issues animating studies of urban education, racial and economic stratification, adolescent identity formation, and educational interventions in marginalized communities. She is specifically interested in the college-going processes of high-performing African American students, with particular attention to students who make less than optimal post-secondary institutional selections. Her work takes into account the institutional mechanisms and processes that contribute to divergent high school experiences, college choices, and educational trajectories among minority students. As a qualitative researcher, she has interests in using narrative-based approaches to examine the interplay of race and constrained social capital in the lives of students in the urban setting. Her work has been supported by grants from the Fahs–Beck Doctoral Dissertation Fund, UChicago Consortium on Chicago School Research, and the Hymen Milgrom Support Group: Successful Pathways from School to Work Grant.

**Mimi Mumm, MSW, PhD, LICSW**, is Professor of Social Work at the Rhode Island School of Social Work and a social worker who specializes in working with children. Mimi has taught at Rutgers University and the University of Maine at Presque Isle. She was a school social worker at Aroostook Academy, a school that specializes in working children with behavioral and emotional disorders. She has also authored numerous professional articles presented at national conferences. Her current research and evaluation efforts center on college persistence for students who have many barriers to academic success.

**Julie O'Donnell, MSW, PhD**, has been Director of Research for the Child Welfare Training Centre in the Department of Social Work at California State University, Long Beach (CSULB), since 1992. She has continually partnered with community agencies to improve children, family, and community well-being, particularly in the downtown Long Beach community. She has written more than $25 million in grants to fund juvenile delinquency prevention, community development, after-school, family involvement, and community school programs. She is a board member for the California Association of School Social Workers and, as chair of the Los Angeles region, led the planning committee that launched the first school social work conference in California. In addition, she has served CSULB's Department of Social Work as the chair of the Personnel Committee, chair and co-chair of the Research Sequence, chair of Strategic Planning, and as a member of the Curriculum and RTP Committees. She currently teaches school social work, thesis, and community projects. She has been the principal investigator on multiple grants that have been funded by organizations such as the W. K. Kellogg Foundation, De-Witt Wallace Reader's Digest Foundation, California Department of Child Abuse Prevention, James Irvine Foundation, California Community Foundation, the Marguerite Casey Foundation, and the Stuart Foundation. She also consults on and evaluates numerous projects that emphasize education and community development in low-income, culturally diverse communities in the Long Beach area.

**Kateri Picard Ray, MSW, PhD, LCSW**, is Core Faculty at Capella University in the master's of social work program. She has a bachelor's degree in social work from Middle Tennessee State University and a master's degree in social work from Florida State University. She recently obtained her PhD in Education from the University of Idaho. She worked as a school social worker before developing her expertise in children's mental health. She worked in children's mental health in various capacities for 13 years before focusing on academia. She is a board member of the National Association of Social Workers, Idaho and the Idaho Federation of Families for Children's Mental Health.

**Jane Piester, MSW, MEd**, is Guidance Counselor at Rock Bridge High School in Columbia, Missouri. She completed her Master's in Social Work at the University of Missouri, Columbia. She also completed her MEd in Guidance and Counseling at Stephens College. She has been a guidance counselor at Rock Bridge High School for 15 years, where she provides support and direction for students in grades 9–12. In addition, she is a field instructor at the University of Missouri and Stephens College. She previously worked as an elementary school social worker and crisis counselor, and she currently maintains a small private practice in Columbia, Missouri.

**Joelle D. Powers, MSW, PhD,** is MSW Program Coordinator, Associate Professor, Boise State University School of Social Work. A former school social worker, she earned her PhD at the University of North Carolina, Chapel Hill, School of Social Work and then worked as the director of student services in the Durham Public Schools. She then became a professor and Associate Dean of Academic Affairs at her alma mater. In 2012, she joined the faculty at the School of Social Work at Boise State University, where she oversees the graduate program. She maintains active memberships in the American Educational Research Association, the Council on Social Work Education, the National Association of School Psychologists, the NASW, the SSWAA, and the Society for Social Work and Research. As a professor, her professional interests remain social work in schools, risk assessment, data-driven school interventions, child and adolescent mental health, and evidence-based practice.

**James C. Raines, MSSW, PhD, LCSW,** is Department Chair of Health, Human Services and Public Policy at California State University, Monterey Bay. He has been a school social worker, managing editor of the *School Social Work Journal*, and president of the Illinois Association of School Social Workers and the Midwest Council of School Social Workers. He has written more than 20 journal articles, numerous book chapters, and three books published by Oxford University Press. He also serves as chair of the College of Professional Studies Curriculum Committee and participates in the Faculty Affairs, Senate Curriculum Council, and Post-Graduate Studies committees.

**Laura Richard, MSW, PhD, LCSW,** is Assistant Professor in the School of Social Work at the University of Southern Mississippi and is a Licensed Clinical Social Worker in Louisiana and Mississippi. She received her MSW from Louisiana State University and has school social work practice experience in Louisiana public schools. She has published her research in peer-reviewed journals such as *Children & Schools*. She is a member of the American Council for School Social Work, the SSWAA, and the Mississippi chapter of the NASW. Her primary areas of research are school social work, school mental health, school mental health policy, and data-driven decision-making.

**Benjamin Roth, MSW, PhD,** is Assistant Professor at the University of South Carolina College of Social Work. He received his PhD in Social Welfare Policy from the University of Chicago. His research focuses on processes of immigrant integration, with particular attention to how local context influences opportunities for social mobility. Current projects include survey research assessing immigrant access to social service organizations in South Carolina and two studies exploring the intersection of youth development and legal status.

**Christine Anlauf Sabatino, MSW, PhD, LICSW, C-SSWS,** is Professor of Social Work, Catholic University of America, and Director of the Center for the Advancement of Children, Youth, and Families. She is a certified school social work specialist (NASW) and a licensed independent clinical social worker in Washington, DC. Her professional experience has been in public and private school systems as a direct practitioner, program director, clinical supervisor, and consultant. Her research interests are school mental health, school consultation, and school social work practice. She has served on several national school social work task forces for the National Association of Social Workers and the School Social Work Association of America. She serves as an editor for *Children & Schools and the Journal of Child and Adolescent Social Work*.

**Mary Sheehan, MSW, LCSW,** is a School Social Worker for the Newport Public Schools in Newport, Rhode Island. She is a licensed clinical social worker and received her MSW from Rhode Island College. Prior to her position as a school social worker she was the Coordinator for an Even Start in Newport, a family literacy program. In addition, her previous work has included, home visiting/community-based work with pregnant and parenting teens, work on adult inpatient psychiatric units and a community mental health center.

**Gary Lee Shaffer, PhD,** associate professor, was a leading experts on social work practice in North Carolina and a staunch advocate for children; particularly advocating against the use of corporal punishment within North Carolina's public schools. He died in 2009 at the age of 62. Shaffer earned his MA from the School of Social Service Administration at the University of Chicago and his PhD from the School of Social Work at the University of Illinois at Urbana-Champaign. Shaffer joined UNC-Chapel Hill's School of Social Work in 1986 as director of the field education program. Shaffer served as a member of the N.C. Professional School Social Work Standards Committee, and also supervised more than 300 MSW students within North Carolina school districts. He was responsible for licensing school social work practitioners through the N.C. Department of Public Instruction. Shaffer demonstrated equally passionate support for an anti-school bullying bill, which North Carolina legislators narrowly adopted in 2008. The act protects students from harassment for numerous reasons, including on the basis of race, religion or disabilities. Some state lawmakers and opponents' groups criticized the law for including language that specifically protects students for actual or perceived sexual orientation. In 2007, Shaffer was named "Social Work Advocate of the Year" by the North Carolina chapter of the National Association of Social Workers.

**Kari Smith, MA, MSW,** is currently a doctoral student at the University of Illinois at Chicago. She has her MA in Teaching, Social Leadership, and she has her MSW from the School of Social Work, University of Illinois at Urbana–Champaign. She received her BA in social work from Arizona State University. She is also President-Elect for the Illinois Association of School Social Workers.

**Susan Stone, AM, PhD,** is an Associate Professor and Catherine Mary and Eileen Clare Hutto Chair for Social Services in Public Education at the School of Social Welfare at the University of California at Berkeley. She is widely published in academic journals. Her publication, *School Social Work: An Evidence-Informed Framework for Practice* (with M. Kelly, J. Raines, and A. Frey; Oxford University Press, 2010), offers school social work students and practitioners a new framework for choosing interventions based on a synthesis of evidence-based practice and recent conceptual frameworks of school social work clinical practice offered by leading scholars and policymakers. An expert on social work in education and its impact on the academic progress of vulnerable youth in schools, her research interests include understanding family and school influences on child and adolescent school performance and dynamics of school-based psycho-social service delivery.

**Frederick Streeck, MSW,** is Executive Director of SSWAA. After receiving his MSW from Washington University in St. Louis, Missouri, in 1973, he worked in community mental health day treatment programs for 6 years as a school social worker in Washington State for 18 years, and as Executive Director of Student Support Services in a Washington State school district for 10 years. In 2008, he began consultation work and university teaching part-time. He has been Executive Director of SSWAA since 2009. He was treasurer of SSWAA at its inception in 1994 and served 8 years in that role. Before 1994, he was president and treasurer of the Washington Association of School Social Workers and was president and a founder of the Western Alliance of School Social Work Organizations.

**Danielle C. Swick, MSW, PhD,** is Assistant Professor at the University of North Carolina at Greensboro. Her areas of interest and expertise include evidence-based practice, school-based interventions, child and adolescent mental health, community-engaged research, and quantitative analysis. Her current research focuses on the impact of school-based mental health services on children's academic and socioemotional outcomes. She has taught such courses that include "Research Designs and Data Analysis for Social Work Practice" and "School Social Work."

**Kevin Tan, MSW, PhD,** is Assistant Professor at the University of Illinois at Urbana-Champaign. He is from Singapore, where he worked as a school social worker for 4 years before pursuing his MSW at the Brown School of Social Work, Washington University in St. Louis. Subsequently, he worked in a suburban school district in St. Louis, Missouri for two years. He received his doctorate from the University of Chicago, School of Social Service Administration. He is an active member of the SSWAA. His primary research interest is on understanding patterns of youth behavioral risk development with attention to social-contextual influences such as those involving the school environment and related interventions.

**Mei Ling Tan-Wu, MS,** is a school social worker, Chair of the School Social Work Chapter and Executive Director, Students Care Service of the Singapore Association of Social Workers. A social worker since her graduation from the Social Work Department, National University of Singapore, she, along with her colleagues, has spearheaded multiple initiatives in school social work in Singapore. These include the Whole School and Community Based School Social Work Approaches. She has also worked with school social work practitioners in the sector to draw up the Core Competencies for the Practice of School Social Work in Singapore. Beyond dedicated service to clients, she is passionate about the social work profession and contributes actively through professional sharing, training, supervisions, and publications. She is currently Executive Director of Students Care Service (a nonprofit organization serving children and youth in Singapore) and a co-chair of the International Committee on School Social Work Collaborations. A Registered Social Worker in Singapore, she received her Master of Social Sciences (Social Work) from the National University of Singapore, with a term completed at the Washington University in St. Louis, Missouri.

**Martell Teasley, MSW, PhD,** is Professor and Chair of the Department of Social Work in the College of Public Policy at the University of Texas at San Antonio. He is the former chair of the Social Work and Disaster Recovery Program at Florida State University College of Social Work. He served in the US Army for 10 years and participated in the first Persian Gulf War as a Licensed Practical Nurse. He is nationally known for his work and research with school-aged children and youth. He received the 2011 Gary Lee Shaffer Award for Academic Contributions to the Field of School Social Work from the SSWAA. He is the editor and coauthor of two books, including *Nation of Cowards: Black Activism in Barack Obama's Post-Racial America* (with David Ikard). He has served on the editorial board of several major social work journals and currently serves on the editorial board of the journal *Children & Schools*. As a Howard University graduate, his primary research interest includes African American adolescent development, cultural diversity, social welfare policy, and Black studies.

**Aaron M. Thompson, MEd, MSW, PhD,** is Associate Professor at the University of Missouri (MU), School of Social Work. Aaron was a former school social worker and principal before he completed his PhD at the University of North Carolina at Chapel Hill. His research interests include the origins of mental and behavioral health issues among youth, training for school-based mental health service providers, and the development and evaluation of early prevention and intervention efforts to improve school readiness and reduce disruptive and aggressive behaviors for high-risk children. Aaron is the developer of the Self-monitoring Training And Regulation Strategy (STARS) and the Self-Management Training and Regulation Strategy (SMART)—both self-management training programs for elementary and secondary school students. Presently, Aaron oversees a second randomized control study of STARS, acts as a scientific advisor to both the Boone County Schools Mental Health Coalition as well as the Family Access Center of Excellence, and he is the Associate Director of Research of the Missouri Prevention Center.

# SCHOOL SOCIAL WORK

# INTRODUCTION

## LETICIA VILLARREAL SOSA, TORY COX, AND MICHELLE ALVAREZ

> If we understand the historical complexity of our profession, then putting our profession into
> action requires that we situate ourselves and our professional development in that complexity.
> Miguel Meza, school social worker, Argentina

A s we wrote the introduction to this book, I (Leticia) was in four different Latin American countries. I spent 2 weeks working with school social workers in Rosario, Argentina, with Miguel Meza, whom I just quoted. Part of my work in Argentina was to provide professional development to school social workers. During one of the workshops that Miguel Meza presented, he made the statement I quoted previously. I quickly wrote it down and decided that it had to be the introduction to this book because this quote reflects our goals for this text and also reflects contributions that can be made to the profession when we see our work through a different lens. Throughout my travels in Latin America, I have had the opportunity to explore social work through the Latin American lens, which can offer a great deal to the challenges we face in the United States.

The profession of school social work in the United States has evolved significantly in the past two decades, with school social workers assuming new roles and visions for the future. This book is an update to a previous edition of *School Social Work: From Theory to Practice*. In this updated edition, we provide a contemporary understanding of school social work practice given numerous changes in practice and policy that have altered the landscape of specialized support services, including school social work services. Due to policy and context changes such as increased privatization, an emphasis on the Common Core, increasing concern about issues of equity and inclusion, and an increasing emphasis on data-based decision-making, the role of school social workers has been and is evolving. Along with these changes, the profession has responded with proactive steps to develop a national model of practice that considers and responds to this changing context. This book is aligned with the newly developed national practice model developed by School Social Work Association of America (SSWAA). Each chapter was designed to align with every aspect of the SSWAA model.

In this book, we hope to give readers special insights into the roles, responsibilities, ethical principles, legal expectations, political landscape, and future of the school social work profession. As primarily employees of educational entities, school social workers face a complex working environment in which educational outcomes are of primary importance, not social services. Within this environment, we have to understand that different motivations regarding the welfare of students exist. In a nuanced approach to his or her work, the skilled school social worker recognizes the political environment of school settings and utilizes his or her relationship- and rapport-building skill set to bridge differences and create coalitions mobilized to support students and families. Of particular interest for school social workers are those marginalized populations that have traditionally faced substandard academic institutions, dilapidated facilities, and inexperienced teachers, all contributing to poor educational outcomes. These marginalized populations can be seen through the lens of the common usage of the phrase "achievement gap" in which Whites and many Asian subgroups have higher standardized test scores than students of different ethnicities or racial groups. This term has become a part of the educational lexicon to the degree that its binary, categorical, and segregationist implications have entered mainstream dialogue and become a paradigm for viewing student potential, remediation, career versus college likelihood, and lowered expectations.

School social workers need to be armed with tools of interpretation and advocacy to combat these paradigms at each tier of the multi-tiered systems of support, with particular focus on students immersed in generational poverty. School social workers carry the responsibility to advocate for different educational futures for children and families in Individual Education Program or Student Success Team meetings; universal prevention activities or targeted interventions; and inclusion, push-in, or pull-out services. Going along with the prevalent school administrator's opinion about a student and his or her family is an insufficient course of action to initiate change. We carry the beacon of belief for students, often being the only person in a room of professionals who can see through the disruptive and defiant behavior and envision the future success for a struggling student. Our strength-based perspective allows us to be merchants of hope for populations trained to believe that bright futures are for the "other kids." We employ systems theory and an ecological perspective in understanding and validating the family stressors that impact educational outcomes while working to build bridges of understanding between school personnel and children, youth, and families who experience cultural dissonance with educational systems. Because we can specialize in direct clinical practice or macro-level program development, grant writing, and school leadership, we have the skill set to change perceptions and expectations that other school professionals may have for students. We may be the last advocate on behalf of a foster youth about to be sent to a continuation school because of credit deficiency; a youth experiencing homelessness who is told he does not belong; or a pregnant teen ostracized by her friends, family, and community. We cannot carry these responsibilities lightly.

Utilizing case studies throughout the book, connections between theory and practice are made, representing school social work throughout the United States in a variety of settings. This book also features, wherever possible, school social work practitioners collaborating with school social work researchers and academics, providing a clear connection between theory and practice as well as modeling the possibilities of academic and practitioner partnerships.

We view this text as a process of entering into dialogue with the evolving changes and perspectives. This dialogue includes a critical understanding of the policy context and neoliberal reforms as presented in Chapter 5 by Stone and Moragne-Patterson. This would also include an emphasis on intersectionality as the approach to issues of diversity, which pushes us to consider the complexity of the lives and various intersecting social identities of our students and of our own social identities.

As a response to efforts to promote equity and appropriately support the needs of an increasingly diverse student body, this book considers issues of diversity from an intersectionality perspective. Understanding students and their lived experience from this intersectional perspective addresses the need for increasing cultural competence among school social workers. Considering issues of social diversity from an intersectional perspective provides the framework for the incorporation of the experiences of marginalized groups as a core feature of the book throughout each chapter rather than an "add on" chapter featuring one or two groups. In this way, we are not considering a particular cultural or ethnic group but, rather, the multiple identities and intersecting systems of oppression that are present in students' lives. This perspective goes beyond race, class, and gender to include, for example, migration, documentation status, language, sexuality, and ability.

An intersectionality perspective is grounded in the work of women of color who insisted that race, class, and gender are interlocking oppressions that are all simultaneously experienced (Mehrotra, 2010). This approach will allow the practitioner to account for the unique experience of students based on migration experience, sexuality, race, ethnicity, and gender, among others. In addition, an intersectionality perspective allows social workers to consider not only individual identity formation as we have been trained to do (i.e., Erikson, Piaget, Phinney, etc.) but also to move to a place where we understand that our students come to us with fluid and hybrid social identities based on the various communities to which they belong. School social workers should understand their students not just from a perspective of who they are as individuals but also from a perspective of who they are as members of a social group, often a social group stigmatized by society, and how that impacts their experience in an educational institution in which stigmatized social identities become salient. For example, a Mexican American student who comes into the school building is not only an individual but also a member of a social group that has had to struggle for educational access and has been viewed within the school system as intellectually inferior. The way in which this student understands his or her own experiences within the school context will be shaped by this knowledge of being a part of this social group that has been historically oppressed.

Additional key elements to an intersectionality approach include placing the lived experiences of marginalized groups at the center of our theorizing, understanding and acknowledging within-group diversity, avoiding the essentializing of social groups, and promoting social justice and social change through acknowledging not just social diversity but also interlocking forms of oppression (Dill-Thornton & Zambrana, 2009). Finally, an intersectional perspective also challenges the practitioner to consider her own social position and understand her own privileged or oppressed identities and how this shapes her own perspectives and work as well as how she is viewed by others. We hope that this approach will provide school social workers with the tools to better understand the lived experiences of their students, help students to navigate these complex social identities, understand how their own social positions shape the work, and advocate for students on a systemic level helping to create schools that value students' various social identities. In doing so, we will further our role as school social workers in promoting educational rights and advocacy, a core feature of the new school social work model developed by SSWAA.

As noted previously, the US educational system has experienced major changes in recent years. With the advent of the Common Core State Standards (CCSS), national standards have been adopted by 90% of the US states, territories, military schools, and the District of Columbia. Although criticism of the CCSS is prevalent, this change in educational policy presents school social workers with the opportunity to further align their work with educational standards. We have the opportunity to establish a new level of collaboration with teachers and administrators tasked with implementing new ways to teaching an increasingly diverse and technologically savvy student population. We encourage school social workers to better understand how their work can link with the expectations of CCSS or their state's standards. We believe that this policy change opens up a doorway of collaboration between school social workers and teachers not seen before, specifically regarding the teaching of standards in which school social workers have specialized skill. Some of these areas include the speaking and listening standards and the national social–emotional learning standards set by SSWAA for school social workers. As we synchronize our work with standards and engage in dialogue with teachers and administrators using their terminology, we become even stronger parts of the safety net of multi-tiered systems of support that children, youth, and families need to succeed.

We have often watched from a distance as principals, vice principals, counselors, and other school-based personnel meted out discipline to students. Some of us may have been asked to take on the disciplinarian role at our schools and can appreciate the challenges of providing therapeutic interventions while balancing the role of enforcement. These types of juxtaposed responsibilities are germane to educational systems and highlight some of the complexities of working in that system. Because studies have confirmed the inequitable distribution and severity of discipline toward non-White children and youth with a particular detrimental target of African American males, school social workers need to intervene when these practices are being carried out in school(s).

The cradle-to-prison pipeline includes a substantial amount of time in schools, particularly in early years when patterns become established and parent–school relationships become entrenched. Disciplinary practices have been used as a means to systemically disenfranchise children and youth as sanctioned by school boards, legislators, and society at large. Whether it is overrepresentation in emotionally disturbed special education classes or inappropriate use of home-based suspensions, these accepted practices of systemic segregation are now being called out and named as inequitable practices. School social workers need to step into this new reality around disciplinary practices and lead in-services on how to appropriately address behavioral issues. We need to harness the elements of trauma-informed care in our consultative and coaching work with teachers and administrators. We can help transform our schools into institutions in which maximal learning can occur because we have ensured safe environments for all students and warm, welcoming, and hospitable interactions with parents.

In this book, we hope to inspire you to pursue school social work as your profession or to enhance your existing skill set by seeking new knowledge about school social work. We hope you critically appraise the information in this text and consider how you might improve your practice by integrating the information into your daily work. We have a vibrant profession built on our contributions to free and appropriate education for all students with a particular focus on those most in need. We need to continue to take this responsibility seriously—to commit our energies and passions to transforming schools into safe learning environments in which children, youth, and their families can thrive and work together for a brighter future.

# REFERENCES

Dill-Thornton, B., & Zambrana, X. (2009). Critical thinking about inequality: An emerging lens. In B. Dill-Thornton & X. Zambrana (Eds.), *Emerging intersections: Race, class, and gender in theory, policy, and practice* (pp. 1–21). New Brunswick, NJ: Rutgers University Press.

Mehrotra, G. (2010). Toward a continuum of intersectionality theorizing for feminist social work scholarship. *Affilia: Journal of Women and Social Work, 25*(4), 417–430.

# CHAPTER 1

# HISTORY OF SCHOOL SOCIAL WORK

## GARY LEE SHAFFER AND RANDY A. FISHER

## INTRODUCTION: ANTECEDENTS OF SCHOOL SOCIAL WORK SERVICES

Social work practice in public schools dates to 1906–1907 with the establishment of visiting teacher services in New York, Chicago, Boston, and Hartford, Connecticut. At its inception in the early 1900s, school social workers were known, among other things, as visiting teachers, school counselors, and home and school visitors. In 1945, a US Office Education survey identified 50 different titles used to designate social workers in the schools. Titles for school social workers continue to vary. Recently, a survey of school social workers in Louisiana found seven different titles in use for school social workers (Richard & Villarreal Sosa, 2014). *School social work services* and *school social worker* are used in this chapter except for historical accuracy.

Settlement workers, women's civic leagues, child welfare practitioners, and others who studied "child maladjustment" viewed the schools as an excellent environment for intervening with "problem children and youth." Although these early programs began at approximately the same time, this field of practice did not spring up spontaneously but, rather, evolved from educational, social, political, and economic developments, such as the establishment of common schools, compulsory education, child labor legislation, and the onset of the Progressive movement in the 1890s. School-age populations increased rapidly, fueled by the flood of immigrants from southern and eastern Europe combined with the migration of African Americans from the agrarian South to the industrialized North. Thus, the considerable ethnic, racial, and socioeconomic diversity of the public schools, coupled with the convergence of new knowledge in such fields as education, psychology, and mental health, pressured schools to change and modify many long-held beliefs and practices.

## THE COMMON SCHOOL MOVEMENT

Common school reformers of the 1830s and 1840s established a pattern of public education that continues to exist in many forms today. Horace Mann lent direction to this movement that replaced the "charity schools" for the poor and provided educational opportunities to the masses that previously had been accessible only to children of the wealthy. The common schools were publicly financed, conservative, bureaucratic, uniform in curriculum and method, and slow to change. The reformers "believed that education could be used to assure the dominance of Protestant Anglo-American culture, reduce tensions between social classes, eliminate crime and poverty, stabilize the political system, and form patriotic citizens" (Spring, 2001, p. 103). Public schools placed a premium on punctuality, standardization, and routinization—skills important for America's industrial revolution.

*[handwritten margin note: problematic clearly]*

## COMPULSORY ATTENDANCE

The first compulsory attendance law was passed by Massachusetts in 1852 when children between 8 and 14 years of age were required to attend school at least 3 months out of the year for a minimum of 6 consecutive weeks. Exceptions were made for poor children, those with mental or physical disabilities, or those able to demonstrate previous mastery of the content. By 1900, more than two-thirds of the states had compulsory attendance laws, and by 1918 compulsory attendance statutes existed in all states. Required ages for attendance, exemptions from attendance, and length of the school year lacked uniformity, and truant enforcement remained uneven for decades because staffing, credentials, administration, and services varied across jurisdictions (Peterson, 1985; Richardson, 1980).

## CHILD LABOR LEGISLATION

Compulsory attendance was both opposed and ignored at times but generally proved to be ineffective without legislation that prohibited or severely limited the workforce participation of children and youth. Industry's demand for child workers was enormous, and by 1900 18% of children 10–15 years old were employed. In 1904, the National Child Labor Committee was organized to investigate and dramatize child labor dangers in concert with lobbying for protective legislation. Organized labor supported such legislation in part because it reduced job competition from the child labor force. Although numerous states outside of the South responded to this lobbying effort, other attempts to secure uniform federal child labor laws were stymied by conservative church and farm organizations as well as the US Supreme Court until passage of the Fair Labor Standards Act of 1939. This legislation limited the number of working hours for school-age children and prohibited child employment in certain industries (Trattner, 1970).

## MIGRATION AND IMMIGRATION

African American migration from the South to the cities of the North, combined with the flood of southern and eastern European immigrants to the cities of the East and Midwest, rapidly expanded the school-age population and exacerbated social unrest. Between 1880 and 1890, immigration increased by 5.25 million people (Cohen, 1958). The immigrants came primarily from eastern and southern Europe; many were Jewish victims of Czarist Russian pogroms. By 1890, two-thirds of the population of New York City lived in hastily constructed tenements that often lacked proper sanitation, utilities for lighting, and fire safety.

It fell to the social settlements, private philanthropies, churches, and local civic authorities to address the urban filth and disease because state and federal governmental intervention was minimal. Congress and the courts objected to involvement in social reforms, and social Darwinism and laissez-faire philosophies were popular. Educational reformers tried to address the needs of the desperately poor, illiterate, and unskilled immigrants and migrants; however, their efforts proved both constructive and destructive. For example, immigrant parents felt their parental authority and respect undermined by the schools' "Americanization" or "deculturation" programs (Nelson, 1987; Spring, 2001).

## THE PROGRESSIVE MOVEMENT AND THE SOCIAL WELFARE EFFORTS IN THE SCHOOLS

Similar to the earlier common schools reformers, the Progressives viewed the schools as a means to address poverty and decrease crime, but their approaches to the situation differed significantly. Common school supporters sought these goals through education in the classroom, whereas the Progressives sought these ends by expanding the social welfare function of the schools. For example, Jacob Riis's widely read and influential muckraking exposés, *How the Other Half Lives* (1890) and *The Children of the Poor* (1892), called for "strengthening and more effective enforcement of compulsory education and child labor laws; municipal provision of truant schools, nurseries, kindergartens, manual skill training, school playgrounds, and the opening of the schools in the evening" (Cohen, 1964, p. 10). However, systems could not respond quickly enough to the rapidly expanding school-age population, and thousands of students in urban settings were turned away as public schools were overcrowded, underfunded, and often in such poor physical repair as to endanger the inhabitants (Spring, 2001).

## CONVERGENCE OF EDUCATION AND SOCIAL WORK

During most of the common school era, children were required to "fit the school," and social services, if they existed, were provided by personnel from outside the school. As the concept of individual differences emerged from the field of psychology, there was greater recognition that individuals could adapt to their environment and that the environment could be altered to meet individual needs (Irwin & Marks, 1924). Social work began to employ new findings from psychology and psychiatry to better understand the mental and emotional life of the child and to emphasize prevention and early intervention in the schools. The mental hygiene movement took root and influenced practice for decades. Educators began to recognize that the home and community influenced the child's education and that academic success required attention to both the intellectual and the social development of the child.

## SCHOOLS AT THE TURN OF THE 20TH CENTURY

By 1900, 44% of the US population was younger than 20 years of age. To best serve the burgeoning young populations, the majority of schools were reorganized into elementary schools with eight separate grades; however, one-room schoolhouses remained dominant in rural communities well into the 20th century. Urban schools were typically overcrowded, with class size, at times, approaching 50 students. Training for teachers was limited, with most teachers in the elementary grades having, at most, 2 years of training in what were called "normal schools." Public school enrollment reached 15.5 million children, equivalent to 72% of the population aged 5–17 years, and all but 519,000 of these children were in kindergarten through eighth grade. The average school year was 144 days, and although 33 states had passed compulsory attendance statutes, truancy was an ongoing problem, with less than 70% of students in attendance on any given school day (Peterson, 1985; Tyack, 1967). Furthermore, only 7% of 17-year-olds were high school graduates. During the next decade, little changed and it was observed that two-thirds of the children who began elementary school dropped out before or by the time they were 13 years old (Harvey, 1914).

## VISITING TEACHERS THE BEGINNING OF SCHOOL SOCIAL WORK

As noted previously, visiting teacher programs were introduced almost simultaneously in four cities in 1906–1907: New York, Chicago, Boston, and Hartford, Connecticut. The New York program was initiated in 1906 by two settlement houses seeking to serve the needs of their children and achieve closer cooperation between home and school. The social settlements had already demonstrated that physical care of children, recreation, and parent education promoted healthy child development; now they wanted to demonstrate that home and school teamwork could better serve pupils. The visiting teacher was strongly supported by the Public Education Association (PEA), an organization of women interested in educational reform and a potent political force in the city. The PEA vigorously lobbied to have the board of education adopt the visiting teacher service and sought to establish high standards for visiting teachers that would employ "methods of social workers," consider needs of the individual child often lost in large classes and highly regimented curricula, and develop community centers in the schools (Oppenheimer, 1925). At approximately the same time, the University of Chicago Settlement and the Chicago Woman's Club placed a full-time social worker in a Chicago school (McCullagh, 2000).

In 1907, the Boston's Women's Education Association employed a "home and school visitor" to improve children's school performance by providing social services and liaison between the home and school. The need for this liaison was highlighted by Oppenheimer (1925):

> Lack of understanding between school and home often results in loss, sometimes in serious injustice to the child, but under the present conditions it is difficult for busy mothers to visit the school, and the large-sized classes make it almost impossible for teachers to know the homes. (p. 3)

The director of the Hartford district's Psychological Clinic established its program in 1907. A "special teacher" was employed to take social histories and to carry out clinic recommendations in regard to social service, physical treatment, or school adjustment (Oppenheimer, 1925). These school social work experiments were viewed as successful, which led other settlement houses and organizations to provide visiting teachers to the schools in their districts in order to create a better understanding between the home and school.

In February 1913, the New York City public school system became the first to fund a visiting teacher service when six staff members were assigned to graded and special needs classes. The board of education in Rochester, New York, hired a visiting teacher in September of the same year, although her services were restricted to girls (Oppenheimer, 1925). Mary Richmond (1922) eloquently noted the importance of the visiting teacher service: It "occupies that strategic ground between home and school over which there is still no well used path" (p. 197). The role of private groups and organizations hiring and financing the visiting teacher service was greatly diminished after 1913 because most school social services, where they existed, became an integral part of the public school system.

## FORMATION OF A NATIONAL ASSOCIATION

The National Conference of Visiting Teachers and Home and School Visitors was organized and held its first conference in 1916, at which it discussed the use of visiting teachers to prevent delinquency and retardation. By 1919, a professional membership association was formed, and a second national conference was held in 1920 (Oppenheimer, 1925). The New York Times ("Visiting Teachers," 1920) reported the following about this meeting: "As a result of their visits the pupils are so improved that they are enabled to advance from grade to grade regularly, whereas if they were left alone they would in many instances fail to do so" (p. 14). Called the National Association of Visiting Teachers from 1919 to 1929, the organization published a journal and later became known as the American Association of Visiting Teachers (1929–1942) and subsequently the American Association of School Social Workers (1942–1945). From 1945 until the formation of the National Association of Social Workers (NASW), the organization was known as the National Association of School Social Workers (NASSW). In 1955, NASSW was one of the seven organizations that merged to form the NASW (Johnson, 1965).

## SKILLS REFLECTIVE OF EARLY SOCIAL WORK PRACTICE

Visiting teachers drew heavily from the tools being defined in the new field of social work. In *What Is Social Case Work?*, a seminal book in the social work profession, Mary Richmond (1922) wrote about the qualifications and roles of the visiting teacher:

> **Case Study.** A visiting teacher is a social worker, preferably one with some classroom experience of teaching. She understands, for a given number of pupils reported to her by the school for poor scholarship, bad health, misconceptions, lateness, irregular attendance, or for what appear to be adverse home conditions, to discover the casual factors in the difficulty and then tries to work out a better adjustment. It is not astonishing to find that, among the measures she most frequently employs, are the exercising of personal influence, winning the cooperation of parents, seeking the

advice and assistance of medical and mental experts, seeking the aid of the various social agencies, utilizing recreational facilities, and changing the child's environment. We have seen repeatedly that these are the measures most frequently used by all social case workers. "Change of environment" may mean a change outside any school, within the present school, or to another school. Such changes within the present school as a promotion, a demotion, and a transfer to a special class, are based on information brought back to the teachers after a study of the individual child in his neighborhood environment and in that of his home. (pp. 198–199)

## THE COMMONWEALTH FUND EXPANDS
## PRACTICE IN THE SCHOOLS

The activities of the Commonwealth Fund during the 1920s encouraged the greatest expansion of visiting teacher activities until after World War II. The Fund established a "Program for the Prevention of Delinquency" in 1921 that included demonstrations of visiting teacher services in 30 selected communities nationwide. Each community paid one-third of the worker's salary and pledged to continue support if the demonstration proved valuable. When the Fund withdrew support in 1930, there were 244 school social workers employed in 31 states (Costin, 1969b; Fink, 1949; Poole, 1947). The Fund published reports of the program widely and offered courses to teachers and others to demonstrate the value of psychiatric study and treatment in serving children with problems. In addition, the Fund provided consultation to other communities and school systems wishing to initiate school social work services.

# PROMISING PRACTICES IN THE 1920S

Publications of the Commonwealth Fund on the visiting teacher demonstration programs and on the Public Education Association of New York City's pioneering visiting teacher efforts provide rich documentation of promising practices during the 1920s (Culbert, 1921, 1929, 1930; Ellis, 1925; Glueck, 1924; Oppenheimer, 1925; Sayles & Nudd, 1925). Jane Culbert, the first president of the National Association of Visiting Teachers and Home and School Visitors, noted that the recommendations drawn from these studies were not meant to be "dogmatic conclusions" or "crystallized standards" but were based "upon careful observation of actual practice . . . not upon academic theory" (1929, p. 109).

The visiting teacher's knowledge of home and community provided a view of the student and family often poorly understood by school staff. Stationing the visiting teacher in the school, rather than in a school-linked agency, enabled her to follow cases on a daily basis, respond to emergencies, provide consultation to school personnel, and use her knowledge of home and community resources to assist individual students and the school. Studies recommended that the visiting teacher be assigned to one or a few small neighboring schools. This assignment would enable her to best represent the interests of the home, school, and the community. Howard Nudd, chairman of the National Committee of Visiting Teachers, noted, "It is important that the visiting teacher . . . not be required to scatter her efforts over too many cases or too wide an area" (Sayles & Nudd, 1925, p. 264). Because many of the visiting teachers served immigrants, foreign languages skills were a great asset. Cultural sensitivity was also important: "The visiting teacher needs to know the nationalities of the children's parents, their customs, traditions, and interests so that she may have a sympathetic approach" (Culbert, 1921, p. 9).

The ratio of visiting teacher to students often defined the depth and breadth of the services she could provide. Oppenheimer's (1925) studies found that the number of cases annually addressed by one visiting teacher

> ranged from 119 to 1,175; the most common number was 500. This means that a visiting teacher can do intensive work on less than half the number of cases and that the others receive short service, which requires but little time. (p. 54)

President Hoover's 1930 White House Conference on Child Health and Protection recommended a ratio of one visiting teacher for every 500 pupils. Typically, one visiting teacher served a school population of 1,500–3,000 students (Leonard, 1935).

Most visiting teachers served elementary schools, composed of first through eighth grades, but many noted that their services were just as needed with older students due to low high school graduation rates, which barely approached 50% by the 1940s (Tynack, 1967). Although half of her time was spent visiting homes, community agencies, and other areas outside of the school, it was considered essential that the visiting teacher have an office in the school where she could be easily approached by parents, students, and school staff. A phone or phone access and locked files were also deemed necessary. Her hours, although similar in duration to those of a teacher, varied considerably. Good diagnosis and casework planning often required additional early morning, evening, Sunday, and even holiday home visits in order to see the whole family and to observe their interactions (Culbert, 1921; Oppenheimer, 1925).

Visiting teachers were advised to maintain close contact and collaboration with the superintendent, principals, and teachers because the case plan and changes sought in the child and school required the support and cooperation of these colleagues. In small systems and rural communities, case interventions depended heavily on the visiting teacher's own skills. In larger districts, the visiting teacher collaborated with school-linked health bureaus, dental clinics, and programs for the gifted, as well as special programs for the "physically defective" and "retarded" children. Vocational guidance personnel, truant officers, and the child study departments responsible for testing and placement of students were frequent referral sources.

The superintendent, his designated representative, or a principal typically provided supervision for the work of the visiting teacher. In some of the larger systems, such as Minneapolis, Rochester, Philadelphia, and New York City, an experienced visiting teacher supervised a staff of 7–14 visiting teachers. Unfortunately, supervisors did not always possess the knowledge or skills needed for this role. Oppenheimer (1925) observed, "as has been the case in other auxiliary services, there is frequently a disposition on the part of boards of education to desire the appointment of people who *do not possess* the necessary qualifications for such positions" (p. 36).

Service was not limited to individual children, and community change resulted from the casework, group work, and community assessment. Visiting teachers occupied a unique role in the community because of their knowledge of both the neighborhood dynamics and the school system. The work of the visiting teacher in the community provided a catalyst for change. In response to identified needs, members of the community were prompted to work together to provide scholarship funds, nurseries, homes for neglected children, better policing, playgrounds, and parks with lights. Changes in the school system led to the establishment of parent's clubs, school lunches, recreational programs, and new courses.

Not surprisingly, the typical visiting teacher was "spread thin" and not all objectives of the program could be achieved. Preventive services did not get the attention needed. Some observed that the visiting teacher's time was consumed by serving "children whose problems have become almost overwhelming because of past oversight or neglect" (Sayles & Nudd, 1925, p. 261). Administrators recognized that situations if attended to earlier might not need further service. It was observed that more time for prevention was afforded in those systems that clearly separated the efforts of attendance (truant) offices and visiting teachers.

The American Association of Visiting Teacher (AAVT) set high standards for the preparation and training of those wishing to serve as visiting teachers. In 1925, AAVT recommended the following: a bachelor of arts degree or a normal (teacher) school certificate or its equivalent, at least 1 year of course work in the theory and practice of casework from a recognized school of social work or 2 years of "well-supervised training" in a recognized social casework agency, and at least 1 year of teaching and 1 year of practice in a family or psychiatric casework agency or 1 year of visiting teacher experience (Culbert, 1930). Not all, of course, met these high standards.

# FROM THE DEPRESSION TO THE COLD WAR: 1930–1960

The 1930s were a period of retrenchment for school social work practitioners in function and method. Casework had little to say in response to the Great Depression, and professionalism took a step back. Grace Abbott (1941), social worker and chief of the Children's Bureau in the US Department of Labor, observed the following:

> The schools were the first to suffer because theirs was the largest item in the social welfare budget. The accounts of the closing of schools and shortening of terms, the increase in pupil–teacher ratios, and the elimination of kindergartens, health supervision, attendance officers, evening schools, continuation schools, opportunity schools or classes, and nursing services have made very discouraging reading. (p. 172)

During the Depression, children commonly lacked food, clothing, school supplies, and shelter. Malnutrition was common, public health problems surged, and students dropped out of school to become the primary breadwinners for their families because parents were unable to secure employment (Amidon, 1937). Private philanthropy failed, local governments went bankrupt, and public attitudes and legal statutes prohibited substantial federal intervention until passage of the Social Security Act in 1935. School social work practitioners returned to their roots as distributors of relief. Health, hot lunches, and clothing shops took precedence (Lide, 1953). The length and depth of the Depression required the schools to cooperate with other community groups to meet the needs of their children and families (Lowry, 1939). Towle (1939) supported this call for community collaboration:

> We are coming not only to recognize the futility of persisting in situations which are beyond the scope of casework help, but to realize also our social responsibility for revealing the inadequacy of social casework in these instances, in order that interest and effort may be directed toward social action. (p. 525)

As the crisis of the Depression era began to recede, school social work services re-emerged. A 1939 survey found school social work practice established in 150 school systems. Casework, not social action, continued to predominate, but examples of educational group work could also be found (Poole, 1947).

With the nation's eventual entry into World War II, school social work was once again faced with circumstances little suited to casework practice. School social work literature of the period does not seem to reflect the immigration of refugees from abroad, the increase in racial and ethnic tensions, the huge migration of families to war industrial centers, or the social-emotional stresses children experienced as family members mobilized for war. Divorces more than doubled between 1940 and 1946, and out-of-wedlock births increased from 71 to 127 per 10,000. School years were shortened and school days compressed to permit children to work in fields, stores, and factories. Rates of school dropouts increased as opportunities to earn wages increased (Cohen, 1958, pp. 224–226).

However, amid this turmoil, legislators established school social work services in Louisiana, Georgia, Virginia, Maryland, Michigan, Illinois, and Puerto Rico. During this time, the National Association of School Social Workers had members in 34 states and Hawaii (Sikkema, 1949). The US Office of Education reported approximately 1,000 full-time visiting teachers in 266 different communities, and visiting teacher services were provided by school personnel not classified as regular visiting teachers in another 102 locations. Other school districts expressed interest in exploring such programs (Poole, 1947).

At this time, Rush Smalley (1947) defined school social work as "a specialized form of social casework. It is identified with and is a part of the program of the public school. It is a method of helping individual children use what the school offers them" (p. 51). Although casework continued to prevail, changes of note did take place in the field during this period. There was a growing awareness that school social work could be as valuable for students in middle and secondary schools as for the elementary programs that were traditionally served. Although first employed to work primarily with the underprivileged, school social work services were now being requested in a variety of schools. Consultation to principals, teachers, and parents continued to be an important function of the program, and prevention was gaining a foothold. Rather than focusing only on "problem children," some schools recognized that all children experienced stress and challenges as they developed socially, emotionally, and physically and school social workers might assist these children in recognizing the problems they were experiencing and what might be done to alleviate their concerns (Fink, 1949). By 1950, the ranks of school social workers had grown to include an estimated 1,700 school social workers employed in 450 cities. The NASSW reported 650 members for this period (Sikkema, 1953). The stresses of the period seemed to foster a resurgence of school social work practice.

Mildred Sikkema's *Report of a Study of School Social Worker Practice in Twelve Communities* (1953) was completed in collaboration with the American Association of Social Workers and the NASSW and gives the most complete overview of school social work practice during this era. Almost one-fourth of the school social work practitioners participated in this research. Her study revealed that there continued to be wide variability in the training and preparation for practice as a school social worker. Other findings in the study showed that informal teacher consultation was viewed as a critical role for the school social worker. Referrals made by the school social worker were most frequently related to student behavior, personality issues, non-attendance, academic problems, home or neighborhood conditions, or parental neglect. Brief "limited service" interventions with students were frequently reported by the participating school social worker.

The merger of the NASSW into the NASW in 1955 marked the beginning of a new era for school social work. Greater political clout was achieved, but visibility of school social work practice was dimmed. Termination of the NASSW *Bulletin*, published since 1925, left this field without a prominent, national voice until the Illinois Association of School Social Workers published its *School Social Work Journal* in 1976 and NASW initiated *Social Work in Education* in 1978 (now titled *Children & Schools*).

# A SEARCH FOR MORE EFFECTIVE PRACTICE ROLES AND MODELS, 1960 TO THE PRESENT, AND THE CRITICAL ROLE OF SCHOOLS OF SOCIAL WORK

Passage of the Education for All Handicapped Children Act (P.L. 94-142) in 1975 led to a substantial increase in school social work practitioners because they were viewed as instrumental in the assessment and placement of children with disabilities and subsequent service delivery to the children and their families. The caseloads of children with disabilities expanded rapidly as well.

In response to a changing social and educational climate, school social workers initiated a search for new and more effective roles and models of practice that continues to the present. A 1969 National School Social Work Workshop by NASW and the National Institute of Mental Health was held to stimulate change and innovation in this practice arena (Sarri & Maple, 1972). State and regional conferences have also promoted new models, methods, and innovative projects. During this period, John Alderson (1972) described and analyzed four models of practice by which school social workers could examine and evaluate their work: (1) the durable traditional-clinical model; (2) the school-change model, whose major focus was the dysfunctional conditions of the school; (3) the community school model, which urged school social workers to employ community organization methods; and (4) the social interaction model, which de-emphasized a specific methodology and required the worker to intervene with the systems interacting with the target system.

To clarify prevalent practice and to guide practitioner training, a series of surveys, reminiscent of those conducted in the 1910s and 1920s by early school social workers, took place in the 1960s, 1970s, and 1980s (Alderson & Krishef, 1973; Allen-Meares, 1977, 1987, 1994; Chavkin, 1985; Costin, 1969a; Mintzies & Hare, 1985; Nelson, 1990). See Chapter 3 for a full description and review of these survey findings.

Costin's (1969a) national survey in the mid-1960s reaffirmed the emphasis that school social work practitioners placed on traditional casework services: "Little recognition was given to the impact of school conditions upon pupil or the total set of circumstances within the school which might be related to his poor adjustment" (pp. 277–278). Costin asserted that changing times and problems required reassessment of even well-established practice and that practitioners could not ignore the impact of school policies and community conditions on pupils. In the early 1970s, she and colleagues at the University of Illinois at Urbana–Champaign developed a "school–community–pupil relations model" that focused on situation rather than personality. The model gave attention to "(1) deficiencies in the school and the community and (2) the interaction between specific characteristics of the system and characteristics of groups of pupils at points of stress in the pupil life circle" (Costin, 1975, p. 135).

Allen-Meares' (1977) replication of Costin's study found only modest evidence of change. However, many school social workers reported activities described as "transitional" between the polar extremes of traditional casework and Costin's approach. Chavkin's 1982 research found, once again, that traditional casework services predominated but that many were employing a wide range of individual, group, family, and community interventions. Chavkin (1985) asserted that greater emphasis was needed in the areas of group intervention, consultation to administrators and students, student's rights, and resource development.

Barriers to education and recommendations to address these barriers were identified in an NASW study carried out in conjunction with its Third National Conference on School Social Work (Mintzies & Hare, 1985). Recommendations included (1) strengthening collaboration and coordination between the school and community, such as mental health and protective services; (2) strengthening pupil services and making services available to the entire school, not just to handicapped and "problem students"; (3) increasing parent involvement and reaching out to those detached from the school; (4) emphasizing early intervention and prevention; (5) expanding the use of school buildings by opening them to after-school programming and community organizations; (6) addressing family barriers by helping students deal with sexual abuse, child abuse, neglect, and family violence; (7) strengthening student self-esteem and increasing opportunities for success; and (8) developing special in-school and alternative programs for "at-risk" groups.

A national study of school social work practitioners, completed in 1989–1990 by NASW and the Educational Testing Service, used a modified version of Meares' 1974 survey (Allen-Meares, 1994; Nelson, 1990). Participants ranked 94 tasks and job responsibilities clustered into five job functions. Maintenance of records, confidentiality, and continuing education were given the highest priorities, followed by home–school liaison and educational counseling to students. Although some evidence of group and family counseling existed, the leadership and policymaking tasks advocated by Costin, Allen-Meares, and others received the lowest mean ranking.

School social workers continue to face the dilemma of practicing in a host setting. In the mid-1930s, Charlotte Towle commented on this challenge when she observed that while working in schools, the school social worker's identity is that of social worker, but there are few social work colleagues to provide support and identification with this profession. Job requirements demand knowledge of education, but while practicing as a social worker, she is not quite accepted in the role of educator. Occasionally, the philosophy of the school conflicts with basic principles of social work, such as confidentiality, informed consent, and self-determination (Lowry, 1939). Towle also noted that the school, with which her clients identify her, is the very same milieu that needs to be modified at times. Dane and Simon (1991) suggested that practitioners in host settings encounter several problems, including (1) discrepancies between professional mission and values, (2) token status in a workplace employing few social workers, and (3) role ambiguity and strain.

Effective child and family advocacy demands school social workers have considerable knowledge of educational legislation, Supreme Court decisions, and case law because they play a major role in defining practice. In addition, it is of critical importance for school social workers to be informed about the following in order to be effective in their practice: knowledge of attendance and exceptional children policies and procedures, child abuse and neglect recognition and reporting, public health and public welfare statutes, the rights of undocumented minors and pregnant and parenting teens, and policies regarding students facing suspension and expulsion. Knowledge of Section 504 of the Rehabilitation Act of 1973 and federal laws such as the Individuals with Disabilities Education Act, the McKinney–Vento Homeless Education Act, the Family Education Rights and Privacy Act, and the No Child Left Behind Act is critical as well.

The field of school social work is currently being driven in multiple directions by the convergence of factors such as changes in federal legislation, shifts in demographics, persistent poverty, diminishing state and local financing, rising public expectations, and a growing emphasis within the social work profession for evidenced-based practice. The restructuring of school-based and school-linked services is in process, and new models of students support and funding options are being proposed, implemented, and evaluated (Dryfoos & Maguire, 2002; UCLA Center for Mental Health in Schools, 2001).

# PROFESSIONAL ASSOCIATIONS, ORGANIZATIONAL HISTORY, AND GROWTH—1956 TO THE PRESENT

During the past 70 years, the profession has matured in regard to the influence that professional associations have had on the field of school social work. The organizational structure of school social work slowly changed from a more passive structure to one that promoted the development of the profession and greatly expanded the number of school social workers in the United States (Fisher, 1993). In addition, many state departments of education began to be more active in supporting the growth of school social work.

## NATIONAL EDUCATION ISSUES (PRIOR TO 1975)

Historically in the United States, education has been the responsibility of state and local governments. States determine if they offer certification for school social work. The requirement for a teaching certificate before becoming a school social worker went by the wayside as social work training became the accepted standard. The visiting teacher programs found in some states began to convert to social work, although in a few states that title lasted into the 1990s. Until 1975, there was no federal acknowledgment of school social work and no national legislation on exceptional children.

## NASSW–NASW–MIDWEST SCHOOL SOCIAL WORK CONFERENCE (1956–1969)

The NASSW was one of the seven founding members of the NASW in 1956. It was difficult for the school social work community to switch from a single focus association no matter how small to a larger umbrella association in which their membership and issues were not the focus of the association. Within 10 years of that formation, there was evidence of disappointment within the school social work community (Staples & Tosby, 1973):

When the National Association of State Consultants in School Social Work held its annual meeting in 1966, concern was expressed about the lack of leadership in school social work within the US Office of Education and the National Association of Social Workers.

One of the outcomes of this disappointment was the formation of the Midwest School Social Work Conference, later renamed the Midwest School Social Work Council. At the time of its formation, the Midwest Conference was made up of six states and the primary leaders were the state school social work consultants. Some Midwest states did have associations in 1967, and others formed within a decade.

## THE FIRST NATIONAL EDUCATION ISSUES
## INVOLVING SCHOOL SOCIAL WORK (1975)

In 1975, there emerged an issue that highlighted the frustration that the school social work community had with NASW. The first national education bill that directly affected school social work was P.L. 94-142 in 1976. This bill, "The Education of All Handicapped Children Act," established education policy for special needs children. School social work was not mentioned in the original bill, and the Midwest Council of School Social Work brought this to the attention of NASW in a forceful way at the annual Midwest School Social Work Conference held in Chicago in 1975.

## NASW AND SCHOOL SOCIAL WORK (1975–1994)

NASW scrambled to ensure school social work was recognized in the rules and regulations of this new law. They began working closely with school social work and continued this path for almost 20 years. Within a few years, NASW hosted a National School Social Work Conference in Denver (1978); developed Standards for School Social Work (1978); and started a quarterly journal, *Social Work in Education* (1978). Between 1975 and the early 1990s, NASW was a significant force within the school social work community because, in large part, the employment of a staff person focused on school social work.

This staff person provided technical support to individual school social workers as well as state and regional associations. NASW held two more standalone school social work conferences in 1981 (Washington, DC) and 1985 (New Orleans). NASW also provided some lobbying efforts in Washington, DC, on various school social work issues. In the late 1980s and early 1990s, two more NASW conferences were held that were the last to include a school social work track. A volunteer leadership structure was put in place at the national level in the 1970s for some of the specialty groups, including school social work. There was also a newsletter for school social workers (*School Social Work Information Bulletin*) published quarterly, a school social work bibliography (1979 and 1981), and a few additional publications focused on school social work during this 19-year period. The only programming failure was that NASW developed a national school social work exam with hopes that state education departments would use the exam in their certification process. That did not happen, and the exam was discontinued in 1998.

## STATE ASSOCIATIONS (1940S–1994)

States such as New York and Georgia had state associations dating back to the 1940s and 1950s. Starting in the 1960s, more states began to form state associations and the Midwest Council (Conference) became a dominant force within school social work. The Illinois Association of School Social Workers (established in 1970) became a leading state association as the number of school social workers grew rapidly in the state. Illinois started the first modern-day professional journal for school social work, *The School Social Work Journal*, in 1976. Some states were able to hire part-time government relations specialists to promote school social work with the state legislatures and state departments of education. State conferences were common, providing in-service learning experiences to current school social workers and orientation to the profession for new school social workers. Certification was a central issue at various times in most states. In lieu of a free-standing state association, some states had a NASW state chapter organization, but those had tended to have less autonomy and less success than the independent state associations.

## STATE DEPARTMENTS OF EDUCATION (1950S–2015)

As evidenced by the formation of the Midwest Conference in the late 1960s, state departments in some instances had a major impact on the growth and development of school social work. Certification was a state issue, and some states employed state school social work consultants. Some of those consultants were social work trained, and others were not. There was a National Association of State School Social Work Consultants for a number of years (1960s–1990s), but the number of state consultants has declined significantly in the past 20 years. A number of states published school social work handbooks that helped shape the profession in those states. Some states require testing in order to receive their school social work certification.

## A NATIONAL VOID (EARLY 1990S)

Two factors weakened the NASW leadership in the eyes of the school social work community. First was the change in staff at the national level. Isadora Hare, the staff person with a focus on and background in school social work, was promoted to the management level and given new responsibilities. Hare's replacement, along with subsequent staffers, had increasingly less responsibility for school social work, until the focus on school social work disappeared. At approximately the same time, the NASW volunteer school social work leadership attached to the specialty group was suspended for a few years. A National Council of School Social Workers was developed at the Midwest School Social Work Conference in 1990 in response and frustration to these developments. The group floundered because it had no revenue source, and it quietly disbanded.

As the void continued, the Midwest Council began to discuss the possibility of starting a national school social work association. An invitational meeting with 60 representatives from 19 states met for 3 days at Southern Illinois University in Edwardsville, Illinois, in July 1994. At the end of gathering, the School Social Work Association of America (SSWAA) was formed with a working interim board of directors. The vote was almost unanimous, with only two dissenting votes. The structure was designed for individual memberships with support from and for the state associations.

## SCHOOL SOCIAL WORK ASSOCIATION OF AMERICA (1994–2015)

After SSWAA was formed in 1994, every effort was made to ensure that the leadership was representative of all school social workers throughout the United States. Within 1½ years, the interim leadership developed a constitution and bylaws, implemented a membership plan (500 members at the end of the first year), and held a second open meeting in the summer of 1995. Soon afterwards, a government relations specialist was hired in Washington, DC, on a part-time basis. An annual summer leadership conference was held each summer in Washington, DC, with attendance of state association representatives as well as SSWAA members. Influencing national education policy and support for state and regional associations were at the center of the summer meetings.

In 1996, a plan was made to host an annual national conference with the support of state and/or regional associations. The first conference was held in Austin, Texas, in 1998. Starting in 2003, SSWAA began to run their conferences without the direct involvement of the state or regional associations.

In 1999, SSWAA hired a new government relations staffer, Myrna Mandlawitz, who was closely tied to the educational lobby in Washington, DC. Since that time, SSWAA's efforts to influence legislation and educational policy have continued to expand. Training and support have been offered by SSWAA to the state and regional leaders each summer, and SSWAA has also held workshops and presented keynote speeches at state and regional events. At the same time, SSWAA's participation and leadership in pupil services coalitions and direct partnership with the National Association of School Psychologists and the American School Counselors Association have increased. The reauthorizations of the Individuals with Disabilities Education Act are closely followed. Support for the Elementary and Secondary School Counseling Program is a high priority on an annual basis when the federal budget comes up for passage. Another example of the national presence is that SSWAA leadership has attended more than a half dozen meetings/conferences at the White House starting in 1998. SSWAA has supported the development of new state associations by providing technical and moral support for the endeavors.

## STATE ASSOCIATIONS (1994–2015)

Currently, 29 states have a state school social work association. All of these state associations have a working agreement with the School Social Work Association of America. Illinois continues to publish the *School Social Work Journal*. The Iowa School Social Work Association published the *Journal of School Social Work* for approximately 15 years before the was journal was eventually merged with the *School Social Work Journal*. Most of the associations have websites, and some continue to hire part-time government relations specialists to represent their interest in their state legislature and state departments of education. Conferences and other in-service opportunities continue to be sponsored by states.

## REGIONAL ASSOCIATIONS (1990–2015)

At the time SSWAA was formed, there were three regional associations: the Midwest School Social Work Council, the Southern Council of School Social Work, and the West Alliance of School Social Work Associations. Within a few years, the Northeastern Council of School Social

Work Associations was formed with the support of SSWAA. The major barrier to a successful regional group was having the income sources to sustain the costs of meeting. The Western Alliance formally disbanded in the 2000s. The southern and the northeastern groups have currently ceased to meet for a number of years. The Midwest Council still meets and hosts an annual conference that is one of their two funding sources.

## NASW (1994–2015)

NASW's school social work section with its volunteer leadership council began again after a short recess, but staffing for school social work has disappeared. NASW offered a certificate in school social work that resembled the certificate by the Academy of Certified Social Workers, but NASW's certificate was not obtained by enough school social workers to make it viable. Its journal continues today under a new title, *Children & Schools*. NASW updated its Standards for School Social Work in 1992 and 2002. The knowledge, skills, and values in the *Standards* (National Association of Social Workers, 2002) reflect best practice in this specialty area and the type of training required. Administrative structures and support necessary for effective school social work programs are also defined by the standards. The 2002 standards reinforce the use of the ecological perspective, evidence-based practice, and assessments based on data obtained through the use of multiple methods and sources. There is also an emphasis on health, resiliency, and protective factors that reflect practice advancements in social work during the past 24 years. Interdisciplinary planning and services delivered through school-based and school-linked programs are recognized as a requirement for effective needs assessment, prevention, early intervention, and responses to chronic and acute problems. Lobbying efforts on behalf of school social work have diminished as well as their participation in educational and pupil service coalitions in Washington, DC.

# INTERNATIONAL SCHOOL SOCIAL WORK

For years at the NASW national school social work conferences (1978, 1981, 1985), some of the annual Midwest School Social Work Conferences, and larger state conferences, there were attendees from Canada and countries in Europe and Asia. In 1999, when SSWAA held its second conference in the Chicago area, this also coincided with the 1st International School Social Work Conference. Leadership of the conference fell to Marion Huxtable, Greg Petty, and Randy Fisher. Huxtable was a leader in the School Social Work Association of Arizona, as well as the Western Alliance of School Social Workers, and British by birth. She had a strong desire to discover more about existing international school social work programs as well as help other school social work programs to begin. By 1992, she had developed the International Network for School Social Work, giving school social workers a way to communicate with peers throughout the world. Petty was the president of the Illinois Association of School Social Workers (the host state association for the conference) as well as one of the key leaders in the formation of SSWAA. Fisher was the current president of the SSWAA and had the initial vision to promote an international conference.

The conference was very successful, with more than 800 school social workers from the United States and 79 participants from 16 other countries. An international steering committee was formed at the conference to select the sites of future international conferences. That informal committee meets during each international conference to plan for the next conference as well as discuss the status of school social work in the respective countries. Huxtable has continued her efforts to build communication throughout the world. She began an electronic monthly international newsletter in 2006. Since in the 1990s, she has sent out a survey to each country with a school social work contact. Data are gathered and published every few years. There is no charge for the newsletter, and it is currently sent to more than 500 individuals in more than 80 countries.

At each subsequent SSWAA national conference, a handful of participants from other countries have attended. International conferences have been hosted by Sweden (2003), South Korea (2006), New Zealand (2009), Ghana (2012), and Mongolia (2015). There is no formal international representative board. School social work is seeing tremendous growth throughout the world, with 50 countries now recognizing the profession. Thirty-four countries responded to Huxtable's 2012 International Survey of School Social Work (Huxtable, 2013). In addition, SSWAA has supported the development of the International Committee on School Social Work Collaborations, whose mission is to address the needs of children in schools globally by ensuring quality school social work services through school social work training and credentialing as well as promoting the exchange of expertise, experience, and resources with a view to strengthening the international presence of school social work.

## CONCLUSION

A review of first 109 years of school social work demonstrates many parallels between the administration, policies, and practices of today and those of earlier periods. Wide variations in education and training, supervision, staffing patterns, and qualifications continue to exist, as does the struggle to establish an effective presence in a host setting. The modern period in school social work has been marked by growth in the numbers of school social workers. Organizations including state associations, regional coalitions, NASW, SSWAA, schools of social work, and the state departments of education have all played a role in this development. They have offered support and leadership in many different formats. The home, school, and community liaison role remains a constant. Practice will continue to evolve in response to changes in social work practice, school funding, educational focus, and political demands. At the same time, school social workers consistently show their value in the schools, and this has led to more positions being established. Professional associations will continue to lead the profession. Growth throughout the world will continue and strengthen the profession. Fortunately and unfortunately, Norma Radin's (1975) words of a quarter century ago ring true today:

> The role of the school social worker is ambiguous; there is typically little supervision and often much misunderstanding by educators who fill the school system. Yet, it is in school social work that one effective worker can have an enormous impact. It is in school that the otherwise hard-to-reach population abounds. It is in school that children can be crippled psychologically for life or aroused to do great things. In spite of the many problems permeating the school, there is enough flexibility in the system today for one creative, energetic school social worker to make a significant difference in the lives of thousands of children. It is a challenge that is irresistible to a particular kind of social worker, and that is the person that school social work needs. (p. 613)

# REFERENCES

Abbott, G. (1941). *From relief to social security: The development of the new public welfare services and their administration.* Chicago, IL: University of Chicago Press.

Alderson, J. J. (1972). Models of school social work practice. In R. C. Sarri & F. F. Maple (Eds.), *The school in the community* (pp. 57–74). Washington, DC: National Association of Social Workers.

Alderson, J. J., & Krishef, C. H. (1973). Another perspective on tasks in school social work. *Social Casework, 54,* 591–600.

Allen-Meares, P. (1977). Analysis of tasks in school social work. *Social Work, 22*(3), 196–201.

Allen-Meares, P. (1987). A national study of educational reform: Implications for social work services in schools. *Children & Youth Services Review, 9,* 207–219.

Allen-Meares, P. (1994). Social work services in schools: A national study of entry-level tasks. *Social Work, 39,* 560–565.

Amidon, B. (1937, January). Children wanted. *Survey Graphic: Magazine of Social Interpretation, 26*(1), 10–15.

Chavkin, N. F. (1985). School social work practice: A reappraisal. *Social Work in Education, 8*(1), 3–13.

Cohen, N. E. (1958). *Social work in the American tradition.* New York, NY: Holt, Rinehart & Winston.

Cohen, S. (1964). *Progressives and urban reform: The Public Education Association of New York City 1895–1954.* New York, NY: Columbia University, Teachers College.

Costin, L. B. (1969a). An analysis of the tasks in school social work. *Social Service Review, 43,* 274–285.

Costin, L. B. (1969b). A historical review of school social work practice: A new model. *Social Work, 20,* 135–139.

Costin, L. B. (1975). School social work practice: A new model. *Social Work, 20,* 135–139.

Culbert, J. F. (1921). *The visiting teacher.* New York, NY: Joint Committee on Methods of Preventing Delinquency. (Reprinted from *Annals of the American Academy of Political and Social Science, 98*(187), November 1921)

Culbert, J. F. (1929). *The visiting teacher at work.* New York, NY: Commonwealth Fund.

Culbert, J. F. (1930). Visiting teachers. In F. S. Hall (Ed.), *Social work year book 1929* (pp. 466–469). New York, NY: Russell Sage Foundation.

Dane, B. O., & Simon, B. L. (1991). Resident guest: Social workers in host settings. *Social Work, 36*(3), 208–213.

Dryfoos, J., & Maguire, S. (2002). *Inside full-service community schools.* Thousand Oaks, CA: Corwin.

Ellis, M. B. (1925). *The visiting teacher in Rochester.* New York, NY: Joint Committee on Methods of Preventing Delinquency.

Fink, A. E. (1949). *The field of social work* (2nd ed.). New York, NY: Holt.

Fisher, R. A. (1993). The future of professional school social work organizations: An inside perspective. *School Social Work Journal, 17*(2), 31–44.

Glueck, B. (1924). *Some extra-curricular problems of the classroom* (Publication No.3). New York, NY: Joint Committee on Methods of Preventing Delinquency. (Reprinted from *School and Society, 19*(476), February 9, 1924)

Harvey, L. D. (1914). Systematic education for those pupils leaving school too soon. *National Education Association of the United States. Meeting: Journal of Proceedings and Addresses of the Annual Meeting, 52,* 119–122.

Huxtable, M. (2013). *A global picture of school social work in 2013.* International Network for School Social Work, Port Townsend, Washington.

Irwin, E. A., & Marks, L. A. (1924). *Fitting the school to the child: An experiment in public education.* New York, NY: Macmillan.

Johnson, A. (1965). Schools (social work practice in). In H. L. Lurie (Ed.), *Encyclopedia of social work* (15th ed., pp. 672–679). New York, NY: National Association of Social Workers.

Leonard, S. (1935). Visiting teachers. In F. S. Hall (Ed.), *Social work year book 1935* (pp. 532–535). New York, NY: Russell Sage Foundation.

Lide, P. (1953). A study of the historical influences of major importance in determining the present function of the school social worker. *Bulletin of the National Association of Social Workers, 29*(1), 18–33.

Lowry, F. (Ed.). (1939). *Reading in social case work 1920–1938: Selected reprints for the case work practitioner.* New York, NY: Columbia University Press.

McCullagh, J. G. (2000, Fall). School social work in Chicago: An unrecognized pioneer program. *School Social Work Journal, 25*(1), 1–15.

Mintzies, P., & Hare, I (1985). *The human factor: A key to excellence in education.* Silver Spring, MD: National Association of Social Workers.

National Association of Social Workers. (2002). *NASW standards for school social work services.* Washington, DC: Author.

Nelson, C. (1990). *A job analysis of school social workers.* Princeton, NJ: Educational Testing Service.

Nelson, F. C. (1987). *Public schools: An evangelical appraisal.* Old Tappan, NJ: Revell.

Oppenheimer, J. C. (1925). *The visiting teacher movement with special reference to administrative relationships* (2nd ed.). New York, NY: Joint Committee on Methods of Preventing Delinquency.

Peterson, P. E. (1985). *The politics of school reform 1870–1940.* Chicago, IL: University of Chicago Press.

Poole, F. (1947). Nationwide developments in school social work. *Bulletin of the National Association of School Social Workers, 22*(3), 4–8.

Radin, N. (1975). A personal perspective on school social work. *Social Casework, 56,* 605–613.

Richard, L., & Villarreal Sosa, L. (2014). School social work in Louisiana: A model of practice. *Children & Schools, 36*(4), 211–220.

Richardson, G. (1980). Variation in date of enactment of compulsory school attendance laws: An empirical inquiry. *Sociology of Education, 53,* 153–163.

Richmond, M. E. (1922). *What is social case work? An introductory description.* New York, NY: Russell Sage: Foundation.

Sarri, R. C., & Maple, F. F. (Eds.). (1972). *The school in the community.* Washington, DC: National Association of Social Workers.

Sayles, M. B., & Nudd, H. W. (1925). *The problem child in school* (Publication No. 4). New York, NY: Joint Committee on Methods of Preventing Delinquency.

Sikkema, M. (1949). An analysis of the structure and practice of school social work today. *Social Service Review, 23*(4), 447–453.

Sikkema, M. (1953). *Report of a study of school social work practice in twelve communities.* New York, NY: American Association of Social Workers.

Smalley, R. (1947). School social work as part of the school program. *Bulletin of the National Association of Social Workers, 22*(3), 51–54.

Spring, J. (2001). *The American school: 1647–2000* (5th ed.). Boston, MA: McGraw-Hill.

Staples, R., & Tosby, G. (1973, November 30). *Midwest School Social Work Conference History.*

Towle, C. (1939). Discussion of Miss Hall's paper. In F. Lowry (Ed.), *Reading in social case work 1920–1939* (pp. 521–526). New York, NY: Columbia University Press.

Trattner, W. I. (1970). *Crusade for the children: A history of National Child Labor Committee and child labor reform in America*. Chicago, IL: Quadrangle Books.

Tyack, D. B. (Ed.). (1967). *Turning points in American educational history*. Waltham, MA: Blaisdell.

UCLA Center for Mental Health in Schools. (2001). *Framing new directions for school counselors, psychologists, & social workers*. Los Angeles, CA: Author.

Visiting teachers meet. (1920, June 29). *The New York Times*, p. 14.

CHAPTER 2

# THE NATIONAL SCHOOL SOCIAL
# WORK PRACTICE MODEL

ANDY J. FREY, JAMES C. RAINES, CHRISTINE ANLAUF SABATINO,
MICHELLE ALVAREZ, BRENDA LINDSEY, ANNE MCINERNEY, AND
FREDERICK STREECK

School social work has its origins in three major developments in the history of American public education. First, the "common school" movement responded to the environmental conditions of the urban slum in the early industrial revolution in the 1820s described by Herbst (1986):

> The growing number of youthful vagrants, petty criminals, orphaned and homeless children, many of them of immigrant parents, had caused consternation and fear among the settled families. Undisciplined, illiterate, without family ties and church attendance, frequently unable to speak or understand the English language, these children threatened an orderly civic life and proved to be inefficient and unreliable as employees in shops, stores, or factories. (pp. 281–282)

The first common schools were described by Horace Mann in 1848 (as quoted in Katz, 1976):

> It knows no distinction of rich and poor, of bond and free, or between those, who, in the imperfect light of this world, are seeking through different avenues to reach the gate of heaven. Without money and without price, it throws open its doors and spreads the table of its bounty for all the children of the State. (p. 16)

Second, compulsory universal education was a new concept when social work started in the late 1870s (Raines, 1999). Child labor laws and compulsory education laws complemented one another (Butler, 1898; Mulkeen, 1986). For example, Illinois passed its first child labor law in 1877 and its first compulsory education law in 1880 (Smith, 1986). Chicago hired its first truant officer in 1855 and had a dozen by 1890. The officers, however, had an unforeseen effect—they brought incorrigible children into an educational system the schools were ill-equipped to handle. By 1900, more than 30 states had legislated compulsory school attendance (Mulkeen, 1986). To assist with the educational changes occurring as a result of compulsory school attendance legislation, districts hired social workers during the 1906–1907 school year in four major cities throughout the United States: Boston; Hartford, Connecticut; New York; and Chicago (Allen-Meares, 2010; McCullagh, 1993, 2000, 2002).

The third development was the introduction of free "appropriate" public education for all children. As early as 1898, C. Loring Brace of the New York Children's Aid Society had taken notice of the needs of children with physical disabilities (as quoted in Shaffer, 1898):

> We determined to establish a class for these children in one of our schools as an experiment; and I think, when you see it, that you will agree that it is very successful. We purchased a wagonette; and the children are brought to school in the morning and taken home in the afternoon by our teacher, receiving a lunch at the school. As we expected, we found children of all ages absolutely ignorant, and we have undertaken to teach them *according to their needs* [emphasis added]. (p. 399)

Unfortunately, this early form of special education was the exception rather than the norm for children with disabilities. The turning point for special education was the US Supreme Court case *Brown v. Board of Education of Topeka, Kansas* (1954). Although this case was about racial justice, its primary importance was that it overturned the *Plessy v. Ferguson* (1898) doctrine of "separate, but equal" and insisted on integrated schools rather than segregated ones (Raines, 1996). Shortly before the Education for All Handicapped Children Act (P.L. 42-142) was passed in 1975, the Midwest School Social Work Council convinced the National Association of Social Workers (NASW) to lobby for school social work to be included as a "related service" for students with disabilities (Raines, 2008). Throughout its more than 100-year history, school social work has taken a student-in-environment perspective; built linkages between schools, homes, and communities; and demonstrated concern for social justice—all with an overarching goal of helping children benefit from the educational process by removing barriers to learning.

For more than a century, school social workers have been providing services to remove barriers to learning that impede children's ability to access and benefit from education, and a number of models and scholarly writings have been presented to guide the practice decisions of this specialized area of social work. The importance of clearly articulating the delivery of school social work has been well documented (Massat, Constable, McDonald, & Flynn, 2009); influential works in this regard include descriptions of school social work roles (Allen-Meares, 2007; Bye & Alvarez, 2007; Kelly, 2008; Massat et al., 2009), surveys of practitioner-reported practice choices (Allen-Meares, 1977, 1994; Costin, 1969; Kelly, Berzin, et al., 2010; Kelly, Frey, et al., 2010; Meares, 1977), and conceptual models (Alderson, 1972; Costin, 1973; Frey & Dupper, 2005). In 1992, NASW developed *Standards for School Social Work Practice*. These were revised in 2003, 2006 and 2012, and they remain a valuable resource to help articulate what school social workers should be able to do (NASW, 2012). Many of the writings in the past two decades have challenged what appears to be an overly individualist orientation, at the expense of the historic commitment to the student-in-environment perspective; linkages between school, home, and community; and social justice. Despite these models and scholarly writings, a clearly articulated model of practice to successfully unify practice, advocacy, certification, and education has remained elusive.

As noted in Chapter 1, numerous changes in practice and policy have altered the landscape of specialized support services, including school social work services, in the past decade. The National School Social Work Practice Model, described later, addresses services provided within a school, and it is not intended to encompass all areas of school social work practice or school social workers' responsibilities to the profession and society (Frey et al., 2013). The model delineates the type of services that might reasonably be expected from certified school social workers, and it is intended as a guide to inform key stakeholders (school social workers, educators, other school professionals, administrators, and policymakers) about professional school social work services. Also, it is hoped that it will unite the profession regarding the roles, skills, and competencies that define this area of social work specialization. Importantly, the model is a vision of school social work services but does not describe everything that school social workers do to support academic and behavioral outcomes. It was created based on and aligned with other recognized national social work documents, such as NASW's *Standards for School Social Work Practice* (2012) and *Code of Ethics* (2008), the Council on Social Work Education's *Educational Policy and Accreditation Standards* (2008), the School Social Work Association of America's (SSWAA) *Ethical Guidelines* (2007), and the *National Evaluation Framework for School Social Work Practice* (2014). The model is intended to be a working document that can be updated to reflect changes in the scope of school social work practice and the evolving landscape of schools.

The model was developed in July 2011 to provide clarity to school social workers, students, school social work faculty, school administrators, and P12 students and families about the value and variety of professional school social work services (Frey et al., 2012). It underwent a number of revisions from November 2011 through March 2012 based on feedback obtained from focus groups convened at national and state social work and school social work conferences, including the Society for Social Work and Research, SSWAA, Midwest School Social Work Association, and the Illinois Association of School Social Workers. The model was also posted for public comment on the SSWAA website; publicized in *Children & Schools* (Frey et al., 2012); and presented to NASW, the National Association of School Psychologists, the National Association of School Counselors, the National Association of School Boards, and national school principal organizations. School social workers' roles and responsibilities vary significantly across schools, districts, states, and countries. The purpose of the School Social Work Practice Model is twofold: (1) to provide a framework for service provision that articulates those skills and services that can reasonably be expected from school social workers; and (2) to promote consistency in pre-service education, continuing professional development, credentialing, and professional practice with the goal of improving academic and behavioral outcomes.

A variety of factors influence the percentage of time that school social workers allocate to these different roles. The most obvious factor is the ratio of full-time equivalency to the number of students. For all of the practice features and key constructs in this model to be implemented effectively, it takes a full-time social worker in a school, or approximately a 1:250 ratio for general education students with few needs. However, when working with students with more needs (e.g., Individualized Education Plan, 504, higher number of suspensions, free and reduced lunch, and attendance concerns), a higher ratio would be considered. This estimate will vary depending on several additional factors, such as the percentage of high-risk students within the school population, the experience and expertise of the school social worker, and the availability of other services—both within the school and the within the community. Additional factors impacting the job description of school social workers are the priorities and expectations of the school/district.

# THE NATIONAL SCHOOL SOCIAL WORK PRACTICE MODEL[1]

The model articulates three practice features and four key constructs, which are described next (Figure 2.1).

## PRACTICE FEATURES

The practice model encourages school social workers to simultaneously (1) provide evidence-based educational, behavioral, and mental health services; (2) promote school climate and culture conducive to learning; and (3) maximize access to school-based and community-based resources. In addition, the model contains four key constructs, which are infused into each practice feature. School social workers are expected to possess advanced knowledge and technical skills to guide their practice in these three areas. The proportion of time school social workers engage in each practice feature varies widely depending on contextual factors, including the needs of the community, school, families, and students served.

## Provide Evidence-Based Education, Behavior, and Mental Health Services

Providing evidence-based education, behavior, and mental health services to support academic and behavior outcomes constitutes the primary direct service component of school social work practice. School social workers have expertise in child and family work that is unique because it also incorporates school and community stressors that interfere with educational success. In addition, school social workers' consultative skills can assist other school staff in implementing interventions with fidelity. This practice feature is accomplished by the following:

- Implementing multi-tiered programs and practices
- Monitoring progress
- Evaluating effectiveness

## Promote a School Climate and Culture Conducive to Student Learning and Teaching Excellence

Promoting school climate and culture conducive to learning refers to the psychosocial environment that fosters academic engagement and achievement. Schools with contexts conducive to learning have (1) policies and procedures that produce safe and orderly environments; (2) capacity-building efforts to promote effective practices; and (3) supportive relationships within and between students, families, school staff, and community partners. Implementing this practice feature is accomplished by the following:

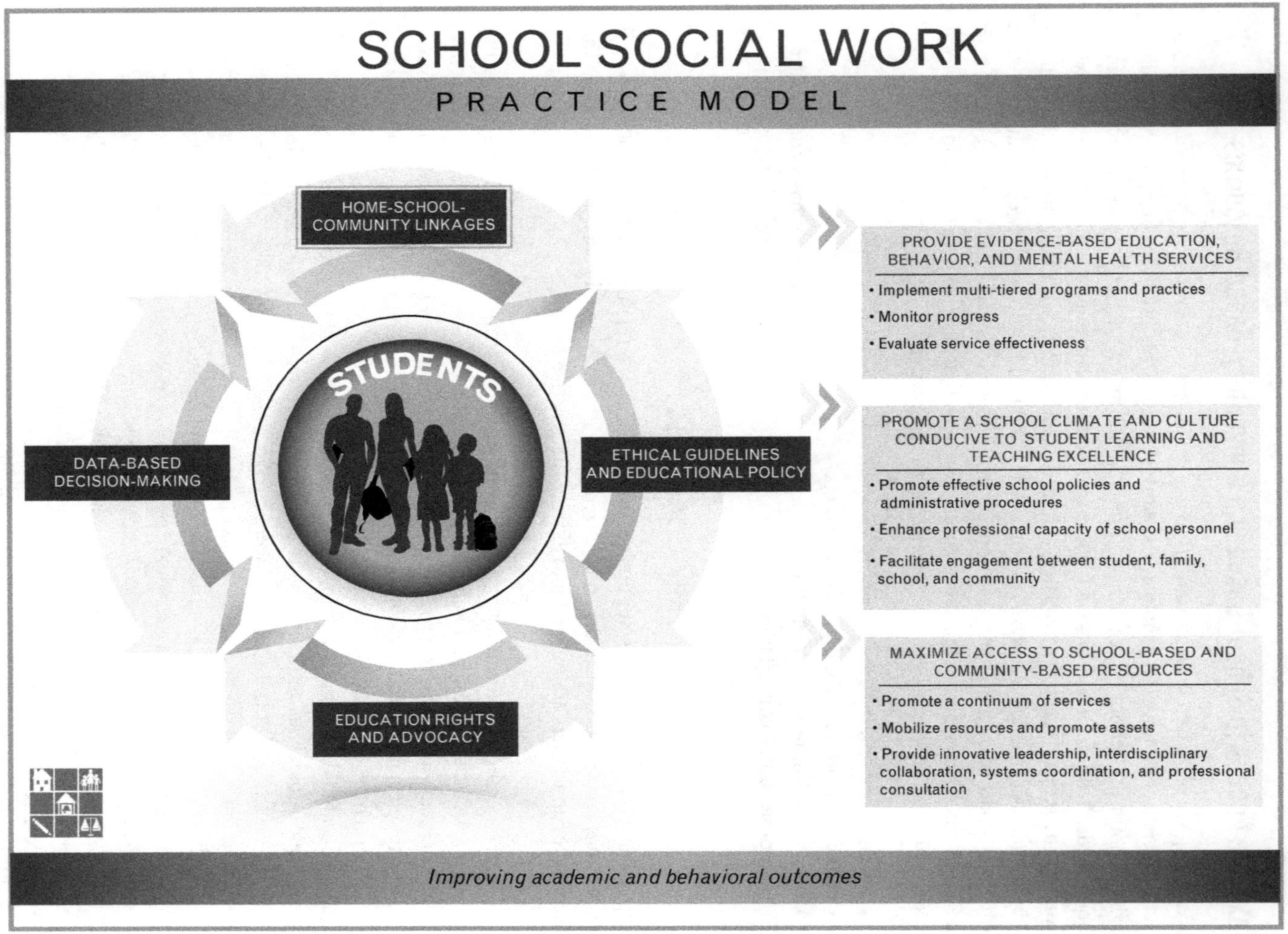

**FIGURE 2.1:** The National School Social Work Practice Model

- Promoting effective school policies and administrative procedures
- Enhancing professional capacity of school personnel
- Facilitating engagement between student, family, school, and community

## Maximize Access to School-Based and Community-Based Resources

Maximizing school-based and community-based resources constitutes the primary indirect or macro-practice component of school social work services. This involves coordinating available services within the school or reaching out to community partners to secure services to meet school needs. School social workers have extensive knowledge about school system services as well as the scope of services available within the community, and they possess the skills to navigate these service delivery systems (e.g., health, mental health, child welfare, and juvenile justice). As a part of their role in the school system, school social workers challenge barriers to accessing school-based and community-based resources that support academic and behavioral success. This practice feature is accomplished by the following:

- Promoting a continuum of services
- Mobilizing resources and promoting assets
- Providing innovative leadership, interdisciplinary collaboration, systems coordination, and professional consultation

### KEY CONSTRUCTS

Each of the practice features is supported by historical school social work scholarship and research that serve to delineate this specialized form of professional social work practice. The following key constructs are infused into each of the practice features:

1. Home–school–community linkages: A hallmark of school social work practice is the belief that academic and behavior achievement are profoundly impacted by the environment, including relationships and interactions across home, school, and community settings. Facilitating communication and promoting linkages across these systems is a central characteristic of school social work practice.

2. Ethical guidelines and educational policy: School social workers pledge to follow professional ethical guidelines and carry out federal and state educational policy to provide the highest level of school social work practice. NASW's *Code of Ethics* (2008) and SSWAA's *Ethical Guidelines* series define expectations for ethical school social work practice. Furthermore, school social work literature facilitates accountability by promoting the use of an ethical decision-making model when applying laws, policies, and codes to specific school dilemmas; school social workers should follow an ethical decision-making model. The Code also emphasizes the need for continuous professional development to keep abreast of evidenced-based practices in the field and also reflection on practice to ensure that evidence-based practices selected fit the context and culture of the school setting.

3. Education rights and advocacy: Educational rights and advocacy require that school social workers address the ways in which structural inequalities and school processes affect school quality and educational outcomes. School social work practitioners are expected to give voice to issues of diversity and also social and economic justice that lead to school failure and educational disparities. As part of their role in the school

system, school social workers should be able to balance their mandate to advocate for students and families in their position as a school employee and work to change policies and practices that undermine the dignity and worth of students.

4.  Data-based decision-making: Data-based decision-making refers to the process of integrating the best current research evidence in designing and implementing interventions. School social work services should be informed by the research literature; adapt empirically supported interventions to fit student needs; and routinely evaluate the effectiveness of policies, programs, and practices.

## IMPLEMENTATION

A recently completed survey of more than 3,500 school social workers in the United States provides some insight into the extent to which the national model is being implemented in practice (Frey, Thompson, Kelly, Alvarez, & Berzin, 2015; Kelly, Frey, Thompson, Klemp, Alvarez, & Berzin, 2016). The authors of this survey project suggest that many components of the model are being actively implemented, according to the responses of the national sample. Specifically, the authors were encouraged by self-reports that indicate the most reliable resources for identifying effective practices (online evidence-based practice sites and online databases) were those that school social workers report using most often. In addition, data indicate that school social workers are in fact implementing education, behavioral, and mental health services at the primary, secondary, and tertiary levels, although the majority of their time is spent providing tertiary support. Results suggest that school social workers most frequently use existing data, standardized scales, and progress monitoring and least often use universal screeners and fidelity monitoring tools.

The authors of the survey also conclude the second practice domain—promoting a school culture conducive to student learning and teaching excellence—is being implemented less frequently than the first and third domains. They suggest there is a need to continue to advocate for intervention approaches that target the environment rather than individuals.

There was substantial evidence in the survey data to suggest the third domain is being implemented. For example, school social workers indicated that they often provide parent workshops and serve on parent–school committees (i.e., advocacy and parent–teacher association). Finally, responses suggest that school social workers promote the development of a continuum of community-based services and engage those services within the school setting.

Unfortunately, the survey did not assess all aspects of the National School Social Work Practice Model. Specifically, the extent to which school social workers follow ethical guidelines, carry out educational policy, or address educational rights and advocate for issues of diversity and social and economic justice that lead to school failure and educational disparities was not captured. Although there are no empirical data to suggest school social workers are or are not addressing issues related to intersecting forms of social diversity, the elevated status of these activities in the model clearly demonstrates their importance to practice.

# SUGGESTIONS FOR DISSEMINATION AND RESEARCH

The National School Social Work Practice Model and other resources are available on the SSWAA website at http://www.sswaa.org/?page=459&hhSearchTerms=%22national+and+

model%22. School social workers are encouraged to share the model and information about the benefits of professional school social work services with teachers, specialized instructional school professionals, principals, superintendents, school board members, as well as children and families (Frey et al., 2012). It represents a milestone in the advancement, practice, and evaluation of school social work. However, additional research is needed to examine the robustness and fidelity of the model. Other critical areas of needed research include determination of an optimal workload ratio of school social workers to students and the impact of school social work services on academic and behavioral outcomes.

## CONCLUSION

The National School Social Work Practice Model was created in the context of education reform and federal policy changes that are altering the landscape of specialized instructional support, including school social work. The model provides a framework for service provision by articulating the skills and services that can reasonably be expected from school social workers; promotes consistency in pre-service education, continuing professional development, credentialing, and professional practice with the goal of improving academic and behavioral outcomes. Recent survey data suggest that all aspects of the model are being implemented by school social workers nationally.

## DISCUSSION QUESTIONS

1. The National School Social Work Practice Model has three practice features. Discuss each practice feature and how it is to be accomplished. How may contextual factors affect the proportion of time a school social worker engages in each feature?

2. The National School Social Work Practice Model has four key constructs: home–school–community linkages, ethical guidelines and educational policy, education rights and advocacy, and data-based decision-making. Explain each construct. How do the constructs support student learning?

3. How might a school social worker demonstrate respect for multiculturalism and diversity through the practice features and key constructs?

---

## CASE STUDIES

### CASE STUDY 1: PRACTICE FEATURES 1 AND 3

John is a fifth-grade student who was identified by the Systematic Screening for Behavior Disorders (SSBD), the school's universal screening tool, is at risk of school failure due to concerns with social–emotional development (Walker, Severson, & Feil, 2014). In addition to being identified as at risk for internalizing behavior problems, a teacher interview completed by the school social worker suggested that John is a very intelligent student and does well academically when he is engaged in learning and gets his work completed and turned in on time. He lives with his parents and sister in a middle-class neighborhood. Both parents work, have graduate degrees, and have high expectations for John. They report that John has been diagnosed with an anxiety disorder; he was evaluated for special education in third grade but did not qualify. The school social worker consulted *School Social Work: An Evidence-Informed Framework for Practice* (Kelly, Raines, Stone, & Frey, 2010) and learned that most of the evidence-supported interventions for elementary-aged children with anxiety problems are tier 2 interventions, which are delivered in small group settings outside of the classroom. Although this resource identified several options, the Cool Kids Program (Mifsud & Rapee, 2005) was selected and implemented with John and seven other children in the school who also scored in the at-risk range on the SSBD (internalizing domain). The program includes eight student sessions (group-based) and two parent sessions. Mid-year SSBD data and teacher report suggested John was doing much better by January. However, John's parents reported to the school social worker that the challenges in the home setting had become more difficult and that John had mentioned wanting to hurt himself on two occasions. In addition, his parents had a difficult time getting him to attend social events, even if they were present. The school social worker referred the parents to a local psychiatrist, who was well known for working with students and coordinating services with schools. The psychiatrist recommended John and his parents to a therapist who specializes in childhood anxiety disorders. The therapist is monitoring John for 6 months before determining if medication is appropriate. The school social worker checks in with John every other week, and he is flagged as an at-risk child to be monitored (SSBD data) quarterly even though he is currently doing well in school.

## CASE STUDY 2: PRACTICE FEATURES 1 AND 2

A school social worker in a large, urban district noticed that more than 35% of the children in her school were being identified as candidates for tier 2 or tier 3 interventions based on universal screening of attendance and office disciplinary referral (ODR) data. To better understand the problem, she identified a five-stage process for improving school climate published from the National School Climate Center, and she obtained permission from the organization to use its Comprehensive School Climate Inventory, which assess 12 dimensions of school. After the survey was administered, she presented the findings to school administration; she also shared the National School Climate Center's five-stage improvement process. The administrators requested she present the same information to faculty to assess buy-in for a multi-year commitment to stages 3 (action planning), 4, (implementation), and 5 (re-evaluation) focusing on the two dimensions of school climate (safety and interpersonal relationships) that were identified during the evaluation as most problematic. The faculty were surprised by the attendance and ODR data, as well as the results of the climate assessment. They were excited about possibilities and agreed to engage in the process. The school social worker remained the lead on the project. She identified all of the school- and community-based supports that were currently in place to foster a healthy school climate, and she made recommendations to the administration for which ones had evidence to support their use and therefore should be retained. She also identified effective climate-enhancing interventions and provided choices to school faculty and staff. Although several interventions were organized and coordinated, the primary addition to the existing school interventions was the Steps to Respect bullying prevention program. The school social worker was responsible for teacher training in the intervention procedures, and she also monitored implementation fidelity and outcomes (using attendance data and ODRs).

## ACKNOWLEDGMENT

The development of the National School Social Work Practice Model was supported, in part, by Minnesota State University, Mankato, through a 2011 Strategic Planning Grant awarded to Michelle Alvarez.

## ADDITIONAL RESOURCES

American School Counselor Association, *ASCA National Model*: http://www.ascanationalmodel.org

National Association of School Psychologists, *NASP Practice Model*: http://www.nasponline.org/standards/practice-model

School Social Work Association of America, *National School Social Work Model*: PowerPoint and graphic, http://sswaa.site-ym.com/?page=459; brochure, http://c.ymcdn.com/sites/www.sswaa.org/resource/resmgr/imported/SSWAA%20Practice%20Model%20Brochure.pdf

## REFERENCES

Alderson, J. (1972). Models of school social work practice. In R. Sarri & F. F. Maple (Eds.), *The school in the community* (pp. 33–36). Washington, DC: National Association of Social Workers.

Allen-Meares, P. (1977). Analysis of tasks in school social work. *Social Work, 22*, 196.

Allen-Meares, P. (1994). Social work services in schools: A national study of entry level tasks. *Social Work, 39*, 560–565.

Allen-Meares, P. (2007). School social work: Historical development, influences, and practices. In P. Allen-Meares (Ed.), *Social work services in schools* (4th ed., pp. 23–51). Boston: Pearson/Allyn & Bacon.

Allen-Meares, P. (2010). *Social work services in schools* (6th ed.). Boston, MA: Pearson.

Butler, A. W. (1898). Indiana [Reports from states]. In I. C. Barrows (Ed.), *Proceedings of the National Conference of Charities & Corrections at the 25th annual session held in the city of New York, May 18–25, 1898* (pp. 45–47). Boston, MA: G. H. Ellis.

Bye, L., & Alvarez, M. (2007). *School social work: Theory to practice*. Belmont, CA: Thompson Brooks/Cole.

Costin, L. B. (1969). An analysis of the tasks in school social work. *Social Service Review, 43*, 274–285.

Costin, L. B. (1973). School social work practice: A new model. *Social Work, 20*, 135–139.

Council on Social Work Education. (2008). *Educational policy and accreditation standards*. Alexandria, VA: Author. Retrieved from http://www.cswe.org/Accreditation/2008EPASDescription.aspx

Frey, A., Alvarez, M., Sabatino, C., Lindsey, B., Dupper, D., Raines, J., . . . Norris, M. (2012). The development of a national school social work practice model. *Children & Schools, 34*, 131–134.

Frey, A., & Dupper, D. R. (2005). A broader conceptual approach to clinical practice for the 21st century. *Children & Schools, 27*, 33–44.

Frey, A. J., Alvarez, M. E., Dupper, D. R., Sabatino, C. A., Lindsey, B. C., Raines, J. C., . . . Norris, M. A. (2013). *National school social work practice model*. University of Louisville. Retrieved from http://sswaa.org/displaycommon.cfm?an=1&subarticlenbr=459

Herbst, J. (1986). Towards compulsory education: The school revival movement in the United States. In G. Genovesi (Ed.), *Introduction, development and extension of compulsory education. Conference papers for the 8th session of the International Standing Conference for the History of Education, Parma, Italy, September 3-6, 1986* (Vol. 1, pp. 281–291). ERIC document ED 279–098.

Katz, M. S. (1976). *A history of compulsory education laws*. Bloomington, IN: Phi Delta Kappa. Eric document ED 119–389.

Kelly, M. S. (2008). *The domains and demands of school social work practice: A guide to working effectively with students, families, & schools*. New York, NY: Oxford University Press.

Kelly, M. S., Berzin, S. C., Frey, A., Alvarez, M., Shaffer, G., & O'Brien, K. (2010). The state of school social work: Findings from the National School Social Work Survey. *School Mental Health, 2*, 132–141. doi:10.1007/s12310-010-903.4-5

Kelly, M. S., Frey, A., Alvarez, M., Berzin, S. C., Shaffer, G. L., & O'Brien, K. (2010). School social work practice choices and response to intervention. *Children & Schools, 4*, 201–210.

Kelly, M. S., Frey, A., Thompson, A., Klemp, H., Alvarez, M., & Berzin, S. C. (2016). Assessing the national *school social work practice model: Findings from the second national school social work. Social Work, 61*, 17–28. doi: 10.1093/sw/swv044.

Kelly, M. S., Raines, J. C., Stone, S., & Frey, A. (2010). *School social work: An evidence-informed framework for practice*. New York, NY: Oxford University Press.

Massat, C. R., Constable, R., McDonald, S., & Flynn, J. P. (2009). *School social work: Practice, policy, and research* (7th ed.). Chicago, IL: Lyceum.

McCullagh, J. G. (1993). The roots of school social work in New York City. *Iowa Journal of School Social Work, 6*, 49–74.

McCullagh, J. G. (2000). School social work in Chicago: An unrecognized pioneer program. *School Social Journal, 25*, 1–15.

McCullagh, J. G. (2002). The inception of school social work in Boston: Clarifying and expanding the historical record. *School Social Work Journal, 26*, 58–67.

Mifsud, C., & Rapee, R. M. (2005). Early intervention for childhood anxiety in a school setting: Outcomes for an economically disadvantaged population. *Journal of the American Academy of Child and Adolescent Psychiatry, 44*, 996–1004.

Mulkeen, T. A. (1986). The compulsory curriculum in industrial America: Connections between past and present. In G. Genovesi (Ed.), *Compulsory education: Schools, pupils, teachers, programs and methods. Conference papers for the 8th session of the International Standing Conference for the History of Education, Parma, Italy, September 3-6, 1986* (Vol. 3, pp. 189–201). ERIC document ED 279–100.

National Association of Social Workers. (2008). *Code of ethics*. Washington, DC: Author. Retrieved from http://www.socialworkers.org/pubs/code/default.asp

National Association of Social Workers. (2012). *Standards for school social work services*. Washington, DC: Author. Retrieved from http://www.socialworkers.org/practice/standards/naswschoolsocial-workstandards.pdf

Raines, J. C. (1996). Appropriate vs. least restrictive: Educational policies and students with disabilities. *Social Work in Education, 18*, 113–127.

Raines, J. C. (1999). Forgotten beginnings? *Social Work, 44*, 400–401.

Raines, J. C. (2008). A retrospective chronicle of the Midwest School Social Work Council: Its vision and influence after forty years. *School Social Work Journal, 33*(1), 1–15.

School Social Work Association of America. (2007). *Ethical guidelines.* London, KY: Author. Retrieved from http://www.sswaa.org/?102

School Social Work Association of America. (2014). *National Evaluation Framework for School Social Work Practice.* London, KY: Author. Retrieved from http://www.cswe.org/Accreditation/2008EPASDescription.aspx

Shaffer, N. M. (1898). The care of crippled and deformed children. In I. C. Barrows (Ed.), *Proceedings of the National Conference of Charities and Correction at the 25th annual session held in the City of New York, May 18–25, 1898* (pp. 393–401). Boston, MA: G. H. Ellis.

Smith, J. K. (1986). Compulsory education in Chicago: Its growth and development from the mid-nineteenth to early twentieth century. In G. Genovesi (Ed.), *Introduction, development and extension of compulsory education. Conference papers for the 8th session of the International Standing Conference for the History of Education, Parma, Italy, September 3–6, 1986* (Vol. 1, pp. 321–331). ERIC document ED 279–098.

Walker, H., Severson, H. H., & Feil, E. (2014). *Systematic screening for behavior disorders (SSBD) (2nd Edition).* Eugene, OR, Pacific Northwest Publishing.

# CHAPTER 3

# CHANGING THE PARADIGM FOR SCHOOL SOCIAL WORK ROLES

## MARTELL TEASLEY AND LAURA RICHARD

This chapter highlights many of the roles and attributes of school social work practice. It outlines information found within research literature in the areas of macro and micro practice, evaluation of services, collaboration, consultation, and the challenges of advocacy for educational equality. It begins with a brief overview of the formative years of school social work as a field of practice, noting the early role development and expansion of school social work practice. Along with a review of research on school social work tasks, their role in special education is discussed with examination of evidence-based methods and culturally competent approaches to practice. Information on self-care for school social workers who sometimes experience stress and burnout is provided. Finally, a case example for teaching and learning is provided highlighting the roles of school social work practice with diverse populations and the need for advocacy for children's educational rights.

## DOMAIN OF PRACTICE

Although the majority of school social workers continue to work within traditional public school settings, there is a changing venue for practice. For example, the continuing flux of education reform measures within the United States with the emerging movement toward marketplace reform creates a new horizon for the field of school social work practice (see Chapter 5). This includes the growing charter school movement in the United States and the growing privatization of local school systems that were once started, owned, and fully staffed with public education professionals and paraprofessionals. There are also parochial and private schools that employ school social work services. Alternative schools are another setting in which school social workers have a known and growing role in practice with youth who have special needs and with youth who have been transferred from the traditional public school settings based on behavioral challenges. However, there is no research or information that provides a description of the numbers and attributes of school social workers in roles outside of traditional public school settings.

Requirements for practice vary by states and regions, with most requiring social work licensure. Although most states and local school districts require a graduate degree in social work in order to be a school social worker, there are localities that allow those with bachelor's degrees in social work to practice in school settings. The expanding role of school social workers has meant that school social work's role has been defined by the school's perception of the social worker's role rather than the social worker's skills and training (Richard & Villarreal Sosa, 2014). Coupled with the changing face of public education, the lack of knowledge that schools and school districts possess about what tasks a social worker performs in a school setting has created a variety of role definitions resulting in role ambiguity in many cases (Richard & Villarreal Sosa, 2014). However, along with the challenge of sorting through the shifting dynamics of public education in the United States, there are new opportunities for school social workers in terms of educational leadership and policymaking in advocating for children's educational rights (Corbin, 2005). Such roles are strongly needed given the increasing public mandate for fiscal austerity in publicly funded programs such as education.

# EARLY ROLES OF SCHOOL SOCIAL WORKERS

Known as "visiting teachers" at the start of the 1906–1907 school year in the cities of Boston, Hartford, Connecticut, New York, and Chicago, school social workers evolved from their initial conception as practitioners benefiting "underprivileged" families and immigrant populations to working with children in early settlement houses (Allen-Meares, 2006). As compulsory school attendance laws were implemented within the United States, the need for school social work services expanded nationwide. The 1920s witnessed the beginning development of a "therapeutic approach for social workers in public schools" (Allen-Meares, 2004, p. 27) only to undergo a shift in focus to that of enforcing compulsory attendance laws in the 1930s. Their role transformed again from 1940 to 1960 with the development of social casework and the clinical approach to practice. Diversity in the school setting became a key issue with the passage of the 1954 *Brown v. Board of Education* Supreme Court verdict outlawing outright segregation of public schools in the United States (Joseph, Slovak, & Broussard, 2010).

The specific role of school social workers was defined in 1949 when Florence Poole associated social work practice with the mission of the school and a child's right to an education (Constable, 2009). Her definition emphasized social casework (Constable, 2009). Group therapy and experimentation with a variety of therapy methods in the 1950s and 1960s led to research on different kinds of school social work practice models: clinical model, school change model, social interaction model, community school model, and the community–school–pupil relations model (see Chapter 1; Allen-Meares, 2006). The community–school–pupil relations model was developed by Lela Costin and established the first set of functions specific to school social workers: direct counseling with individuals, groups, or families; advocacy; consultation; community linkage; interdisciplinary team coordination; needs assessment; and program policy development (see Chapter 1; Constable, 2009).

During the 1970s, new and changing educational legislation regarding early childhood education and the education of children with disabilities led to the expansion of school social work (Allen-Meares, 2010). National standards and qualification requirements for school social work practice were enacted in the 1990s as a response to the challenge of educating a more diverse student population along with the growing challenge of childhood poverty and its impact on school readiness (Allen-Meares, 2006; Dupper & Evans, 1996).

School social work roles began to shift—roles that remain a staple of practice today—with the reauthorizations of the Elementary and Secondary Act (ESEA) in 1975 and its subsequent development into the Individuals with Disabilities Education Act (IDEA) (Whitted, Rich, Constable, & Massat, 2009). Both laws were established to ensure equal educational opportunity and access for all children regardless of their background. The ESEA has been reauthorized seven times, with the most recent reauthorization in January 2002 as the No Child Left Behind (NCLB) Act (New America Foundation, 2010). Because IDEA is reauthorized by the US Congress, it continues to define the role of school social workers and other service professionals as *related services personnel* in working with children and youth with disabilities. For example, among other descriptive sections within IDEA (2006), Statute Title I/A/ Sec. 602(26) (US Department of Education (http://www.ed.gov) states that

> the term related services means transportation, and such developmental, corrective, and other supportive service (including speech–language pathology and audiology services, interpreting services, psychological services, physical and occupational therapy, recreation, including therapeutic recreation, social work services, school nurse services designed to enable a child with a disability to receive a free appropriate public education).

Teasley and Cruz (2014) note that related services personnel are "multiskilled practitioners who provide preventive, therapeutic, and crisis intervention; developmental guidance; and individual and group counseling" (p. 32). Their main task is to stop obstacles that impede a child's chance of succeeding in life, to enhance educational opportunity, and to work collaboratively in doing so.

# PRIOR RESEARCH ON ROLE DEFINITIONS FOR SCHOOL SOCIAL WORK

Kelly and Stone (2009) note that studies of school social work practice have not moved beyond a description of the tasks, activities, and services that school social workers perform to analyze what shapes social workers' choice of tasks, activities, and services. In a review of state and national surveys, Kelly and Stone determined that a lack of adherence to national standards for school social work practice contributes to the difficulty of determining defined roles for school social workers. Several state and national surveys provide examples of the existence of role definition inconsistencies. Four national and three state surveys have been conducted in the United States (Allen-Meares, 1977, 1994; Costin, 1969; Dibble, 2008; Kelly, 2007; Kelly et al., 2010; Richard & Villarreal Sosa, 2014; Whittlesey-Jerome, 2012).

In 1967, a rating scale with 107 items was administered to a random sample of 368 school social workers, out of a population of 1,456, from 40 states and the District of Columbia that employed school social workers (Costin, 1969). Data collected from December 1966 to March 1967 resulted in 238 questionnaires in the analysis of school social work tasks. A factor analysis identified the following nine factors loading at least .40 on the factor and having at least five items: leadership and policymaking, casework service to the child and his parents, clinical treatment of children with emotional problems, educational counseling with the child and his parents, liaison between the family and community agencies, interpreting the child to the teacher, interpreting school social work, and case load management (Costin, 1969).

Using the 1967 survey, Allen-Meares (1977) reduced the list of 107 tasks to 85 tasks and distributed the survey to school social workers nationwide. A total of 832 participants were randomly selected from a population of 4,497 school social workers from 39 states. A factor analysis indicated that the description of school social work was changing from traditional casework to a systems-change model such as a school–community model (Allen-Meares, 1977). The survey showed very little emphasis on larger scale practice but instead focused on individuals and casework (Allen-Meares, 1977).

Another national survey of school social workers was conducted in 1994 by Paula Allen-Meares that updated her prior work on tasks school social workers must be able to perform and tasks school social workers prefer to perform (Allen-Meares, 1994). The survey was based on Allen-Meares' (1994) survey instrument and had a 49.5% response rate. The random sample was drawn from the National Association of Social Workers (NASW), state social work associations, employers, and state commissions, with the majority of respondents living in the east north central United States (25%), Middle Atlantic (19%), South Atlantic (18%), or New England (10%). Receiving the lowest mean task rating was policymaking and leadership. School, community, and pupil relations were important to the respondents, with prevention, cultural diversity, and development of community services and social supports viewed as necessary to meet educational goals (Allen-Meares, 1994).

In 2007, a statewide school social work survey designed by Kelly (2007) was conducted in Illinois to determine the nature of school social work practice in that state (which has the largest number of school social workers in the United States), the influence of best practice literature on practice, and the influence of organizational factors on practice choices. The survey had a cross-sectional sample of 821 randomly selected school social workers from Illinois. It was found that individual and small group treatments were used the most with students, with a large majority of social workers providing at least half of their time serving students with Individualized Education Plans (IEPs) and having a caseload of 20–50 regular and special education students per week. Few school social workers reported using best practice literature to guide their practice, but most believed school social workers had adequate support from other school personnel and were pleased with their practice (Kelly, 2007).

A longitudinal analysis of school social work practice in Wisconsin was conducted by the Wisconsin Department of Instruction (WDI) in 2008 using combined results from school social work surveys completed in 1998–1999, 2001–2002, 2004–2005, and 2007–2008 to identify areas of responsibility for Wisconsin school social workers and strategies they used to address those areas of responsibilities (Dibble, 2008). A census sample of school social workers was gathered by the WDI each year, making the survey available to as many school social workers as possible (Dibble, 2008). The average number of respondents in each survey was 230 (45%). The top areas of responsibility addressed most often were children at risk, attendance, truancy, dropouts, behavior management, special education, and basic human needs. The top five strategies used to address these issues were advocacy for students and families, consultation, individual student counseling, referral and information giving, and case management. Systemwide, Wisconsin school social workers were involved with school–community collaborative partnerships 91% of the time in their practice (Dibble, 2008).

In 2008, another national survey ($N$ = 1,639) was conducted to determine the interventions school social workers relied on, the use of school social workers' time, and the demographic characteristics of respondents (Kelly et al., 2010). The survey found that most respondents were female (89%), White (79%), and practiced in public schools (89%). The most common referral reasons were behavioral problems, emotional problems, attendance issues, and academic problems. The survey also found that school social workers spent most of their time doing individual or group counseling for students with mental health needs who did not receive any other services outside of the school setting (Kelly et al., 2010).

In 2010, a statewide survey of New Mexico school social workers was commissioned by NASW in an attempt to strengthen their practice specialty area through advocacy with the New Mexico state legislature (Whittlesey-Jerome, 2012). A total of 64 (32%) of the 210 respondents answered the open-ended questions on the survey used for analysis. Issues most impacting the practice of school social work in New Mexico were the economy, large caseloads, and the feeling of overwork and uncertainty about the future of practice. The author placed a strong emphasis on interdisciplinary collaboration as becoming a central role in the future of school-based practice given the economic forecast aimed at defunding school-based services. In such an environment, school social workers worry about engaging in more case management and less direct services (Whittlesey-Jerome, 2012).

Also in 2010, a statewide survey of Louisiana school social workers was conducted for the Louisiana Department of Education (Richard, 2011). The survey provided a comprehensive view of the roles of school social workers in Louisiana. It also highlighted areas needing improvement. The following factors hindered school social work practice effectiveness: large caseload size, lack of supervision by a social worker, and lack of a clear role definition (Richard, 2011). According to this survey, school social workers were functioning under a variety of titles, and some were not properly credentialed. Evaluations of social work performance were conducted but were not specific to social work practice and did not provide a means of accountability for school social work practice, thus diminishing the value of the profession. Students were consistently referred for services to address behavior concerns, but many school social workers were practicing outside their training to provide interventions in academic areas (Richard, 2011). Based on the survey, school social work practice in Louisiana could be broken down into four major areas of practice: supervision of other social workers, macro practice (school- or districtwide program design and management), evaluation/coordination for special education, and micro practice (individual and group mental health treatment or behavior intervention) (Richard & Villarreal Sosa, 2014).

In summary, although the previously discussed surveys did not ask the exact same questions, typical and multiple roles were identified for school social workers: educational and mental health counseling, collaboration, policymaking and advocacy, behavioral intervention, service to children with disabilities, and monitoring school truancy. The reality of high caseloads and the challenge of working in the host setting dominated by teachers and school administrators were also common themes. The description of roles across state and national surveys that were identified indicated ambiguity in role definitions and practices within and among states (Richard & Villarreal Sosa, 2014). There is little consistency of tasks performed in different states, meaning that there is no clear role definition and model of practice across domains for school social workers. In addition, representative research samples among states on national surveys has been a problem. For example, on the 2008 survey, of all 50 states, only 10 had more than 50 respondents to the survey: Florida, Georgia, Illinois, Iowa, Kansas, Minnesota, Missouri, North Carolina, Texas, and Wisconsin (Loyola University Chicago, 2008). More research that includes sustained longitudinal efforts at national, state, and local levels is needed in the examination of roles for school social workers.

# ROLES OF SCHOOL SOCIAL WORKERS TODAY

Today, school social workers are considered an integral link between the home, school, and community (Allen-Meares, 2010). School social work is a growing field of practice aimed at facilitating academic achievement and healthy developmental outcomes for children and youth. School social workers work directly with schoolteachers, administrators, and other school-based personnel to facilitate student success. With each new and expanding role, the definition of school social worker shifts, calling for a larger skill set that meets the needs of the particular context of a given school setting. Because of continued changes in public education including increasing levels of childhood poverty, greater reliance on alternative school settings, and market-based education reform measures, the expanding role for school social workers calls for high flexibility on a daily basis. School social work scholar Cynthia Franklin (2005) remarks that school social workers need to have the skills necessary to practice within their school setting and within a larger political context of reforms. Conversely, given the high demand for flexibility and the multiple skills needed for the practice setting, serving as the home–school–community liaison marks the signature role of school social work practice. School social workers must be able to work across practice levels (macro and micro) and be actively involved in the evaluation of practices and programs while taking leadership roles within and outside school settings.

## DIRECT CLINICAL SERVICES PROVIDER

As direct clinical services providers, the practice of school social workers consists of working with individuals or families (Zastrow & Kirst-Ashman, 2013). Clinical practice in school settings can take the form of services for students and families; case management; crisis intervention; staff consultation and collaboration; and special education assessment, evaluation, and intervention services. The growing ranks of school-aged children with diagnosed learning disabilities and mental health concerns continues to be a challenge for related services personnel. Students with mental health concerns bring additional challenges to classroom management and the need for school-based services. According to 2007 data from the US Department of Health and Human Services (USDHHS), nationally, 11.3% of children aged 2–17 years were diagnosed with a mental health condition (see Chapter 12). Problem behaviors were common in 19% of children with emotional, behavioral, or developmental problems, and less than half (45.6%) of these children received treatment or counseling from a mental health professional (USDHHS, 2007). This direct clinical service role requires attention to guidelines in the NCLB and IDEA laws, indicating a need for evidence-based interventions to be implemented with fidelity, following all guidelines for implementation, and used when making decisions in both general and special education (Louisiana Department of Education, 2009; see Chapter 10). Thus, this role includes viewing oneself as an evidence-based practitioner and comfort with data collection and analysis needed to evaluate one's practice.

## MULTI-TIERED SYSTEMS OF SUPPORT

One of a school social worker's primary roles in working with schoolteachers is to assist in the identification of classroom behavioral strategies. Multi-tiered systems of support (MTSS) or response to intervention (RTI) provisions are outlined in IDEA (2004) for the purpose of implementing evidenced-based measures to address problematic behaviors. MTSS is used mainly with students who display learning disabilities and often as an early instructional support screening tool starting as early as elementary school (Gersten, 2008; Greenwood et al., 2014); RTI is to be used within the educational setting with students prior to referral for special education services (see Chapter 9). As a form of evidence-based intervention, RTI includes pre- and post-intervention methods and is said to help reduce the systematic overreliance on "identify and place" in special education, help reduce the overrepresentation of minority students in special education, and provide behavioral support for children experiencing behavioral problems and emotional disturbances (Thompson, Greenwood, et al., 2014).

However, in the movement toward evidence-based intervention as an approach to school social work practice, there are several challenges. First, there is limited use of evidence-based interventions within this field of practice (Thompson, 2008). Thompson's systematic review of evidence-based intervention to reduce problem behavior found few studies among related services personnel that demonstrate the intended use of RTI. Kelly et al. (2010) determined that school social workers did make use of MTSS; however, practices indicated a preference for primary or individualized treatment instead of universal interventions—a problem that continues to reduce the effectiveness and efficiency of school social workers (Joseph et al., 2010). Furthermore, high caseloads inhibited appropriate use of evidence-based interventions, centralized intervention mandates in some school systems precluded the use MTSS, and there was a lack of data-based decision-making or data analysis by school social workers—a factor central to effective implementation of MTSS. Moreover, supportive systems were not always in place for school social workers to engage in MTSS. However, Kelly et al. concluded that the successful implementation of RTI by school social workers will bolster their leadership, visibility, and credibility in the education setting.

## CASE MANAGEMENT

According to the *NASW Standards for Social Work Case Management* (NASW, 2013), case management is defined as "a process to plan, seek, and advocate for, and monitor services from different social services or health care organizations and staff on behalf of a client" (p. 13). For school social workers, this means "organizing, coordinating, and sustaining activities designed to optimize the functioning of students and/or families" (NASW, 2002, p. 7). School social workers link families and students with resource providers to address needs the family or student may have that cannot be met within the school setting. Resources range from financial assistance and housing to medical referrals. Case management consists of working with a family or individual to develop a plan and then ensuring the family or individual is able to follow the plan to receive the needed assistance. Case management can also involve coordinating the services of several agencies to assist a family or individual, thus providing continuity of services and reducing overlap (Zastrow & Kirst-Ashman, 2013). Mental and behavioral health, special education, child welfare, and foster care are some of the areas in which case management becomes the role of the school social worker.

## FAIR SCHOOL DISCIPLINE ADVOCATE

Cameron's (2006) review of the literature revealed the need for school social workers to engage in advocacy for schoolchildren subject to unfair and overly punitive discipline; educating teachers and administrators about the potential harm associated with conventional disciplinary practices; and educating school personnel about effective, punitive approaches to school disciplinary measures. Teasley and Cruz (2014) note that "school social workers are also expected by school administrators to increase school attendance and decrease school discipline problems" (p. 54).

This is another area in which diversity in practice is essential to improving educational equality. The track record of school social workers in the development of nonpunitive measures, including a reduction in the disproportionate school suspension and expulsion of minority children and youth, is absent from the research literature. African American students are suspended and expelled almost twice as much as other races of students, with even more suspended more than once (Office for Civil Rights, 2012).

## CRISIS INTERVENTION SPECIALIST
## AND RESOURCE MOBILIZATION

In general, one of the roles of school social workers is to diminish or ameliorate crisis in the school setting, particularly for individuals who may be experiencing difficulty in processing a situation such as bullying or a death in the family (Allen-Meares, 2010). However, crisis intervention can address a wide range of issues, including student misbehavior in the classroom, violent outbursts, the spread of a communicable disease, and natural disasters. School social workers can be called on to intervene in a crisis situation or consult with a teacher on how to handle a particular behavior being displayed in the classroom or in the aftermath of a crisis within the classroom.

Resource mobilization in times of crisis intervention is central to school social work practice. As part of a crisis team, school social workers can mobilize the resources needed to support the school system, the community, and individuals. They can broker goods and services needed by others through advocacy and collaboration via intervention networks at local and state levels. Social workers not only can obtain monetary resources but also can garner support for the school or district through volunteers, professional organizations, fundraising, and grant research and writing. Indeed, resource mobilization as an ongoing component of school social work practice can become a salient feature of school social workers' worth to school systems.

## SPECIAL EDUCATION SERVICE PROVIDER AND ADVOCATE

Special education assessment and evaluation is a commonly assigned task for school social workers (for an expanded discussion of the role of the school social worker in special education, see Chapter 7). Social workers are an integral part of the special education department, performing tasks that range from serving as part of a multidisciplinary team that performs pre-referral interventions to performing a biopsychosocial assessment that can include a medical review, behavioral screenings, and gathering information from parents, teachers, and students to inform a special education evaluation. Special education is also an area in which the school social worker can play a critical role in addressing disproportionality. The overrepresentation of Black and Hispanic children and youth continues to worsen in the US public education system. Studies have also demonstrated the overrepresentation of Native American children with a special education diagnosis (Morrier & Gallagher, 2012). Although IDEA mandates nondiscriminatory assessment and evidence-based methods in the identification and placement of children and youth with disabilities, minority children continue to be overidentified and disproportionately placed in special education programs.

Combined with poverty and other risk factors for poor school performance, a litany of social and cultural factors contribute to disparities in special education diagnosis and treatment (Oswald, Coutinho, Best, & Singh, 1999). Racial bias, cultural misunderstanding, and outright draconian approaches to school discipline factor into the oversuspension and overplacement in special education programs of African American and Hispanic (Latino) children and youth. The perceptions and stereotypes of minority children, particularly Black and Hispanic children, are more negative than those of White children: "There is some indication that teachers do make differential judgments about achievement and behavior based on racially conditioned characteristics" (Skiba et al., 2011, p. 87). Once referred to a school administrator, Black and Hispanic children experience harsher punishment (including arrests and referral to law enforcement) in comparison to their White counterparts for similar school violations (Office for Civil Rights, 2012).

Despite more than three decades of research on the subject, mainly by education scholars, there continues to be disproportionality of students of color in special education programs (Fenning & Rose, 2007; Joseph et al., 2010). It is troubling that given the continued disproportionality of students of color, no body of research adequately assesses the roles of school social workers in addressing this issue. Suffice it to say that the track record of school social workers with regard to the reduction of minority student disproportionality in special education programs is absent from the research literature.

The challenge for school social workers as culturally competent practitioners is to understand diversity within the context of special education assessment and diagnosis. In their roles as education advocates, policy analysts, and consultants, school social workers must work to dispel stereotypes aimed at racial, ethnic, gender, and sexual minorities at the individual and organizational levels within school systems (Bean, 2011). The normality of special education placement as a response to structural inequalities within public education in US society must end (Joseph, Slovak, & Broussard, 2014; Teasley & Cruz, 2014). School social workers should be aware of disparities in special education enrollment, and they should advocate for school reform and appropriate resource procurement. Working collaboratively, engaging in self-awareness, consulting with others, understanding state and local IDEA implementation, informing parents and children of their rights, understanding community dynamics, and appropriately using evidence-informed practices in the assessment and development of IEPs are all necessary activities in which school social workers can make a difference (Teasley & Cruz, 2014). School social workers should have an organized and executable advocacy plan for ameliorating racial and ethnic disparities in special education programs as part of their commitment to social justice (Joseph, Slovak, & Broussard, 2014; Teasley & Cruz, 2014).

## CONSULTANT AND COLLABORATOR

Staff consultation and collaboration can require a considerable amount of time for school social workers, but are extremely important to efficient and effective practice. Consultation involves a social worker meeting with someone (school personnel, families, community agencies, etc.) to discuss a problem, provide an answer to a question, or share insight into a situation (Barker, 1999). Collaboration involves working together with someone to achieve an outcome for an individual, family, group, or community (Barker, 1999).

Consultation can be facilitated through formal means such as a written request from a teacher as well as more informally through day-to-day interactions with school staff. Social workers should not only consult with other social workers but also be available and amenable to consulting with other school professionals. Sharing the knowledge and skills that social workers possess with other professionals creates a mutual respect and understanding of the role each plays within the school district. It also reveals ways to partner on common issues facing schools, again solidifying the social worker's place at the table in future discussions. Often, social workers in schools have conversations with individuals involved with schools (e.g., parents and staff) and provide guidance and ideas for those individuals without need for further intervention or collaboration. If a social worker begins working together with an individual or entity toward a specific outcome for a student or group, it becomes collaboration.

Collaboration of services helps to reduce fragmentation and barriers to services, facilitates positive change, and creates greater workplace efficiency. Roles garnered in the collaborative process with other related service personnel include mental health and child welfare service coordination, community outreach, program evaluation, collective advocacy, planning and managing programs, networking, and grant writing (Teasley & Cruz, 2014; Villarreal Sosa & McGrath, 2013). As home, school, and community liaisons, it is the role of school social workers to initiate collaborative practices in order to reduce gaps in services and enhance educational opportunities for school-aged children and youth.

## MACRO PRACTITIONER

In a school setting, macro practice can involve collaborating with all of the external systems affecting a student's life. Understanding and advocating for the educational rights of students is one area of macro practice that distinguishes social workers from other school professionals and is a foundational principle of social work practice (NASW, 2012). School social workers should also be aware of policies affecting children's educational rights and well-being, as well as how policies affect school social work practice. As advocates for educational equality and individual rights, social workers have the ability to develop needed policies and lobby for change with local, state, and federal leaders and should be constantly aware of their role in this process. Although research studies shed little light on the subject of school social work and policymaking or advocacy, by taking the lead on the development of policy initiatives affecting local education districts, social workers can place themselves in the forefront of the school leadership and become indispensable as education advocates at the local, regional, and state levels. National school social work organizations such as the School Social Work Association of American (SSWAA) advocate for student rights and legislation supporting and expanding school social work services. In particular, SSWAA has a government relations director who regularly reports information on national legislation affecting school social work practice.

School social workers can also be key players in development and implementation of schoolwide and districtwide interventions (see Chapter 9). Trained in systemic practice, social workers in a school setting also serve as the intermediaries among families, staff, and communities. School social workers can bridge the divide that sometimes exists and make connections that are often difficult to make when dealing with multiple systems. In this way, they can work to acquire resources and create programming opportunities or improve parent involvement with schools. They can also collaborate with community agencies to procure services needed by students, families, and schools to ensure the best educational experience for all involved.

## PRACTITIONER/RESEARCHER

Just as teachers are required to prove effectiveness, so are other school-based personnel, including school social workers. School practitioners are increasingly asked to provide accountability for outcomes of their work. Social workers are trained to research, plan and design, implement, and evaluate programs, including tasks such needs assessment. In a school setting, this could take the form of districtwide programs such as suicide prevention, anti-bullying, or parent involvement or programs designed for the individual needs of students such as interventions for anger management or autism support. By engaging in the role as a practitioner/researcher, school social workers can help schools meet their standards of performance and demonstrate how school social work is a part of the overall school mission of gaining the best outcomes possible for students (Franklin, 2005). Social workers have an obligation to evaluate their practice and also any programs they implement in a school or a district. It is not only good practice but also can provide the needed information to school districts that will ultimately preserve the jobs of school social workers in those districts (see Chapter 11). Greater use of hard data is necessary to provide evidence of a given intervention's merit, thus solidifying the school social worker's role in the school setting (Kelly et al., 2010).

## LEADER

The most important role a social worker can play in a school setting is that of a leader. Leadership for school social workers means addressing multisystemic needs that no other profession can fully address (Kelly, 2008). Leadership roles that social workers should undertake in a school setting are program development for staff and students, professional consultation and supervision, leading multidisciplinary teams, and capacity building of school and district personnel. Leading multidisciplinary teams is a natural role for school social workers, given their knowledge of the systems involved in students' lives within and outside of the school setting. School social workers can use this knowledge to assist school-based teams in their efforts to design appropriate interventions for students (Franklin, 2005). Most important, social workers should always be at the table for decision-making and policy development involving staff and student needs. If necessary, school social workers should consider developing town hall meetings to inform the public about important issues. Leadership for school social workers also means providing information on district school social work activities and reporting on state and national school social work organizations.

## SELF-CARE PROVIDER

There is no doubt that workplace stress can be a salient component of practice in educational settings. Work-related stress occurs when an individual's response to emotional and physical demands on the job is incongruent with his or her resources, abilities, or workplace needs (Arrington, 2008). For instance, Aronsson, Astvik, and Gustafsson's (2014) investigation of working conditions associated with stress for school social workers found that high caseloads, a lack of adequate resources, demanding schedules, and a lack of innovation in the work climate were factors related to workplace stress. If unchecked over time, "work-related stress can result in burnout, increased risk for workplace injury, impaired performance, poor mental health, impaired cognitive functioning, decreased concentration, and health-related problems for social workers" (Wharton, 2015, p. 1).

Understanding the link between stress and school social work practice and also the importance of self-care is paramount to the success and longevity of school-based practice. In addition to self-care strategies such as setting limits between work and personal life, exercise, and meditation (Arrington, 2008), the development of a supportive environment with a collaborative network of professional practitioners can be therapeutic and serve as a resource for negotiating workplace stressors (Villarreal Sosa & McGrath, 2013). Local and regional school social work organizations can be outlets for reducing the isolation and feelings of inadequacies typical of social workers in schools as "host settings."

# CONCLUSION

This chapter highlighted many of the roles and attributes of school social work practice. It outlined information found within research literature in the areas of macro and micro practice, evaluation of services, collaboration, consultation, and the challenges of advocacy for educational equality. As school social work continues to adapt to changes in public education, new opportunities to lead and define social work practice in schools are available. Social work training has created a robust landscape of social workers with the skills necessary to remove obstacles and enhance experiences in the educational setting. As education laws change and expand, social workers should stay abreast of those changes and utilize them to further the profession. Social work practice in schools will continue to maintain its niche as the link between the home, school, and community practicing on both the micro and macro level. It is this niche that opens the door for more and better leadership by school social workers for the educational settings in which they work.

# DISCUSSION QUESTIONS

1. Think about developing a school social work program for a district that currently does not have one. What steps would you take to determine the needs of the district?
2. Identify the roles that a school social worker can take in a school. Describe each. Why did you select those roles?
3. What are the ways that school social workers can collaborate with other related services personnel, such as school psychologists and school counselors?

4.  How can a school social worker advocate for his or her job in a school district? Where can data be obtained and how can the data be used to support the social worker's position?
5.  Discuss the disproportionality of minority children and youth in special education programs. What can school social workers do to reduce the disparity?

# CASE STUDY

## ATTENTION DEFICIT/HYPERACTIVITY DISORDER AND EDUCATIONAL RIGHTS

Sarah Lopez is a second-generation Latina 10-year-old girl in the fourth grade. Sarah's teacher has contacted the school social worker because she believes that Sarah has behavioral issues due to possible attention deficit/hyperactivity disorder (ADHD). The teacher states that Sarah has been interrupting class by switching seats from her assigned seat, tapping on her desk with her pencil, and daydreaming when given in-class assignments. The teacher goes on to say that Sarah does not interact with students at recess. She is often found walking in the field or swinging on the swings by herself. Sarah receives C's and D's on her report card.

In her discussion with Sarah, the school social worker records the following. She often feels that her parents do not understand her. She states that all they care about is why she cannot follow her parents' and teachers' instructions. Sarah states that other kids do not like her, which is why she does not play with them. She seems to have low self-esteem and does not have many friends. Sarah also mentions that the kids at recess ignore her because she is a "bad kid" who always gets in trouble with the teacher. When asked about her homework, Sarah says that her homework "takes too long" and is "boring."

The school social worker decides to contact Sarah's parents to have a meeting about her behavioral issues. Her parents tell the social worker that Sarah rarely finishes her homework unless someone sits with her the entire time—and even that takes several hours a night. She also has difficulty following through on requests made by her parents, such as doing chores, and seems to "forget" what she is asked to do. After some time, Sarah is tested and diagnosed with attention deficit disorder, non-hyperactivity by a medical doctor. Her parents tell the school social worker they are worried that Sarah will be made fun of at school and be "labeled" if she gets diagnosed with a mental health disorder. They fear she will not be able to attend college. The school social worker tries to ease the parents' fears by telling them that Sarah is not failing school and that there are programs that can help her with schoolwork. Sarah's parents question the need for Sarah to receive possible special education services at school. The school social worker assures them that an Individualized Accommodation Plan or an IEP, if needed, can help Sarah to have an equal learning experience and can provide her with needed services that can help improve her academic experiences. Also, the school social worker tells the parents about mental health services available for free or at minimal cost for low-income families. The parents give written permission to move forward with the special education/504 referral process, and they state that they want the best for their daughter and her future.

In a meeting with the principal of the school, the school social worker discusses Sarah's situation and tells him that her parents have consented to move forward with the special education/504 referral process. The principal states that there are funding issues and that the school cannot afford to put every student on an IEP. He further states that Sarah has satisfactory grades and can do her work without special education services. The school social worker informs the principal of the facts surrounding the lack of support experienced by minority children with regard to disability services and educational support from schools, in addition to voicing her concern that minority students are often overrepresented in receipt of services. Further, the law states that schools must abide by IDEA policies, which provide a process of collaboration and intervention to address a student's needs prior to the initiation of any testing.

Discuss the various roles that were undertaken by the school social worker. Also, identify future roles she might take with Sarah, Sarah's family, and the school.

## ADDITIONAL RESOURCES

### LEADERSHIP

TED: http://www.ted.com/talks/simon_sinek_why_good_leaders_make_you_feel_safe?language=en

University of North Carolina, School of Social Work: http://ssw.unc.edu/files/web/pdf/Leadership DefinitionandElements.pdfSS

WHYY: http://www.whyy.org/podcast/010710_110630.mp3

## REFERENCES

Allen-Meares, P. (1977). Analysis of tasks in school social work. *School Social Work, 22*(3), 196–201.

Allen-Meares, P. (1994). Social work services in schools: A national study of entry-level tasks. *Social Work, 39*(5), 560–565.

Allen-Meares, P. (2004). *Social work services in school* (4th ed.) Boston, MA: Allyn & Bacon.

Allen-Meares, P. (2006, Summer). One hundred years: A historical analysis of social work services in schools [Special Issue]. *School Social Work Journal, 24*–43.

Allen-Meares, P. (2010). *Social work services in schools* (pp. 48–87, 191–221). Boston, MA: Allyn & Bacon.

Aronsson, G., Astvik, W., & Gustafsson, K. (2014). Work conditions, recovery and health: A study among workers within pre-school, home care and social work. *British Journal of Social Work, 44*(6), 1654–1672.

Arrington, P. (2008). *Stress at work: How do social workers cope? NASW Membership Workforce Study.* Washington, DC: National Association of Social Workers.

Barker, R. L. (1999). *The social work dictionary.* Washington, DC: NASW Press.

Bean, K. (2011). Social workers' role in the disproportionality of African American students in special education. *Advances in Social Work, 12*(2), 363–375.

Burdette, P. (2007). *Response to interventions as it relates to early intervening services: Recommendations.* Retrieved from http://nasdse.org/DesktopModules/DNNspot-Store/ProductFiles/26_515e0af4-52a4-435f-b1be-505438639cb4.pdf

Cameron, M. (2006). Managing school discipline and implications for school social workers: A review of the literature. *Children & Schools, 28*(4), 219–227.

Constable, R. (2009). The role of the school social worker. In C. R. Massat, R. Constable, S. McDonald, & J. P. Flynn (Eds.), *School social work: Practice, policy, and research* (pp. 1–29). Chicago, IL: Lyceum.

Corbin, J. (2005). Increasing opportunities for school social work practice resulting from comprehensive school reform. *Children & Schools, 27*(4), 239–246.

Costin, L. B. (1969). School social work: An analysis of function. *Psychology in the Schools, 6*(4), 347–352.

Dibble, N. (2008). *Longitudinal analysis of school social work practice in Wisconsin: Wisconsin school social worker survey.* Madison, WI: Wisconsin Department of Public Instruction.

Dupper, D. R., & Evans, S. (1996). From Band-Aids and putting out fires to prevention: School social work practice approaches for the new century. *Social Work in Education, 18*(3), 187–192.

Fenning, P., & Rose, J. (2007). Overrepresentation of African American students in exclusionary discipline: tThe role of school policy. *Urban Education, 42*(6), 536–559. doi:10.1177/0042085907305039

Franklin, C. (2005). The future of school social work practice: Current trends and opportunities. *Advances in School Social Work, 6*(1), 167–181.

Gersten, R., Compton, D., Connor, C. M., Dimino, J., Santoro, L., Linan-Thompson, S., & Tilly, W. D. (2008). *Assisting students struggling with reading: Response to intervention and multi-tier interventions for reading in the primary grades. A practice guide* (NCEE 2009-4045). Washington, DC: National Center for Education Evaluation and Regional Assistance, Institute of Education Sciences, US Department of Education. Retrieved from http://ies.ed.gov/ncee/wwc/practiceguide.aspx?sid=3

Greenwood, C. R., Carta, J. J., Goldstein, H., Kaminski, R. A., McConnell, S. R., & Atwater, J. (2014). Developing evidence-based tools for a multi-tier approach to preschool language and early literacy instruction. *Journal of Early Intervention, 36*(4), 246–263.

Joseph, A. L., Slovak, K., & Broussard, C. A. (2010). School social workers and a renewed call to advocacy. *School Social Work Journal, 35*(1), 2–20.

Kelly, M. S. (2007). *Illinois school social workers' use of practice interventions: Results from a statewide survey.* Unpublished doctoral dissertation, University of Illinois at Chicago, Chicago, IL.

Kelly, M. S. (2008). *The domains and demands of school social work practice: A guide to working effectively with students, families, and schools* (pp. 31–53). New York, NY: Oxford University Press.

Kelly, M. S., Frey, A. J., Alvarez, M., Berzin, S. C., Shaffer, G., & O'Brien, K. (2010). School social work practice and response to intervention. *Children & Schools, 32*(4), 201–209.

Kelly, M. S., & Stone, S. (2009). An analysis of factors shaping interventions used by school social workers. *Children & Schools, 31*(3), 163–176.

Loyola University Chicago. (2008). *School social work practice 2008 national survey data.* Retrieved from http://etd.lsu.edu/docs/available/etd-01172013-144551/unrestricted/Dissertation.pdf

Morrier, M. J., & Gallagher, P. A. (2012). Racial disparities in preschool special education eligibility for five southern states. *Journal of Special Education, 46*(3), 152–169.

National Association of Social Workers. (2002). *NASW standards for school social work services.* Washington, DC: NASW Press.

National Association of Social Workers. (2013). *NASW standards for social work case management.* Washington, DC: NASW Press.

New America Foundation. (2010). *No Child Left Behind: Overview.* Retrieved from http://febp.newamerica.net/background-analysis/no-child-left-behind-overview

Office for Civil Rights, US Department of Education. (2012). *The transformed civil rights data collection (CRDC).* Retrieved from http://www2.ed.gov/about/offices/list/ocr/docs/crdc-2012-data-summary.pdf

Oswald, D. P., Coutinho, M. J., Best, M. M., & Singh, N. N. (1999). Ethnic presentation in special education: The influence of school related economic and demographic variables. *Journal of Special Education, 32,* 194–206.

Richard, L. (2011). *School social workers: Effectiveness measures.* Unpublished manuscript, School of Social Work, Louisiana State University, Baton Rouge, LA.

Richard, L. A., & Villarreal Sosa, L. (2014). School social work in Louisiana: From role ambiguity to a model of practice. *Children & Schools, 36*(4), 211–220.

Skiba, R. J., Horner, R. H., Chung, C.-G., Rausch, M. K., May, S. L., & Tobin, T. (2011). Race is not neutral: A national investigation of African American and Latino disproportionality in school discipline. *School Psychology Review, 40*(1), 85–107.

Teasley, M., & Cruz, D. (2014). Diversity and related services personnel: Challenges, strategies, and solutions through culturally competent collaborative practice. *School Social Work Journal, 39*(1), 51–72.

Villarreal Sosa, L., & McGrath, B. (2013). Collaboration from the ground up: Creating effective teams. *School Social Work Journal, 38*(1), 34–48.

Wharton, T. C. (2015). Compassion fatigue: Being an ethical social worker. *The New Social Worker: The Social Work Careers Magazine.* Retrieved June 2015 from http://www.socialworker.com/feature-articles/ethics-articles/Compassion_Fatigue%3A_Being_an_Ethical_Social_Worker

Whitted, B. R., Rich, M. C., Constable, R., & Massat, C. R. (2009). Educational mandates for children with disabilities: School policies, case law, and the school social worker. In C. R. Massat, R. Constable, S. McDonald, & J. P. Flynn (Eds.), *School social work: Practice, policy, and research* (pp. 1–29). Chicago, IL: Lyceum.

Whittlesey-Jerome, W. (2012). Selling the need for school social work services to the legislature: A call for advocacy. *School Social Work Journal, 36*(2), 44–55.

Zastrow, C. H., & Kirst-Ashman, K. K. (2013). *Understanding human behavior and the social environment* (9th ed.). Belmont, CA: Brooks/Cole.

# CHAPTER 4

# THE EVIDENCE BASE FOR SCHOOL SOCIAL WORK

KEVIN TAN, MIMI MUMM, STEFAN BATTLE, AND MARY SHEEHAN

Evidence exists that school social workers influence a wide variety of student academic, social, emotional, and behavioral issues (Allen-Meares, Montgomery, & Kim, 2013; Early & Vonk, 2001; Franklin, Kim, & Tripodi, 2009; Sabatino, Mayer, Timberlake, & Rose, 2009; Staudt, Cherry, & Watson, 2005). Across these domains, studies suggest that school social workers have the greatest influence on academic outcomes. For instance, an analysis of published studies suggests that school social work practice is associated with medium to large improvements in student performance (e.g., increases in grade point averages and student knowledge) (Franklin et al., 2009). Another study on published research observed that most school social work interventions on academic achievement reported success in achieving students' intervention goals (Sabatino et al., 2009). Research further indicates that the influence of school social workers on student outcomes is relevant across cultural and political contexts. Cross-national reviews of school social work contributions to student outcomes suggest numerous positive effects across a variety of student issues in international settings (Allen-Meares & Montgomery, 2014; Allen-Meares et al., 2013).

The evidence that school social workers have influence on student outcomes continues to emerge in the literature. A review of recently published articles suggests promise for the future of school social work. Notable research highlighting the important influence of school social workers on student academic success includes studies based on data from the 100 largest US school districts. Studies indicate that the number of school social workers in these school districts is positively associated with academic outcomes such as the number of students who complete high school (Alvarez, Bye, Bryant, & Mumm, 2013). Another study reveals that the number of school social workers is positively associated with average freshmen graduation rates, after taking into account district poverty level and district size (Tan, Battle, Mumm, Eschmann, & Alvarez, 2015).

Other encouraging evidence includes a study that found that school social workers can influence student outcomes through collaborative work with teachers (Berzin, O'Brien, & Tohn, 2012). Another study further suggests that teachers can emulate the distinctive characteristics of the social work profession to promote student success (Bair, 2014). Research also suggests that school social workers can achieve success with a wide range of student populations, such as high-risk students (Wisner, 2013), homeless students (Canfield, 2014), students with disabilities (Rueda, Linton, & Williams, 2014), and ethnic minority youths (Montañez, Berger-Jenkins, Rodriguez, McCord, & Meyer, 2015; Sale, Weil, & Kryah, 2012).

Due to the increasing evidence of the effectiveness of school social work practice, numerous state, national, and global initiatives have emerged to better understand and conceptualize the work that school social workers perform that relates to student success. Some of these projects include state surveys of school social workers (Dupper, Rocha, Jackson, & Lodato, 2014; Richard & Sosa, 2014); national surveys of school social workers (Kelly et al., 2010, 2015); the development of a national school social work practice model (see Chapter 2); and international reviews of school social work trends in practice, policy, and research (Allen-Meares & Montgomery, 2014).

These initiatives represent the profession's strong commitment to the scientific knowledge base of its practice and also its obligation to provide services to help students achieve success in schools. The profession's efforts to foster, better organize, and understand the evidence base of its practice will undoubtedly grow, and all school social workers must actively contribute to these efforts.

## THE SCHOOL SOCIAL WORKER'S TYPICAL DAY

The evidence that school social workers can contribute to student success is extremely important for the profession. The primary mission of schools is to educate students (Alvarez et al., 2013; Franklin et al., 2009), and school social workers help achieve this purpose through an array of intervention approaches. School social workers have multiple responsibilities in the course of a typical day, and it warrants practitioners' reflection on the evidence basis of their practice in supporting students' academic successes.

School social workers provide direct service work with students, complete student assessments and observations, offer consultations with teachers and parents, and make community connections and referrals. School social workers are often members of educational teams, and they work collaboratively with school administrators, teachers, and parents to assist students in making academic progress.

School social workers primarily focus on addressing factors that influence a student's ability to be successful in learning. Many schools adopt a response to intervention (RTI) model that utilizes interventions with strong empirical support. These interventions start with universal (tier 1) programs and progress to more strategic (tier 2) interventions and then intensive (tier 3) interventions (Clark & Alvarez, 2010). A schoolwide Positive Behavior Intervention and Support program is an example of an evidence-based universal program that promotes student learning (Sugai & Horner, 2009). Typically, if a student is not making adequate progress, school social workers use a more targeted or individualized intervention. School social workers are often involved in teams planning for and monitoring interventions through the RTI model (Clark & Alvarez, 2010).

School social workers can assist in gathering information to plan for interventions. They may meet with a parent or guardian or complete student observations to better understand the presenting problem. Gaining a more complete picture allows the educational team to make better decisions about the appropriate intervention. Implementing the intervention with fidelity is important, as is the collection of data to evaluate the success of the intervention.

Although substantial evidence in the published literature indicates that school social workers are associated with student success, school social workers must constantly demonstrate their contributions toward educational outcomes within the school districts. This is especially important in light of the current emphasis on the Common Core State Standards (see Chapter 6). The pressure on districts to demonstrate student academic progress will likely be heightened. School social workers must provide evidence of their contributions to student academic outcomes to key personnel influential in deciding whether their services are needed in schools (Franklin, 2005; Garrett, 2006). Case Study 1 discusses the challenges and illustrates a process that school social workers can undertake to provide evidence of their contributions toward student outcomes.

# CASE STUDY 1: IS SCHOOL SOCIAL WORK EFFECTIVE?

Sarah Ann is a school social worker at Angelina Grimke Middle School and Abbey Kelley Elementary School. She spends half of each day at one of the schools, attending an average of two Individualized Educational Plan (IEP) meetings and running two or three groups each week, counseling individual students, consulting with teachers on behavioral management plans, attending faculty meetings, and responding to crises in her "assigned" schools as well as other schools in the district, as needed.

Recently, her direct supervisor, the special education director, told her, "The school board is thinking about cutting the Specialized Instructional Support Personnel budget. At the school board meeting, we need to present why your services are crucial for the school. We both know they are, but the board wants documentation." Faced with this news, Sarah Ann's first reaction was panic. She heard the word "evaluation" and thought back to her Master of Social Work (MSW) course on research and evaluations. After the panic subsided, she realized she could present documentation of her practice effectiveness.

She remembered that the first step of a research project is a clearly written question, and she had such a question in mind: Which school social work services are crucial for the school? She remembered that the second step is to define the concept: What does crucial mean? She then thought about the stakeholders, the people interested in and benefiting from the answers to these questions: school board members, administration, teachers, her supervisor, her students, and their parents. Sarah Ann started with the school board. She researched her school district's website for information on the school board's goals and the district's strategic plan (Dibbles, 2014). This document provided a rich source of information on what is important to the school district. Sarah Ann then queried her building's administrators about what activities and outcomes they viewed as "crucial," and she thought about her interactions with the teachers. Finally, she recalled the content of recent IEP meetings and the topics that arose during those discussions as important to students and their family members.

Based on this information, Sarah Ann defined "crucial" as relating to services that improve the educational outcomes for the children the school district serves. Educational outcomes include increases in attendance, graduation rates, standardized test scores, and faculty knowledge when responding to children with mental health and behavioral issues. In addition, important academic outcomes include decreases in the achievement gap between students of color and White students, the number of out-of-school placements due to mental health issues, and disruptive behavioral issues.

Once Sarah Ann clearly defined her SMART (specific, measurable, attainable, realistic, time frame) goals, it was time to explore the interventions that she had been using to achieve these goals. Although it is important to document all activities in which the social worker participates, Sarah Ann knew the list of activities would not impress the school board as much as actual educational outcomes. She quickly looked at the time study that the district required her to conduct each month. The study allowed her to see the activities she performs, but this alone would not connect the activities to the outcomes. She remembered her research professor explaining the difference between process and outcome evaluations. Although both have their place, Sarah Ann knew that her research question was asking for the impact of these services.

Sarah Ann still needed to portray the connection between the social work services and the outcomes for students. She began to think about other data she had collected that might document outcomes, and she realized that she had been remiss in her documentation. Although she knew it was important to collect outcomes, she had not taken the time to document the results of her work. She remembered, however, that plenty of data are collected in a school setting. She knew, for example, that teachers collect data on attendance, grades, turned-in homework, disruptive behaviors, and test scores. Thus, Sarah Ann called her former research professor and asked for help in creating a database of the teacher-collected information. She was pleasantly surprised: Her former professor was happy to be remembered and willing to consult on the project.

The professor suggested that Sarah Ann read meta-analysis articles that highlighted the evidence basis of school social work practice (e.g., Allen-Meares et al., 2013; Franklin et al., 2009; Sabatino et al., 2009). The professor believed that these articles could help Sarah Ann consider the impact of her work across the various student domains (e.g., academic, social, emotional, and behavioral). The professor also recommended research evaluating the work of school social workers with different student populations (e.g., Canfield, 2014; Wisner, 2013). Based on these articles, the professor advised Sarah Ann to consider the different ways she could document her work with students. The professor also suggested that Sarah Ann consult an RTI guidebook for school social workers (e.g., Clark & Alvarez, 2010). The professor believes that reading the chapters can help Sarah Ann understand the relation between her services and students with varying needs.

The professor guided Sarah Ann on how she could develop a spreadsheet that the information management staff (IMS) could easily populate for her. Sarah Ann consulted with the IMS, who shared the information they had with her. She decided to collect data on those students with whom she had worked over the course of the school year. She organized this student list in various ways—for instance, students who struggled academically (e.g., those students who had been failing in the first quarter of the previous year) or those who were referred for behavioral issues (e.g., who were disruptive in the classroom). She also indicated whether these students (or their faculty members) received social work services (i.e., individual counseling, group counseling, classroom intervention, and behavior plan development, or faculty professional development and consultation). Sarah Ann started to identify how her services relate to the various tiers of the RTI model.

Sarah Ann then explored whether there might be an association between the services she provided and the outcomes for the students. She focused on academic outcomes such as students' grade point averages and other student academic measures (e.g., standardized test scores). She also included other measures (e.g., attendance and disciplinary records) that the IMS populated for her. What do you think Sarah Ann found?

## THE EVIDENCE-BASED PROCESS IN PRACTICE

In Case Study 1, Sarah Ann took several steps to answer the school board's question using an evidence-based process (Figure 4.1). Such a process also involves integrating into practice prior interventions and programs that have proven effective with students. Thus, evidence-based practice (EBP) is "the process of continually infusing practice with the current research" (Drake et al., as cited in Raines, 2008, p. vii). A critical aspect of the evidence-based *process* is the integration of research into school social work *practice* to provide evidence of its effectiveness.

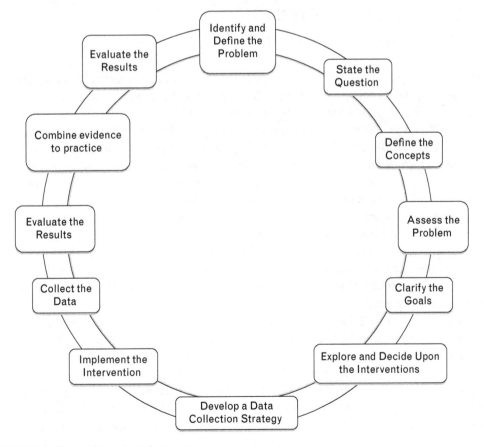

**FIGURE 4.1:** The evidence-based process.

The evidence-based process varies somewhat, depending on the author, but many components are similar from author to author. To illustrate, Bloom, Fischer, and Orme (2009, pp. 455–459) outlined six steps in developing EBP:

Step 1: Develop a question
Step 2: Find the evidence
Step 3: Analyze the evidence
Step 4: Combine the evidence with your understanding of the client and situation
Step 5: Application to practice
Step 6: Monitor and evaluate results

Raines' (2008) model has one less step than that of Bloom et al. Although Raines did not explicitly state that evidence is applied to practice (step 5 of Bloom et al.), he did imply it. The evidence-based process we are using combines the historical perspective of Perlman's (1957) problem-solving process (engagement, data collection/assessment, planning/contracting, intervention, and evaluation/termination) with Bloom et al.'s and Raines' evidence-based processes. The details of the evidence-based process are not elaborated here, and the reader is recommended to consult resources such as Raines (2008) and Bloom et al. (2009).

# CULTURALLY COMPETENT EVIDENCE-BASED PRACTICE

Evidence-based practice also involves integrating culturally sensitive practices targeting different aspects of the school system (Franklin & Kelly, 2009). Attention to student diversity and cultural issues is of paramount importance because social work professionals have an ethical responsibility to ameliorate academic disparities and promote culturally competent practices (Teasley & Cruz, 2014). Traditionally, school social workers provide direct student-focused interventions based on the presenting problem. However, aspects of school social workers' duties and responsibilities articulated in their job descriptions may require them to provide a macro-systemic approach for the betterment of the school district.

To provide this macro-systemic approach, the senior-level administration of their respective school districts can ask school social workers to take part in systemwide initiatives that involve addressing issues such as the diversity and cultural competence of school staff. These issues are especially important to consider because the Latino and immigrant-student populations are growing rapidly, are facing high rates of academic underachievement, and school social workers are likely to encounter these students in their practice (Franklin, 2005).

Individual stereotypical ideologies, beliefs, and attitudes about marginalized groups among students and staff can make intervention work on diversity issues challenging and complex. Cultural issues are subjective to individuals and can evolve based on social contexts and interactions with others (Jani, Pierce, Ortiz, & Sowbel, 2011). Providing culturally competent practices to the increasingly diverse student populations may require additional knowledge and training (Teasley & Cruz, 2014). For instance, school social workers must consider the intersections of their own cultural identity with others when planning and implementing interventions

(Jani et al., 2011). Furthermore, cultural competent practice may involve collaboration with other professionals such as administrators, teachers, and parents to reduce barriers influencing classroom instruction and enhance positive student experience in school (Teasley & Cruz, 2014). Because little has been published in the literature regarding how school social workers can provide evidence of their practice based on student diversity and cultural issues, Case Study 2 illustrates this process.

## CASE STUDY 2: WHO ARE OUR STUDENTS?

Henry is a Black American school social worker at an urban middle school. Due to budgetary constraints, he is the only social worker at the school. The student population is 650 students, of which 70% are students of color. Twenty percent of the teacher population is of color.

The district superintendent and the principal, who are both White, approached Henry about a concern in his school. Specifically, the superintendent had been receiving phone calls and meeting requests from parents of color about the perceived insensitivity of some White teachers interacting with their children in the classroom. It is clear from the superintendent's perspective that a group of parents had rallied to articulate their concerns privately—outside of the school—and wanted some type of response. The parents based their information on what their children reported to them. One set of parents also cited a comment made to them about their son during a teacher–parent conference as evidence of intolerant behavior. The superintendent and principal requested that Henry provide them with information regarding whether there was a lack of cultural competency among the teachers and how this issue may adversely influence student learning.

As the school's social worker, Henry felt a strong ethical professional responsibility to address this issue. Furthermore, based on his own personal experience of being a student in a school in which the majority of teachers and students were White, with a limited number of students of color, he could relate to the issues raised by the parents and students.

Henry recalled his school social work internship experience. His placement was in a large suburban school district with a demographic profile similar to that of the schools he attended while growing up. His supervisor was a White female school social worker who was most concerned about the experiences of students of color in her school. Henry's supervisor observed that the majority of students who dropped out of school were Black and Latino students. His supervisor believed in being a strong advocate for these students because many had shared with her that they felt misunderstood by their administrators, teachers, and peers, and they disliked being in school.

Henry remembered being impressed with the work of his supervisor. He remembered the numerous after-school activities involving creative and performing arts, which his supervisor organized for those students of color to keep them interested in attending school. He recalled how his supervisor made further efforts to enhance their school experience through organizing schoolwide events that provided a platform for them to perform. He remembered attending many of those events and saw how the whole school community enjoyed the experience. He also participated in the numerous "pizza parties" organized by his supervisor to celebrate the academic accomplishments of these students. It was often at these events that he met the students' families, friends, teachers, and administrators .

To address the concerns raised by his superintendent and the principal, Henry had a vision of fostering a school environment similar to his internship experience. He also recalled his social work professor introducing the importance of the evidence-based process in practice. Henry wanted to ensure that any programs he recommended were efficacious and capable of improving student outcomes.

He remembered that the first step in this process is to identify the problem. Henry asked the following question: How do you practice cultural competence in your classroom? With this question, Henry was trying to define the concept and formulate an understanding of what *cultural competence* meant to the teachers. Henry was also interested in the extent to which teachers engaged in and promoted cultural competence practices with students from minority groups. As Henry moved forward in collecting data to address this question, he recognized that the people who would most benefit from this information were the superintendent, the principal, the teachers, the parents who brought their concerns to the superintendent, and these parents' children.

To assess the problem, Henry examined the school district's current goals and objectives that addressed the need for diversity and cultural competence awareness among teachers and staff. After he researched the district goals and objectives, Henry met jointly with the superintendent and principal to gather additional information about their perspectives on diversity and cultural competence practice needs.

By examining the district goals and objectives, and based on discussion with the superintendent and principal, Henry formulated goals to address the problem. The goals were for the teachers to develop an increased understanding of the following:

- Cultural competence and social construct norms
- Societal stereotypes that can perpetuate cultural competence insensitivity in the classroom among marginalized groups
- Classroom strategies that will eradicate cultural insensitivity in teacher–student relationships

Henry evaluated the teachers' level of cultural sensitivity and their understanding of societal stereotypes using the Cultural Diversity Awareness Inventory (Turner, 2007). This instrument assesses knowledge of strategies that promote cultural sensitivity between teachers and students. To assess the teachers' strategies to support cultural competence among their students, the following five question prompts explored each teacher's methods within the classroom:

- How do you promote cultural competence dialogue within the classroom, when able?
- How do you create a safe environment for students in your classroom who are culturally diverse?
- How do you promote culturally competent awareness and advocacy to your students so they can gain sensitivity and understanding of cultural differences?
- How do you encourage students to ask questions of one another about cultural competence complexities that may be different from those of their own culture?
- How do you assist students in engaging in a bias-free process of understanding and awareness about other students in the classroom who are culturally different from each other?

To develop a data collection strategy, Henry developed a matrix using an Excel spreadsheet to tabulate responses. The matrix helped (1) identify how teachers responded overall, (2) assist in connecting the responses to the goals established to increase the understanding of cultural competence, and (3) determine how to proceed in offering diversity and cultural competence training to teachers based on parental concerns.

Henry examined the data collected, evaluated the results, and presented the data at a faculty meeting. During this presentation, Henry shared examples of diversity issues based on his social work practice with students. Using self-disclosure, exposure, and personal history, combined with his professional practice, Henry articulated how the importance of cultural competency greatly needing discussion in his school had been overlooked. One important area highlighted by Henry to the faculty was the need to be more attentive to the relevance of the curriculum and instruction to the students' cultural experience.

Henry subsequently followed up with a joint meeting with his superintendent and principal. Based on their previous conversations, Henry determined that they greatly valued his assessment of diversity issues in the district. In this meeting, Henry provided anecdotal examples that supported the parents' concerns about the fragmentation and lack of cultural competence toward students of color among teachers. Henry strongly recommended professional development sessions to help faculty gain greater awareness of how their interactions with students may adversely affect students. The superintendent and principal agreed and asked Henry to recommend programs. What programs would Henry recommend?

---

## CHALLENGES AND FUTURE DIRECTIONS

Despite prevailing evidence of the relation between school social workers and student academic outcomes, studies indicate that school social workers are not doing enough to demonstrate their relevance toward academic outcomes (Bye, Shepard, Partridge, & Alvarez, 2009). Most school social workers are also not actively involved in school-level, data-driven decision-making processes, a key component of the evidence-based process (Kelly et al., 2010). Therefore, it is not surprising that school social workers are largely relegated to peripheral roles in the leadership hierarchy of schools (Shaffer, 2006). For more information on this topic, see Chapter 13.

School social work practice can be complex to evaluate (Franklin, 2005; Garrett, 2006), and practitioners may initially be overwhelmed in trying to document practice effectiveness (e.g., Case Study 1). Furthermore, the failure to recognize the contributions of school social workers on student outcomes may be related to the lack of an integrated data system that considers other outcomes along with academic success (Jonson-Reid, 2009). For instance, student social dimensions (e.g., school climate on cultural awareness as illustrated in Case Study 2) and health measures (e.g., depressive symptoms) are important aspects to consider in relation to academic success. For school social workers to be strong advocates for students, it is essential that they remain relevant to the demands of the prevailing educational climate. This means that school social workers must document evidence of their practice across an array of outcomes involving educational success. This is important given the lack of consensus among federal and state agencies regarding the ideal measure to evaluate student academic success (Rumberger, 2011). In addition, school social workers must demonstrate the relevance of their services across a spectrum of students, especially immigrants and students of color, who are most vulnerable to poor academic outcomes (Franklin, 2005).

Providing culturally competent evidence-based practice, as highlighted in Case Study 2, requires strong support from school leaders. There needs to be strong recognition from school administrators on the links between cultural sensitivity, student experience, and academic success. Without strong support, multicultural programs and accountability measures may not be effectively enforced (Teasley & Cruz, 2014). School social workers interface among students, teachers, and parents, so they have a distinct perspective of schools' climate. School social workers can be a catalyst for positive change. The challenge is for school social workers to provide evidence and recognition of their abilities to promote inclusive practices supporting the academic needs of minority students. This requires school social workers to be strong advocates to district officials when working with these students. School social workers should also conscientiously monitor, document, and present the academic progress of these students to school leaders.

In addition to the two case studies presented in this chapter, there are other examples of how school social workers can effectively organize data and present them to key district stakeholders (Clark & Alvarez, 2010; Jonson-Reid, Kontak, Citerman, Essma, & Fezzi, 2004; Jonson-Reid, Kontak, & Mueller, 2001). These strategies may not necessarily be complex research designs that merit the gold standards of evidence-based practice (e.g., random controlled clinical trials). In fact, without strong infrastructural support, it is unrealistic to expect practitioners to conduct such rigorous research (Franklin et al., 2009). Nonetheless, the absence of research resources should not be an excuse for school social workers to fail to examine their contributions toward student success. School social workers should be encouraged to collaborate with university professors who can help to develop evaluation designs and assist with the analysis (e.g., Case Study 1). It is critical that school social workers continually infuse, and review, research into their practice. Not only is this an ethical mandate as professionals but also the future of the school social work profession depends on this process (Alveraz et al., 2013).

## CONCLUSION

To provide effective social work services to students, school social workers should integrate effective, culturally competent, and sensitive evidence-based processes into their practices. This chapter began with a review of the evidence base of school social work practice. Studies indicate that school social work is important in influencing student outcomes.

This chapter also proposed an evidence-based approach that school social workers can incorporate into their practice and illustrated the model through two case studies. The first case study detailed how school social workers can collect and organize data to document the effectiveness of their practices. The second case study exemplified how school social workers should integrate cultural considerations into the evidence-based process and presented measures to evaluate cultural competency practices. In implementing these practices, school social workers must be aware of and address cultural influences that are barriers to student success. This chapter concluded with a discussion of the challenges and implications of the evidence-based process for school social workers.

## DISCUSSION QUESTIONS

1. A typical day in a school social worker's life is presented at the beginning of this chapter. Is this day consistent with your experience in a school?

2. Examine the evidence-based model in Figure 4.1.
   a. How could you use the evidence-based model to examine a topic in your school setting?
   b. What are the greatest challenges you experience in thinking about implementing this model?
3. Getting "buy-in" from teachers is an important component of school social work practice. What strategies discussed in this chapter could you implement?
4. In Case Study 1, Sarah Ann realized that she had been remiss in her documentation. What could she do differently to capture the outcomes of her work?
5. In Case Study 2, Henry responded to the concerns raised by the superintendent and principal. As part of his assessment process, are there other individuals or groups with which he could connect to ensure he has a clear understanding of the concerns expressed by parents?
6. What evidence-based practice data from Henry's assessment of the lack of cultural competence in the classroom would he need to provide the superintendent and principal to support the need for teachers to be involved in professional development training?

## ADDITIONAL RESOURCES

Campbell Collaboration (social, behavioral, and educational issues): http://www.campbellcollaboration.org

National Center for Learning Disabilities: https://www.ncld.org/learning-disability-resources

Office of Juvenile Justice and Delinquency Prevention, model programs: http://www.ojjdp.gov/mpg

Substance Abuse and Mental Health Services Administration, National Registry of Evidence-Based Programs and Practices: http://www.nrepp.samhsa.gov

What Works Clearinghouse: http://ies.ed.gov/ncee/wwc

## REFERENCES

Allen-Meares, P., & Montgomery, K. L. (2014). Global trends and school-based social work. *Children & Schools, 36*(2), 105–112.

Allen-Meares, P., Montgomery, K. L., & Kim, J. S. (2013). School-based social work interventions: A cross-national systematic review. *Social Work, 58*(3), 253–262.

Alvarez, M. E., Bye, L., Bryant, R., & Mumm, A. M. (2013). School social workers and educational outcomes. *Children & Schools, 35*(4), 235–243.

Bair, M. A. (2014). Teacher professionalism: What educators can learn from social workers. *Mid-Western Educational Researcher, 26*(2), 28.

Berzin, S., O'Brien, K., & Tohn, S. (2012). Working on what works: A new model for collaboration. *School Social Work Journal, 36*(2), 15–26.

Bloom, M., Fischer, J., & Orme, J. G. (2009). *Evaluating practice guidelines for the accountable professional* (6th ed.). Boston, MA: Pearson.

Bye, L., Shepard, M., Partridge, J., & Alvarez, M. (2009). School social work outcomes: Perspectives of school social workers and school administrators. *Children & Schools, 31*(2), 97–108.

Canfield, J. P. (2014). Examining perceived barriers and facilitators to school social work practice with homeless children. *Children & Schools, 36*(3), 165–173.

Clark, J. P., & Alvarez, M. (2010). *Response to intervention: A guide for school social workers.* New York, NY: Oxford University Press.

Dibbles, N. (2014). *Using data to document the impact of school social work services to school boards: How to reach them & how to teach them.* Paper presented at the School Social Work Conference, March 23, 2014, Chicago, IL.

Drake, B., Hovmand, P., Jonson-Reid, M., & Zayas, L.H. (2007). Adopting and teaching evidence-based practice in master's-level social work programs. *Journal of Social Work Education, 43*(3), 431–446.

Dupper, D. R., Rocha, C., Jackson, R. F., & Lodato, G. A. (2014). Broadly trained but narrowly used? Factors that predict the performance of environmental versus individual tasks by school social workers. *Children & Schools, 36*(2), 71–77.

Early, T. J., & Vonk, M. E. (2001). Effectiveness of school social work from a risk and resilience perspective. *Children & Schools, 23*(1), 9–31.

Franklin, C. (2005). The future of school social work practice: Current trends and opportunities. *Advances in Social Work, 6*(1), 167–181.

Franklin, C., & Kelly, M. S. (2009). Becoming evidence-informed in the real world of school social work practice. *Children & Schools, 31*(1), 46–56.

Franklin, C., Kim, J. S., & Tripodi, S. J. (2009). A meta-analysis of published school social work practice studies 1980–2007. *Research on Social Work Practice, 19*(6), 667–677.

Garrett, K. J. (2006). Making the case for school social work. *Children & Schools, 28*(2), 115–121.

Jani, J. S., Pierce, D., Ortiz, L., & Sowbel, L. (2011). Access to intersectionality, content to competence: Deconstructing social work education diversity standards. *Journal of Social Work Education, 47*(2), 283–301.

Jonson-Reid, M. (2009). Redefining the outcome for education. *Children & Schools, 31*(3), 131–133.

Jonson-Reid, M., Kontak, D., Citerman, B., Essma, A., & Fezzi, N. (2004). School social work case characteristics, services, and dispositions: Year one results. *Children & Schools, 26*(1), 5–22.

Jonson-Reid, M., Kontak, D., & Mueller, S. (2001). Developing a management information system for school social workers: A field–university partnership. *Children & Schools, 23*(4), 198–211.

Kelly, M. S., Berzin, S. C., Frey, A., Alvarez, M., Shaffer, G., & O'Brien, K. (2010). The state of school social work: Findings from the National School Social Work Survey. *School Mental Health, 2*(3), 132–141.

Kelly, M. S., Thompson, A. M., Frey, A., Klemp, H., Alvarez, M., & Berzin, S. C. (2015). The state of school social work: Revisited. *School Mental Health, 7*(3), 174–183.

Montañez, E., Berger-Jenkins, E., Rodriguez, J., McCord, M., & Meyer, D. (2015). Turn 2 Us: Outcomes of an urban elementary school-based mental health promotion and prevention program serving ethnic minority youths. *Children & Schools, 37*(2), 100–107.

Perlman, H. H. (1957). *Social casework: A problem solving process.* Chicago, IL: University of Chicago Press.

Raines, J. (2008). *Evidence based practice in school mental health.* New York, NY: Oxford University Press.

Richard, L. A., & Sosa, L. V. (2014). School social work in Louisiana: A model of practice. *Children & Schools, 36*(4), 211–220.

Rueda, H. A., Linton, K. F., & Williams, L. R. (2014). School social workers' needs in supporting adolescents with disabilities toward dating and sexual health: A qualitative study. *Children & Schools, 36*(2), 79–90.

Rumberger, R. W. (2011). *Dropping out: Why students drop out of high school and what can be done about it.* Cambridge, MA: Harvard University Press.

Sabatino, C. A., Mayer, L. M., Timberlake, E. M., & Rose, T. Y. (2009). Evidence for the effectiveness of school social work practice. In C. Massat, R. Constable, S. McDonald, & J. Flynn (Eds.), *School social work: Practice, policy, and research* (7th ed.). Chicago, IL: Lyceum.

Sale, E., Weil, V., & Kryah, R. (2012). An exploratory investigation of the Promoting Responsibility through Education and Prevention (PREP) after school program for African American at-risk elementary school students. *School Social Work Journal, 36*(2), 56–72.

Shaffer, G. L. (2006). Promising school social work practices of the 1920s: Reflections for today. *Children & Schools, 28*(4), 243–251.

Staudt, M. M., Cherry, D. J., & Watson, M. (2005). Practice guidelines for school social workers: A modified replication and extension of a prototype. *Children & Schools, 27*(2), 71–81.

Sugai, G., & Horner, R. H. (2009). Responsiveness-to-intervention and school-wide positive behavior supports: Integration of multi-tiered system approaches. *Exceptionality, 17*(4), 223–237.

Tan, K., Battle, S., Mumm, M., Eschmann, R., & Alvarez, M. (2015). The impact of school social workers on high school freshman graduation among the one hundred largest school districts in the United States. *School Social Work Journal, 39*(2), 1–14.

Teasley, M. L., & Cruz, D. (2014). Diversity and related services personnel: Challenges, strategies, and solutions through culturally competent collaborative practice. *School Social Work Journal, 39*(1), 51–72.

Turner, M. M. (2007). *Multicultural teacher attitudes and cultural sensitivity: An initial exploration of the experiences of individuals in a unique alternative teacher certification program.* Doctoral dissertation, University of Notre Dame, Notre Dame, IN.

Wisner, B. L. (2013). Less stress, less drama, and experiencing Monkey Mind: Benefits and challenges of a school-based meditation program for adolescents. *School Social Work Journal, 38*(1), 49–63.

# CHAPTER 5

# THE CHANGING CONTEXT OF SCHOOL SOCIAL WORK PRACTICE

## SUSAN STONE AND Y. KAFI MORAGNE-PATTERSON

This chapter discusses some key contextual forces shaping social work practice in schools. Given that the term "context" in social work varies in meaning and application, we discuss context from two points of view. We first consider schools as social systems, from both organizational and institutional perspectives. We then consider education policy as a context and focus particularly on the contemporary standards-based reform movement. A theme that we weave throughout the chapter is that although current federal education policy aims to raise achievement levels among *all* students (a fairly novel policy goal), basic institutional arrangements significantly shape the delivery of educational and other services in schools. These basic arrangements are often taken for granted and often not subject to critique. These organizational and institutional forces present a unique set of opportunities and challenges for social work practitioners to identify, elaborate, and address issues of educational equity. Specifically, this chapter (1) discusses key organizational and institutional features of the US education system and (2) traces the standards-based reform to its most current manifestation in federal No Child Left Behind legislation and the current rollout of the Common Core Standards. Throughout the chapter, we also highlight implications for the structure and delivery of school social work services.

## CONCEPTUAL FRAMEWORKS RELATED TO SCHOOLS AND EQUITY

### SCHOOLS AS ORGANIZATIONS

An important strand of scholarship seeks to understand how the experience of attending school influences students in the short and long term across a variety of domains, including academic progress and achievement, educational attainment, occupational outcomes, and, recently, health outcomes (for review, see Teddlie & Reynolds, 2000). In fact, a long-standing debate considers whether schools exert influences on students beyond their own and their families' background characteristics (Konstantopoulos & Borman, 2011). Although most contemporary scholars would reframe this debate from "whether" to "how" schools matter to students, one important by-product of this discussion is a general conceptual framework—often referred to as "school effects"—for understanding how schools shape students' educational trajectories. Scholars generally apply this framework to explain student performance on standardized tests of achievement, but we and other scholars concur that it is also useful as a heuristic for understanding key categories of important school characteristics and student outcome domains (Rutter & Maughan, 2002).

The school effects framework integrates three strands of research on the influence of schools on students, highlighting three conceptual domains of school characteristics. A first strand, developed and utilized mostly by economists, is referred to as the "education production function" and focuses on how allocations of school resources influence student outcomes. A second strand investigates how demographic and structural attributes of schools influence students. A final strand of research, often referred to as "school effectiveness" research, emphasizes organizational features of schools linked to student engagement and achievement. This strand of research directly informs school improvement research, which concentrates on interventions to improve schools.

Integration of these strands of research suggests that schools influence students' outputs (short-term effects such as achievement or grades) and outcomes (long-term effects such as educational or occupational attainment) through three sets of factors or conceptual domains. "Input" factors include those that the school is "given" (i.e., public school personnel do not typically choose students to serve). These include the sociodemographic characteristics of the student body (often called compositional effects), the human capital characteristics of teachers and other school staff, and the fiscal resources that are available. Efforts to ensure that all students receive instruction from credentialed teachers represent an example of an "input" reform. "Structural" factors refer to how schools are structured to serve students (e.g., classroom and school sizes and grade span). Finally, "process" factors represent the core focus of school effectiveness research. These process characteristics include the beliefs and behaviors of actors in a school community.

Scholars pay particular attention to process characteristics; they are believed to be malleable and, thus, amenable to intervention. A useful exemplar of research on process characteristics appears in the work of Anthony Bryk and colleagues (for a summary, see Bryk, 2010). They find that schools are most likely to positively influence student engagement and achievement under specific conditions. The first condition is strong relational trust across a school community, and the second is strong principal leadership. The third condition is the presence of both strong parent–school–community ties and an instructional climate characterized by "student centeredness" (orderliness, high levels of expectations for achievement (often termed "academic press"), and supports (usually defined as teacher–student relationships) for learning). A final and crucial condition includes coherent instructional programming linked to teacher professional development and also a culture of innovation across staff members.

The school effects framework implies that school effects are complex, including influences of the school environment, classrooms, teachers, parents, and peer groups on students and vice versa (Rutter & Maughan, 2002). Grubb's (2008) work on school resources helps tie the core concepts of school effects research together. He defines four categories of school resources that account for school effects on student outcomes. Simple resources reflect school "inputs" (i.e., financial and human capital—for example, per-pupil revenues and teacher educational background). Compound resources are combinations of two or more resources (e.g., relatively high per-pupil revenues and a high percentage of well-qualified teachers). Process characteristics reflect complex school resources, which often must be created through investments in professional development and collaboration. Finally, abstract resources refer to the "web of relationships and practices" among members of the school community (Grubb, 2008, p. 108).

Bryk's line of research provides evidence of the potential benefits of complex and abstract school resources. For example, strong principal leadership, high levels of trust and strong working relationships among school staff, the extent to which staff hold high expectations and show strong support for students, the extent to which staff are oriented toward learning and innovation, and the extent to which staff are engaged with parents and the school community are associated with growth in student achievement (Bryk, 2010).

Although few studies directly consider the influence of schools on school social workers and their practices, there is evidence of school effects on school social worker practices. Kelly and Stone (2009) link school characteristics to school social workers' reports of their practice strategies, including whether they most often engage in individual casework with students versus other practice modalities. Other research demonstrates that school-level compositional and organizational features shape the delivery of psychosocial services in schools. For example, school features such as rates of concentrated poverty and teacher turnover, urbanicity, size, and principal support relate to the quality of implementation of school-based prevention programs (Payne, 2009).

Although often not explicitly considered in the discussion of the roles and practices of school social workers, the concept of school resources provides an important rationale that the addition of a school social worker to a school community could potentially shape both school and student outputs (Phillippo & Stone, 2011). For example, school social workers strongly contribute to school reform efforts in terms of their critical role in building complex and abstract resources (e.g., in strengthening parent, teacher, school, and community ties), particularly with communities of color (Teasley, 2004).

Consider the following case excerpt[1] and reflect on the types of compound, complex, and abstract resources that could be deployed on behalf of the focal student, his family, his teachers, and the wider school and community:

*Background*: Born in Mexico, Javier (age 9) arrived in California in February of 2010. Javier was classified as an English language learner and assigned to a fourth grade class in a school that was composed equally of Latino and African American students. Javier's fourth and fifth grade teachers had similar assessments of him. Both described him as a shy student who didn't try very hard in school. Javier's grades were poor and he participated very little in classroom activities. His fifth grade reading and mathematics achievement test scores suggested that his performance was below the tenth percentile of students tested statewide. His fifth grade teacher expressed surprise at how little English Javier was picking up.

Javier didn't seem to be making much progress in socializing with his peers. His only friend was Jeffrey, a Spanish-speaking, bilingual student in his class who was more competent than Javier both academically and socially. Javier often seemed withdrawn and unengaged, as observed by his tendency to put his head down on his desk and hum to himself while the classroom activities

---

[1] Adapted from case material provided by Megan Goss, PhD.

went on around him. When Javier was in a group with just Jeffrey and another adult to speak with, and was allowed to speak some Spanish, he would likely be described as a boy full of spunk and humor.

Javier was walked to and from school every morning by his mother. According to Javier, his mother didn't allow him or his sisters to play outdoors in their neighborhood. He revealed that his family was very afraid of their African American neighbors and that his mother demanded that he stay away from them. She told Javier that they would be a bad influence on him.

*Class observation 1*: Seated in a horseshoe of desks in a sunny, second-story classroom, the 29 fifth grade students seem unable to sit still. Their teacher repeatedly and distractedly calls for order just as often as she requests an answer from last night's math homework. Even those students who are not engaged in offering answers to the teacher are engaged in some form of communication with a nearby peer—laughing, tickling, whispering, or writing notes. Javier has his head on his desk and is humming to himself. He is seated near several especially rambunctious boys. The teacher, apparently tired of telling this particular group to be quiet, suddenly walks over to this section of the class and says, "I want someone from this side of the room to answer!" Javier looks up at her quickly, then down again. The boy next to him says, "Well, don't ask Javier!" He pronounces the name as an English-speaker would. As the group start to snicker at the mispronunciation of Javier's name, the boy continues: "He doesn't know *anything*!" The entire class now erupts in laughter. Javier's teacher chuckles with them for a few moments then continues on with the homework exercise. Javier gives a small smile and looks around the room at his peers. It is unclear if he understands that that they are laughing at him.

*Class observation 2*: The teacher was returning papers to the students, who were sitting at their desks, waiting for their papers to arrive. Javier was given a series of three papers, and each seemed to be identical. They were all book reports written on the same form. Javier had written the same book report over, word for word, three times, turning them in on successive weeks. Across the bottom, the teacher had written the same comment on each report: "This needs to be longer." The book reports were all concerning a graphic comic book.

This brief case excerpt raises many potential issues on which a school social worker might focus his or her attention: Javier's withdrawal in the classroom, his relationships with peers, his relationship with teachers, the nature and quality of instruction Javier is receiving both related to his English language development and in general, his relationship with his parents, and his parent's relationships with other members of the school community. The point we want to make is that a singular focus on Javier's social skills, for example, would miss important opportunities for a social worker to creatively combine and deploy resources to address Javier's needs as well as to simultaneously enhance his and his peer's classroom and school experience.

## EQUITY FRAMEWORKS

The concepts presented previously provide insight into how schools may influence students' outputs and outcomes and the potential role of school social work in those influences. However, as social workers concerned with issues of social justice, we also need a framework that helps us understand differences among social groupings of students in achieving particular outputs and outcomes. School social workers express long-standing concerns about unequal school outcomes represented in persistent "achievement gaps" across ethno-racial groupings of students and across levels of family income and education.

Farrell (2013) suggests that unequal outcomes may emerge across many points over students' academic careers. Inequalities of access occur when social groupings (variously defined) show differential access to schools. Inequalities of survival refer to differences in completion of cycles (e.g., staying on an academic track or high school completion). Inequalities of opportunities to learn refer to differential access to valued school resources (e.g., high-quality teachers or curricula). Inequalities of output refer to differentials in learning outcomes. Inequalities of outcome refer to differentials in quality of life.

How one seeks to address such inequalities can be termed an "equity framework." We view analysis of equity frameworks as inextricably tied to our discussion of school resources outlined previously. To address achievement differentials, is it best to distribute resources so that they are equal across all schools and students? Or, is it best to compensate particular subgroups of students (i.e., divert more resources to them)? Most crucially, what is the "resource" to be distributed? Therefore, determining both the source of the inequality and the nature of the resource problem is important. School effects and resource frameworks presented previously also anticipate that sources of inequality may vary quite substantially between schools.

# INSTITUTIONAL FEATURES OF SCHOOLS

So far, our discussion has considered schools as organizations, focusing on the beliefs and behaviors of actors within schools and across relevant community stakeholders. Another vantage point from which to view schools is through an institutional lens. This lens enables us to inspect the often taken-for-granted aspects of how our society views and organizes education in general. Overall, an institutional lens suggests four enduring forces characterizing our education system.

## SCHOOLS REFLECT DOMINANT
## AND CONFLICTING SOCIAL VALUES

As a key socializing institution, the education system reflects dominant cultural values (Cuban, 2012). However, the American citizenry actually has multiple (and often conflicting) goals about the purposes and outcomes of education. For example, Americans differ substantially in their views about the purpose of education. Is the role of education to inculcate particular forms of moral behavior, prepare responsible voters, teach students codes of power and power relations, teach basic skills, create critical thinkers, improve social conditions, some combination of these, or some other role not mentioned? Not surprisingly, Americans also differ considerably in terms of their views of equity in education.

As a consequence, dominant beliefs about the potential for the education system as well as policy goals appear to cycle over time. Tyack (1991) highlights enduring debates reflecting this dynamic, including whether education serves as an equalizing function in society, the relative benefits of common versus differentiated standards and curriculum, as well as whether educational resources should be distributed equally or equitably. In short, an important institutional dynamic is that education goals and practices represent contested domains within American society.

## SCHOOLS WERE DESIGNED FOR ENROLLMENT

Given enduring tensions concerning educational goals and practices, educational historians generally concur that schools were originally designed to achieve mass enrollment. Indeed, historian Patricia Graham (1993) argues that most federal and state education policy (at least until recently) focuses on issues of school access. To achieve mass enrollment, schools exhibit relatively homogenous structural features. Tyack (1991) extensively discusses these features. With few exceptions, the students served by school social workers, the students' parents, and their grandparents likely encountered very similar school organizational arrangements. Examples of this include age grading (students typically enter kindergarten at age 5 years and tend to be educated in homogenous age groups), a sequential curriculum (addition is typically taught before multiplication and algebra), and the tendency for students to be educated in similar ability groups. Students typically encounter similar promotion criteria with fairly narrowly constructed views of success or failure (e.g., grades and high school exit exams). Schools typically utilize centralized methods of bureaucratic control (district administrators typically oversee principals, who oversee the school staff). Particular views of teaching, learning, and knowledge imbue schools. Students generally spend time in self-contained classrooms with one teacher, and teachers tend to work in isolation from other school staff (including teachers and school social workers). Teachers largely direct the content and pacing of learning and also take almost full responsibility for appraising student performance. We take for granted and rarely challenge these very basic features of schools, although they may not always serve all students equally well (Deschenes, Cuban, & Tyack, 2001).

## SCHOOLS ARE DIFFICULT TO REFORM

Given the aforementioned institutional features, one can understand why schools, and particularly classrooms, are difficult to reform. Elmore (2002) argues that the "holy grail" of educational reform is "decreasing interruption of instruction, encouraging richer intellectual and personal connections between teachers and students, and increasing classroom time for ambitious teaching and active engaged learning" (p. 24). However, this is an elusive goal. Many attribute the difficultly in achievement of this goal to the underlying institutional forces and arrangements discussed previously.

## SCHOOL SYSTEMS RELIABLY CONSTRUCT
## DIFFERENCES AMONG STUDENTS

This is the most important enduring institutional feature. Implementation of strategies to identify and intervene with students perceived as "misfitting" by educators is a central feature of universal, bureaucratized education (Deschenes et al., 2001). Such interventions, moreover, often take place separately from the mainstream of classroom instruction.

Deschenes et al. (2001) trace explanations forwarded about misfitting students over time. These include accounts that suggested that students were morally weak, that their families were morally weak, or that the cultures of schools and some families were incompatible. Regardless of the explanation, students and families (vs. the arrangement of schools or instruction) almost always represent the source of difference to be addressed. Such institutional features sparked an important critique of the term "achievement gap" and the label of "at-risk" status. This critique takes up how students of color are differentially labeled and treated within schools.

Processes of labeling achievement differences through tracking, placement in special education, discipline problems, and punitive suspension and expulsion policies are highly racialized in the school setting (O'Connor, Hill, & Robinson, 2009). Specifically, a growing body of research documents that students of color and low-income students are more likely than their White and more affluent peers to be enrolled in lower track classes (Skiba, Michael, Nardo, & Peterson, 2002), enrolled in special education (Harry & Klingner, 2014; Milofsky, 1974; Skiba et al., 2008), identified for disciplinary action (Noguera, 2009), and suspended and/or expelled from school (Fabricant & Fine, 2012).

These racialization processes are of concern for students of color. Evidence indicates that they are disproportionately restricted from the general education program and receive punitive treatment. At the same time, because of resource constraints in their own communities, they are also more in need of the potential supports and resources embedded in their school networks (Farmer-Hinton, 2002). This vicious cycle of race-based overrepresentation in negative behavioral measures coupled with a lack of critical intervention means that many students of color have poor long-term educational outcomes, which impact their opportunities for social mobility. Moreover, this pattern of findings suggests that many schools may be failing to engage a large portion of their student population in ways that reflect cultural and structurally competent responses.

## STANDARDS-BASED REFORM

Our discussion of schools through organizational and institutional lenses sets the general background for recent contemporary education policy initiatives. As such, we foreground our discussion of "standards-based reform" in critical policy scholarship. This additional institutional context sets a general backdrop for educational and related policy developments designed to, at least in part, respond to the achievement gap. Briefly, the term "standards-based reform" refers to educational policies rooted in the notion that performance-based testing and accountability measures are the most efficient mechanism for closing racialized achievement gaps.

### NEOLIBERAL INFLUENCES ON EDUCATION
### AND SOCIAL WELFARE POLICY

Fundamental to this reform strategy is a dominant neoliberal mindset that emphasizes the privatization of public goods; individualism and meritocracy; market deregulation; and decreased spending on social services such as health care, education, and welfare. In this section, we locate schooling within the historical and political manifestations of policies in the current post-Keynesian neoliberal state.

Beginning in the 1970s, and propelled by the Reagan administration of the 1980s, an influx of neoliberal economic and social policies contributed to the demise of the preexisting Keynesian welfare reforms that began decades earlier under the socially liberal tenure of the Franklin D. Roosevelt administration. The Keynesian welfare state, characterized by a stable post-war economy supported by government intervention in the devolution of public services, combined economic growth with market regulation. In other words, the government bore some responsibility for ensuring that citizens had the opportunity to receive services (e.g., education and health care) that could potentially enhance their life outcomes (Darling-Hammond, 2007). The dawning of the neoliberal social and economic agenda was particularly felt in the context of schools, where harsh accountability-based measures and sanctions prescribed by national reform boards aimed to eliminate the achievement gap on the surface while simultaneously reducing governmental education spending, moving toward the privatization of education, and unapologetically contributing to the gentrification of urban space (Lipman & Haines, 2007). Charter schools thus became "the organizational instrument expected to transform a deregulated public education marketplace into an engine for academic achievement" (Fabricant & Fine, 2012, p. 63).

Taking advantage of soaring rates of parental disillusionment with traditional public schooling options, poor education outcomes in resource-drained communities, and even natural disasters (as evidenced by the use of charter schools in the aftermath of Hurricane Katrina), neoliberal restructuring largely viewed charter schools as the best means for providing parents with "choice" and raising public education standards. This strong pro-charter sentiment continues to be espoused even though data increasingly demonstrate that the mandatory testing and accountability measures invoked by standards-based reform have not generally improved the quality of education or increased student outcomes across either traditional or charter settings (Fabricant & Fine, 2012). In addition, although national evaluation data overwhelmingly indicate that the vast majority of charters are doing the same or even worse than traditional public schools, charters continue to be allocated resources while traditional public schools remain underfunded (Schemo, 2004; Zimmer & Buddin, 2009).

In addition to mediocre achievement gains at best, in an effort to meet the aggregate passing score regulated by standards-based reform measures, both traditional and charter schools have been known to encourage students experiencing academic challenges to leave so they do not lower the schools' overall score (Dobbs, 2003; Hursh & Martina, 2003). Specifically, Darling-Hammond (2007) found that there are actual accountability stipulations in standards-based reform guidelines that create the conditions for schools to benefit from the demotion or expulsion of students who need additional academic supports. Coupled with existing charter policies notorious for overly punitive responses to academic and behavioral challenges with students of color, particularly Black males, the vast majority of charters contribute to a racially stratified, highly privatized education system that overlooks the critical needs of students who lack political prestige, particularly students with special needs, English language learners, and students with academic or behavioral challenges (Frankenberg, Siegel-Hawley, & Wang, 2010).

By drawing on the impoverished circumstances and fears of low-income and minority parents, neoliberal governments adopt a business model aimed at increasing efficiency while isolating and shaming low-performing schools and students. By using the rhetoric of "choice," the expansion of charter schools allows the government to dismiss any responsibility for the current state of public education, and failures squarely rest on the shoulders of schools, educators, students, and their families. Little discussion is given to educational equity or to providing the resources needed to position schools for higher achievement, likely due to the fact that the closure of failing public schools makes room for additional charters (Lipman, 2011).

## CURRENT EDUCATIONAL POLICIES AND RELATED INITIATIVES

The passage of No Child Left Behind (NCLB) in 2002 punctuated a significant shift in US educational policy (Dee & Jacob, 2010). It marked an expanded federal role in that it required states to (1) set standards for student academic performance, (2) assess and make transparent student performance in relationship to those standards, and (3) create accountability systems—particularly focused on schools enrolling critical densities of low-income children. It also changed the performance expectations for schools from the historic emphasis on equality of *access* to schooling to equality of *outputs*, as measured by performance on standardized tests (for a review of this history, see Graham, 1993). More recent initiatives include rapid state adoption (45 of 50 states) of the rigorous Common Core Standards for student learning (Phillips & Wong, 2010) and President Obama's Race to the Top initiative, which offers competitive funds to improve low-performing schools and districts (McGuinn, 2012).

Ongoing efforts to improve access to and quality of health and mental health care are also important to note. Health care reform and debate in the United States implicates schools as potentially important sources of access to care (Keeton, Soleimanpour, & Brindis, 2012). In addition, the New Freedom Commission, convened by former President Bush, proposed six national goals for mental health. This report specifically heightened attention to how best to coordinate mental health service delivery across education and other child serving systems (McCabe, Wertlieb, & Saywitz, 2013).

The literature reflecting on the logic of these policies and their relative impacts on schools and students indicates that they generally heighten pressures on schools to not only raise student achievement levels but also simultaneously play key roles as access points for the delivery of health and mental health services to youth. These policies result in increased scrutiny of teachers and their effectiveness (Darling-Hammond, 2010; Hanushek & Rivkin, 2010) and have (perhaps inadvertently) increased demands to demonstrate a relationship between providing access to health and mental health care and academic success (Keeton et al., 2012). On the one hand, these simultaneous pressures on schools may be interpreted in a positive light in that, taken together, they reflect a holistic approach to children's needs. On the other hand, simultaneous pressure to standardize the curricular experiences while increasing responsiveness to factors that differentiate student experience (e.g., responsiveness to student health and mental health characteristics) may create the kind of incompatibility that is reflected in the historically enduring and unresolved tensions between standardization and customization as educational institutional goals (Cuban, 2012).

# CONCLUDING COMMENTS: SCHOOL SOCIAL WORK DELIVERY IN CONTEXT

We conclude by reflecting on school social work service delivery through the frameworks presented throughout this chapter. Delivering health, psychosocial, and other related support services to student populations represents a long-standing tradition in schools. Examining this history reveals, however, several underlying tensions related to these services, which have been viewed by educators and the public mainly as ancillary to the core academic mission of schools (Adelman & Taylor, 2006; Tyack, 1992). As such, they have not been consistently funded as a core component of programming and are driven by other agendas; when these services are funded from the school budget, they are typically the first to be cut or reassigned in lean budgetary times. School social work services may be co-opted to serve organizational and institutional goals (Tyack, 1992). In short, there are a variety of ways in which schools resource, administer, and structure health, psychosocial, and other supports for students. Thus, in part due to these "host" setting policy and institutional dynamics, contemporary school social work is unevenly funded, and the nature and quality of services vary significantly across school districts, states, and regions. Examining school social work services alongside our discussion of the school organizational, institutional, and policy context suggests the importance of continuous reflection on how stated goals of social work and related services may become displaced over time and/or pottentially serve as "sorting" mechanisms for children from non-dominant ethno-racial groups.

Given these institutional constraints, it is also illuminating to view school social work and social workers as complex school resources. This would lead practitioners to consider local school conditions and reflect on what set of specific resources and interventions, combined together, would best enhance overall school functioning and best serve the needs of students.

Finally, it also suggests that school social workers attend to the "contested" nature of schooling and education and critically reflect on how schools as institutions and logics underlying education policy actually serve students and communities. At a minimum, the current context suggests that school social workers may be particularly well positioned in facilitating "power sharing" among school staff, parents, and students, particularly toward the objective of creating shared visions of the purpose of schooling and school goals and practice.

## ADDITIONAL RESOURCES

The following resources are geared toward educators but are written to be directly applied to practice in schools. For these reasons, we view them as particularly applicable to school social workers.

Details strategies to promote equity in school practices:

McKenzie, K. B., & Scheurich, J. J. (2004). Equity traps: A useful construct for preparing principals to lead schools that are successful with racially diverse students. *Educational Administration Quarterly, 40*(5), 601–632.

One of the seminal investigations that sparked more contemporary studies into race and discipline in education:

Children's Defense Fund. (1975). *School suspensions: Are they helping children?* Cambridge, MA: Washington Research Project.

A solid resource for social workers and educators attempting to put critical theory into practice:

Ladson-Billings, G., & Tate IV, W. (1995). Toward a critical race theory of education. *The Teachers College Record, 97*(1), 47–68.

Investigation into the ongoing discussion of racial equity and disproportionate punishment:

Carter, P., Skiba, R., Arredondo, M., & Pollock, M. (2014). *You can't fix what you don't look at: Acknowledging race in addressing racial discipline disparities.* Discipline Disparities Series: Acknowledging Race. The Equity Project at Indiana University, Center for Evaluation and Education Policy, Bloomington, IN.

Solid discussion of the tensions between standards-based reform and social justice:

Darling-Hammond, L. (1994). Performance-based assessment and educational equity. *Harvard Educational Review, 64*(1), 5–31.

A podcast illustrating school organizational dynamics and school social work services within an urban community marked by violence.

Lutton, L., Calhoun, B., & Kotlowicz, A. (2013a, February 15). *Harper High School, Part One. This American life podcast.* Podcast retrieved from http://www.thisamericanlife.org/radio-archives/episode/487/harper-high-school-part-one

Lutton, L., Calhoun, B., & Kotlowicz, A. (2013b, February 22). *Harper High School, Part Two. This American life podcast.* Podcast retrieved from http://www.thisamericanlife.org/radio-archives/episode/488/harper-high-school-part-two

# REFERENCES

Adelman, H., & Taylor, L. (2006). Mental health in schools and public health. *Public Health Reports, 131,* 294–298.

Bryk, A. S. (2010). Organizing schools for improvement. *Phi Delta Kappan, 91,* 23–30.

Cuban, L. (2012). Standards vs. customization: Finding the balance. *Educational Leadership, 69,* 10–15.

Darling-Hammond, L. (2007). Race, inequality and educational accountability: The irony of "No Child Left Behind." *Race Ethnicity and Education, 10,* 245–260.

Darling-Hammond, L. (2010). *The flat world and education: How America's commitment to equity will determine our future.* New York, NY: Teachers College Press.

Dee, T. S., & Jacob, B. A. (2010). The impact of No Child Left Behind on students, teachers, and schools. *Brookings Papers on Economic Activity, 2010*(2), 149–207.

Deschenes, S., Cuban, L., & Tyack, D. (2001). Mismatch: Historical perspectives on schools and students who don't fit them. *Teachers College Record, 103,* 525–547.

Dobbs, M. (2003, November 9). Education "miracle" has a math problem. *The Washington Post.*

Elmore, R. (2002). Hard questions about practice. *Educational Leadership, 59,* 22–25.

Fabricant, M., & Fine, M. (2012). *Charter schools and the corporate makeover of public education: What's at stake?* New York, NY: Teachers College Press.

Farrell, J. P. (2013). Equality of education: Six decades of comparative evidence seen from a new millennium. In R. F. Arnove, C. A. Torres, & S. Franz (Eds.), *Comparative education: The dialectic of the global and the local* (pp. 149–174). Lanham, MD: Rowman & Littlefield.

Farmer-Hinton, R. (2002). The Chicago context: Understanding the consequences of urban processes on school capacity. *The Journal of Negro Education, 71*(4), 313–330.

Frankenberg, E., Siegel-Hawley, G., & Wang, J. (2010). *Choice without equity: Charter school segregation and the need for civil rights standards.* Los Angeles, CA: The Civil Rights Project/Proyecto Derechos Civiles at UCLA. Retrieved from https://www.civilrightsproject.ucla.edu

Graham, P. A. (1993). What America has expected of its schools over the past century. *American Journal of Education, 101,* 83–98.

Grubb, W. N. (2008). Multiple resources, multiple outcomes: Testing the "improved" school finance with NELS88. *American Educational Research Journal, 45,* 104–144.

Hanushek, E. A., & Rivkin, S. G. (2010). Generalizations about using value-added measures of teacher quality. *American Economic Review, 100*, 267–271.

Harry, B., & Klingner, J. K. (2014). *Why are so many minority students in special education? Understanding race & disability in schools.* New York, NY: Teachers College Press.

Hursh, D., & Martina, C. (2003). Neoliberalism and schooling in the U.S.: How state and federal government education policies perpetuate inequality. *Journal of Critical Education Policy Studies, 1*, 2.

Keeton, V., Soleimanpour, S., & Brindis, C. D. (2012). School-based health centers in an era of health care reform: Building on history. *Current Problems in Pediatric and Adolescent Health Care, 42*, 132–156.

Kelly, M., & Stone, S. (2009). An analysis of factors shaping interventions used by school social workers. *Children & Schools, 31*, 163–176.

Konstantopoulos, S., & Borman, G. D. (2011). Family background and school effects on student achievement: A multilevel analysis of the Coleman data. *Teachers College Record, 113*, 97–132.

Lipman, P. (2011). *The new political economy of urban education: Neo-liberalism, race and the right to the city.* New York, NY: Routledge.

Lipman, P., & Haines, N. (2007). From accountability to privatization and African American exclusion: Chicago's "Renaissance 2010." *Educational Policy, 21*, 471–450.

Lutton, L., Calhoun, B., & Kotlowicz, A. (2013a, February 15). *Harper High School, Part One. This American life podcast.* Podcast retrieved from http://www.thisamericanlife.org/radio-archives/episode/487/harper-high-school-part-one

Lutton, L., Calhoun, B., & Kotlowicz, A. (2013b, February 22). *Harper High School, Part Two. This American life podcast.* Podcast retrieved from http://www.thisamericanlife.org/radio-archives/episode/488/harper-high-school-part-two

McCabe, M. A., Wertlieb, D., & Saywitz, K. (2013). Promoting children's mental health: The importance of collaboration and public understanding. In A. McDonald (Ed.), *Child and family advocacy* (pp. 19–34). New York, NY: Springer.

McGuinn, P. (2012). Stimulating reform: Race to the top, competitive grants and the Obama education agenda. *Educational Policy, 26*, 136–159.

Milofsky, C. D. (1974). Why special education isn't special. *Harvard Educational Review, 44*(4), 437–458.

Noguera, P. A. (2009). *The trouble with black boys: . . . And other reflections on race, equity, and the future of public education.* San Francisco, CA: Jossey-Bass.

O'Connor, C., Hill, L., & Robinson, S. (2009). Who's at risk in school and what's race got to do with it? *Review of Research in Education, 33*, 1–34.

Payne, A. A. (2009). Do predictors of the implementation quality of school-based prevention programs differ by program type? *Prevention Science, 10*, 151–167.

Phillippo, K., & Stone, S. (2011). Toward a broader view: A call to integrate knowledge about schools into school social work research. *Children & Schools, 33*, 71–81.

Phillips, V., & Wong, C. (2010). Tying together the common core of standards, instruction, and assessments. *Phi Delta Kappan, 91*, 37–42.

Rutter, M., & Maughan, B. (2002). School effectiveness findings 1979–2002. *Journal of School Psychology, 40*, 451–475.

Schemo, D. (2004, August 16). Charter schools trail in results, U.S. data reveals. *New York Times,* p. A1.

Skiba, R. J., Michael, R. S., Nardo, A. C., & Peterson, R. L. (2002). The color of discipline: Sources of racial and gender disproportionality in school punishment. *The Urban Review, 34*(4), 317–342.

Skiba, R. J., Simmons, A. B., Ritter, S., Gibb, A. C., Rausch, M. K., Cuadrado, J., & Chung, C. G. (2008). Achieving equity in special education: History, status, and current challenges. *Exceptional Children, 74*(3), 264–288.

Teasley, M. (2004). School social workers and urban education reform with African American children and youth: Realities, advocacy, and strategies for change. *School Community Journal, 14*(2), 19–38.

Teddlie, C., & Reynolds, D. (Eds.). (2000). *The international handbook of school effectiveness research.* New York, NY: Farmer Press.

Tyack, D. (1991). Public school reform: Policy talk and institutional practice. *American Journal of Education, 100,* 1–19.

Tyack, D. (1992). Health and social services in public schools: Historical perspectives. *The Future of Children, 2,* 19–31.

Zimmer, R., & Buddin, R. (2009). Is charter school competition in California improving the performance of traditional public schools? *Public Administration Review, 69,* 831–845.

# CHAPTER 6

# CONTEMPORARY FEDERAL POLICY AND SCHOOL SOCIAL WORK

*Implications for Practice and Opportunities for Leadership*

## ANDREW BRAKE AND BENJAMIN ROTH

Recent federal legislation initiatives in the United States underscore the complex and dynamic relationship that exists between social policy and social work practice in schools. This chapter analyzes three federal policy domains to assess how they impact some of the most marginalized youth in the country, the schools they attend, and the critical roles that school social workers play in this complex relationship. Together, these policy domains represent efforts to engage students holistically, address social dynamics obstructing academic success, and ensure that all students experience public education as a safe and dependable springboard for pursuing their long-term goals. Specifically, we examine the following:

1. The 2012 Deferred Action for Childhood Arrivals (DACA), the 2014 Deferred Action for Parent Arrivals (DAPA), and supporting unauthorized youth and families in schools
2. The 2013 Safe Schools and Improvement Act and ensuring anti-discrimination and anti-bullying protections for lesbian, gay, bisexual, transgender, and questioning/queer (LGBTQ) youth in schools
3. The 2014 School Discipline Guidance Package and strategies for closing the school-to-prison pipeline

These three policy domains are not explicitly interrelated, nor do they represent an exhaustive list of legislative initiatives to improve school quality for marginalized youth. However, given their focus and target populations, they offer a useful heuristic for (re)examining the importance of school social workers as leaders within the school context. Although not all of these initiatives have successfully become law, each has important implications for the services that school social workers provide. Each policy has potential to greatly improve supports for low-income youth of color, immigrant youth, LGBTQ youth, and youth who may identify across a combination of these intersecting identities and experiences. In light of these policy domains, we also highlight key leadership opportunities for school social workers as they help their schools understand, articulate, and leverage their strengths, as well as find innovative ways to work through their limitations. We map important future directions and potential for better serving and advocating for some of our schools' most underserved youth.

## THE CONTEMPORARY POLICY CONTEXT AND SCHOOL SOCIAL WORK

The year 2014 marked the 30th anniversary of John I. Goodlad's (1984) acclaimed critique of schooling in the United States, *A Place Called School*. In it, Goodlad made four specific goals for national education policy to strive to achieve by 2001: (1) reorganize schools into smaller learning communities, particularly secondary schools, to focus on and support individual student needs, interests, knowledge, and talents; (2) make a major shift in focus toward technology; (3) develop a closer alignment of national curriculum and workplace preparedness in the new economy; and (4) lead a greater investment in the multiple benefits of highly educated students, including their problem solving, social awareness, equity, technical skills, and citizenship. Although Goodlad's call provides a prophetic window into the direction that much of the national education reform agenda has taken during the past three decades, by 2002, as enormous reform efforts to overhaul America's schools were well underway, Goodlad (2002) also took note of another danger. Specifically, he warned of what he called "eduviruses"—reform efforts built on the mythology of "failing schools" that quickly and insidiously spread across the educational landscape with a promise of success that often far exceeds the actual outcomes they deliver. Rather than committing to a policy agenda aimed at developing a workforce of qualified, caring, and competent teachers, during the past three decades we have witnessed a long and costly series of so-called silver-bullet fixes that have brought about limited substantive changes in narrowing achievement outcomes for marginalized youth, particularly in large urban school districts (Payne, 2008).

Today, even as the wake of the destructive policies of No Child Left Behind (NCLB) retreats into the recent past, the threat of eduviruses remains high for America's schools and classrooms. As Burris and Aja (2014) note, much of the rhetoric that surrounds the promises to fix America's failing schools can still be found in contemporary education policy. Closely tied to the claim that the key to fixing schools lies mostly in the drive to "raise the standards," Burris and Aja highlight that potentially costly remnants of NCLB still ripple through President Obama's 2009 Race to the Top initiative—a federal carrot held out to states with the guarantee of funds to initiatives that aim to ensure college and career readiness for all students, particularly the most marginalized. Five years into the Race, however, this initiative continues to prioritize policies and programs that align increased standards with high-stakes testing and a strict accountability regime—a "scared straight" approach that threatens schools with the punitive specter of being closed unless their students' achievement improves significantly.

Despite emerging evidence showing that such heavy-handed efforts do little to narrow the achievement gap, school turnaround and closure initiatives have continued apace, along with a heavy investment in charter schools, particularly in large, urban school districts. Research on school turnaround has shown little success in improving the engagement and performance of many marginalized youth (Peck and Reitzug, 2014), while school closures appear to have accelerated student mobility (Gwynne & de la Torre, 2009). In turn, the rapid expansion of charter schools has largely filled the void left by shuttered schools. In effect, charter schools have reinforced racial isolation among the majority of their students (Frankenberg, Siegel-Hawley, & Wang, 2010); lowered student academic performance and achievement (Institute on Metropolitan Opportunity, 2014); increased disciplinary referrals for largely minor behavioral infractions (Ahmed-Ullah & Richards, 2014); and created more privatized, formerly public, charter schools with less accountability to effectively serve their students (see Chapter 5).

Within this volatile and unpredictable education policy context, school social workers continue to forge ahead. Guided by ethical standards and core practices that aim to create educational equity and achieve social justice for marginalized youth in schools, now, more than ever, school social workers must also be knowledgeable of the policies and practices that directly impact these youth. This chapter outlines three such federal policy domains and considers their impact on schools, school social work practice, and marginalized youth. In addition, it makes recommendations for the field of school social work to assume greater leadership in helping schools better use these policies to improve how we serve them.

# THE 2012 DEFERRED ACTION FOR CHILDHOOD ARRIVALS, THE 2014 DEFERRED ACTION FOR PARENT ARRIVALS, AND SUPPORTING UNAUTHORIZED YOUTH AND FAMILIES IN SCHOOLS

A large and growing number of immigrant children and youth are growing up in the United States without legal status, and many US-born children have at least one parent who is unauthorized (also commonly referred to as "undocumented"). Unauthorized children are particularly disadvantaged. Although they are legally entitled to a public education through the 12th grade, they are unable to work legally in the United States or receive federal financial aid to pay for college. In many states, they are charged nonresident tuition at public colleges and universities, and in several states they are prohibited from attending these institutions at all. In response, the Development, Relief, and Education for Alien Minors (DREAM) Act was introduced to the Senate in 2001 to provide a pathway to citizenship for unauthorized immigrants brought to the United States before the age of 16 years. Although passage of the DREAM Act has failed repeatedly since it was originally introduced, it has come to represent a movement spurred by a new generation of immigrant rights activists who call themselves DREAMers. DREAMers and their allies have raised significant awareness about the need for reform, including relief from deportation, increased access to higher education, and new pathways to citizenship (Nicholls, 2013; Zimmerman, 2012).

The compelling momentum of the DREAMer movement contributed to President Obama's executive order in June 2012 to defer the deportation of certain unauthorized immigrants who came to the United States as children. Deferred Action for Childhood Arrivals (DACA) provides temporary deportation relief for an estimated 2.1 million unauthorized immigrants (Batalova et al., 2010) provided they

(1)   arrived in the United States prior to age 16 years;

(2)   continuously resided in the United States without legal status since June 15, 2007;

(3)   were younger than age 31 years as of June 15, 2012, and at least age 15 years at application (unauthorized immigrants younger than 15 years but in removal proceedings are also eligible to apply);

(4)   are currently enrolled in school, have already graduated high school or obtained a general development certificate (GED), or are an honorably discharged veteran; and

(5)   have not been convicted of a felony or multiple or serious misdemeanors and do not pose a threat to national security or public safety. (US Citizenship and Immigration Services, 2015)

In addition to a 2-year reprieve from deportation, DACA offers eligible young people temporary Social Security numbers and 2-year work permits they can use to obtain jobs and paid internships anywhere in the United States and more easily access limited financial and other resources. Indeed, DACA presents a significant shift in the life opportunities available to unauthorized young people, and as of 2015 1,017,977 DACA-eligible youth have either applied or renewed (US Citizenship and Immigration Services, 2015; Gonzales & Bautista-Chavez, 2014; Gonzales, Terriquez & Ruszczyk, 2014). Many unauthorized youth will become eligible for DACA once they age into the program. These young people are currently coming up through primary and secondary schools and—provided they meet the other criteria to receive DACA—will be eligible to apply once they reach age 16 years.

President Obama announced the expansion of DACA in November 2014. Currently, DACA expansion is on hold while its legality is debated in the courts. If the expansion is authorized, DACA eligibility criteria will no longer stipulate that applicants be younger than 31 years old, provided they have lived continuously in the United States since January 1, 2010. In addition, DACA recipients must reapply every 3 years, rather than every 2 years, lowering the cost of reapplying and, therefore, potentially encouraging more who are eligible to apply.

In addition to expanding DACA in 2014, President Obama also created a program to defer deportation for select unauthorized immigrants who came to the United States as adults. The program, called DAPA, is for unauthorized immigrants who have lived in the United States continuously since January 1, 2010, have a son or daughter who was a US citizen or lawful permanent resident, and are not an enforcement priority for removal from the United States (US Citizenship and Immigration Services, 2015). Similar to DACA, DAPA provides deportation relief and work authorization for 3 years.

Neither DACA nor DAPA provide a pathway to lawful status. Furthermore, they are programs made possible through executive order rather than policies enacted by Congress. In other words, DACA and DAPA offer a limited set of temporary rights to unauthorized immigrants, and even these rights could be rolled back at any time. Nonetheless, these programs provide one of the only avenues by which unauthorized youth and families can afford to attend college (through in-state tuition) and participate legally in the mainstream labor market.

## IMPLICATIONS FOR PRACTICE AND
## OPPORTUNITIES FOR LEADERSHIP

The Pew Research Center (2015) estimated that as of 2012, more than 11 million unauthorized residents were living in the United States, 60% of whom were children younger than age 18 years. Unauthorized children and families are a uniquely vulnerable population, with specific concerns, needs, and strengths. In addition to social mobility barriers on the way to young adulthood, unauthorized immigrant youth experience fear and stigma (Abrego, 2011) and obstructed access to a range of resources and institutions because of their legal status (Yoshikawa, Godfrey, & Rivera, 2008; Gonzales, 2010). The potential negative effects on the mental health and educational aspirations of unauthorized youth, particularly as they grow increasingly aware of the financial and career constraints brought on by their status during adolescence, is of special concern to school social workers (Gonzalez, Suárez-Orozco, & Dedios-Sanguineti, 2013). Young children are also affected. An estimated 5.5 million children—many of whom are US citizens—grow up with unauthorized parents; these children encounter numerous developmental barriers, including obstructed access to public programs and anxiety stemming from fear of deportation (Yoshikawa, Kholoptseva, & Suárez-Orozco, 2013). Indeed, the negative effects brought on by deportation can break up families and have devastating impacts on family systems (Mahatmya & Gring-Pemble, 2014). Although uncertain legal status has a significant impact on children and families, the vulnerable position of these families creates a conundrum for school social workers, teachers, and administrators. On the one hand, legal status *should* be overlooked by school social workers. Because of the Supreme Court's ruling in *Plyler v. Doe* (1982), unauthorized youth can legally attend public schools just like their citizen peers and they should not be flagged or identified in any way that invites discrimination or bias. On the other hand, school social workers are less able to effectively serve and advocate for unauthorized students and their families if they are unaware of the legal status of these students and families. It is critical that school social workers learn to navigate this conundrum so they are able to consider how each immigrant family's unique composition is potentially affected by the legal status of one, some, or all of its members.

In addition to providing direct services for youth and families coping with the challenges of being unauthorized, school social workers can take a leadership role in learning about the benefits of DACA and DAPA policies and actively share this information with their school community. School social workers can also learn more about lesser known alternatives for unauthorized youth in unique circumstances. For example, the Violence Against Women Act (VAWA) can provide pathways to citizenship for spouses and children who have been victims of domestic violence and child abuse at the hands of a spouse who is a legal resident or an American citizen. Similarly, Special Immigrant Juvenile Status (SIJS) and certain visas for victims of domestic violence and trafficking can be particularly helpful to specific subgroups of unauthorized youth and families. School social workers can refer immigrants to qualified legal service professionals for consultation on their eligibility for these and other protections. At the very least, school social workers can take the lead on informing unauthorized youth and families—as well as teachers and administrators—about specific eligibility requirements and availability of services and resources through DACA and DAPA. Other tasks may include sponsoring attorney-led workshops so that immigrant families can understand the specific guidelines and benefits of DACA and DAPA and current state and institutional policies governing access for unauthorized immigrants to colleges and universities. Finally, school social workers should be apprised of existing and emerging scholarships, changes in in-state tuition policies, community funds that might make it possible for unauthorized youth to attend college and prepare for the labor force, and critical ways to cultivate a more welcoming environment in their schools for unauthorized youth and their families.

# THE 2013 SAFE SCHOOLS AND IMPROVEMENT ACT AND ANTI-DISCRIMINATION AND ANTI-BULLYING PROTECTIONS FOR LGBTQ YOUTH IN SCHOOLS

The Safe Schools and Improvement Act (SSIA), put forth to Congress by Senator Robert Casey (D-PA) in January 2015, includes a federal anti-discrimination policy that aims to reduce the threat of bullying for LGBTQ youth in schools. Although the policy has yet to pass, it has gained significant momentum after years of advocacy efforts from a broad coalition of anti-bullying groups led by the Gay, Lesbian & Straight Education Network (GLSEN). The SSIA would require public kindergarten through 12 schools to enact all-inclusive anti-bullying policies in all schools throughout the United States (GLSEN, 2013). Specifically, SSIA would amend the Elementary and Secondary Education Act of 1965 and would require states to direct their local districts to create policies that prevent and prohibit bullying and harassment that limits students' ability to participate in afterschool programs or creates a hostile or abusive environment that adversely affects their education. In addition, districts and schools would be required to (1) give annual notice of their prohibited and disciplinary polices, (2) outline specific grievance procedures, and (3) provide annual public data on the incidence and frequency of related disciplinary infractions at the school and district level. Finally, SSIA would require the Secretary of Education to evaluate policies that aim to combat bullying in elementary and high schools, and it would require the Commission for Education Statistics to track these data with an independent review (Civic Impulse, 2015).

## IMPLICATIONS FOR PRACTICE AND OPPORTUNITIES FOR LEADERSHIP

National research on bullying has found that disproportionate rates of LGBTQ students are victims of bullying (Human Rights Campaign, 2015). National surveys of youth in schools report that 69% of LGBTQ youth still feel unsafe in schools, 85% have experienced verbal harassment in school, and 62% of reported incidents received no response from school staff (GLSEN, 2013). However, there is also evidence that anti-bullying policies are effective. Schools that enact inclusive anti-bullying policies and practices create safer, more welcoming school environments for LGBTQ youth, and these environments are associated with a reduced risk for suicide attempts among these youth (Hatzenbuehler & Keyes, 2013).

Until legislation such as SSIA is enacted, school social workers must continue to take critical leadership roles in helping schools develop specific policies and practices that support LGBTQ youth. To begin, school social workers should become familiar with and knowledgeable of the common concerns of LGBTQ youth regarding their experience in schools and share this information with their school communities. A number of leading organizations provide valuable national, regional, and district data about how LGBTQ youth experience safety, harassment, bullying, and peer and staff support in schools. Next, social workers should help schools use student surveys to assess their climate of support for all youth. These data can provide critical insights into the experiences of youth who identify in various ways. Student survey data can also inform interventions for LGBTQ youth and identify key areas of need and success.

Building on findings from their school assessment, school social workers can help create safe spaces in schools where LGBTQ youth can find peer support and explore and express their concerns and strengths. Research conducted by the Gay, Lesbian & Straight Education Network (2015) found that schools report significantly higher levels of safety and academic performance among LGBTQ youth to the extent they meet three conditions. First, such schools have active student organizations dedicated to creating safe space for LGBTQ youth, such as the Gay–Straight Alliance and similar groups. Second, they have clearly articulated and enforced anti-bullying and anti-harassment policies. Third, schools with the most success at supporting LGBTQ students have course curricula that include topics relevant to the LGBTQ students. However, because few schools have any of these supports in place (GLSEN, 2015), social workers must take leadership in creating and implementing these policies and supports in schools.

School social workers can also help lead schools in understanding the implicit gendered assumptions that are encoded in our language and school policies and practices. Recent efforts by transgender advocates underscore how traditionally gendered binary language (e.g., he/she and him/her) can serve to marginalize youth who may not conform physiologically, or in their expressed identity, to the identity or expression that was traditionally associated with their assigned sex at birth (National Center for Transgender Equality, 2015). A close examination of many operating school traditions suggests they all assume a gender binary that can be uncomfortable, hostile, or act as a barrier to opportunity for transgender and gender nonconforming youth. These traditions include gendered school uniforms, bathrooms and locker rooms, participation in team sports, and applications for college financial aid. As a general rule, school staff should ask students the gender pronoun with which they wish to identify. School social workers can facilitate conversations among members of the school community about how the language used in schools and in teaching and learning may privilege traditional students and marginalize transgender students. They can also provide professional development trainings to schools staff about how best to support transgender students, create alternative restroom spaces and places available for transgendered students if they wish to use them, and involve transgender students' parents in helping their children prepare for transitions into new school contexts (National Center for Transgender Equality, 2015).

# THE 2014 SCHOOL DISCIPLINE GUIDANCE PACKAGE AND STRATEGIES FOR CLOSING THE SCHOOL-TO-PRISON PIPELINE

Recent studies of school disciplinary practices designed to make schools safer have revealed troubling and persistent patterns of ineffectiveness and even harm, particularly in the area of ethnic and racial disparities. Zero tolerance discipline policies, in particular, have been shown to be largely ineffective at making schools safer (Chin, Dowdy, Jimerson, & Rime, 2012; Stinchcomb, Bazemore, & Riestenberg, 2006; Teske, 2011; Wald & Losen, 2003). Moreover, Black, Latino, and Native American youth disproportionately attend schools that continue to use zero tolerance policies and practices. As a result, they are significantly more likely than students of other backgrounds to be referred for discipline problems and to receive out-of-school suspension or expulsion as punishment (Hannon, DeFina, & Bruch, 2013; Krezmien, Leone, & Achilles, 2006; Skiba et al., 2011; Wallace, Goodkind, Wallace, & Bachman, 2008; Welch & Payne, 2010). Compounding this problem are findings from the US Department of Education Office for Civil Rights (2014) that boys receive more than two out of three suspensions, and students with disabilities are more than twice as likely as students without disabilities to receive out-of-school suspensions. Zero tolerance and exclusionary discipline sanctions also often have adverse effects on students' academic and life trajectories and can be directly traced to increased school dropout rates (Fabelo et al., 2011; Rausch, Skiba, & Simmons, 2004; Skiba et al., 2003). In short, as researchers and advocates have highlighted, the discipline policies and practices most often used in urban school districts contribute to low student achievement, higher school dropout rates, and increased involvement in the criminal justice system—in effect, facilitating the school-to-prison pipeline for many youth of color.

On January 8, 2014, US Secretary of Education Arne Duncan and Attorney General Eric Holder, in a joint initiative between the US Department of Education and the US Department of Justice, released the 2014 School Discipline Guidance Package. It outlined a set of principles and resources, as well as provided a compendium of existing laws and regulations, designed to assist and remind public schools of their legal obligation to provide fair and equitable discipline practices. Responding to years of efforts by advocates expressing grave concerns over inequitable disciplinary practices across age, race, and gender in public schools, this initiative aimed to incentivize and renew efforts among districts and schools to closely examine disparities in discipline outcomes and to develop and implement more equitable policies and practices. Although it provides no new legislative mandates, the Guidance Package has helped to raise national concern for this issue. Its introduction also signals to schools and districts the legislative direction and legal accountability measures that the federal government could take if significant changes in these disparities remain unaddressed.

## IMPLICATIONS FOR PRACTICE AND OPPORTUNITIES FOR LEADERSHIP

Since its announcement, advocates have applauded the arrival of the Guidance Package for beginning the process of challenging districts and schools to closely examine their own disparate discipline outcomes, as well as to identify and implement more effective and equitable practices. School social workers are also well positioned and trained in practices that can help guide schools in their school discipline reform efforts. An important starting point is for school social workers to lead schools in carefully examining their own exclusionary disciplinary practices (e.g., their suspension and expulsion rates) across all grade levels, as well as across students of different races and ethnicities, genders, and academic abilities. In addition, encouraging schools to disseminate empirically validated school climate surveys that examine students' experiences with, and perceptions of, school safety, disciplinary policies and practices, and peer and staff supports can provide valuable insights into addressing issues of safety, mutual respect, and trust between students, peers, and school staff.

School social workers' knowledge base and training in the implementation of positive behavioral supports and use of comprehensive assessments of student behavior—such as functional assessments and manifestation determination processes—is also highly valuable in beginning to reduce exclusionary discipline outcomes and disproportionality. Together, they reinforce the importance of utilizing consistent and systematic individualized behavior plans and practices that have been found to reduce disproportionality, especially for students receiving special education services (Moreno & Bullock, 2011; Moreno & Gaytán, 2013; Peguero & Shekarkhar, 2011; Skiba et al., 2006, 2008; Van Acker, Borenson, Gable, & Potterton, 2005).

School social workers can also take a leadership role by advocating for the implementation of the most effective approaches in their schools and being knowledgeable of how their and other school districts are reforming their own policies and practices. Research on successful implementation of school discipline reforms suggests that increased school safety and reduced disciplinary infractions are tied to central office and school-level administrative support of proactive and preventive behavior interventions and school–community–family partnerships (Gregory, Allen, Mikami, Hafen, & Pianta, 2013; Monroe, 2006; Skiba et al., 2011). Skiba and colleagues (2003) have also noted that administrators' support of universal interventions (e.g., peer mediation and social skill programs) was negatively associated with the suspension of students of color. Other researchers theorize that certain types of professional development—focused on culturally responsive teaching, for example, or implementing Positive Behavioral Intervention and Supports (PBIS) and restorative justice practices (RJP)—foster stronger family–community–school connections and reduce the odds of harsher discipline consequences for minority students (Bohanon & Wu, 2011; Houchins, Shippen, & Murphy, 2012; Monroe, 2006; Sharkey & Fenning, 2012; Sugai & Horner, 2009).

Most of these interventions have not yet undergone rigorous empirical testing, and emerging evidence appears to suggest that the implementation of PBIS alone is insufficient for protecting against racial and gender disparities in school discipline (Bradshaw, Koth, Thornton, & Leaf, 2009; Skiba et al., 2011; Vincent, Sprague, & Gau, 2013). Therefore, school social workers should work closely with school leaders to actively and carefully pursue effective approaches that meet the particular and unique needs of their school. For example, prevention programs designed to teach anger management and remediate social skill deficits (Durlak, Weissberg, Dymnicki, Taylor, & Schellinger, 2011; Kelly, Raines, Stone, & Frey, 2010; Walker, Kerns, Lyon, Bruns, & Cosgrove, 2010; Wilson, Gottfredson, & Najaka, 2001) appear to provide promise for reducing conflict in schools, as do interventions designed to address harassment and school bullying (Ttofi & Farrington, 2012). Finally, perhaps the most important role that school social workers can take is to help school staff recognize that all members of a school community have a stake in positively shaping student behaviors and making school discipline policies and practices more equitable.

## CONCLUSIONS AND RECOMMENDATIONS

Outside of the family, schools remain the primary institution for guiding the development of youth; ensuring their safety; and providing them critical educational, nutritional, physical, and mental health services and supports. However, across the landscape of public schools in the United States, the distribution of resources, the quality of policies and practices, and the priorities placed on supporting youth from all backgrounds are far from equal. School social workers can play a key leadership role as knowledgeable and qualified practitioners and as strong advocates for supporting marginalized youth and families. Indeed, doing so is at the core of our guiding ethical standards. However, in the contemporary policy context, the challenges that social workers face in supporting marginalized youth in schools are great. Moreover, not all policymakers, districts, schools, and educators share the vision that schools should act as institutions that work toward equity and social justice for marginalized youth. In light of this context, it is imperative that school social workers stay current and knowledgeable of contemporary policies that support this goal. Doing so can aid social workers in not only helping youth develop critical skills essential for their college and career goals but also guiding them in developing a deep engagement and a holistic stake in shaping the valuable problem-solving, technical, and self- and social-awareness skills essential for their future.

## QUOTES FROM THE FIELD

As the educational achievement gap widens I think our roles as social workers continues to become more expansive and critical. Despite the constraints placed on us in schools, it is imperative that we continue to not only become more knowledgeable of the available resources, but also build supports within systems and communities in order to appropriately serve our students and families, both inside and outside the school walls.

Alejandra Gutiérrez, School Social Worker, Cicero Public Schools District 99

This past year, our school examined suspension and expulsion data to discern patterns and identify areas of change. I partnered with the discipline team to create alternate to suspension programs such as peer mediation and peer mentoring. We also created a suspension re-entry process that incorporated restorative practices to facilitate a student's re-entry and decrease the likelihood of a repeat suspension. Our expulsion rate has dropped by 50% this year.

Faiza Omer, School Social Worker, DRW College Prep,
Chicago Public Schools District 299

## CASE STUDY 1: KRISTINA

Kristina is an 11th grade student who emigrated from Bosnia to the United States when she was 18 months old. She attends the local high school, where you work as a school social worker. The school is located in a working-class neighborhood in an older suburb that has seen few immigrant families living there during the past 50 years. Kristina has a reputation of doing very well in her classes and often speaks in class about her positive experience coming to the United States as an immigrant. Kristina and most of her peers expect to go to college, and their high school has a strong record of college attendance among its graduates. Halfway through the school year, Kristina is referred to you by her English teacher, who has had to calm Kristina down twice this week after her emotional outbursts during class debates that were designed to improve students' argumentation skills. The issues debated included Affirmative Action, need-based financial aid, and the recent increase of immigrant deportations in the United States. When you meet Kristina, she is sullen and describes feeling targeted by her teacher and peers, who "just don't understand what it's like to be Bosnian in this school." At the time, you are also unaware that Kristina is an undocumented immigrant and that she, her mother, and her brother have experienced severe physical abuse at the hands of her father, an American citizen.

## CASE STUDY 2: TERRY

Terry is an African American male ninth grade student who is referred to you the first month of the school year. As a social worker, the classroom teacher assumes you are the best person in the building to "deal with Terry" but provides little other details. When you first meet, Terry seems calm and kind, and he explains that he has recently been questioning whether or not he would prefer to be referred to as "he" or "she." Terry also explains that a few close friends have become accepting of Terry's preference for being referred to as "she" but does not think her classmates will be so supportive. Terry also tells you that yesterday she got into a shoving match with two boys in the hallway after she stood up for herself when they called her "gay" for wearing eyeliner. In your conversation, Terry explains that she does not have a problem sticking up for herself and that she will "fight anyone who tries me." You also learn that Terry has been sleeping on her 20-year-old cousin's couch since this summer because her mother threw her out of the house when she learned of Terry's new identity.

## ADDITIONAL RESOURCES

### SUPPORTING UNDOCUMENTED IMMIGRANT YOUTH AND FAMILIES

BestColleges.com, *College Guide for Undocumented Students*: http://www.bestcolleges.com/resources/undocumented-students-guide

Educators for Fair Consideration: http://e4fc.org

Immigrant Youth Justice League: http://www.iyjl.org

National Immigrant Justice Center: http://www.immigrantjustice.org/dreamer-resource-hub

National Immigration Law Center: https://www.nilc.org/issues/daca.html

US Citizenship and Immigration Services, *Citizenship Eligibility Through the Violence Against Women Act (VAWA)*: https://www.uscis.gov/humanitarian/battered-spouse-children-parents

US Citizenship and Immigration Services, *Deferred Action for Childhood Arrivals (DACA)*: https://www.uscis.gov/humanitarian/consideration-deferred-action-childhood-arrivals-daca

US Citizenship and Immigration Services, *Deferred Action for Parents of Americans and Lawful Permanent Residents (DAPA)*: https://www.uscis.gov/immigrationaction#2

### CREATING SAFE SCHOOLS FOR LGBTQ YOUTH

Gay, Lesbian & Straight Education Network (GLSEN): http://www.glsen.org

Gay, Lesbian & Straight Education Network (GLSEN), State-by-state snapshot results of the 2013 National School Climate Survey: http://glsen.org/statesnapshots

Human Rights Campaign, *Supporting and Caring for Our Gender-Expansive Youth*: http://www.hrc.org/youth-report/supporting-and-caring-for-our-gender-expansive-youth#VNepJcaVhNJ

National Center for Transgender Equality, *Model School District Policy on Transgender and Gender Nonconforming Students*: http://transequality.org/PDFs/Trans_ModelPolicy_2014.pdf

## IMPROVING SCHOOL DISCIPLINE AND CLOSING THE SCHOOL-TO-PRISON PIPELINE

Illinois Criminal Justice Information Authority, *Implementing Restorative Justice: A Guide for Schools*: http://www.icjia.state.il.us/publications/implementing-restorative-justice-a-guide-for-schools

National Center on Safe Supportive Learning Environments (NCSSLE), *School Climate Survey Compendia*: https://safesupportivelearning.ed.gov/topic-research/school-climate-measurement/school-climate-survey-compendium

National Clearinghouse on Supportive School Discipline: http://supportiveschooldiscipline.org

National Education Policy Center, *Discipline Policies, Successful Schools, and Racial Justice*: http://nepc.colorado.edu/publication/discipline-policies

US Department of Education, *Regulations Enforced by the Office for Civil Rights*: http://www2.ed.gov/policy/rights/reg/ocr/index.html

# REFERENCES

Abrego, L. J. (2011). Legal consciousness of undocumented Latinos: Fear and stigma as barriers to claims-making for first-and 1.5-generation immigrants. *Law & Society Review, 45*(2), 337–370.

Ahmed-Ullah, N., & Richards, A. (2014, February 6). CPS: Expulsion rate higher at charter schools: Disparity sure to become fuel in ongoing education debate. *The Chicago Tribune*. Retrieved from http://articles.chicagotribune.com/2014-02-26/news/ct-chicago-schools-discipline-met-20140226_1_charter-schools-andrew-broy-district-run-schools

Bohanon, H., & Wu, M.-J. (2011). Can prevention programs work together? An example of school-based mental health with prevention initiatives. *Advances in School Mental Health Promotion, 4*(4), 35–46.

Bradshaw, C., Koth, C., Thornton, L., & Leaf, P. (2009). Altering school climate through school-wide positive behavioral interventions and supports: Findings from a group-randomized effectiveness trial. *Prevention Science, 10*(2), 100–115.

Burris, C., & Aja, A. (2014, March 10) Quoted in Strauss, V. The myth of Common Core equity. *The Washington Post*. Retrieved from http://www.washingtonpost.com/blogs/answer-sheet/wp/2014/03/10/the-myth-of-common-core-equity

Chin, J. K., Dowdy, E., Jimerson, S. R., & Rime, W. J. (2012). Alternatives to suspensions: Rationale and recommendations. *Journal of School Violence, 11*(2), 156–173.

Civic Impulse. (2015). *S. 403-113th Congress: Safe Schools Improvement Act of 2013*. Retrieved from https://www.govtrack.us/congress/bills/113/s403

Durlak, J. A., Weissberg, R. P., Dymnicki, A. B., Taylor, R. D., & Schellinger, K. B. (2011). The impact of enhancing students' social and emotional learning: A meta-analysis of school-based universal interventions. *Child Development, 82*(1), 405–432.

Fabelo, T., Thompson, M. D., Plotkin, M., Carmichael, D., Marchbanks III, M. P., & Booth, E.(2011). *Breaking schools' rules: A statewide study of how school discipline relates to students' success and juvenile justice involvement.* New York; College Station, TX: Council of State Governments Justice Center; Public Policy Research Institute at Texas A&M University. Retrieved February 12, 2015, from https://www.ncjrs.gov/App/Publications/abstract.aspx?ID=266653

Frankenberg, E., Siegel-Hawley, G., & Wang, J. (2010). *Choice without equity: Charter school segregation and the need for civil rights standards.* Los Angeles, CA: Civil Rights Project/Proyecto Derechos Civiles.

Gay, Lesbian & Straight Education Network. (2013). *2013 National School Climate Survey.* New York, NY: Author.

Gonzales, R. G. (2010). On the wrong side of the tracks: Understanding the effects of school structure and social capital in the educational pursuits of undocumented immigrant students. *Peabody Journal of Education, 85*(4), 469–485.

Gonzales, R. G., & Bautista-Chavez, A. M. (2014). *Two years and counting: Assessing the growing power of DACA* [Special Report]. Washington, DC: American Immigration Council.

Gonzales, R. G., Suárez-Orozco, C., & Dedios-Sanguineti, M. C. (2013). No place to belong: Contextualizing concepts of mental health among unauthorized immigrant youth in the United States. *American Behavioral Scientist, 57,* 1174–1199.

Gonzales, R. G., Terriquez, V., & Ruszczyk, S. P. (2014). Becoming DACAmented: Assessing the short-term benefits of Deferred Action for Childhood Arrivals (DACA). *American Behavioral Scientist, 58*(14), 1852–1872.

Goodlad, J. 1. (1984). *A place called school: Prospects for the future.* New York, NY: McGraw-Hill.

Goodlad, J. I. (2002). Kudzu, rabbits, and school reform. *Phi Delta Kappan, 84*(1), 16–23.

Gregory, A., Allen, J. P., Mikami, A. Y., Hafen, C. A., & Pianta, R. C. (2013). The promise of a teacher professional development program in reducing racial disparity in classroom exclusionary discipline. In *Closing the school discipline gap: Equitable remedies for excessive exclusion* (p. 166). Los Angeles, CA: Civil Rights Project/Proyecto Derechos Civiles.

Gwynne, J., & de la Torre, M. (2009). *When schools close: Effects on displaced students in Chicago public schools.* Chicago, IL: UChicago Consortium on School Research.

Hannon, L., DeFina, R., & Bruch, S. (2013). The relationship between skin tone and school suspension for African Americans. *Race and Social Problems, 5*(4), 281–295.

Hatzenbuehler, M. L., & Keyes, K. M. (2013). Inclusive anti-bullying policies and reduced risk of suicide attempts in lesbian and gay youth. *Journal of Adolescent Health, 53*(1), S21–S26.

Houchins, D. E., Shippen, M. E., & Murphy, K. M. (2012). Evidence-based professional development considerations along the school-to-prison pipeline. *Teacher Education and Special Education, 35*(4), 271–283.

Human Rights Campaign. (2015). *Safe Schools Improvement Act.* Retrieved from http://www.hrc.org/resources/entry/safe-schools-improvement-act

Institute on Metropolitan Opportunity, University of Minnesota Law School. (2014). *Charter schools in Chicago: No model for education reform.* Minneapolis, MN: Author.

Kelly, M. S., Raines, J. C, Stone, S. I., & Frey, A. J. (2010). *School social work: An evidence-informed framework for practice.* New York: Oxford University Press.

Krezmien, M. P., Leone, P. E., & Achilles, G. M. (2006). Suspension, race, and disability: Analysis of statewide practices and reporting. *Journal of Emotional and Behavioral Disorders, 14*(4), 217–226.

Mahatmya, D., & Gring-Pemble, L. M. (2014). DREAMers and their families: A family impact analysis of the DREAM Act and implications for family well-being. *Journal of Family Studies, 20*(1), 79–87.

Monroe, C. R. (2006). African American boys and the discipline gap: Balancing educators' uneven hand. *Educational Horizons, 84*(2), 102–111.

Moreno, G., & Bullock, L. M. (2011). Principles of positive behaviour supports: Using the FBA as a problem-solving approach to address challenging behaviours beyond special populations. *Emotional and Behavioural Difficulties, 16*(2), 117–127.

Moreno, G., & Gaytán, F. X. (2013). Reducing subjectivity in special education referrals by educators working with Latino students: Using functional behavioral assessment as a pre-referral practice in student support teams. *Emotional and Behavioural Difficulties, 18*(1), 88–101.

National Center for Transgender Equality. (2015). *Model district policy on transgender and gender non-conforming students.* Retrieved from http://transequality.org/PDFs/Trans_ModelPolicy_2014.pdf

Nicholls, W. (2013). *The DREAMers: How the unauthorized youth movement transformed the immigrant rights debate.* Stanford, CA: Stanford University Press.

Payne, C. M. (2008). *So much reform, so little change.* Cambridge, MA: Harvard Education Press.

Peck, C., & Reitzug, U. C. (2014). School turnaround fever: The paradoxes of a historical practice promoted as a new reform. *Urban Education, 49*(1), 8–38.

Peguero, A. A., & Shekarkhar, Z. (2011). Latino/a student misbehavior and school punishment. *Hispanic Journal of Behavioral Sciences, 33*(1), 54–70.

Pew Research Center. (2015). Retrieved from http://www.pewhispanic.org/2012/12/06/unauthorized-immigrants-11-1-million-in-2011/

Rausch, M. K., Skiba, R. J., & Simmons, A. B. (2004). *The academic cost of discipline: The relationship between suspension/expulsion and school achievement .* Unpublished manuscript, Center for Evaluation and Education Policy, School of Education, Indiana University, Bloomington, IN.

Sharkey, J. D., & Fenning, P. A. (2012). Rationale for designing school contexts in support of proactive discipline. *Journal of School Violence, 11*(2), 95–104.

Skiba, R. J., Horner, R. H., Chung, C. G., Karega Rausch, M., May, S. L., & Tobin, T. (2011). Race is not neutral: A national investigation of African American and Latino disproportionality in school discipline. *School Psychology Review, 40*(1), 85.

Skiba, R. J., Simmons, A. B., Ritter, S., Gibb, A. C., Rausch, M. K., Cuadrado, J., & Chung, C. G. (2008). Achieving equity in special education: History, status, and current challenges. *Exceptional Children, 74*(3), 264–288.

Skiba, R., Simmons, A., Ritter, S., Kohler, K., Henderson, M., & Wu, T. (2006). The context of minority disproportionality: Practitioner perspectives on special education referral. *The Teachers College Record, 108*(7), 1424–1459.

Skiba, R. J., Simmons, A., Staudinger, L., Rausch, M., Dow, G., & Feggins, R. (2003, May). *Consistent removal: Contributions of school discipline to the school–prison pipeline.* Paper presented at the School to Prison Pipeline Conference, Boston, MA.

Stinchcomb, J. B., Bazemore, G., & Riestenberg, N. (2006). Beyond zero tolerance: Restoring justice in secondary schools. *Youth Violence and Juvenile Justice, 4*(2), 123–147.

Sugai, G., & Horner, R. H. (2009). Responsiveness-to-intervention and school-wide positive behavior supports: Integration of multi-tiered system approaches. *Exceptionality, 17*(4), 223–237.

Teske, S. C. (2011). A study of zero tolerance policies in schools: A multi-integrated systems approach to improve outcomes for adolescents. *Journal of Child and Adolescent Psychiatric Nursing, 24*(2), 88–97.

Ttofi, M. M., & Farrington, D. P. (2012). Risk and protective factors, longitudinal research, and bullying prevention. *New Directions for Youth Development, 2012*(133), 85–98.

US Citizenship and Immigration Services (2015). *Consideration for Deferred Action for Childhood Arrivals (DACA).* Retrieved from https://www.uscis.gov/humanitarian/consideration-deferred-action-childhood-arrivals-daca

US Department of Education, Office for Civil Rights. (2014, March). *Civil rights data collection, data snapshot: School discipline* (Issue Brief No. 1). Retrieved from http://www2.ed.gov/about/offices/list/ocr/docs/crdc-discipline-snapshot.pdf?utm_source=JFSF+Newsletter&utm_campaign=0f6e101c7e-Newsletter_July_2013&utm_medium=email&utm_term=0_2ce9971b29–0f6e101c7e-195307941

Van Acker, R., Borenson, L., Gable, R., & Potterton, T. (2005). Are we on the right course? Lessons learned about current FBA/BIP practices in schools. *Journal of Behavioral Education, 14*(1), 35–56.

Vincent, C. G., Sprague, J. R., & Gau, J. M. (2013). Effectiveness of schoolwide positive behavior interventions and supports in reducing racially inequitable disciplinary exclusion. In *Closing the school discipline gap: Equitable remedies for excessive exclusion* (p. 207). Los Angeles, CA: Civil Rights Project/Proyecto Derechos Civiles.

Yoshikawa, H., Godfrey, E. B., & Rivera, A. C. (2008). Access to institutional resources as a measure of social exclusion: Relations with family process and cognitive development in the context of immigration. *New directions for child and adolescent development, 121*, 63–86.

Yoshikawa, H., Kholoptseva, J., & Suárez-Orozco, C. (2013). The role of public policies and community-based organizations in the developmental consequences of parent undocumented status. *Social Policy Report, 27*(3), 1–17.

Wald, J., & Losen, D. J. (2003). Defining and redirecting a school-to-prison pipeline. *New Directions for Youth Development, 2003*(99), 9–15.

Walker, S. C., Kerns, S. E., Lyon, A. R., Bruns, E. J., & Cosgrove, T. J. (2010). Impact of school-based health center use on academic outcomes. *Journal of Adolescent Health, 46*(3), 251–257.

Wallace Jr., J. M., Goodkind, S., Wallace, C. M., & Bachman, J. G. (2008). Racial, ethnic, and gender differences in school discipline among US high school students: 1991–2005. *Negro Educational Review, 59*(1–2), 47.

Welch, K., & Payne, A. A. (2010). Racial threat and punitive school discipline. *Social Problems, 57*(1), 25–48.

Wilson, D. B., Gottfredson, D. C., & Najaka, S. S. (2001). School-based prevention of problem behaviors: A meta-analysis. *Journal of Quantitative Criminology, 17*(3), 247–272.

Zimmerman, A. (2012). *Documenting DREAMs: New media, unauthorized youth and the immigrant rights movement. A case study report working paper.* Media, Activism and Participatory Politics Project Civic Paths, Annenberg School for Communication and Journalism, University of Southern California, Los Angeles.

# CHAPTER 7

# SPECIAL EDUCATION

## JOELLE D. POWERS, DANIELLE C. SWICK, AND JANET B. CHERRY

School social workers are charged with supporting the success of all students within the schools in which they work. This includes students participating in regular education programming as well as those who qualify for special education services and accommodations. In order to effectively and efficiently promote academic and school achievement, school social workers must be knowledgeable about the legislation that guides a complex special education evaluation and service delivery model within the school environment (Altshuler, 2007). Social workers can be critical advocates and agents of change for vulnerable students and their families when participating in this process. This chapter discusses the role of the history of the special education process, the current status of policy that guides special education within public schools, Individual Education Programs (IEPs) and special education services, the development of functional behavioral analysis (FBA), behavior intervention plans (BIPs), adaptive behavior assessments, and the role of the social worker. The challenges to special education, including racial disproportionality in identification and placement, are discussed. The chapter also includes helpful resources for practitioners and educators.

## HISTORY OF SPECIAL EDUCATION SERVICES AND LEGAL MANDATES

Prior to the 1970s, there were no major federal laws in the United States that protected the civil or constitutional rights of individuals with disabilities (Aron & Loprest, 2012). In 1970, only one in five US children with disabilities was educated in a public school. In addition, several states had laws that excluded children with disabilities from schools, including children who were deaf, blind, emotionally disturbed, or intellectually disabled (US Department of Education, Office of Special Education and Rehabilitative Services, 2010). This changed under the passage of Section 504 of the Vocational Rehabilitation Act of 1973, which stated that excluding or segregating a person with a disability was discriminatory (Aron & Loprest, 2012).

Section 504 protected the rights of individuals with disabilities in programs and activities that receive federal financial assistance from the US Department of Education, including public school districts. This law stated that children with disabilities have the right to a public education comparable to that of children who do not have disabilities (US Department of Education, Office for Civil Rights, 2010).

In 1975, additional legislation was enacted to protect the educational rights of children with disabilities. Originally named the Education for All Handicapped Children Act of 1975 (Public Law 94-142), this law was amended and renamed the Individuals with Disabilities Education Act (IDEA) in 1990. This piece of legislation sets forth that (1) all students with disabilities are to have access to free and appropriate public education; (2) all students with disabilities have the right to a nondiscriminatory evaluation of their strengths and needs; (3) schools must individualize each student's education to address the specific needs of each student and they are to be documented in the student's Individualized Education Program (IEP); (4) students with disabilities should be educated in the least restrictive educational placement possible; (5) parents have the right to consent or object to the identification, evaluation, or placement of a child; and (6) parents have the right to participate in the planning and decision-making process of their child's education program (Altshuler, 2007; Turnbull & Turnbull, 1998).

One major difference between the current implementation of IDEA and Section 504 is the eligibility requirements. Under IDEA, a student is eligible for services only if his or her disability adversely affects his or her educational performance. However, under Section 504, a student is eligible for services if the student's disability substantially limits a major life activity; therefore, unlike IDEA, there is no requirement under Section 504 that the disability specifically adversely affects the child's education performance (deBettencourt, 2002).

## CATEGORIES OF DISABILITY AND SPECIAL EDUCATION SERVICES

According to IDEA, special education is defined as "specifically designed instruction, at no cost to the parents, to meet the unique needs of a child with a disability" (IDEA, 2004). In accordance with IDEA, students with disabilities must be educated in the least restrictive environment that is most appropriate for them. In addition, Section 504 requires schools to provide a "free appropriate public education" (FAPE) to children with disabilities. An appropriate education is defined by the following components: (1) education services designed to meet the education needs of students with disabilities to the same extent of their peers without disabilities, (2) educating students with disabilities with their peers without disabilities to the maximum extent possible, (3) ongoing evaluation procedures that ensure proper placement of students, and (4) due process procedures that involve the parent and guardians in evaluation and placement decision (US Department of Education, Office for Civil Rights, 2010).

The following 14 disability categories are currently defined under IDEA (2004):

1.  Autism
2.  Deaf-Blindness
3.  Deafness
4.  Developmental Delay

5.  Emotional Disturbance
6.  Hearing Impairment
7.  Intellectual Disability (formerly known as Mental Retardation)
8.  Multiple Disabilities
9.  Orthopedic Impairment
10. Other Health Impairment
11. Specific Learning Disability
12. Speech or Language Impairment
13. Traumatic Brain Injury
14. Visual Impairment Including Blindness

Schools must individualize each student's education to address the specific needs of each student because students with the same disability may still have different needs (Marx et al., 2014). These needs, and the services to address these needs, are documented in each student's IEP. The types of services provided to students with disabilities will vary by the individual student's needs (U.S. Department of Education, Office for Civil Rights, 2010). These services may include education in regular classes, education in regular classes with the use of aids and services, consultation provided by special educators to the general education teacher, collaborative instruction in the general education classroom through co-teaching by the general and special education services, or special education and related services in separate classrooms for all or parts of the school day. Related services may include speech therapy, occupational and physical therapy, psychological counseling, and medical diagnostic services necessary to the student's education (US Department of Education, Office for Civil Rights, 2010).

# OVERVIEW OF REFERRAL AND TESTING PROCESSES FOR QUALIFICATION

Services provided by IDEA are primarily intended to provide supplemental education supports in addition to the general education programming (Spiel, Evans, & Langberg, 2014). In order to qualify for these supports, the following 10-step process for referral and testing outlined under IDEA is completed for each student (US Department of Education, Office of Special Education and Rehabilitative Services, 2000):

1.  The student is identified as potentially requiring special education services. This can occur in multiple ways because a teacher or a parent can request evaluation.
2.  The student is evaluated. The results of the evaluation will be used to determine eligibility so the assessment must test all areas that are suspected to relate to the disability. If a parent is dissatisfied with the evaluation, he or she can request an independent education evaluation and ask the school district to cover the expense.
3.  A multidisciplinary group of school professionals will review the evaluation results and determine eligibility for special education services.
4.  If the student is determined to qualify for special education services under IDEA, an IEP team must meet within 30 calendar days to write an IEP for the student.
5.  The school schedules and facilitates an IEP meeting. Parents must be notified of the purpose for and invited to the meeting. The meeting should be scheduled at a time

and place amenable to them, and parents should be told they can invite others of their choosing to the meeting.

6. The IEP meeting takes place, and the IEP is written for the student. Once the plan is written, if the parents agree and give consent, services will begin as soon as possible for the student. If the parents do not agree, they can work with the multidisciplinary team to develop an agreeable plan. If they cannot accomplish this, the parents can ask for mediation, file a complaint with the district and the state, and request a due process hearing.

7. The student begins receiving special education services according to the agreed upon IEP. The parents, teachers, and additional service providers all have access to the IEP. The school ensures that all services, accommodations, supports, and modifications are provided in accordance with the IEP.

8. The student's progress is measured and reported. Progress made toward the IEP goals is measured regularly. Progress reports are sent to parents at least as often as children who do not qualify for special education receive progress reports.

9. The IEP is reviewed. The IEP for any student receiving special education services is reviewed annually and more often if the school or parents request it. Parents and IEP team members attend these meetings, and modifications to the plan can be made if agreed upon by all.

10. The student is re-evaluated. At a minimum, the student is re-evaluated every 3 years. This meeting is called the *triennial* and is used to determine if the student still qualifies under IDEA as requiring special education services. This re-evaluation can take place more often if requested.

Just as IDEA outlines a process for special education referral, evaluation, and identification, it also defines content that must be included within each IEP in order to guide service provision and meet the unique educational goals of students (US Department of Education, Office of Special Education and Rehabilitative Services, 2000). Each student receives an IEP created specifically for him or her and, according to federal regulations, the IEP must include the following content:

- The current performance of the student: Evidence from multiple sources is included in the IEP to describe how the disability impacts involvement in the general curriculum. This evidence can include evaluation results from the eligibility testing; classroom tests and assignments; and observations from teachers, parents, and service providers.
- The IEP annual goals: These are academic, behavioral, physical, or social goals that the student can reasonably accomplish in 1 year. Goals must be measurable and broken down into smaller benchmarks.
- The services to be provided: All special education or related services or modifications to be provided to the student must be included. In addition, any supports or professional development training to be provided to school personnel to support the child should be included as well. Common related services as listed in IDEA include (but are not limited to) the following:
  - Audiology services
  - Counseling services
  - Early identification and assessment of disabilities in children

- Medical services
- Occupational therapy
- Orientation and mobility services
- Parent counseling and training
- Physical therapy
- Psychological services
- Recreation
- Rehabilitation counseling services
- School health services
- Social work services in schools
- Speech–language pathology services
- Transportation
- Student participation with nondisabled peers: The IEP must specify the extent of any time that the student will not participate with students in the regular education classroom and other school activities.
- Student participation in district and state testing: If a student will not be participating in a test that is regularly given to students in his or her grade, the IEP must clearly articulate why the testing is inappropriate and how the student will be alternatively assessed.
- Service dates and places: The IEP must provide service provision logistics such as the date when they will begin, times, locations, and duration.
- Student transition service needs: For students ages 14 years or older (or younger if appropriate), the IEP must address the courses required to reach post-school goals in a statement of transition services. This statement must subsequently be included in every future IEP.
- Needed transition services: Beginning at age 16 years, the IEP must state which transition services the student will need to prepare for leaving school.
- Age of majority (only required in states that transfer rights at the age of majority): One year before the student reaches the age of majority, the IEP must include a statement that the student has been made aware of any rights that will transfer at the age of majority.
- Measuring student progress: The IEP must clearly articulate how progress will be evaluated and also reported to parents.

The multidisciplinary team is critical to the success of students who qualify for special education services because the team is responsible for evaluating the student and creating and implementing the IEP. IDEA specifies certain people who must be involved. *Parents* are among these and are considered key members of the IEP team. They should be considered the experts on the student because they have insight into their child's strengths and functioning within the home. Each of the student's *primary regular and special education teachers* must be included on the team (regular education teachers should be included if the student is participating at all in general education programming). This allows for expertise about both implementation and modification of regular education curriculum to better support the student. An *individual representing the school system* should participate. This person is often a school administrator because he or she is expected to be able to commit school resources when appropriate and have authority to oversee service provision. An *individual who can interpret what the child's evaluation results mean* is another key member of the team because he or she can talk about the implications of results for education planning.

This person is often a school psychologist who works in the district. An *individual with knowledge or special expertise about the child* should also be included. This may be an advocate invited by the parents or another professional who works closely with the student, such as a school social worker, speech therapist, or nurse. When appropriate, a *representative from transition service agencies* can be important to the team because this person can assist with planning transition services and can also provide resources for the implementation of these plans in the future. Finally, *the student* may also be a critical member of the IEP team because this allows for participation and self-determinism in the student's education (Barnard-Brak & Lechtenberger, 2010).

## FUNCTIONAL BEHAVIORAL ANALYSIS AND BEHAVIOR INTERVENTION PLANS

The reauthorization of IDEA in 1997 mandated the use of FBAs and BIPs for any student in special education whose behavior resulted in suspension, a change in placement, or removal to an alternate placement (Couvillon, Bullock, & Gable, 2009; Murdick, Gartin, & Stockall, 2003). The goal of the FBA is to describe and predict the behavior but also to aid in understanding the function or purpose of the disruptive behavior. Once completed, the FBA is then used to inform the development of an appropriate BIP to address the behavior displayed by the student that is negatively impacting his or her education (Van Acker, Boreson, Gable, & Potterton, 2005). The following steps are included in the FBA-to-BIP process: (1) Identify target behaviors that need to be addressed; (2) observe student to identify antecedents of target behaviors; (3) observe peer(s) of similar age and sex for comparison; (4) identify the function of the behaviors; (5) develop a BIP; and (6) implement, monitor, and evaluate the BIP (Murdick et al., 2003).

The BIP is a support plan for students that must include positive behavioral support rather than punishment (Van Acker et al., 2005). The plan should be focused on skill building for the student and evaluated on effectiveness. The BIP should be dynamic because it requires regular review and revision based on the progress of the student.

The use of FBA and BIP procedures has proven to be effective in increasing appropriate skills and reducing challenging behaviors (Lo & Cartledge, 2006). They also promote individualized and unique interventions specific to each student. Unfortunately, those on multidisciplinary teams who are tasked with developing these plans are not always adequately trained, so ongoing support and professional development opportunities for school staff are critical (Couvillon et al., 2009). Many states and school districts are developing their own training for effective FBA and BIP development and management in order to better comply with the mandates outlined in the law (Van Acker et al., 2005).

## DISPROPORTIONALITY

Schools in the United States are overidentifying subgroups of the student population to qualify for special education, particularly with regard to race, socioeconomic status, gender, and language status (Knotek, 2003; Sullivan & Bal, 2013). In fact, disproportionality is considered by some to be the most significant problem in special education today (Skiba, Poloni-Stowdinger, Simmons, Feggins-Azziz, & Chung, 2005). It has been well documented during the past 30 years that males, students of color, and those from disadvantaged backgrounds are overrepresented in special education programs (Albrecht, Skiba, Losen, Chung, & Middelberg, 2012; Lo & Cartledge, 2006). For example, there have been consistent findings of racial disproportionality within specific categories of disability, including learning disabilities, emotional and behavioral disabilities (Bean, 2013), and cognitive impairment (Donovan & Cross, 2002). This is significant because using race as a factor in identification for special education is discriminatory (Skiba et al., 2005). However, it may not be overt and direct racism or discrimination that leads to disproportionality but, rather, the bias and stereotyping of boys of color in particular that leads to harsher and more frequent disciplinary interventions, bias in the classroom, and lower achievement levels.

Special education provides additional resources to students with disabilities, but it may also unintentionally lead to stigma and segregation, which is why disproportionality is so problematic (Donovan & Cross, 2002). To combat and prevent overrepresentation, new monitoring requirements were included in the 1997 and 2004 amendments of IDEA requiring states to report on racial disproportionality (Albrecht et al., 2012). Unfortunately, disproportionality and educational inequity are still common in schools and require awareness and vigilant intervention to prevent.

## CHALLENGES TO SPECIAL EDUCATION

Providing a free and appropriate education within the least restrictive environment to all students can be difficult for schools, and often complex challenges must be overcome to deliver services appropriately. Staffing deficits in schools can present a substantial challenge for special education. The individual members of the multidisciplinary teams that oversee the IEP process each play a critical role in supporting students. Unfortunately, due to budgetary restraints, not every school has a full-time social worker, psychologist, and nurse. Often, these positions serve multiple schools within a district, making the scheduling of meetings, service provision, and ongoing evaluation difficult.

Another challenge to the special education process is the logistical task of scheduling IEP meetings. There is a clear emphasis in IDEA that parents be included throughout the special education process (Weishaar, 2010). However, it can be difficult for working parents or parents with very young children to come to the school for multiple hours for multiple meetings throughout the school year. Parents who do not have access to reliable transportation may also struggle to make it to the school. Another common difficulty with regard to scheduling meetings is language barriers between the multidisciplinary team members and parents. In these situations, a translator would also need to be present to ensure meaningful communication during the meetings. Finally, multidisciplinary teams often invite community providers to the IEP meetings when appropriate. For example, if a student has been working with a counselor from a community agency, it might be highly beneficial to invite the counselor to the IEP meeting to include his or her experiences and perceptions with the team. It can also serve to promote consistency for the student and family when all service providers are working toward the same goals. Unfortunately, again, it can be very difficult for a community-based provider to attend multiple meetings throughout the academic year.

# THE ROLE OF THE SCHOOL SOCIAL WORKER

In many ways, the school social worker can play a vital role in promoting the success of students who receive special education services. First, actively working from a strengths-based approach can have a major impact on the relationship between home and school. The special education process can be daunting and overwhelming for families, so making a concerted effort to start each meeting by addressing the strengths and abilities of the student is a gentle reminder to all involved that the meeting should not be deficit-focused (Weishaar, 2010). IEP goals can be written with a strengths-based approach by phrasing them in terms of abilities and skills gained or appropriate behaviors increased rather than focusing only on decreasing the undesired behaviors.

The social worker certainly plays a major role in setting up family members for success as they move through the IEP process. Educating parents on their rights as well as what to expect throughout the process and in individual meetings may reduce stress and anxiety for them. Ensuring that families are invited and feel welcome as a partner to IEP meetings is critical. Scheduling meetings according to parent availability is another key piece to ensuring that the home–school partnership is strong. Eliminating transportation barriers may increase participation in the process. Certainly, the social worker would also be well positioned to help connect the family with additional resources in the community as appropriate.

The social worker can work to set up the student for success in the same way that he or she does for the family. Taking the time to ensure the student knows what special education means and framing it is positive terms such *a resource for learning* can eliminate shame or embarrassment. Ensuring that the student knows what to expect with upcoming assessments and meetings can alleviate anxiety for the student. The social worker can also help with resulting transitions for the student, whether it is managing a change to the student's typical schedule, a change in classrooms, or even a move to a new school (Rosenkoetter, Hains, & Dogaru, 2007).

The school social worker can actively participate in the assessment process for the determination of eligibility and service delivery. Whether it is classroom or playground observations, interviewing parents to obtain an in-depth family history or biopsychosocial assessment, or completing other standardized assessments, the social worker can be a major asset in the data collection phase. The social worker can then be written into the IEP for related services such as counseling. However, even if services are not formally written into the IEP, the social worker may provide them for additional support as needed.

The social worker can also play a critical role in reducing disproportionality in special education. Providing important information to school administration and staff about the critical nature of overidentification to ensure awareness can be a key first step. The social worker can then collaborate with other members of the multidisciplinary team to develop a plan to closely monitor the race, gender, socioeconomic status, and language status of students referred for testing and those identified as eligible. Regular and ongoing review of these data is useful for identifying and preventing potential overidentification patterns.

# CONCLUSION

School social workers are well positioned to play active and important roles within the special education process. Being knowledgeable about the legal mandates and provisions governed by recent policy is one of the first steps to meeting the unique needs of often vulnerable students and families who would benefit from additional support beyond the general curriculum. Social workers work collaboratively in the assessment, intervention, and evaluation phases with other multidisciplinary school staff, community service providers, families, and students. These components of the special education process provide opportunities for the social worker to be an advocate, change agent, and truly promote the academic and school success of all students.

---

# CASE STUDY: ALICE

Alice is 6 years old and new to her school. This is her second kindergarten placement this academic year. Within the first few days, Alice's teacher noticed challenging behavior that was detracting from Alice's ability to concentrate and learn in class. Specifically, Alice had difficulty recalling and retrieving information, and she was unable to follow directions due to inattention. In addition, she was unable to recognize the letters in the alphabet and had difficulty expressing herself when in conversation. The teacher invited Alice's mother to the school for a conference to discuss these concerns and to get the mother's feedback about her observations. During the conference, the mother shared that Alice had attended four different preschools since the age of 4 years due to her acting out and distractible behaviors. The teacher talked with the mother about special education services and the testing process. She explained that if Alice qualified, it would provide her with additional resources and support to promote her educational success at school. The teacher was careful to explain that the mother would be a critical part of the team, and that nothing would happen without her consent and approval. Alice's mother expressed her interest and is going to meet with the teacher again next week after taking time to read and think about the special education materials she was given during the meeting.

---

# DISCUSSION QUESTIONS

1. Regarding the case study, what do you think are some of the most critical aspects of special education for the teacher to talk about with Alice's mother?
2. How are IDEA provisions and 504 accommodations different?
3. What does FAPE stand for and how would you define it?
4. What are the greatest contributions of social workers within the special education process in schools?

# COMMON SPECIAL EDUCATION ACRONYMS

| Acronym | Description |
| --- | --- |
| ADA | Americans with Disabilities Act |
| ADD | Attention deficit disorder |
| ADHD | Attention deficit/hyperactivity disorder |
| ADLs | Activities of daily living |
| AEP | Alternative education placement |
| AG | Annual goal |
| APE | Adapted physical education |
| APR | Annual performance report |
| ARRA | American Recovery and Reinvestment Act of 2009 |
| ASD | Autism spectrum disorders |
| ASL | American Sign Language |
| AT | Assistive technology |
| AYP | Adequate yearly progress |
| BD | Behavioral disorder |
| BIP | Behavior intervention plan |
| BOE | Board of education |
| CAP | Corrective action plan |
| CAPD | Central auditory processing disorder |
| CBA | Curriculum-based assessment |
| CBM | Curriculum-based measurement |
| CD | Cognitive disability |
| CFR | Code of Federal Regulations |
| CIFMS | Continuous improvement and focused monitoring system |
| CSHCN | Children with special health care needs |
| CST | Child study team |
| DB | Deaf-blindness |
| DD | Developmental delay; developmental disability |
| DPI | Department of Public Instruction |
| DSM | *Diagnostic and Statistical Manual of Mental Disorders* |
| ED | Emotional disturbance |
| ECE | Early childhood education |
| EI | Early intervention |
| ESL | English as a Second Language |
| FAPE | Free appropriate public education |
| FBA | Functional behavioral assessment |
| FC | Facilitated communication |
| FERPA | Family Educational Rights and Privacy Act |
| FOIA | Freedom of Information Act |
| GE | General education |
| HI | Hearing impairment |
| ID | Intellectual disabilities |
| IDEA | Individuals with Disabilities Education Act |
| IEP | Individualized Education Program |
| IFSP | Individualized Family Service Plan |

| | |
|---|---|
| LD | Learning disability |
| LEA | Local education agency |
| LEP | Limited English proficiency |
| LRE | Least restrictive environment |
| MD | Multiple disabilities |
| NCLB | No Child Left Behind |
| OCR | Office of Civil Rights |
| ODD | Oppositional defiant disorder |
| OHI | Other health impairment |
| OI | Orthopedic impairment |
| OSEP | Office of Special Education Programs, US Department of Education |
| OSERS | Office of Special Education and Rehabilitative Services |
| OT | Occupational therapy |
| PBIS | Positive Behavioral Intervention and Supports |
| PD | Physical disability |
| PT | Physical therapy |
| RTI | Response to intervention |
| SDD | Significant developmental delay |
| Section 504 | Section 504 of the Rehabilitation Act |
| SED | Serious emotional disturbance |
| SLD | Specific learning disability (formerly LD) |
| SLI | Speech/language impairment |
| SST | Student study team; student support team |
| TBI | Traumatic brain injury |
| VI | Visual impairment |

## ADDITIONAL RESOURCES

Autism Speaks: https://www.autismspeaks.org

Center for Parent Information and Resources: http://www.parentcenterhub.org

Disability.gov: https://www.disability.gov

National Center for Homeless Education: http://center.serve.org/nche/ibt/sc_spec_ed.php

National Center for Learning Disabilities: http://www.ncld.org

PACER Center: Champions for Children with Disabilities: http://www.pacer.org

Special Education Guide: http://www.specialeducationguide.com

Special Education Resources: http://www.specialednet.com/Resources.htm

The Arc: http://www.thearc.org

US Department of Defense Education Activity (DoDEA), *Special Education*: http://www.dodea.edu/Curriculum/specialeduc/index.cfm

US Department of Education, *A Guide to the Individualized Education Program*: http://www2.ed.gov/parents/needs/speced/iepguide/index.html

US Department of Education, Office of Special Education and Rehabilitative Services: http://www2.ed.gov/about/offices/list/osers/osep/index.html

# REFERENCES

Albrecht, S. F., Skiba, R. J., Losen, D. J., Chung, C. G., & Middelberg, L. (2012). Federal policy on disproportionality in special education: Is it moving us forward? *Journal of Disability Policy Studies, 23*(1), 14–25.

Altshuler, S. (2007). Everything you never wanted to know about special education . . . and were afraid to ask (I.D.E.A.). *Journal of Social Work in Disability & Rehabilitation, 6*(1–2), 23–33. doi:10.1300/J198v06n01_02

Aron, L., & Loprest, P. (2012). Disability and the education system. *Future Child, 22*(1), 97–122.

Barnard-Brak, L., & Lechtenberger, D. (2010). Student IEP participation and academic achievement across time. *Remedial & Special Education, 31*(5), 343–349.

Bean, K. F. (2013). Disproportionality and acting-out behaviors among African American children in special education. *Child & Adolescent Social Work Journal, 30*(6), 487–504. doi:10.1007/s10560-013-0304-6

Couvillon, M. A., Bullock, L. M., & Gable, R. A. (2009). Tracking behavior assessment methodology and support strategies: A national survey of how schools utilize functional behavioral assessments and behavior intervention plans. *Emotional and Behavioural Difficulties, 14*(3), 215–228.

deBettencourt, L. U. (2002). Understanding the differences between IDEA and Section 504. *Teaching Exceptional Children, 34*(3), 16–23.

Donovan, M. S., & Cross, C. T. (Eds.). (2002). *Minority students in special and gifted education.* Washington, DC: National Academies Press.

Individuals with Disabilities Education Act, 20 U.S.C. § 1400 (2004).

Knotek, S. (2003). Bias in problem solving and the social process of student study teams. *Journal of Special Education, 37*(1), 2.

Lo, Y. Y., & Cartledge, G. (2006). FBA and BIP: Increasing the behavior adjustment of African American boys in schools. *Behavioral Disorders, 31*(1), 147–161.

Marx, T. A., Hart, J. L., Nelson, L., Love, J., Baxter, C. M., Gartin, B., & Whitby, P. J. S. (2014). Guiding IEP teams on meeting the least restrictive environment mandate. *Intervention in School and Clinic, 50*(1), 45–50.

Murdick, N., Gartin, B., & Stockall, N. (2003). Step by step: How to meet the functional assessment of behavior requirements of IDEA. *Beyond Behavior, 12*(2), 25–30.

Rosenkoetter, S., Hains, A., & Dogaru, C. (2007). Successful transitions for young children with disabilities and their families: Roles of school social workers. *Children & Schools, 29*(1), 25–34.

Skiba, R. J., Poloni-Stowdinger, L., Simmons, A. B., Feggins-Azziz, R., & Chung, G. (2005). Unproven links: Can poverty explain ethnic disparities in special education? *Journal of Special Education, 39*(3), 130–144.

Spiel, C. F., Evans, S. W., & Langberg, J. M. (2014). Evaluating the content of individualized education programs and 504 plans of young adolescents with attention deficit/hyperactivity disorder. *School Psychology Quarterly, 29*(4), 452–468. doi:10.1037/spq0000101

Sullivan, A. L., & Bal, A. (2013). Disproportionality in special education: Effects of individual and school variables on disability risk. *Exceptional Children, 79*(4), 475–494.

Turnbull, H. R., & Turnbull, A. P. (1998). *Free appropriate public education: The law and children with disabilities* (5th ed., pp. 273–274). Denver, CO: Love Publishing.

US Department of Education, Office for Civil Rights. (2010). *Free appropriate public education for students with disabilities: Requirements under Section 504 of the Rehabilitation Act of 1973.* Washington, DC: Author.

US Department of Education, Office of Special Education and Rehabilitative Services. (2000). *A guide to the individualized education program.* Washington, DC: Author.

US Department of Education, Office of Special Education and Rehabilitative Services. (2010). *Thirty-five years of progress in educating children with disabilities through IDEA.* Washington, DC: Author.

Van Acker, R., Boreson, L., Gable, R. A., & Potterton, T. (2005). Are we on the right course? Lessons learned about current FBA/BIP practices in schools. *Journal of Behavioral Education, 14*(1), 35–56.

Weishaar, P. M. (2010). Twelve ways to incorporate strengths-based planning into the IEP process. *Clearing House, 83*(6), 207–210. doi:10.1080/00098650903505381

# CHAPTER 8

# ETHICAL AND LEGAL FOUNDATIONS FOR SCHOOL SOCIAL WORK PRACTICE

## JAMES C. RAINES AND NIC T. DIBBLE

The School Social Work Association of America's (SSWAA) *School Social Work Practice Model* identifies ethical guidelines and educational policy as foundations of practice nationwide (Frey et al., 2013). This chapter explores how school social workers can have a firm foundation for their practice based on professional ethics and national educational policy. Professional ethics can be found in the National Association of Social Workers' (NASW) *Code of Ethics* (2008), SSWAA ethical guidelines, and the ethical codes of other student services personnel, such as school counselors and school psychologists (Raines & Dibble, 2011). The *Supplemental Ethical Standards for School Social Work Practice* (Midwest School Social Work Council, 2015) are designed to be applied in conjunction with the NASW *Code of Ethics* to provide expectations for ethical behavior in important areas on which the NASW *Code of Ethics* is silent (see the Appendix). National educational policy can be found in the US Constitution, federal statutes, regulations, administrative guidance, executive orders, and case law (Redfield, 2002). Because the US Constitution (i.e., the 10th amendment) leaves states with the primary responsibility for educating citizens (Alexander & Alexander, 2012), national education policy works indirectly through state education agencies that accept federal funds. School social work practice is based on the interaction between professional ethics and both state and national educational policy. We place professional ethics first because "sometimes, the law is wrong" (Stefkovich, 2014, p. 33) and professionals are obligated to lobby for changes or engage in civil disobedience.

## PROFESSIONAL VALUES

First, the NASW *Code of Ethics* is founded on six primary social work values: dignity and worth of the person, social justice, service, importance of human relationships, integrity, and

Table 8.1:  Common Social Work Values and Corresponding Ethical Principles

| Value | Ethical Principle |
|---|---|
| Truthfulness and full disclosure | Social workers should be completely honest with their clients. |
| Dignity and worth of the person | Social workers should treat each client in a caring and respectful manner. |
| Privacy and confidentiality | Social workers should only seek to acquire relevant information and should keep that material sacrosanct. |
| Social justice | Social workers should pursue social change, particularly with and on behalf of vulnerable and oppressed groups. |
| Protection of life | Social workers should seek to protect and prolong a client's biophysical life. |
| Service | Social workers should seek to help people in need and address social problems above any self-interest. |
| Equal treatment | Social workers should treat clients in similar circumstances in a similar manner. |
| Importance of human relationships | Social workers should seek to strengthen relationships among people to enhance the well-being of families, groups, and communities. |
| Least harm | When faced with possibly negative outcomes, social workers should choose the least harmful, least permanent, or most easily reversible option. |
| Integrity | Social workers should behave in a trustworthy manner, congruent with professional values and ethics. |
| Quality of life | Social workers should seek to promote the highest quality of life for both clients and their environments. |
| Competence | Social workers should practice within their areas of knowledge and skills while constantly striving to improve their expertise. |
| Autonomy/freedom | Social workers should respect clients' rights to control or contribute to decisions that affect them. |

*Source: Adapted with permission from Raines and Dibble (2011).*

competence. There are other values, however, that are *implied* within the NASW *Code* rather than *explicitly* stated. For example, the NASW *Code* permits social workers to violate confidentiality when a client is a danger to self or others, thus implying that protection of life is an inherent value. Thus, Loewenberg, Dolgoff, and Harrington (2000) identify seven other values that are also consistent with the explicit values in the NASW *Code*. Raines and Dibble (2011) combined both lists of professional values and corresponding ethical principles that school social workers should consider; these are shown in Table 8.1.

The *Supplemental Ethical Standards for School Social Work Practice* provide beliefs on which the 13 supplemental ethical standards are based. These beliefs address (1) the development and growing autonomy of children and adolescents and how that growing autonomy interacts with key ethical responsibilities to clients delineated in the NASW *Code of Ethics*; (2) parents' rights, roles, and responsibilities in relationship to their children; (3) minor students' rights to determine their involvement in school-based activities; and (4) the responsibilities of school social workers and other school officials to students.

## DEFINING THE CLIENT

Social workers use the term "client" very often but seldom define it. Even the NASW *Code of Ethics* only mentions who *can* be a client without ever defining the term. We have defined a *client* as someone who knowingly enters into a trust-based or fiduciary relationship with the social worker (Raines & Dibble, 2011). This is in keeping with the ethical value about the importance of human relationships. Some clients may be voluntary or self-referred, but many will be involuntary or referred by others. There are students, parents, faculty, and staff with whom social workers interact on a daily basis who are *not* clients. They may only become clients if they have entered into a fiduciary relationship with a professional (Kutchins, 1991). Fiduciaries are then expected to be familiar with and uphold the standards of their profession (e.g., the NASW *Code of Ethics* and the NASW *Standards for School Social Work*).

In a Response to Intervention (RTI) model, the "client" may be a client system, including an entire classroom, small group, or client pair. It should be acknowledged, however, that as the client system increases in size, the level of confidentiality decreases. For example, one can hardly guarantee that what is shared during a classroom discussion will remain within the classroom (Raines, 2008a).

Loewenberg et al. (2000) identify three other roles that are common in any systemic practice, and Sabatino (2014) identifies a fourth. First, there are *supplicants*—those who request professional help. Teachers fit into this category when they refer a student for services. Second, there are *targets*—those whose attitudes, knowledge, or behavior we hope to modify often on behalf of our clients. Administrators frequently fit into this category, but they are not clients because they usually hold more power than school social workers. Third, there are *beneficiaries*—those who benefit from our work with the client. Parents and school systems often fit into this category, but they are not usually considered clients. Fourth, there are *consultees*—those other professionals who seek help regarding a job-related problem, such as classroom management. Teachers or other special education specialists often fall into this group (Sabatino, 2014). Finally, any of these other students, parents, faculty, and staff might also be considered stakeholders. Raines (2009) defines *nonclient stakeholders* as concerned parties with a vested interest in the outcome of services but warns that they should not be viewed as competing clients.

It is important to remember the context of school social work practice when identifying clients and other stakeholders. Stated missions of schools typically articulate their primary purpose as educating students and helping prepare them for life following graduation from high school. The *Supplemental Ethical Standards for School Social Work Practice* state that a school social worker's primary ethical obligation is to students, with secondary ethical obligations to other stakeholders.

## INFORMED CONSENT

Informed consent must possess three qualities: capacity, information, and voluntariness. *Capacity* is the ability to comprehend the information and appreciate the consequences of a decision. Capacity is always decision specific; in other words, it applies only to a specific treatment offered at a specific time (Schacter, Kleinman, & Harvey, 2005). *Information* refers to the adequacy of one's knowledge. An important part of this information should be a clear explanation of the limits to confidentiality. *Voluntariness* is the freedom from coercion, constraint, or compulsion. A person must be free to choose either to participate or not to participate.

Voluntariness requires some explanation for involuntary clients. Generally, the best approach to involuntary clients is an honest admission of the bind that they face. For example, for a student who otherwise faces suspension or expulsion from school, the social worker may say, "I know it's not your idea to be here and that's okay with me, but since we have to spend some time together, what would you prefer to talk about?" This allows involuntary clients to set the agenda and become willing recipients of social work services on their own terms. In one case, the social worker allowed a referred adolescent to set the agenda. He wanted orthodontic treatment but his family could not afford braces. After the social worker obtained free services from a dental school, the student began to voluntarily open up about his mental health issues.

The concept of informed *assent* is not synonymous with informed *consent*. It has been generally defined as minors' ability to participate in treatment decisions. In other words, it is never assumed that they have complete autonomy, such as the right to refuse treatment. Assent simply means that practitioners should treat children as agentic human beings (Conroy & Harcourt, 2009). This should be done with sensitivity to the child's developmental capacity.

Schools have a long history of using passive consent. For example, in general education, schools often notify parents that their children will be given instruction about sexual development. Unless parents specifically object, schools presume that the parents have given passive consent. Note that passive consent still requires the same level of information as active consent (*Rhoades v. Penn-Harris*, 2008). The *Supplemental Ethical Standards for School Social Work Practice* specify that school social workers are to "obtain active or passive consent to provide services to students consistent with federal and state statutes and local school district policy and practice" (p. 3). However, examples of services that may not require consent are provided, including observations, progress monitoring, consultation, and crisis intervention.

Special education functions slightly differently. Although the Individuals with Disabilities Education Act (IDEA) does allow screening for *instructional* purposes without consent (34 CFR 300.302), school social workers should be cautious about assuming that all screening is permitted. Behavioral screening that gathers information from existing data or classroom teachers does not require parental consent. The federal Protection of Pupil Rights Amendment does, however, require school districts to (1) obtain prior written consent from parents before their children are required to participate in screening, assessment, or treatment that would involve gathering information from students about sensitive topics, including "mental or psychological problems"; and (2) allow children to opt out of any such activity (34 CFR Part 98). Furthermore, the 1973 federal case *Merriken v. Cressman* articulated numerous concerns about the use of passive consent for student-completed screening for behavioral health problems, such as depression (Fisher, 2004). The most recent cases that have also weighed in on this issue are *C.N. v. Ridgewood* (2005), *Fields v. Palmdale* (2005, 2006), and *Rhoades v. Penn-Harris* (2008). Given the continued controversy with universal screening instruments, Box 8.1 provides guidelines for school districts implementing a survey such as the Columbia Teen Screen program.

Universal behavioral health screening is a tier 1 strategy. Following these guidelines can help (1) ensure that behavioral health screening is conducted in both a legal and an ethical manner and (2) reduce the likelihood of objections from parents or the community following the screening.

---

**BOX 8.1: Passive Consent Guidelines for Schools Regarding Behavioral Health Screening Surveys**

1. Become familiar with the federal guidelines in the Protection of Pupil Rights Amendment available at http://www2.ed.gov/policy/gen/guid/fpco/ppra/index.html.
2. Be sure that all notices about the screening survey clearly describe essential points, including (but not limited to) the following:
   a. The purpose and nature of the questions on the survey (e.g., sexual experience, substance abuse, or suicidal thoughts)
   b. Potential benefits (catharsis or receiving help) and risks (embarrassment or feeling stigmatized) associated with participation
   c. Potential benefits (more study time) and risks (not receiving timely help) associated with nonparticipation
   d. Limits to confidentiality if identifying information is requested (e.g., if a student is identified as a danger to self or others or if the student alleges child abuse/neglect)
   e. How and with whom the results will be shared (including parents)
   f. How results will be safeguarded and when the results will be destroyed
3. Use multiple notification methods, including (but not limited to) open school board meetings, parent–teacher association presentations, letters sent home, or mention in the student handbook.
4. Provide an "opt out" form for both parents and students in middle and upper grades. Be sure to clarify that there are no penalties for nonparticipation or incentives for participation.
5. On the day of the survey, allow an alternate neutral event for nonparticipating students (e.g., a study hall).
6. Be sure that the information in the survey also conveys that participation is optional and voluntary.
7. Be sure that those administering the survey verbally explain the purpose and voluntary nature of the survey.

---

# SCHOOL SOCIAL WORK SERVICES

The commentary on the IDEA regulations provides the following guidance about the scope of school social work services (US Department of Education, Office of Special Education and Rehabilitative Services (OSERS), 2006a):

> The definition of social work services in schools includes examples of the types of social work services that may be provided. It is not a prescriptive or exhaustive list. The child's IEP Team is responsible for determining whether a child needs social work services, and what *specific* [emphasis added] social work services are needed in order for the child to receive FAPE [free appropriate public education]. (p. 46575).

Because no two local education agencies (LEAs) will define a school social worker's role exactly the same way, we have identified some common tasks that social workers routinely perform, and we provide the ethical and legal foundations. Although not universal, many LEAs also involve school social workers in non-IDEA services—for example, involvement with multi-tiered interventions such as Positive Behavior Interventions and Supports (PBIS).

## ASSESSMENT

School social workers perform several types of assessments. From an ethical standpoint, this is related to our values on social justice and the dignity and worth of the person. First, they often assist with eligibility determinations for students with emotional disturbances as part of the Individualized Education Program (IEP) team and provide the psychosocial context for students experiencing other challenges such as learning disabilities (Raines, 2013). Second, they help with manifestation determinations for students with discipline problems. Third, they complete functional behavioral assessments for students with emotional or behavioral disorders. The primary ethical values undergirding social work assessments should be social justice, service, and equal treatment. The *Supplemental Ethical Standards for School Social Work Practice* specify that "school social workers utilize reliable and valid assessment and screening instruments and strategies that (1) they are competent to utilize, (2) are appropriate for the student(s), and (3) achieve the purpose(s) of the screening or assessment" (p. 3). There are education policies that affect each type of assessment.

## Eligibility Determinations for Emotional Disturbance

Although RTI approaches have been permitted for eligibility determinations for learning disabilities, RTI has also been applied to eligibility determinations for emotional and behavioral disorders (Gresham, 2007) and has been effective in improving the behavior of students who were not responsive to generic classroom management practices (Fairbanks, Sugai, Guardino, & Lathrop, 2007). However, Smith, Katsiyannis, and Ryan's (2011) review of judicial decisions about the application of RTI procedures for students with emotional and behavioral problems found that RTI may lead to delays in service delivery. These delays then lead to more restrictive interventions, such as utilizing law enforcement officers, suspension, or expulsion (Lospennato, 2009; Rabinowitz, 2006). An OSERS letter (2011) clarifies that data from an RTI process is "only one component of a full and individual evaluation" for students with emotional disturbances (pp. 2–3). Clopton and Etscheidt (2009) conclude that teacher-completed screening measures such as the Systematic Screening for Behavior Disorders (Walker et al., 1990) or the Student Risk Screening Scale (Lane, Parks, Kalberg, & Carter, 2007) should lead to expedited eligibility determinations, especially in disciplinary situations.

## Eligibility Under Section 504

Section 504 of the Rehabilitation Act of 1973 uses a functional definition of disability rather than a list of disabilities as presented in IDEA. Specifically (US Department of Education, Office of Civil Rights, 2012), an individual is considered to have a disability if he or she: (1) has a physical or mental impairment that substantially limits one or more major life activities of that person; (2) has a record of such an impairment; or (3) is regarded as having such an impairment. (p. 1)

Examples of impairments include alcoholism, cancer, depression, diabetes, drug addiction, food allergies, heart disease, HIV and AIDS, and orthopedic impairments (US Department of Education, Office of Civil Rights, 2012; US Department of Health and Human Services, 2013). Zirkel (2009) notes three considerations for eligibility: (1) Conditions that are episodic or in remission must be measured when they are active, (2) mitigating measures (except eyeglasses or contact lenses) should not be considered, and (3) "life activities" should be broadly defined.

## Manifestation Determinations

Manifestation determinations (MDs) decide whether a student's disability interfered with (1) the capacity to understand the consequences of the behavior or (2) the ability to control the behavior (Knoster, 2000). IDEA based this provision on a US Supreme Court ruling in *Honig v. Doe* (1988). IDEA 2004 requires an MD (1) whenever a student with a disability is suspended out of school for more than 10 days or (2) if the student is removed to an Interim Alternative Education Setting for possession of drugs, weapons, or causing serious bodily injury (Katsiyannis, Losinski, & Prince, 2012). IEP teams are expected to review all relevant information and whether the services provided were consistent with the student's IEP. OSERS (2003) clarifies that an MD review "could include consideration of a previously unidentified disability of the child" (p. 1) and provides the following illustration:

> For example, where a student is being re-evaluated to determine the existence of an additional disability, such as emotional disturbance, and engages in misbehavior prior to the completion of the evaluations, it may be appropriate for the IEP team to convene the review within the ten-day timeline, but decide to continue the review at a later time in order to consider the results of the completed evaluations. (p. 2)

Katsiyannis and Maag (2001) review the legal rulings regarding MDs and recommend that IEP teams attempt to answer four questions, to which Knoster (2000) adds a culminating fifth question:

1. Does the student have the necessary social skills to use an appropriate behavior?
2. Can the student engage in appropriate problem-solving steps?
3. Does the student tend to distort social realities?
4. Can the student control his or her own behavior?
5. Was the misbehavior a manifestation of the student's disability?

Zirkel (2010) also provides a model checklist for IEP teams to derive a legal conclusion.

## Functional Behavioral Assessments

Functional behavioral assessments (FBAs) focus on the purpose or function of a student's misbehavior. FBAs use a person-in-environment approach that uses direct observation to study the function of the misbehavior (Filter & Alvarez, 2011; McIntosh, Brown, & Borgmeier, 2008; Raines, 2002). Legally, an IEP team must *consider* doing an FBA anytime a student's behavior interferes with learning by self or others (Zirkel, 2011). According to a US Department of Education (2002) report to Congress, disciplinary problems are relatively rare despite their high visibility; only 14% of students with disabilities are ever suspended or expelled during their school careers. However, nearly 50% of these students are labeled with emotional disturbances. Furthermore, African American students are disproportionally represented at 28%. Disproportional representation of minority students in special education and disciplinary hearings is a persistent and serious concern nationally and is addressed in more detail in Chapter 6 of this text (Beratan, 2008; Fenton, 2012; OSERS, 2007; Redfield & Kraft, 2012).

FBAs must be *conducted* when the discipline of students with disabilities results in a significant change to their educational placement (Maag & Katsiyannis, 2006; Zirkel, 2011). While OSERS (2008a) has acknowledged that not every school assessment is an evaluation requiring parental consent, an FBA does require informed consent "if the evaluation is specific to an individual child and is '. . . crucial to determining a child's continuing eligibility for services or *changes* [emphasis added] in those services'" (p. 2). Based on their review of judicial decisions, Losinski, Katsiyannis, and Ryan (2014) suggest that FBAs,

> at a minimum, should include (a) a clear description of problem behavior; (b) identification of the events, times, and situations that predict the behaviors; (c) identification of the consequences that maintain the problem behaviors; (d) developing a hypothesis regarding the problem behavior; and (e) collection of direct observation data that support the hypothesis. (p. 254)

## INTERVENTION PLANNING

School social workers regularly conduct two types of intervention planning. First, they may serve on IEP teams. Second, they may collaborate to construct behavior intervention plans (BIPs). Note that even though parents may give informed consent to an assessment, they must give a *separate* consent to the provision of services. This IDEA requirement is consistent with the ethical value of autonomy/freedom and the NASW (2008) insistence on client self-determination.

## Individualized Education Programs

IEPs are required under IDEA and associated with a student's due process rights under the 14th Amendment to the US Constitution. There are two types of requirements for IEPs. First, *procedural* requirements obligate schools to follow seven aspects of the law: (1) prior written notice to the parents, (2) keeping state-mandated timelines, (3) involving parents in the decision process, (4) conducting complete individualized evaluations, (5) having all required personnel attend the IEP meeting, (6) specifying appropriate content in the IEP, and (7) making sure the IEP is implemented as written (Bateman, 2011; Yell, 2012). Yell, Katsiyannis, and Losinski (2013) provide three helpful forms to ensure fidelity to the due process requirements: an IEP Meeting Worksheet, Parent IEP Planning Worksheet, and Student IEP Planning Worksheet. School social workers can play an important role in ensuring that the IEP process is conducted in an ethical as well as a legal manner. For instance, some school districts mail the consent for

IEP assessment form and list of due process rights to parents and ask them to sign and return the form. This process is enhanced if a school social worker personally meets with the parent to explain the IEP process and due process rights and to answer any questions the parent may have. If a social developmental study is part of the IEP evaluation, that can be conducted at the same time to expedite the evaluation.

Second, *substantive* requirements obligate schools to follow five aspects of the law: (1) an assessment of the student's academic and functional needs, (2) annual goals based on those needs, (3) measurable goals and objectives, (4) provision of related services based on peer-reviewed research, and (5) regular progress monitoring (Etscheidt, 2003; Yell, 2012). These activities are consonant with the ethical values of service and competence. Rosas, Winterman, Kroeger, and Jones (2009) have developed a 9-point rubric for verifying compliance with substantive requirements, consisting of (1) present levels of performance, (2) measurable annual goals, (3) benchmarks or short-term objectives, (4) periodic reports to parents, (5) adequate related services, (6) least restrictive environment, (7) classroom accommodations, (8) transition services, and (9) technical information.

## 504 Plans

Parallel to IEPs, Section 504 plans should enable students with disabilities to be educated with their nondisabled peers as much as possible. This least restrictive environment requirement is in keeping with the ethical value of equal treatment. For example, a student with depression may need accommodations, such as extended time for assignments, but remain within a general education classroom. Schools must provide FAPE with "reasonable accommodations" to enable students with disabilities to fully participate in major life activities (US Department of Education, Office of Civil Rights, 2012). Furthermore, the commentary on Americans with Disabilities Act regulations clarifies that "public school systems must provide program accessibility to parents and guardians with disabilities to these programs, activities, or services, and appropriate auxiliary aids and services whenever necessary to ensure effective communication" (US Department of Justice, 2010, §1.184).

## Behavioral Intervention Plans

Under IDEA, positive behavioral interventions must be *considered* by the IEP team anytime a student's behavior impedes his or her performance or the performance of other students (US Department of Education, 2006a, p. 46790) and, when appropriate, should lead to a BIP (p. 46721). FBAs and/or BIPs must be *conducted* whenever the discipline of a student results in a significant change to his or her educational placement and the behavior is a manifestation of the child's disability (p. 46798). In the absence of clear regulatory guidance, Etscheidt (2006) analyzed 52 court decisions regarding BIPs and identified the following five judicial guidelines: (1) BIPs should occur whenever student behavior interferes with student learning, (2) BIPs should be based on a functional behavioral assessment, (3) BIPs must be individualized to meet student needs, (4) BIPs must utilize positive behavioral interventions and supports (although aversive interventions are not disallowed), and (5) BIPs must be implemented as written and progress must be monitored. Maag and Katsiyannis (2006) add a sixth requirement: BIPs should be conducted in the least restrictive environment.

The ethical value of autonomy and freedom is honored when students are included in the process to develop a BIP.

# INTERVENTIONS

In this section, we clarify the quality and types of common school social work interventions. After addressing scientifically based interventions, we discuss early intervening services, positive behavior intervention and supports, bullying prevention, and mental health services.

## SCIENTIFICALLY BASED INTERVENTIONS

The NASW (2008) *Code of Ethics* states that "social workers should critically examine and keep current with emerging knowledge relevant to social work" (section 5.02(d)). IDEA adopts the same definition of scientifically based research as the No Child Left Behind Act, but it alternatively requires the IEP to use "peer-reviewed" interventions "to the extent practicable" (US Department of Education, 2006a, p. 46788). Zirkel (2008) differentiates the term "scientifically based" from similar terms—"peer-reviewed," "research-based," and "evidence-based"—and concludes that whereas peer-reviewed represents an overlapping standard, the rest represent a lower standard. The commentary on the IDEA regulations (US Department of Education, 2006a) provides the following definition of peer-reviewed research: " 'Peer-reviewed research' generally refers to research that is reviewed by qualified and independent reviewers to ensure that the quality of the information meets the standards of the field before the research is published" (p. 46664). In a topic brief, the US Department of Education (2006b) clarifies that "practitioner journals or education magazines are not the same as peer-reviewed academic journals" (p. 2). The commentary on the IDEA regulations seems suspicious of other terms: "The Act does not refer to 'evidenced-based practices' or 'emerging best practices,' which are generally *terms of art* [emphasis added] that may or may not be based on peer-reviewed research" (US Department of Education, 2006a, p. 46665).

## EARLY INTERVENING SERVICES

Under IDEA 2004, *early intervening services* are activities for children in kindergarten through grade 12 who have not been identified as needing special education but who do need supplemental academic or behavioral support. They are not to be confused with early *intervention* services that are designed for children younger than age 3 years who have been identified as needing special education. They specifically required to reduce disproportional representation of minority students in special education (Carothers, 2008). LEAs must focus "particularly, but not exclusively, on children in those groups that were significantly overidentified" (US Department of Education, 2006a, p. 46805).

There are two types of early intervening activities. First, professional development training can be provided for teachers or other staff to enable them to deliver scientifically based academic or behavioral interventions. Staff development is a tier 1 strategy. Second, school personnel can provide educational and behavioral evaluations, services, and supports to at-risk students (i.e., tier 2 interventions). In a guidance letter to chief state school officers, OSERS (2008b) provides the following illustration of early intervening services: "For example, an LEA might provide behavioral interventions to nondisabled students who receive a certain number of disciplinary office referrals, perhaps as part of a Positive Behavioral Interventions and Supports (PBIS) initiative" (p. 3).

## POSITIVE BEHAVIOR INTERVENTIONS AND SUPPORTS

Under the IDEA regulations (US Department of Education, 2006a), each state must review its policies on PBIS whenever it determines that children with disabilities are disproportionally affected by suspensions or expulsions. Likewise, each IEP team must *consider* the use of PBIS anytime a student with a disability exhibits behavior that impedes the child's learning or that of others. PBIS falls under both psychological and social work services in IDEA, but this is not to be construed as meaning that all psychologists or social workers are automatically qualified or that other related services personnel are unqualified (p. 46569) (Box 8.2).

In a position paper funded by the US Department of Education Office of Special Education Programs, Sugai and colleagues (1999) identify four core components of PBIS: (1) systemic changes (policies, structures, and routines), (2) change of school environments, (3) change of both student and adult behavior, and (4) change in appreciation of appropriate behavior of all involved (students, families, and school staff).

---

### BOX 8.2:  What Do You Mean School Social Workers Are Not Automatically Qualified?

We surmise two reasons behind this thrice-stated assertion in the IDEA regulations. First, as stated in this chapter, the federal role in education is secondary to that of the states. Even when the No Child Left Behind Act tried to improve educator qualifications, the strongest language it could use was that states were required to use "high, objective, uniform *state* standards of evaluation." As Altshuler and Webb (2009) discovered, there is a great inconsistency across states regarding pre-service educational requirements for school social workers. Among the 30 states that have clear pre-service educational requirements, one-third of these require only a Bachelor of Social Work (BSW) degree, and two-thirds require a Master of Social Work (MSW) degree. Eighty percent require some form of internship, whereas 20% do not. Only 3 states (Illinois, Tennessee, and Washington) require candidates to pass an advanced subject area exam. Second, state representatives who represent large rural populations have consistently advocated for federal flexibility due to the difficulties in hiring and retaining highly qualified personnel (Eppley, 2009; Mollenkopf, 2009), a fact acknowledged by NASW's (2012) rural policy statement.

## BULLYING PREVENTION

In a Dear Colleague letter, OSERS (2013a) states that because students with disabilities are disproportionately affected by bullying, students without disabilities who are victimized "may trigger a school's child find obligations under IDEA" (p. 2). Likewise, students with disabilities who are victimized may create a denial of FAPE that must be remedied because it limits such students from receiving services in the least restrictive environment. OSERS (2013b) attached an enclosure on evidence-based practices for preventing bullying that recommends a "comprehensive, multi-tiered behavioral framework used to establish a positive school environment" (p. 1). It also describes eight core components of effective programs: (1) teach appropriate behaviors and how to respond, (2) provide active adult supervision, (3) train and provide ongoing support for staff and students, (4) develop and implement clear policies to address bullying, (5) monitor and track bullying behaviors, (6) notify parents when bullying occurs, (7) address ongoing concerns, and (8) sustain bullying prevention over time. Components 1–4 are tier 1 strategies, whereas components 5–7 are usually applied at tier 2 or 3.

## MENTAL HEALTH SERVICES

In the Elementary and Secondary Education Act (P.L. 107-110), school social workers are listed under one of three types of "school based mental health services providers" that also include school counselors and school psychologists (section 4151(9)). Accordingly, schools can employ school social workers under the Elementary and Secondary School Counseling Program, a competitive grant that aims to establish or expand school-based counseling services in underserved communities (section 5421). Schools that receive the grant are expected to

> ensure a team approach to school counseling in the schools served by the local educational agency by working toward ratios recommended by the American School Health Association of one school counselor to 250 students, one school social worker to 800 students, and one school psychologist to 1,000 students. (section 5421(c)(2)(K))

School social workers employed under this grant must hold the following two qualifications:

> (a) a master's degree in social work from a program accredited by the Council on Social Work Education; and (b) either (i) is licensed or certified by the State in which services are provided; or (ii) in the absence of such State licensure or certification, possesses a national credential or certification as a school social work specialist granted by an independent professional organization. (section 5421(e)(5))

Mental health services are mentioned only once in IDEA, in which states that choose to reserve a portion of their allocations for other state-level activities are required "to assist LEAs in providing positive behavioral interventions and supports and *mental health services* for children with disabilities" (US Department of Education, 2006a, p. 46807). Since 1983, federal courts have recognized psychotherapy as a related service under IDEA (*T.G. v. Board of Education of Piscataway*, 1983). The major problem for school social workers is that students with emotional disturbances are underidentified and underserved (SSWAA, 2005). Part of the problem is that the federal definition deliberately excludes children who are "socially maladjusted" without defining this term unless they also had an emotional disturbance. It is not clear whether the emotional disturbance must be prior in onset or comorbid with social maladjustment. Currently, 73% of state educational agencies maintain this exclusion, and these have significantly lower identification rates (Wery & Cullinan, 2013). Only four states provide any guidance on the meaning of socially maladjusted.

The Protection of Pupil Rights Amendment (PPRA) defines psychiatric or psychological treatment as follows: "an activity involving the planned, systematic use of methods or techniques that are not directly related to academic instruction and that is designed to affect behavioral, emotional, or attitudinal characteristics of an individual or group" (34 CFR 98.4(a)). Individual and small group counseling provided by school social workers addressing social–emotional–behavioral issues may be included in this definition and fall under the requirements of the PPRA.

Addressing mental health through an RTI process started approximately a decade ago. Heathfield and Clark (2004) recommend that school-based professionals should take a proactive preventive approach. They identify a three-tier approach in which the universal level focuses on all students and addresses such common issues as violence prevention and stress management. Selected programs should aim at targeted groups of at-risk students (e.g., those exposed to trauma or parental divorce). Finally, indicated programs should aim at specific students with intensive interventions designed to reduce negative consequences, such as school suspensions, grade failure, or expulsion. Note that the 2006 IDEA regulations warn that "RTI is only one component of the process to identify children in need of special education and related services. Determining why a child has not responded to research-based interventions requires a comprehensive evaluation" (US Department of Education, 2006a, p. 46647). Landrum (2011) identifies four components of a comprehensive evaluation for a student suspected of having an emotional disturbance: (1) biological factors (e.g., mental disorders among blood relatives, traumatic brain injury, or temperament), (2) family factors (e.g., parental discipline, familial substance abuse, or child abuse or neglect reports), (3) school factors (e.g., ineffective instruction, harsh discipline, or outdated curriculum), and (4) cultural factors (e.g., excessive media or community violence). At the elementary level, strategies such as direct social skill instruction, classwide peer tutoring, and self-regulation strategy development should be considered. At the secondary level, group or individual strategies aimed at substance abuse, early sexual activity, and juvenile delinquency should be weighed. Finally, an individualized transition plan should be developed.

# PROGRESS MONITORING AND (RE)EVALUATION

The NASW (2008) *Code of Ethics* recommends that "social workers . . . fully use evaluation and research evidence in their professional practice" (section 5.02(c)). Students in special education should be re-evaluated whenever (1) significant progress has been made, (2) parents or teachers make a request, or (3) 3 years have passed since the last evaluation. After the initial evaluation for services, the IDEA regulations do not require parental consent when school personnel review "existing data" (US Department of Education, 2006a, p. 46784). Progress monitoring is an integral part of the RTI process and can help to ensure students receive the services they need in the least restrictive environment, promoting the ethical value of quality of life. Raines (2008b) recommends unobtrusive measures such as school attendance, tardiness, disciplinary referrals, grades, in-class observations, nurse visits, and universal test results (e.g., state assessments).

The IDEA regulations require that an IEP delineate how progress on annual measurable goals will be measured. Raines (2008b) recommends triangulating these measures to meet the IDEA requirement that no single measure be used as the sole criterion for determining eligibility or appropriate related services. Parents are to receive quarterly reports about a child's progress to the annual measurable goals that are concurrent with report cards for general education.

## ETHICAL DECISION-MAKING STEPS

Because school social workers engage in a variety of roles, it is common for them to experience a conflict between professional ethics and educational policies. We address the process of ethical decision-making in great detail and in summary form elsewhere (Raines & Dibble, 2011, 2013). We recommend seven essential steps. An opportunity to work on these steps is provided in the case study at the end of the chapter. The steps are as follows:

1. Know yourself and your professional responsibilities.
2. Analyze the predicament (especially the conflicting values).
3. Seek consultation (regarding ethics, laws, and clinical concerns).
4. Identify at least three courses of action (avoid "either–or" thinking).
5. Manage the clinical concerns (put people ahead of problems).
6. Implement the best ethical decision available.
7. Reflect on the process and re-engage as needed.

## CONCLUSION

School social work practice rests on a trifold foundation of professional ethics, state education policy, and national education policy. We focused on the professional ethics and national policy because they are the greatest common denominator for school social workers nationally. We believe that school social workers should be active in their state professional associations and that these associations have a responsibility to provide professional development regarding important state policy directions and case law decisions.

## CASE STUDY: ZERO TOLERANCE POLICIES

Maria is a school social worker at a junior high school in a high-poverty town known for its gang violence and drug problems. With the election of a new school board, the district has adopted a "zero tolerance" policy for student violence or drug possession. Upon arriving at school, Maria learns that one of her students, Arthur, was found to be in possession of a miniature Swiss army knife while passing through the newly installed metal detectors. Arthur had just received the knife from his grandfather on his 12th birthday and wanted to show it to his friends because it contained a nail file, screwdriver, mini-scissors, plastic toothpick, and tweezers. He did not even think about the 1.75-inch blade. The principal has decided to send Arthur to a highly restrictive correctional school for 45 days. Maria is upset because Arthur has been diagnosed with a reading disability and attention deficit/hyperactivity disorder. She is sure that he just brought the knife to school on an impulse and did not mean to hurt anyone. Arthur's mother calls her frantically because both she and Arthur's father work full-time and they said they do not want him "hanging out with the wrong crowd." They are sick with worry. Because Maria knows this is her third male student of the same ethnicity to be removed this year, she decides to consult the principal, and he provides her with the following quote from the IDEA regulations (2006):

(g) Special circumstances. School personnel may remove a student to an interim alternative educational setting for not more than 45 school days *without regard to whether the behavior is determined to be a manifestation of the child's disability*, if the child—(1) carries a weapon to or possesses a weapon at school, on school premises, or to or at a school function under the jurisdiction of an SEA or an LEA.

Maria is dissatisfied with the principal's response and decides to consult a local attorney. The lawyer tells Maria that the principal's quote is taken out of context. IDEA defers to another section of the US Code for its definition of a weapon:

USC 18:930(d)(2) The term "dangerous weapon" means a weapon, device, instrument, material, or substance, animate or inanimate, that is used for, or is readily capable of, causing death or serious bodily injury, except that such term does not include a pocket knife with a blade of less than 2½ inches in length.

## DISCUSSION QUESTIONS

1. In the case study, the race or ethnicity of the student was not mentioned. How did you picture Arthur? Why?
2. What ethical values might be in conflict in this situation? Who is the primary client and who are the other stakeholders in this situation?
3. Who else should Maria consult before making a decision about what to do?
4. With this legal knowledge, what are three different courses of action that Maria might take to help Arthur and other students like him?
5. What clinical issues need to be addressed with Arthur and his family?
6. Of the three courses of action given in response to Question 4, which one is the best choice?
7. How would you determine whether the result was a successful outcome for Arthur? What else might you do?

## ADDITIONAL RESOURCES

American School Counselor Association ethical standards: http://www.schoolcounselor.org/asca/media/asca/home/EthicalStandards2010.pdf

Americans with Disabilities Act regulations: http://www.ada.gov/regs2010/titleII_2010/titleII_2010_regulations.pdf

Bullying: https://www2.ed.gov/policy/speced/guid/idea/memosdcltrs/bullyingdcl-8-20-13.pdf

Discipline: http://idea.ed.gov/object/fileDownload/model/TopicalBrief/field/PdfFile/primary_key/6

Disproportionality/overidentification: http://www2.ed.gov/policy/speced/guid/idea/tb-overident.pdf

Due process hearings: http://idea.ed.gov/explore/view/p/%2Croot%2Cdynamic%2CTopicalBrief%2C16%2C

Early intervening services: http://idea.ed.gov/explore/view/p/%2Croot%2Cdynamic%2CTopicalBrief%2C8%2C

Evaluation and re-evaluation: http://idea.ed.gov/explore/view/p/%2Croot%2Cdynamic%2CTopicalBrief%2C4%2C

Family Educational Rights and Privacy Act (FERPA) and the PATRIOT Act: http://www2.ed.gov/policy/gen/guid/fpco/pdf/htterrorism.pdf

IDEA regulations: http://idea.ed.gov/explore/view/p/%2Croot%2Cregs%2C

IEPs: http://idea.ed.gov/explore/view/p/%2Croot%2Cdynamic%2CQaCorner%2C14%2C

Least restrictive environment: http://www2.ed.gov/policy/speced/guid/idea/letters/revpolicy/tplre.html

Manifestation determination: https://www2.ed.gov/policy/speced/guid/idea/letters/revpolicy/tpman-det.html

NASW *Code of Ethics*: http://www.socialworkers.org/pubs/code/code.asp

National Association of School Psychologists ethical principles: http://www.nasponline.org/standards/2010standards/1_%20Ethical%20Principles.pdf

Procedural safeguards: http://idea.ed.gov/explore/view/p/%2Croot%2Cdynamic%2CTopicalBrief%2C15%2C

Response to Intervention: http://www2.ed.gov/policy/speced/guid/idea/memosdcltrs/osep11-07rtimemo.pdf

Restraints and seclusion: http://www2.ed.gov/policy/seclusion/restraints-and-seclusion-resources.pdf

SSWAA ethical guidelines: http://sswaa.org/displaycommon.cfm?an=1&subarticlenbr=102

Supplemental ethical standards for school social work practice: http://midwestssw.org

US Department of Education, Family Policy Compliance Office: http://www2.ed.gov/policy/gen/guid/fpco/index.html

US Department of Education, Office for Civil Rights: http://www2.ed.gov/about/offices/list/ocr/index.html

US Department of Education, Office of Special Education Programs: http://www2.ed.gov/about/offices/list/osers/osep/index.html?src=mr

# REFERENCES

Alexander, K., & Alexander, M. D. (2012). *American public school law* (8th ed.). Belmont, CA: Wadsworth/Cengage.

Altshuler, S. J., & Webb, J. R. (2009). School social work: Increasing the legitimacy of the profession. *Children & Schools, 31*(4), 207–218.

Bateman, B. D. (2011). Individualized education programs for children with disabilities. In J. M. Kauffman & D. P. Hallahan (Eds.), *Handbook of special education* (pp. 77–90). Philadelphia, PA: Taylor & Francis/Routledge.

Beratan, G. D. (2008). The song remains the same: Transposition and disproportionate representation of minority students in special education. *Race, Ethnicity, & Education, 11*(4), 337–354.

Carothers, L. R. (2008). Here's an IDEA: Providing intervention services for at-risk youth under the Individuals with Disabilities Education Act. *Valparaiso University Law Review, 42,* 543–585.

Clopton, K. L., & Etscheidt, S. (2009). Using the convergence of data for expedited evaluations: Guidelines for school psychologists. *Psychology in the Schools, 46*(5), 459–470.

*C.N. v. Ridgewood Board of Education,* 430 F.3d 159 (3rd Cir. 2005).

Conroy, H., & Harcourt, D. (2009). Informed agreement to participate: Beginning the partnership with children in research. *Early Child Development and Care, 179*(2), 157–165.

Eppley, K. (2009). Rural schools and the highly qualified teacher provision of No Child Left Behind, a critical policy analysis. *Journal of Research in Rural Education, 24*(4), 1–11.

Etscheidt, S. (2003). An analysis of legal hearings and cases related to Individualized Education Programs for children with autism. *Research & Practice for Persons with Severe Disabilities, 28*(2), 51–69.

Etscheidt, S. (2006). Behavior intervention plans: Pedagogical and legal analysis of issues. *Behavioral Disorders, 31*(2), 223–243.

Fairbanks, S., Sugai, G., Guardino, D., & Lathrop, M. (2007). Response to intervention: Examining classroom behavior support in second grade. *Exceptional Children, 7*(3), 288–310.

Fenton, Z. E. (2012). Disabling racial repetition. *Law & Inequality, 31,* 77–121.

*Fields v. Palmdale School District,* 427 F.3d 1197 (9th Cir. 2005).

*Fields v. Palmdale School District,* 447 F.3d 1187 (9th Cir. 2006).

Filter, K. J., & Alvarez, M. E. (2011). *Functional behavioral assessment: A three-tiered model.* New York, NY: Oxford University Press.

Fisher, C. B. (2004). Informed consent and clinical research involving children and adolescents: Implications of the revised APA Code of Ethics and HIPAA. *Journal of Clinical Child and Adolescent Psychology, 33*(4), 832–839.

Frey, A. J., Alvarez, M. E., Dupper, D. R., Sabatino, C. A., Lindsey, B. C., & Raines, J. C., . . . Norris, M. A. (2013). *School social work practice model.* London, KY: School Social Work Association of America.

Gresham, F. M. (2007). Response to intervention and emotional and behavioral disorders: Best practices in assessment for intervention. *Assessment for Intervention, 32*(4), 214–222.

Heathfield, L. T., & Clark, E. (2004). Shifting from categories to services: Comprehensive school-based mental health for children with emotional disturbance and social maladjustment. *Psychology in the Schools, 41*(8), 911–920.

*Honig v. Doe,* 108 S. Ct. 592 (1988).

Katsiyannis, A., Losinski, M., & Prince, A. M. T. (2012). Litigation and students with disabilities: A persistent concern. *NASSP Bulletin, 96*(1), 23–43.

Katsiyannis, A., & Maag, J. (2001). Manifestation determination as a golden fleece. *Exceptional Children, 68*(1), 85–96.

Knoster, T. P. (2000). Understanding the difference and relationship between functional behavioral assessments and manifestation determinations. *Journal of Positive Behavior Interventions, 2*(1), 53–58.

Kutchins, H. (1991). The fiduciary relationship: The legal basis for social workers' responsibility to clients. *Social Work, 36*(2), 106–113.

Landrum, T. J. (2011). Emotional and behavioral disorders. In J. M. Kauffman & D. P. Hallahan (Eds.), *Handbook of special education* (pp. 209–220). New York, NY: Routledge/Taylor & Francis.

Lane, K. L., Parks, R. J., Kalberg, J. R., & Carter, E. W. (2007). Systematic screening at the middle school level: Score reliability and validity of the Student Risk Screening Scale. *Journal of Emotional and Behavioral Disorders, 15*(4), 209–222.

Loewenberg, F. M., Dolgoff, R., & Harrington, D. (2000). *Ethical decisions for social work practice* (6th ed.). Itasca, IL: Peacock.

Losinski, M. L., Katsiyannis, A., & Ryan, J. B. (2014). Recent case law regarding functional behavioral assessments: Implications for practice. *Intervention in School & Clinic, 49*(4), 251–154.

Lospennato, R. K. (2009). Multifaceted strategies to stop the school-to-prison pipeline. *Clearinghouse Review: Journal of Poverty Law and Policy, 42*, 528–550.

Maag, J. W., & Katsiyannis, A. (2006). Behavior intervention plans: Legal and practical considerations for students with emotional and behavioral disorders. *Behavioral Disorders, 31*(4), 348–362.

*Merriken v. Cressman*, 364 F. Supp. 913 (E.D. Pa. 1973).

Midwest School Social Work Council. (2015). *Supplemental ethical standards for school social work practice*. Louisville, KY: Author.

Mollenkopf, D. L. (2009). Creating highly qualified teachers: Maximizing university resources to provide professional development in rural areas. *Rural Educator, 30*(3), 34–39.

National Association of Social Workers. (2008). *Code of ethics*. Silver Spring, MD: Author.

National Association of Social Workers. (2012). Rural policy statement. In *Social work speaks* (9th ed., pp. 296–301). Silver Spring, MD: Author.

Protection of Pupil Rights Amendment, Pub. L. No. 95-561, 92 Stat. 2355.

Rabinowitz, J. (2006). Leaving homeroom in handcuffs: Why an overreliance on law enforcement to ensure school safety is detrimental to children. *Cardozo Public Law, Policy & Ethics Journal, 4*, 153–201.

Raines, J. C. (2002). Brainstorming hypotheses for functional behavioral assessment: The link to effective behavioral intervention plans. *School Social Work Journal, 26*(2), 30–45.

Raines, J. C. (2008a). *School social work & group work*. Part of the SSWAA Ethical Guideline Series. Approved by the SSWAA Board of Directors on July 16, 2008.

Raines, J. C. (2008b). *Evidence-based practice in school mental health*. New York, NY: Oxford University Press.

Raines, J. C. (2009). The process of ethical decision making in school social work: Confidentiality. In C. R. Massat, R. Constable, S. McDonald, & J. P. Flynn (Eds.), *School social work: Practice, policy, and research* (pp. 71–94). Chicago, IL: Lyceum.

Raines, J. C. (2013). Improving the self-esteem and social skills of students with learning disabilities. In C. Franklin, M. B. Harris, & P. Allen-Meares (Eds.), *School social work and mental health worker's training and resource manual* (2nd ed., pp. 237–250). New York, NY: Oxford University Press.

Raines, J. C., & Dibble, N. T. (2011). *Ethical decision making in school mental health*. New York, NY: Oxford University Press.

Raines, J. C., & Dibble, N. T. (2013). Ethical decision making in school mental health. In C. Franklin, M. B. Harris, & P. Allen-Meares (Eds.), *School social work and mental health worker's training and resource manual* (2nd ed., pp. 37–49). New York, NY: Oxford University Press.

Redfield, S. E. (2002). *Thinking like a lawyer: An educator's guide to legal analysis and research*. Durham, NC: Carolina Academic Press.

Redfield, S. E., & Kraft, T. (2012). What color is special education? *Journal of Law & Education, 41*, 129–202.

*Rhoades v. Penn-Harris-Madison School Corp.*, 574 F. Supp. 2d 888 (N.D. Ind. 2008).

Rosas, C., Winterman, K. G., Kroeger, S., & Jones, M. M. (2009). Using a rubric to assess Individualized Education Programs. *International Journal of Applied Educational Studies, 4*(1), 47–57.

Sabatino, C. A. (2014). *Consultation theory and practice: A handbook for school social workers*. New York, NY: Oxford University Press.

Schacter, D., Kleinman, I., & Harvey, W. (2005). Informed consent and adolescents. *Canadian Journal of Psychiatry, 50*(9), 534–540.

School Social Work Association of America. (2005). *Resolution statement: Education for students with social maladjustment.* Washington, DC: Author. Retrieved May 19, 2014, from http://www.sswaa. org/?52

Smith, C. R., Katsiyannis, A., & Ryan, J. B. (2011). Challenges of servings students with emotional and behavioral disorders: Legal and policy considerations. *Behavior Disorders, 36*(3), 185–194.

Stefkovich, J. A. (2014). *Best interests of the student: Applying ethical constructs to legal cases in education* (2nd ed.). New York, NY: Routledge/Taylor & Francis.

Sugai, G., Horner, R. H., Dunlap, G., Hieneman, M., Lewis, T. J., & Nelson, C. M. (1999). *Applying positive behavior support and functional behavioral assessment in schools.* Retrieved February 14, 2014, from http://digitalcommons.calpoly.edu/cgi/viewcontent.cgi?article=1030&context=gse_fac

*T.G. v. Board of Education of Piscataway,* 576 F. Supp. 420 (1983).

US Department of Education, Office of Civil Rights. (2012, January 19). *Frequently asked questions about Section 504 and the Education of children with disabilities.* Retrieved February 28, 2014, from http://www2.ed.gov/about/offices/list/ocr/504faq.html

US Department of Education, Office of Special Education Programs. (2002). *24th annual report to Congress on the implementation of IDEA, Section III: Programs and services.* Retrieved February 14, 2014, from http://www2.ed.gov/about/reports/annual/osep/2002/section-iii.pdf

US Department of Education, Office of Special Education and Rehabilitative Services. (2003, August 1). *Letter to Geoffrey A. Yudien.* Retrieved January 11, 2014, from http://www2.ed.gov/policy/speced/ guid/idea/letters/2003-2/yudien080103discip2q2003.pdf

US Department of Education, Office of Special Education and Rehabilitative Services. (2006a, August 14). Assistance to the states for the education of children with disabilities and preschool grants for children with disabilities: Final rule. 34CFR Parts 300 and 301. *Federal Register, 71*(156), 46540–46845.

US Department of Education, Office of Special Education Programs. (2006b, October 4). *Topic: Early intervening services.* Retrieved February 5, 2014, from http://idea.ed.gov/explore/view/p/%2Croot% 2Cdynamic%2CTopicalBrief%2C8%2C

US Department of Education, Office of Special Education and Rehabilitative Services. (2007, April 24). *Memo to state directors of special education.* Retrieved February 24, 2014, from http://www2.ed.gov/ policy/speced/guid/idea/letters/2007-2/osep0709disproportionality2q2007.pdf

US Department of Education, Office of Special Education and Rehabilitative Services. (2008a, May 5). *Letter to Sarzynski.* Retrieved January 11, 2014, from http://www2.ed.gov/policy/speced/guid/idea/ letters/2008-2/sarzynski050608consent2q2008.doc

US Department of Education, Office of Special Education and Rehabilitative Services. (2008b, July 28). *OSEP memo on coordinated early intervening services.* Retrieved February 5, 2014, from https://www2.ed.gov/policy/speced/guid/idea/letters/2008-4/ceis-guidance072808eis4q2008.pdf

US Department of Education, Office of Special Education and Rehabilitative Services. (2011, January 6). *Letter to Perry A. Zirkel.* Retrieved January 11, 2014, from http://www2.ed.gov/policy/speced/guid/ idea/letters/2011-1/zirkel010611rti1q2011.doc

US Department of Education, Office of Special Education and Rehabilitative Services. (2013a, August 20). *Dear colleague letter on bullying.* Retrieved February 5, 2014, from http://www2.ed.gov/policy/ speced/guid/idea/memosdcltrs/bullyingdcl-8-20-13.pdf

US Department of Education, Office of Special Education and Rehabilitative Services. (2013b, August 20). *Effective evidence-based practices for preventing and addressing bullying.* Retrieved February 14, 2014, from http://www2.ed.gov/policy/speced/guid/idea/memosdcltrs/ bullyingdcl-enclosure-8-20-13.pdf

US Department of Health and Human Services, Office of Civil Rights. (2013). *Fact sheet: Your rights under Section 504 of the Rehabilitation Act*. Retrieved February 28, 2014, from http://www.hhs.gov/sites/default/files/ocr/civilrights/resources/factsheets/504.pdf

US Department of Justice. (2010, September 15). *Americans with Disabilities Act, Title 2 regulations: Nondiscrimination on the basis of disability in state and local government services*. Retrieved February 28, 2014, from http://www.ada.gov/regs2010/titleII_2010/titleII_2010_regulations.pdf

Walker, H. M., Severson, H. H., Todis, B. J., Block-Pedego, A. E., Williams, G. J., Haring, N. G., et al. (1990). Systematic screening for behavior disorders (SSBD): Further validation, replication, and normative data. *Remedial and Special Education, 11*(2), 32–46.

Wery, J. J., & Cullinan, D. (2013). State definitions of emotional disturbance. *Journal of Emotional and Behavioral Disorders, 21*(1), 45–52.

Yell, M. L. (2012). *The law and special education* (3rd ed.). Upper Saddle River, NJ: Pearson/Merrill.

Yell, M. L., Katsiyannis, A., & Losinski, M. (2013). Avoiding procedural errors in Individualized Education Program development. *Teaching Exceptional Children, 46*(1), 56–64.

Zirkel, P. A. (2008). A legal roadmap of SBR, PRR, and related terms under the IDEA. *Focus on Exceptional Children, 40*(5), 1–4.

Zirkel, P. A. (2010). Manifestation determinations under the new Individuals with Disabilities Education Act: An update. *Remedial & Special Education, 31*(5), 378–384.

Zirkel, P. A. (2009). Section 504: Student eligibility update. *The Clearing House, 82*(5), 209–211.

Zirkel, P. A. (2011). State special education laws for functional behavioral assessments and behavior intervention plans. *Behavior Disorders, 36*(4), 262–278.

# CHAPTER 9

# MULTI-TIERED SYSTEMS OF SUPPORT

*Schoolwide Evidence-Based Interventions*

## AARON M. THOMPSON AND TORY COX

Throughout this book, it is well documented that many promising school social work practices exist to address a range of challenging social, emotional, and behavioral problems with students in school settings. Much of this knowledge has been generated in response to an increase in incidents of school violence and declining student performance during the past several decades. These issues prompted a wave of sweeping educational reforms in the United States and other developed nations, including No Child Left Behind (NCLB), and the revised Individuals with Disabilities Education Act (IDEA) as well as the more recent Every Student Succeeds Act (2015). The intent of these reforms was to accelerate the academic and social performance of students, which is often reflected in specific frameworks for both academic and behavioral interventions. These frameworks, known generally as multi-tiered systems of support (MTSS) and specifically by more popular iterations such as Response to Intervention (RTI) or Positive Behavioral Interventions and Supports (PBIS), depict graduated approaches to address significant barriers to student success. Viewed as a pyramid-shaped design, MTSS takes the concept of universal prevention programs for all, selective group interventions for some, and indicated or targeted individual interventions for a few and applies it to both academic and behavioral intervention models. Of principal importance in this chapter, MTSS helps practitioners and educators view the powerful work of universal prevention at the primary, universal, or tier 1 level.

To expedite successful outcomes, MTSS explicitly requires educators and school-based professionals (i.e., school social workers, psychologists, counselors, and nurses) to rely on evidence-based practices to address student social, emotional, behavioral, and academic difficulties. It is important to distinguish between *evidence-based practice* and *evidence-based programs* in both this chapter and Chapter 10. Evidence-based practice (EBP) is a comprehensive framework to approach effective school social work practice. Evidence-based programs, on the other hand, are research-supported or evidence-based treatments (EBTs) or interventions (EBIs) that have been tested repeatedly in rigorous scientific studies and found to improve student and school educational and behavioral outcomes.

This chapter shapes the discussion of EBP for school social workers (SSWers) by presenting a model of EBP as it applies to school settings. EBP school social work is operationalized using the MTSS framework, a common model of prevention and intervention services currently adopted by many schools. Using this model, screening, assessment, and ongoing data collection are discussed along with available tools and instruments to collect these data in school settings. Then, the chapter presents a discussion on how screening and assessment data are used to select, organize, and deploy a continuum of EBTs at the universal, selective, and indicated levels. This chapter provides an overview of schoolwide or universal EBTs. Chapter 10 focuses more on targeted EBTs (i.e., selective and indicated).

# EVIDENCE-BASED SCHOOL SOCIAL WORK PRACTICE

The concept of EBP was originally developed in the medical profession (Sackett, Rosenberg, Gray, Haynes, & Richardson, 1996) and was brought to social work as an alternative to authority-based practice (i.e., practice guided by history, policies, and authority figures; Gambrill, 1999). The EBP model, broadly speaking, has been described as a "process of lifelong learning" in which practitioners ask questions regarding direct practice, seek the "best evidence" related to each question, and then take appropriate action guided by that evidence (Gibbs, 2003, p. 6).

However, the EBP model defined here lacks the specificity required to guide SSWers to apply EBP strategies in school settings. That is, school settings are unique contexts in which federal, state, and local policies and events shape school culture, daily practice, and create barriers to applying the EBP framework as described by many authors. These conditions require a reconceptualization of what EBP looks like for school settings. In short, SSWers wanting to apply EBPs in school settings must master two broad skill sets. First, SSWers must possess and maintain an understanding of existing research on school-based EBTs. Second, SSWers must possess the fundamental practice knowledge and skills to operate effectively in school settings. The elements underlying these two broad skill sets are defined next in a model of EBP for school social work.

# EVIDENCE-BASED PRACTICE MODEL FOR SCHOOL SOCIAL WORK

The broad skill sets described previously are depicted in Figure 9.1 in the form of an hourglass. As suggested by Figure 9.1, EBP SSWers operate in the space between two distinct worlds of evidence—evidence derived from research findings (i.e., *evidence-informed practice*) and evidence derived from evaluations (i.e., *practice-based evidence*; Green, 2006). The information from these two distinctly different worlds flows through the evidence-based school social worker in a bidirectional manner dependent on which way the hourglass is tipped.

In the research-driven, evidence-informed practice world, SSWers must maintain an awareness of existing and trending knowledge that cuts across several streams of research. Some

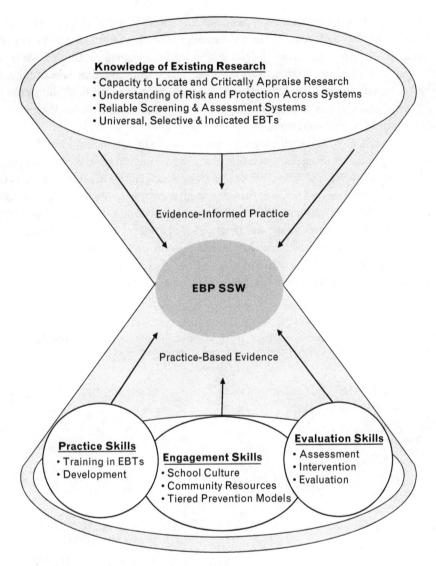

**FIGURE 9.1**: Evidence-based school social work practice model.

research streams focus on descriptive studies of the social and environmental risk factors associated with poor student social, behavioral, and academic outcomes. Knowledge from these studies can highlight areas of need and risk factors relevant to any particular school setting. Other streams of research focus on the development and testing of quality psychosocial and behavioral measurement instruments. Knowledge from these studies can assist SSWers in selecting the most reliable instruments to assess relevant risk factors in a school. Other streams of research focus on testing the effectiveness of universal, selective, or indicated EBTs. Knowledge from this stream of research can arm SSWers with a tool box of evidence-informed strategies from which to address a range of social and behavioral issues. Last, simply locating a study in any of these streams of research is never adequate because an EBP SSWer must also be adept at critically appraising the quality of any study (Howard, McMillen, & Pollio, 2003). To critically appraise a study, SSWers must understand research methods and how issues of sampling, measurement, and design impact the external, conceptual, and internal validity (i.e., trustworthiness) of any study's findings.

In the practice-based, evaluation-informed world, professional SSWers must possess skills in the areas of practice, engagement, and evaluation. In the area of practice, SSWers must be able to competently deliver effective strategies that address challenging student behaviors across the developmental spectrum. Next, SSWers must be adept at understanding school culture and engaging key players in the school setting (i.e., teachers and administrators) and in the community. Finally, SSWers must master the capacity to use trustworthy evaluation methods to appraise the impact of their own work.

In summary, EBP SSWers rely on research-driven evidence to inform and direct their practice by (1) identifying and measuring relevant risk factors and (2) selecting an array of EBTs to mitigate those risk factors. However, EBP SSWers must also competently engage in practice-driven evaluation strategies that produce evidence that the selected EBTs are improving school, group, and student outcomes. In this way, well-trained EBP SSWers commonly flip the direction of the hourglass and adeptly draw upon research-based and practice-based evidence to guide their efforts. To be sure, the goal of EBP is to close the research-to-practice gap in school settings. Doing so is a complex endeavor. As such, EBP SSWers need to frame these concepts and their work using MTSS, which mirrors a public health framework (Reinke, Herman, & Tucker, 2006). Figure 9.2 shows

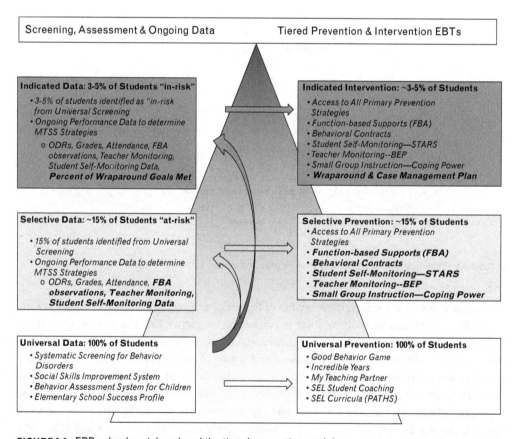

**FIGURE 9.2:** EBP school social work and the tiered prevention model.

*Source: Adapted from Thompson, A. M., Reinke, W. M., & Herman, K. C. (2016). The value, practice, and evaluation of teaching social emotional learning to students with and without disabilities. In C. R. Massat, M. S. Kelly, & R. Constable (Eds.), School social work: Practice, policy, and research (8th ed.). New York, NY: Oxford University Press.*

the MTSS model concept along with each of the EBTs discussed in this chapter and Chapter 10 adjacent to the practice-based types of evidence collected and used to evaluate the strategies and needed to drive decisional systems regarding the allocation of services within the model.

## MULTI-TIERED SYSTEMS OF SUPPORT: A FRAMEWORK FOR SCHOOL SOCIAL WORK EVIDENCE-BASED PRACTICE

An MTSS typically utilizes data (e.g., screening and progress monitoring data) to select, organize, and monitor the impact of a continuum of EBTs. Contemporary perspectives on MTSSs are organized into three levels that are characterized by an increasing degree of implementation intensity and support needed to meet a variety of student needs at each tier. The first tier, commonly referred to as *universal prevention*, includes EBTs that are low-intensity and are provided to all students in school settings (e.g., monitoring hallways, praising appropriate behavior and delivering social emotional curricula). Tiers 2 and 3—often referred to as targeted interventions—are discussed in more detail in Chapter 10 and include selective prevention and indicated intervention. *Selective prevention* includes more intensive supports targeting subgroups of youth identified as being "at-risk" for experiencing poor outcomes (e.g., self or teacher monitoring and small groups). The third tier, commonly referred to as *indicated intervention*, organizes the most intensive supports delivered to youth who may be showing early signs or symptoms of an oncoming disorder or disability (Cicchetti & Cohen, 2006; Offord, Kraemer, Kazdin, Jensen, & Harrington, 1998; Thompson, 2012; Thompson, Reinke, & Herman, 2016). Properly implemented MTSSs include all three levels of prevention and intervention in one data-driven model. Randomized studies suggest properly implemented MTSSs are associated with mild to modest improvements in school safety (ES[1] = 0.23), academic achievement (ES = 0.24–0.38), positive student behaviors (ES = 0.30), improved school climate (ES = 0.29), and increased staff collaboration (ES = 0.26) (Bradshaw, Reinke, Brown, Bevans, & Leaf, 2008; Horner et al., 2009).

One might ask how the use of an MTSS approach impacts specific subgroups such as children and youth in foster care, experiencing homelessness, living in poverty, and identifying as LGBT, who have historically experienced marginalization in educational settings. Although MTSS is not an approach rooted in student rights, advocacy, or cultural competency, per se, it does have particular elements that support marginalized youth and families and, in some ways, equalize the educational landscape. For example, one of the core principles of MTSS is that a student's failure to learn is due to improper instruction and not to the student's innate inability to learn (Harlacher, Sakelaris, & Kattelman, 2014). This perspective is categorically different than that found in many US public education classrooms and student support teams, in which students are blamed for their inability to learn and systematically lost throughout the years in

---

1. ES = effect size, a statistic communicating the strength of an intervention to influence a desirable outcome. ES = 0.2 is considered mild, ES = 0.5 is considered moderate, and ES = 0.8 is considered strong (Rubin & Babbie, 2012).

the educational system (Harlacher et al., 2014). Taking the focus off the student and placing it onto the system that created the incorrect instruction can help change teacher perceptions of student abilities and address the isolation and self-blame that many students feel when they are not learning at the pace of other students.

Another principle of MTSS that promotes the spirit of equity is the clear use of data to inform decision-making (Harlacher et al., 2014). The use of data helps remove many inherent biases that may cloud the judgment of administrators and teachers and helps students and their families see clearer rationale for decisions (Harlacher et al., 2014). The last principle of MTSS is that the whole school participates in MTSS prevention and intervention efforts. This principle emphasizes building unity, breaking down barriers between people, and creating collaborative experiences (Harlacher et al., 2014). These three principles help create a perspective of the whole school taking responsibility for the whole child with particular needs due to his or her specific circumstances (Sugai & Horner, 2009). This philosophy is the operational embodiment of an intersectional approach to students in which their individuality is celebrated and supported by a responsive system attuned to their unique qualities.

On balance, implementing an MTSS model follows a stepwise intervention process that generally includes screening, identification, implementation, and evaluation. These steps are briefly described as follows:

1. Screen all students using reliable tools to assess risk/protective factors.
2. Identify risk factors and subgroups using the data.
   a. Identify the greatest universal risk factors.
   b. Identify subgroups of students "at-risk" (~15%) and in need of selective supports.
   c. Identify students "in-risk" (~3–5%) who need of indicated supports.
      i. Conduct in-depth assessments with in-risk students to gauge the type and magnitude of risk.
3. Implement a continuum of EBTs at the universal, selective, and indicated levels with the following conditions:
   a. Universal EBTs address the key risk factors in the whole population of students as identified in the screening data.
   b. Targeted EBTs (discussed in Chapter 10)
      i. Selective EBTs target risk factors for groups of "at-risk" students (~15%) as identified in the screening data.
      ii. Indicated EBTs, following an in-depth assessment, should target individualized needs for "in-risk" students (~3–5%).
4. Apply EBP evaluation skills to determine if the EBTs effectively improve outcomes (discussed in detail in Chapter 10).
   a. Compare pre- and post-differences at each level.
      i. Universal—Compare school-level data sources to determine effectiveness of universal EBTs.
      ii. Selective—Compare group-level screening scores and ongoing progress monitoring data sources to determine the effectiveness of selective EBTs.
      iii. Indicated—Compare individual student pre- and post-test assessment scores, screening scores, and progress monitoring data.

In summary, EBP SSWers must clearly understand the MTSS model to be proficient at organizing and executing each of the steps listed previously. To deepen SSWers understanding of the EBP model using a tiered prevention approach, measurement tools and EBTs at the universal level are suggested in this chapter, and measures for selective and indicated levels are included in Chapter 10. Data collection and evaluation strategies at these levels are also discussed in these two chapters. However, these chapters do not present an exhaustive view of all tools and strategies currently available. The purpose is to shape a discussion of how these tools may be used to (1) collect data using reliable instruments tapping relevant risk factors so that (2) EBTs may be selected at multiple levels (universal, selective, and indicated) with the intent of (3) evaluating the effectiveness of the supports on school-, group-, and student-level outcomes.

School social workers can play an important role in the development of programs and practices of universal prevention by involving and including all key stakeholders. Given their understanding of systems theory and ecological approaches, SSWers should take the lead in ensuring that feedback loops are built into program design. They will need to emphasize social diversity and cultural competency as key considerations of every program. With an end goal of building capacity in schools and districts so that programs become self-sustaining, SSWers can facilitate administrator, teacher, and staff buy-in at the local and district levels. SSWers will need to ensure that progress is monitored (see Chapter 13) in ways that allow for mid-course corrections to reflect changing conditions. Finally, SSWers should continue to hone their skills in evaluation around service effectiveness, use data to inform decision-making, and measure academic and behavioral outcomes to appraise the impact of intervention efforts.

## STEP 1: SCREENING, ASSESSMENT, AND ONGOING PERFORMANCE MONITORING

Tiered prevention models include EBTs, but the selection of those EBTs is informed by early screening data. The purpose of early screening is to identify areas of risk at the school level so that SSWers may (1) select universal prevention programs to mitigate those concerns and (2) pinpoint subgroups of "at-risk" and "in-risk" students who may benefit from selective and indicated EBTs, respectively. For in-risk students being considered for indicated EBTs, EBP SSWers should conduct an in-depth assessment to determine the nature and magnitude of the risk factors impeding the students' functioning.

An effective universal screening and assessment system needs to rely on technically accurate and sensitive measures (i.e., valid and reliable) that answer important questions (e.g., What risk factors are affecting which students?) in an efficient manner. The data should yield information to guide the selection and organization of EBTs across universal school, selective group, and indicated student levels of prevention and intervention.

## Tools for Universal Screening and Assessment

Several systems for universal screening are available to identify what risk factors are impacting which students. For instance, the Systematic Screening for Behavior Disorders (Walker & Severson, 1992), the Social Skills Improvement System (Gresham & Elliott, 1990), the Behavior Assessment System for Children (BASC) (Kamphaus & Reynolds, 2007), and the Elementary

Table 9.1:  Risk Factors by Developmental Domain

| Developmental Domain | Risk Factors |
| --- | --- |
| Home and family | • Family management problems<br>• Coercive parenting practices<br>• Sibling dropped out of school<br>• Substance use<br>• Low education engagement |
| Neighborhood | • Availability of drugs or weapons<br>• High neighborhood crime and violence<br>• Community norms toward aggression/crime<br>• Low neighborhood collective efficacy<br>• High neighborhood social disorganization<br>• Saturation of low income |
| Peers | • Peer rejection/acceptance<br>• Friends with problem behavior<br>• Friends' acceptance of problem behavior |
| School | • Early academic failure<br>• Lack of behavioral, cognitive, and academic engagement<br>• Poor teacher–student relationship<br>• Large school/classroom |
| Individual/health | • High psychosomatic complaints<br>• Absences from school for illness<br>• Poor cognitive concentration |
| Individual/behavioral | • Early aggression<br>• Authority acceptance problems<br>• Poor social competency |

School Success Profile (ESSP) (Bowen, Thompson, & Powers, 2012) are commercially available screening systems. Other free systems are also available, such as those offered by the Community and Youth Collaborative Institute (CAYCI; available at http://cayci.osu.edu). These systems rely on Likert-type rating scales to gauge risk factors associated with poor social, emotional, behavioral, and academic outcomes. However, each system focuses on different risk factors and practitioners must determine which scales are appropriate for their settings. For example, the BASC focuses on child-level internalizing and externalizing behaviors (e.g., authority problems, aggressive behaviors, and withdrawnness). By contrast, the ESSP and CAYCI tools focus on child behavior and contextual risk factors that create problems (e.g., poor peer–teacher relations, coercive parenting practices, caustic contextual influences, and disengagement) (Table 9.1).

## Differences Between Screening, Assessment, and Ongoing Performance Data

A distinction needs to be made between screening and assessment and what is often referred to as "ongoing performance data." Many school personnel using MTSS models utilize existing types of data as "screening" data to identify students who are at- or in-risk. For example, office disciplinary referrals, attendance rates, truancy referrals, dropout rates, free and reduced lunch participation, grades, and achievement scores are common sources of data used in MTSS models. These data, which are regularly collected and readily available in school settings, are then used to drive decisional systems surrounding the allocation resources and the application of EBTs for struggling students. Although these data are excellent indicators of ongoing progress monitoring, *they are not screening tools*. Highlighting this misperception, the National Center on Response to Intervention lists 48 "screening" tools that actually measure concurrent academic performance. Similarly, the Technical Assistance Center for PBIS lists office referrals, attendance rates, and grades as "screening" indicators (2013, http://www.rti4success.org/). However, measures of concurrent student academic (i.e., test scores and grades) or behavioral performance (e.g., office referrals and classroom observations) are *reactive* types of information describing the intensity and frequency of an existing problem. These measures can assist us to monitor the effect of EBTs at the universal, selective, and indicated levels of prevention. However, these sources of data do not proactively identify (or screen) youth at- or in-risk of developing poor outcomes. If a school is relying on these data as "screening" tools, the problem is already in place and the question then becomes "How large is the problem?" or "Are these efforts reducing the influence of the problem?" To properly build an evidence-based MTSS model, SSWers should use early screening tools to identify individual and contextual risk factors that are predictive of later problems (Bowen et al., 2012).

## STEP 2: IDENTIFYING UNIVERSAL, SELECTIVE, AND INDICATED CONCERNS

Using a screening and assessment system, EBP SSWers can examine the aggregate student scores to identify universal risk factors (Table 9.2). Conversely, SSWers can disaggregate the data to identify subgroups and individual students requiring more targeted supports. These data direct EBP SSWers to (1) identify universal EBTs that address the highest school-level risk factors, (2) identify students in need of more targeted selective and indicated EBTs (discussed in Chapter 10), (3) identify specific domains of risk for those groups and individual students, and (4) develop a work plan to identify EBTs to mitigate those risks. These data also provide school teams with a baseline for comparing post-test screening and assessment scores to appraise the effect of those efforts.

### Table 9.2:  Step 2 Assessment Resources

| Area of Concern | Instruments |
| --- | --- |
| Multidomain screening systems | • Strengths and difficulties questionnaire<br>• Elementary school success profile |
| Social, behavioral, and emotional assessments | • Child behavior checklist<br>• Behavior assessment system for children<br>• Social skills improvement system |
| Classroom behavior and attention | • Direct behavior rating<br>• Vanderbilt ADHD diagnostic scales |
| Depression and anxiety (including suicide screening) | • Children's depression inventory<br>• Center for epidemiologic studies depression scale<br>• Columbia health and suicide screen |
| Exposure to trauma | • Child posttraumatic stress reaction index |

### STEP 3: IMPLEMENTING A CONTINUUM OF EVIDENCE-BASED TREATMENTS: UNIVERSAL, SELECTIVE, AND INDICATED LEVELS

Following screening, assessment, and identification, school professionals should use those data to select universal, selective, and indicated supports. The ESSP, for example, offers a free online database of EBTs that are connected to the domains of risk assessed by the ESSP (https://www.schoolsuccessonline.com/resources/best-practices.aspx). The CAYCI project also has information on EBTs connected to concerns that are assessed at the school level using the CAYCI tools (http://cayci.osu.edu/surveys/your-results). Using data from the ESSP or CAYCI tools, school personnel can identify schoolwide and targeted (selective and indicated) risks or areas of concern. Once the concerns are noted, SSWers can select EBTs that target those risk factors. Although many tiered EBTs or prevention supports are practices (e.g., formative feedback, praise, well-defined expectations), other supports consist of programs that are manualized and packaged for broader dissemination. In this chapter, only a few universal or schoolwide EBTs are addressed. For information on targeted selective and indicated EBTs, see Chapter 10.

## Universal Evidence-Based Treatments: Schoolwide, Classroom Management, and Curricula

Universal prevention approaches facilitate effective and nurturing school environments in which students can engage in appropriate social exchanges amid supportive adults (Sprick, Garrison, & Howard, 2002; Sugai & Horner, 2006). Common elements of effective universal EBTs that facilitate supportive school cultures include

- establishing clear social and behavioral expectations in all school settings;
- teaching those expectations on a regular basis;
- providing high rates of positive attention and positive teacher–student interactions when students are observed meeting those expectations; and
- enforcing consistent and equitable consequences for student conduct violations.

Schoolwide prevention programs focus on a variety of areas, including school safety, bullying prevention, trauma awareness, crisis intervention, threat assessment, inclusion policies, and parent involvement. Many additional resources are available to assist SSWers to select universal schoolwide EBTs (c.f. www.pbis.org or http://www.interventioncentral.org). Two widely used tier 1 strategies are described next, followed by examples of classroom management programs and evidence-based curricula to address school-level risks.

## Positive Behavioral Intervention Supports

This approach to creating positive school climate is essentially MTSS applied to social behavior. It emphasizes several elements in common with MTSS, including universal screening, continuous progress monitoring, data-based decision-making, implementation fidelity, and evidence-based interventions (see http://www.pbis.org/school/swpbis-for-beginners/pbis-faqs). PBIS is built on five key elements that define the process of systems interacting within school settings to optimize school climate and student behavior possibilities: (1) team-based leadership, (2) data-based decision-making, (3) continuous monitoring of student behavior, (4) regular universal screening, and (5) effective ongoing professional development. In this approach, which is not a curriculum or set of manualized steps, school administrators and faculty set goals of achieving positive school climate through clear behavioral instruction, non-escalating methods of intervention and application of consequences for misbehavior, preemptively facilitating positive student interactions instead of reacting to misbehavior, evaluating the processes and outcomes, and establishing a feedback loop so that the system of supports for positive school climate continuously improves (Barrett, Bradshaw, & Lewis-Palmer, 2008; Bui, Quirk, & Almazan, 2010). This whole-school approach to changing student and teacher interactions often focuses on changing staff and faculty behavior toward students who misbehave. Outcome data often referenced in support of PBIS are reductions in office referrals, suspensions, expulsions, and dropouts from school prior to graduation (Bradshaw et al., 2008; Bui et al., 2010). Studies in Maryland, North Carolina, and Iowa on schools implementing PBIS have shown office disciplinary referrals declined by as much as 33–42% while fidelity remained high across the years in all districts studied in those three states (Bui et al., 2010).

## Safe & Civil Schools

This schoolwide approach to improving school climate and culture shares much of the same structure as PBIS. Led by Dr. Randy Sprick from the University of Oregon, *Safe & Civil Schools* focuses on changing staff–student interactions from punitive and reactive to positive and proactive through the establishment of clear behavioral expectations (see http://www.safeandcivilschools.com). The program utilizes the acronym STOIC to guide site-based decisions on how best to improve school climate and culture. STOIC stands for *s*tructure for success, *t*each expectations, *o*bserve student behavior, *i*nteract positively, and *c*orrect fluently. According to the evaluation of a large urban school district implementing the Safe & Civil Schools program, school suspensions declined and staff perceptions of student behavior improved versus those of control group schools that had not yet entered the program (Ward & Gerstein, 2013).

---

## CASE STUDY

In a large urban school district in California, teams of elementary school administrators, key teachers, and the SSWers participated in a series of trainings presented by the Safe & Civil Schools team. For one particular kindergarten through eighth grade school, SSWer Dominique played an active role as the team created behavioral expectations for students, developed methods for ensuring that all students understood the expectations, and posted those expectations so that students would see them daily. The team identified problem areas on the physical campus where misbehavior and lack of supervision coexisted regularly, according to data gathered by the team. These areas included the bathrooms, certain hidden areas on the playground that were just out of the sightlines of playground supervisors, the cafeteria, and certain passageways in between buildings that were used during times of student transitions from one activity to another. By redesigning the zones of supervision, much of these unwatched areas became more public, and the misbehavior decreased simply by increasing oversight.

The team also created signage reinforcing the behavioral standards of the school by applying the perspective that behavioral expectations have to be taught. The team understood the assertion by the Safe & Civil Schools' trainers that most educators assume students know how to behave and only act out due to personal feelings toward staff and administrators. Through data culled from schoolwide surveys, the team learned that students felt unsafe and that their misbehavior primarily stemmed from that feeling of insecurity. Dominique helped reinforce this understanding, utilizing her expertise in the ecological perspective and trauma-informed schools to support the rest of the team in devising solutions.

As the team returned to the school site after each monthly training session, there were grumblings from school staff regarding the amount of time that the team was spending in training. During on-site staff meetings in which the plan to transform the school's climate and culture was regularly presented, teachers openly expressed frustration at another quick-fix solution being handed down from administration. Teachers viewed the program as one more way to force them to keep students who disrupted class in the classroom without being able to utilize the principal's office as a respite. Many of them interpreted these new expectations as administration abdicating its responsibilities. And yet the number of office disciplinary referrals began to decline, instructional time increased, the number of fights on the playground decreased, and the number of out-of-school suspensions declined. The school climate began to improve.

The SSW worked with teachers on how to deliver the behavioral expectations to their classes, helping them understand what the team had understood regarding the importance of safety in anchoring students' behaviors and abilities to meet expectations (see also the next section). She worked with teachers to find creative ways to interact positively with students five times more often than interacting negatively, including encouraging them to implement a greeting system for individual students as they entered class. This simple but effective method pushed teachers to maximize class time by being prepared and emotionally ready for the start of school each day. Dominique worked with a small group of students and teachers to help them learn a new song that incorporated the newly created school behavioral expectations, and she organized a contest across the grade levels in which classes presented the song in the most creative way during a specially created assembly celebrating safety.

Meanwhile, other members of the team addressed playground supervisors' resistance to the new zones of supervision, teachers' uncertainty about the new changes, parents' curiosity and desire for involvement in developing the changes, and students' testing the willingness of the whole school to adhere to the new expectations. As each team member accomplished his or her assigned tasks and continued in monthly training with technical assistance as needed, the school transformed and referrals, suspensions, and truancies were all reduced by 37–54%. Although not the driving force behind the complete change in culture, Dominique was an important team member whose expertise helped the team take the important step from skepticism to acceptance of new ways of teaching students and improving climate.

## Classroom Management Supports

Teachers need guidance and support from SSWers to focus on positive student behaviors. Several studies have highlighted that teachers are more likely to react to negative student behaviors than to praise positive student interactions (Beaman & Wheldall, 2000; Chalk & Bizo, 2004; Clunies-Ross, Little, & Kienhuis, 2008; Reinke, Herman, & Stormont, 2013). To accurately rebalance these responses, it is recommended that teachers provide five positive student interactions to every admonishment for inappropriate behaviors (Clunies-Ross et al., 2008). Engaging in this simple practice can have positive classwide effects on student behaviors. Beyond classroom support strategies, classroom management programs focus on encouraging positive and expected student behaviors. For example, the Good Behavior Game—renamed PAX—was developed in the 1960s to encourage effective classroom management skills (Barrish, Saunders, & Wolf, 1969). PAX has been rigorously evaluated in more than 20 randomized studies, with results favoring treatment groups on a range of proximal and distal outcomes (Biglan, Flay, Embry, & Sandler, 2012; Dolan et al., 1993; Embry, 2002; Medland & Stachnik, 1972).

Other packaged programs exist to assist teachers to learn effective classroom management strategies. For example, the Incredible Years Teacher Classroom Management (IY TCM) program aims to cultivate effective classroom environments. Sharing many of the concepts targeted by PAX, the IY TCM extends strategies to promote positive teacher–student interactions using a video-based and peer teacher coaching format. Randomized studies suggest IY TCM increased prosocial behaviors, emotional regulation skills, and school readiness among students (Webster-Stratton, Reid, & Stoolmiller, 2008).

Beyond the elementary level, similar effects have been found for teacher training programs on middle and high school student outcomes. For instance, a teacher consultation program called My Teaching Partner (MTP) was tested, and the results of the study were published in the journal *Science*. A robust study, the findings from MTP suggested the program increased academic achievement of middle school students. Indeed, the improved academic outcomes were caused by increases in student autonomy, a program target of MTP (Allen et al., 2011). That is, although MTP did not provide students with explicit academic or autonomous instructional supports, the program taught strategies and skills to teachers that increased their capacity to promote student autonomy and that, in turn, encouraged increases in academic and social competence. In summary, EBP SSWers do not need to be experts in classroom management, but they do need to know where to find evidence of existing EBTs or programs that target improvements in teacher classroom management skills.

## Curricula

With regard to teaching students social and emotional competencies, there are many social-emotional learning (SEL) programs that have been evaluated in rigorous studies. However, not all SEL programs are equal. In a review of more than 200 SEL programs, the Collaborative for Academic, Social, and Emotional Learning (Durlak, Weissberg, Dymnicki, Taylor, & Schellinger, 2011) recommended 22 "select" programs for use in schools (see http://www.casel.org). Common elements of successful programs included (1) the creation of safe, caring, and well-managed learning environments; and (2) an increase in student knowledge of self-awareness, social awareness, self-management, relationship skills, and responsible decision-making. Recommended programs that address these aspects of successful SEL programs include Second Step (SS) for elementary students (Grossman et al., 1997) and Promoting Alternative THinking Strategies (PATHS) for middle and high school students (Greenberg, Kusche, Cook, & Quamma, 1995).

This chapter describes PATHS in more detail given its widespread application and rigorous research conducted in the United States and other nations. PATHS is a comprehensive SEL curriculum for children in pre-kindergarten through sixth grade. PATHS skills are designed to be taught by a classroom teacher or SSWers using two or three in-class sessions per week. Skills are sequenced and organized to impart knowledge regarding self-control, emotional understanding, positive self-esteem, relationships, and interpersonal problem-solving skills. PATHS lessons are scripted, include active learning lessons, and the program has been rigorously evaluated over 30 years. In one study, students in special education were observed to have lower risk for internalizing and externalizing symptoms during a 3-year period (Kam, Greenberg, & Kusche, 2004). However, relatively recent studies in the United States and Europe have reported mixed findings for SEL programs (Ross, Sheard, Cheung, Elliott, & Slavin, 2011; SACD, 2010). Though mixed, the balance of findings from early efficacy trials, systematic reviews, and recent effectiveness studies suggest that SEL programs mildly improve student and school outcomes (Durlak et al., 2011; Heckman & Kautz, 2012).

See Chapter 10 for more details on evaluating MTSS elements and SSW EBP.

## CONCLUSION

As a profession, school social work has been drawn into the delivery of special education services that have primarily placed our skill set in the context of mental health services to children and youth with Individualized Educational Programs. Training at the university level has focused more on clinical skill development than on macro practices such as program development or evaluation. Utilizing the MTSS framework, the largest area of intervention impacting the most people is clearly identified at the tier 1 level, where universal prevention and school climate improvement have the widest impact. As school reform efforts tackle inequitable disciplinary practices, the impact of trauma on student functioning, and the training and expectations of teachers in addressing student mental health behaviors, SSWers should spend consistent time weekly focusing on tier 1 programs and interventions. Because they have a systems perspective with an understanding and appreciation for the impact of the environment, their voices need to be heard by principals and key school stakeholders.

This chapter introduced the ideas of EBIs and EBTs as foundational perspectives to guide the macro practices associated with tier 1 work. Because school social work is a profession that often responds to one crisis after another, this chapter is intended to stress the importance of SSW involvement in program development impacting the whole school community. As the discussion turns from tier 1 prevention work to more targeted approaches in tiers 2 and 3 (see Chapter 10), the authors encourage the reader to continue to explore how tier 1 work should be considered in all problem situations on campus.

## REFERENCES

Barrett, S. B., Bradshaw, C. P., & Lewis-Palmer, T. (2008). Maryland statewide PBIS initiative: Systems, evaluation, and next steps. *Journal of Positive Behavior Interventions, 10*(2), 105–114.

Barrish, H. H., Saunders, M., & Wolf, M. M. (1969). Good behavior game: Effects of individual contingencies for group consequences on disruptive behavior in a classroom. *Journal of Applied Behavior Analysis, 2*(2), 119–124.

Beaman, R., & Wheldall, K. (2000). Teachers' use of approval and disapproval in the classroom. *Educational Psychology, 20*(4), 431–446.

Biglan, A., Flay, B. R., Embry, D. D., & Sandler, I. N. (2012). The critical role of nurturing environments for promoting human well-being. *American Psychologist, 67*(4), 257.

Bowen, N. K., Thompson, A. M., & Powers, J. D. (2012). A quasi-experimental test of the elementary-school success profile model of assessment and prevention. *Journal of the Society for Social Work and Research, 3*(3), 178–196.

Bradshaw, C. P., Reinke, W. M., Brown, L. D., Bevans, K. B., & Leaf, P. J. (2008). Implementation of school-wide Positive Behavioral Interventions and Supports (PBIS) in elementary schools: Observations from a randomized trial. *Education and Treatment of Children, 31*(1), 1–26.

Bui, X., Quirk, C., & Almazan, S. (2010). *Positive Behavioral Interventions and Supports*. Hanover, MD: Maryland Center on Inclusive Education.

Chalk, K., & Bizo, L. A. (2004). Specific praise improves on-task behaviour and numeracy enjoyment: A study of year four pupils engaged in the numeracy hour. *Educational Psychology in Practice, 20*(4), 335–351.

Cicchetti, D., & Cohen, D. (2006). *Developmental psychopathology*. Hoboken: NJ: Wiley.

Clunies-Ross, P., Little, E., & Kienhuis, M. (2008). Self-reported and actual use of proactive and reactive classroom management strategies and their relationship with teacher stress and student behaviour. *Educational Psychology, 28*(6), 693–710.

Dolan, L. J., Kellam, S. G., Brown, C. H., Werthamer-Larsson, L., Rebok, G. W., Mayer, L. S., ... Wheeler, L. (1993). The short-term impact of two classroom-based preventive interventions on aggressive and shy behaviors and poor achievement. *Journal of Applied Developmental Psychology, 14*(3), 317–345.

Durlak, J. A., Weissberg, R. P., Dymnicki, A. B., Taylor, R. D., & Schellinger, K. B. (2011). The impact of enhancing students' social and emotional learning: A meta-analysis of school-based universal interventions. *Child Development, 82*(1), 405–432.

Embry, D. D. (2002). The Good Behavior Game: A best practice candidate as a universal behavioral vaccine. *Clinical Child and Family Psychology Review, 5*(4), 273–297.

Gambrill, E. (1999). Evidence-based practice: An alternative to authority-based practice. *Families in Society, 80*(4), 341–350.

Gibbs, L. E. (2003). *Evidence-based practice for the helping professions: A practical guide with integrated multimedia* (Vol. 1). Pacific Grove, CA: Brooks/Cole.

Green, L. W. (2006). Public health asks of systems science: To advance our evidence-based practice, can you help us get more practice-based evidence? *American Journal of Public Health, 96*(3), 406.

Greenberg, M. T., Kusche, C. A., Cook, E. T., & Quamma, J. P. (1995). Promoting emotional competence in school-aged children: The effects of the PATHS curriculum. *Development and Psychopathology, 7*, 117–117.

Gresham, F. M., & Elliott, S. N. (1990). *Social skills rating system: Preschool, elementary level*. Circle Pines, MN: American Guidance Service.

Grossman, D. C., Neckerman, H. J., Koepsell, T. D., Liu, P.-Y., Asher, K. N., Beland, K., ... Rivara, F. P. (1997). Effectiveness of a violence prevention curriculum among children in elementary school. *JAMA, 277*(20), 1605–1611.

Harlacher, J. E., Sakelaris, T. L., & Kattelman, N. M. (2014). Multi-tiered system of support. In *Practitioner's guide to curriculum-based evaluation in reading* (pp. 23–45). New York, NY: Springer.

Heckman, J. J., & Kautz, T. (2012). Hard evidence on soft skills. *Labour Economics, 19*(4), 451–464.

Horner, R. H., Sugai, G., Smolkowski, K., Eber, L., Nakasato, J., Todd, A. W., & Esperanza, J. (2009). A randomized, wait-list controlled effectiveness trial assessing school-wide positive behavior support in elementary schools. *Journal of Positive Behavior Interventions, 11*(3), 133–144.

Howard, M. O., McMillen, C. J., & Pollio, D. E. (2003). Teaching evidence-based practice: Toward a new paradigm for social work education. *Research on Social Work Practice, 13*(2), 234–259.

Kam, C.-M., Greenberg, M. T., & Kusche, C. A. (2004). Sustained effects of the PATHS curriculum on the social and psychological adjustment of children in special education. *Journal of Emotional and Behavioral Disorders, 12*(2), 66–78.

Kamphaus, R., & Reynolds, C. (2007). *Behavior Assessment System for Children—Second Edition (BASC-2): Behavioral and Emotional Screening System (BESS).* Bloomington, MN: Pearson.

Medland, M. B., & Stachnik, T. J. (1972). Good-behavior game: A replication and systematic analysis. *Journal of Applied Behavior Analysis, 5*(1), 45–51.

Offord, D. R., Kraemer, H. C., Kazdin, A. E., Jensen, P. S., & Harrington, R. (1998). Lowering the burden of suffering from child psychiatric disorder: Trade-offs among clinical, targeted, and universal interventions. *Journal of the American Academy of Child & Adolescent Psychiatry, 37*(7), 686–694.

Reinke, W. M., Herman, K. C., & Stormont, M. (2013). Classroom-level positive behavior supports in schools implementing SW-PBIS: Identifying areas for enhancement. *Journal of Positive Behavior Interventions, 15*(1), 39–50.

Reinke, W. M., Herman, K. C., & Tucker, C. M. (2006). Building and sustaining communities that prevent mental disorders: Lessons from the field of special education. *Psychology in the Schools, 43*(3), 313–329.

Rubin, A., & Babbie, E. R. (2012). *Brooks/Cole empowerment series: Essential research methods for social work.* Pacific Grove, CA: Brooks/Cole.

Sackett, D. L., Rosenberg, W., Gray, J., Haynes, R. B., & Richardson, W. S. (1996). Evidence based medicine: What it is and what it isn't. *British Medical Journal, 312*(7023), 71–72.

Social and Character Development Research Consortium. (2010). *Efficacy of schoolwide programs to promote social and character development and reduce problem behavior in elementary school children.* Washington, DC: National Center for Education Research, Institute of Education Sciences, US Department of Education.

Sprick, R., Garrison, M., & Howard, L. (2002). *Foundations: Establishing positive discipline policies: Module I: The process; Module II: Behavior in the common areas; Module III: Safety, discipline and behavior support.* Eugene, OR: Pacific Northwest Publishing.

Sugai, G., & Horner, R. R. (2006). A promising approach for expanding and sustaining school-wide positive behavior support. *School Psychology Review, 35*(2), 245.

Sugai, G., & Horner, R. H. (2009). Responsiveness-to-intervention and school-wide positive behavior supports: Integration of multi-tiered system approaches. *Exceptionality, 17*(4), 223–237.

Thompson, A. M. (2012). Improving classroom conflict management through positive behavior supports. In M. B. H. Cynthia Franklin & Paula Allen-Meares (Eds.), *The school services sourcebook: A guide for school-based professionals* (2nd ed., pp. 491–506). New York, NY: Oxford University Press.

Thompson, A. M., Reinke, W. M., & Herman, K. C. (2016). Promoting social emotional learning for children with special needs. In C. R. Massat, M. S. Kelly, & R. Constable (Eds.), *School social work: Practice, policy, and research* (8th ed.). Chicago, IL: Lyceum.

Walker, H. M., & Severson, H. H. (1992). *Systematic screening for behavior disorders.* Longmont, CO: Sopris West.

Ward, B., & Gersten, R. (2013). A randomized evaluation of the safe and civil schools model for positive behavioral interventions and supports at elementary schools in a large urban school district. *School Psychology Review, 42*(3), 317.

Webster-Stratton, C., Reid, J. M., & Stoolmiller, M. (2008). Preventing conduct problems and improving school readiness: Evaluation of the Incredible Years teacher and child training programs in high-risk schools. *Journal of Child Psychology and Psychiatry, 49*(5), 471–488.

# CHAPTER 10

# MULTI-TIERED SYSTEMS OF SUPPORT

## *Targeted Evidence-Based Interventions*

### AARON M. THOMPSON AND JANE PIESTER

Chapter 9 discussed the application of universal or schoolwide evidence-based practices and interventions within a multi-tiered system of support (MTSS) to address social and academic concerns at the schoolwide level or the universal level. Although prior research suggests that schoolwide interventions applied with fidelity can effectively support a majority of students in a school, some students will require more intensive group and individualized supports. Therefore, the goal of this chapter is to expand the discussion of MTSS beyond schoolwide evidence-based practice and programs by focusing on targeted interventions, specifically selective (secondary) and indicated (tertiary) supports.

Because the knowledge here builds on the content of Chapter 9, readers should review the previous chapter. Failure to fully understand how all of the elements of an MTSS converge to create a comprehensive service model will not only result in a partial understanding of how MTSS models operate, how data are used to drive decisional systems within an MTSS, and how students with varying needs are served but also lead a school social worker to be less effective in his or her job. To continue the building of this discussion, we refer to Figure 9.2. Whereas Chapter 9 focused on school-level efforts to expose 100% of students to effective practices and programs (the base of the pyramid in Figure 9.2), this chapter focuses on the targeted interventions. Targeted interventions consist of selective or secondary group interventions for 15% of students and indicated or individualized interventions for 3–5% of students.

Furthermore, concepts discussed in Chapter 9 regarding the distinctions between evidence-based practice (EBP) and the application of evidence-based treatments (EBTs) hold true here as well. That is, EBP requires EBTs, but EBP is more than just the application of EBTs. School social workers (SSWers) can apply scientifically supported EBTs throughout their practice, but those SSWers will only be practicing from an EBP perspective if they are utilizing the data collection and practice evaluation strategies discussed in this chapter.

The goal of this chapter is to expand upon universal or schoolwide EBP by focusing on the application of selective and indicated EBTs for students who require additional supports. Before discussing these strategies, we address two caveats associated with targeted interventions: (1) the iatrogenic or unintended negative consequences referred to as *deviancy training* and *peer rejection* and (2) the need to increase cultural awareness and concerns about disproportional representation of low-income and non-White children in targeted interventions. Following these brief caveats, we discuss scientifically based selective and indicated treatment approaches. Last, we continue the discussion of the EBP model for SSWers by addressing evaluation strategies to determine the effect of EBTs on school, group, and student outcomes. The chapter concludes with a brief discussion of common barriers to applying the EBP model in school settings along with resources to address those barriers.

# CAVEAT 1: DEVIANCY TRAINING AND PEER REJECTION

In typical selective or secondary support services, youth with similar social, emotional, or behavioral concerns are grouped together and exposed to treatments targeting common risk factors. In these groups, concerns about iatrogenic effects due to peer contagion or "deviancy training" are often raised. Under such conditions, youth attending small group sessions acquire, practice, and reinforce each other's antisocial behaviors (Dishion & Tipsord, 2011). Beyond group interventions and in the case of students in need of intensive indicated or tertiary level supports, those students may be at risk of peer rejection due to their participation in the individualized supports. To be sure, some studies have suggested any intended efforts to convey positive knowledge and skills on students using selective group and indicated individualized treatments may be offset by the unintended consequences of deviancy training and peer rejection (Dishion, McCord, & Poulin, 1999; Fo & O'Donnell, 1975). However, the only existing meta-analysis on the topic does cast doubt on both the strength of the effect and the quality of the widely cited research supporting the phenomena of peer contagion in group and individualized treatments for youth with challenging behaviors (Weiss et al., 2005). Nonetheless, because research findings are mixed on the issue—and it is plausible that targeted interventions can cause unintended negative effects—precautions should be followed so that interventions intended to help students do not unintentionally do harm.

To reduce the plausibility of peer contagion, care must be taken to observe certain research-supported implementation protections. These protective mechanisms include considerations for participant age, group leader skills, positive relations with students, integrating positive peers, and reliance on structured formats (Dishion & Dodge, 2005; Gifford-Smith, Dodge, Dishion, & McCord, 2005). First, EBT interventions targeting younger students (<11 years; Weiss et al., 2005) suggest contagion effects are less likely to occur compared to targeted interventions with older students. Second, when intervention agents (i.e., school counselors, social workers, and psychologists) have adequate training and knowledge of the intervention and evidence-based strategies for leading groups, the likelihood that challenging student behaviors will be curtailed during training is increased. Third, school-based professionals are better equipped to address deviant verbal and nonverbal communications that reinforce unacceptable behaviors and interactions between students in small groups. Fourth, including positive peers in small groups or in individualized interventions reduces concerns about peer contagion and rejection (Hawken & Horner, 2003). Last, SSWers who rely on research-based, highly structured and active approaches to teaching will be more successful at curtailing any deviancy training in a group intervention (Dishion & Dodge, 2005; Gifford-Smith et al., 2005). Note that in prior studies of several of the interventions discussed in this chapter (e.g., Self-Management Training And Regulation Strategy and Coping Cat), no peer contagion effects were observed and both teachers and students reported favorable outcomes (Lochman, Barry, & Pardini, 2003; Magee, 2006; Thompson, 2014; Thompson & Webber, 2010).

## CAVEAT 2: CONCERNS FOR CULTURAL MINORITY YOUTH IN TARGETED INTERVENTIONS

Many youth requiring targeted interventions are struggling with cultural and behavioral expectations in school settings. Research strongly indicates that those students are frequently from low-income and non-White families (Skiba & Peterson, 2000; Smith, 2009). Because US schools predominately employ White, middle-class educational professionals, the expectations and rules that schools are predicated on reflect White, middle-class values. As such, these youth require support and guidance to unpack what Lisa Delpit (2006) calls the "culture of power." There are five aspects of the culture of power in schools: (1) The culture of power is played out in schools and classrooms; (2) there are unwritten rules defining participation in the culture of power; (3) those rules are defined by those who are in power; (4) explicit and honest training in those rules makes participating in the culture of power easier; and (5) those with power are least aware of the culture of power, whereas those without power are most aware of it (Delpit, 2006).

To help low-income and minority youth participate in the culture of power underlying school success, use direct language, help students clearly understand the expectations, and provide explicit instruction in how those students can achieve success. Be aware of how stereotype threat affects decisions (e.g., internalized belief structures that girls are not good at science or, conversely, Asian students are good at math). Last, adapt a "growth" mindset by cultivating the belief that competence is developed, talent is shaped, learning and change require practice and work, and mistakes and failure are clues to success rather than negative outcomes (Dweck, 2006).

## TARGETED EVIDENCE-BASED INTERVENTIONS: SELECTIVE AND INDICATED INTERVENTIONS

SSWers frequently coordinate targeted EBTs. As shown in Figure 9.2, targeted EBTs focus on providing direct services to students with elevated social, emotional, and behavioral concerns.

These services are in addition to universal supports. Furthermore, targeted EBTs are divided into selective (group) and indicated (individual) supports.

## SELECTIVE EVIDENCE-BASED INTERVENTIONS: FUNCTIONAL ASSESSMENT, SELF-MANAGEMENT, AND GROUP INSTRUCTION

Selective supports are usually small group interventions for students at risk of similar academic and/or behavior problems. Regardless, prior to considering selective social–emotional learning (SEL) supports for students, EBP SSWers must examine the implementation integrity or fidelity of universal EBTs. If a student has been truant from school or is not receiving exposure to schoolwide universal supports, then the SSWer should refrain from applying additional services to the student without first attempting to provide the student with exposure to existing schoolwide supports. In schools with effective universal EBTs (Figure 10.1), studies suggest that approximately 15% of students need more intensive selective supports. Next, several selective EBTs are described, specifically functional assessment strategies, self-management supports, and small group practices.

## Functional Assessment-Driven Interventions

It is important to consider the underlying function of a behavior before choosing a selective intervention for a student. In theory, all rational human behavior has an underlying function. In general, there are three common functions of human behavior: attention (from adults and/or peers), power/revenge (to be in or maintain control), and escape/avoidance of a situation (tasks or social situations). As such, determining the function or purpose of the behaviors displayed by a student in need of selective EBTs is relatively simple. SSWers may gather observational data to define the behavior and pinpoint what happens prior to the behavior (i.e., the antecedent) as well as what happens after the behavior (i.e., the consequence). These data can suggest environmental alterations before and after the target behavior that will facilitate a reduction in the occurrence of the behavior (Stormont, Reinke, Herman, & Lembke, 2012).

For example, a student who is aggressive (behavior) with peers may find peer interactions (antecedent) difficult and that engaging in aggression ends the interactions (consequence and function). The behavior may be due to the youth misinterpreting unclear social cues as antagonistic (e.g., believing peers are taunting when they are not), or it may be that the youth lacks the self-management or coping skills to regulate appropriate responses or to deal with peers who may indeed be taunting him or her. In either case, this student may benefit from a small group instructional approach targeting problem-solving, coping skills, and self-management skills.

## Self-Management

Self-management EBTs are useful approaches for assisting students to effectively manage their own behaviors. Some efficient strategies for supporting student development in these skill domains include behavioral contracting, self-monitoring, and teacher monitoring strategies. SSWers may use behavioral contracts (i.e., agreements defining expected behaviors and outcomes if the student meets the agreement). Using behavioral contracts has long been shown to be effective for increasing student self-control and productivity (Kelley & Stokes, 1984; White-Blackburn, Semb, & Semb, 1977). Behavioral contracts can be effective for students in need of selective supports when the function of behavior is considered. To increase the likelihood that the intervention will be effective, SSWers should connect reinforcements to the function of the behavior. That is, when a student exhibits a problem behavior that appears to be power maintained, a relevant reinforcement might be to offer the child a free "homework pass" to be used as he or she sees fit. Contracts are more effective when they include (1) student input, (2) goals that are achievable and provide ample opportunities for the student to meet the goals, and (3) direct instruction in the skills needed so that the student can perform the behavior. The contract should be typed; signed by the social worker, teacher, and student; and a copy should be provided to everyone involved (see Figure 10.1). Once implemented, if the contract does not improve the targeted behaviors, SSWers should revisit the plan to ensure the student is able to perform the expected behaviors, the terms of the contract are clear, and the reinforcers motivate and encourage positive student behavior.

---

## Behavior Contract

**TO:** PARENT/GUARDIAN AND STUDENT

[Aaron M. Thompson] will begin this contract on  today 9–17–15   to help him be successful at school related tasks.

**GOALS FOR STUDENT:**

1. *I will keep my body parts to myself.*

2.

3.

**REWARDS IF GOALS ARE MET:**

1. *Free get out of 1 homework assignment pass to be used at my discretion.*

2.

3.

We will review the terms of this contract on this date:  9–22–15

By signing this contract all parties agree to the stipulations in the document and will following accordingly.

_____*Aaron Thompson*_____
(Signature of Student                          Date

_____*Ms. Penny*_____
(Signature of Teacher)                         Date

_____*Mom* --------_____
(Signed Name of Parent/Guardian)       Date

_____*Mr. Doolittle*_____
(Signature of Principal)                       Date

_____*Jane Piester*_____
(Signature of School Social Worker)     Date

**FIGURE 10.1:** Sample behavior contract.

Self-monitoring is a multistage self-management intervention composed of self-assessment and goal setting, self-monitoring, self-recording, and self-evaluation (Thompson, 2010, 2014; Thompson, Ruhr, Maynard, Pelts, & Bowen, 2013; Thompson & Webber, 2010). During the self-assessment stage, students identify, define, and set goals to reduce or increase target behaviors. During the self-observation stage, students prompt themselves, reflect upon their behavior, and discriminate whether or not the behavior aligned with the goals. The self-recording stage consists of students documenting the observations using forms that span developmental age ranges from preschool to middle and high school (Figure 10.2). During the self-evaluation stage, students compare the performance with a predetermined goal. The self-evaluation stage may also include graphing observations, comparing current data with prior self- or current teacher observations, and using the data to formulate a new goal.

Meta-analyses suggest that self-monitoring is related to improvements in both academic and behavioral outcomes with large effects (effect size (ES) = 2.30–4.11) (Briesch & Chafouleas, 2009; Fantuzzo, Polite, Cook, & Quinn, 1988). To encourage increased autonomy support and direct student involvement, the Self-Management Training and Regulation Strategy (STARS) was developed by the first author (Thompson, 2012a, 2012b, 2014; Thompson & Webber, 2010). STARS is intended to be delivered by SSWers to students in need of selective EBTs. The program aims to promote student autonomy; increase student social competency; and improve relations between SSWers, teachers, and students. Two studies—a multiple-baseline, single-subject study across 10 students and a randomized control design with 108 students with challenging behaviors—suggest that STARS is feasible for students and teachers (Thompson, 2012a; Thompson & Webber, 2010). Furthermore, STARS has been shown to improve student behaviors (ES = 0.46), increase authority acceptance (ES = 0.47), expand social competencies (ES = 0.55), and enrich student relations with teachers (ES = 0.39).

|  | Before Lunch | After Lunch |
|---|---|---|
| Raise Hand | 😊 😐 ☹️ | 😊 😐 ☹️ |
| Stayed in Seat | 😊 😐 ☹️ | 😊 😐 ☹️ |

| Time | Completed Work | | Accepted Direction | | Stayed in Assigned Area | |
|---|---|---|---|---|---|---|
| 8:00-8:30 | Yes | No | Yes | No | Yes | No |
| 8:31-9:00 | Yes | No | Yes | No | Yes | No |
| 9:01-9:30 | Yes | No | Yes | No | Yes | No |
| 9:31-10:00 | Yes | No | Yes | No | Yes | No |
| 10:01-10:30 | Yes | No | Yes | No | Yes | No |

FIGURE 10.2: Sample self-monitoring recording sheets for elementary and secondary students.

## Teacher Monitoring

A teacher monitoring program called the Behavior Education Program (BEP) is a selective EBT (Crone, Hawken, & Horner, 2010) that is based on the check-in/check-out system (Cheney et al., 2009). BEP relies on daily progress monitoring to provide feedback to students. Expectations for student behaviors are defined, and students are provided immediate reinforcement for meeting behavioral expectations. Home–school communication is also emphasized by sending a progress report home each day to be signed and returned. The central elements of the BEP can be managed by SSWers and include (1) clearly defined expectations, (2) positive reinforcement for meeting expectations, (3) contingent consequences for problem behavior, (4) increased supportive contact with an adult at school, and (5) increased home–school communication. Research suggests that BEP is most effective in supporting students with problem behaviors maintained by attention (Mitchell, Stormont, & Gage, 2011).

## Small Group Instruction

Small group instruction is most useful for students who react to social cues in maladaptive ways. A number of social skills curricula can be used to support students in small group training formats. For example, the Coping Power Program (Lochman & Wells, 2002) is a small group-based selective prevention program designed for parents and their children who are in elementary school (grades 3–5). Social competence, self-regulation, and positive parental involvement are targeted by Coping Power. The program lasts 15–18 months and relies on small student and parent groups. Student topics include goal setting, anger management, perspective taking, self-awareness, mindfulness training, problem-solving, coping, and relationship skills. Parent group sessions are also available for SSWers who work as school outreach personnel with parents to develop positive parenting strategies such as giving effective feedback, rewarding appropriate child behavior, establishing effective home rules, and applying effective penalties for inappropriate child behaviors. Coping Power has been shown to increase positive behaviors and has been related to reductions in substance use and behavior problems at home and in school (Lochman et al., 2010; Lochman & Wells, 2002).

For younger children, the Incredible Years Small Group Dinosaur School Program (Webster-Stratton, Reid, & Hammond, 2004) was developed as a secondary support for students in preschool and early elementary grades. The program is delivered in 2-hour weekly small group sessions with approximately six children across 22 weeks. The program may be delivered by SSWers to teach students appropriate classroom behaviors, problem-solving strategies, social skills, feelings literacy, and emotional self-regulation skills. Ideally, it is offered in conjunction with the 2-hour weekly Incredible Years Parent Group sessions. Research indicates that the program increases student use of prosocial skills, improves social competence, and decreases aggressive behavior (Webster-Stratton et al., 2004).

## INDICATED EVIDENCE-BASED INTERVENTIONS: WRAPAROUND AND CASE MANAGEMENT

Indicated supports necessitate a team-based approach and should utilize all assessment, screening, and ongoing data collected from existing universal and selective responses to EBTs at those levels (e.g., discipline referrals, attendance, grades, functional assessment data, and self- and teacher monitoring data). Given the individualized nature of indicated strategies, student input is essential to developing a well-rounded plan. The most widely used indicated supports include special education and "wraparound" or intensive case management. Before proceeding to allocate indicated services, SSWers should examine the fidelity of universal and selective EBTs to be certain those practices are being fully implemented as designed. Because special education identification is a broader area with many procedural and substantive legal considerations beyond the scope of this chapter, here we discuss only wraparound services.

Wraparound is endorsed by the US Department of Health and Human Services, the Substance Abuse and Mental Health Services Administration, the National Institute of Mental Health, and consumer organizations such as the Federation of Families for Children's Mental Health and the National Alliance on Mental Health as an evidence-based approach to care for youth presenting challenging social, emotional, and behavioral issues. Although wraparound was designed as a community-based approach to mental health treatment for adults and youth, it has been successfully adapted for use in school settings (Eber, Sugai, Smith, & Scott, 2002). Also, although research has yet to unpack the most effective elements in the wraparound process, several randomized studies suggest school-based wraparound promotes higher rates of participation among team members compared to community-based wraparound. Studies have also suggested that school-based wraparound improves school attendance and reduces school suspensions, rearrests, and incidents of aggression (Carney & Buttell, 2003; Clark & Clarke, 1996; Clark, Lee, Prange, & McDonald, 1996). Importantly, from a case management perspective, wraparound improves linkages between schools, families, and community agencies; increases parent engagement at school; and assists students with challenging behaviors.

School-based wraparound does require SSWers to access training in the process to optimize the coordination of school, family, and community resources into a child and family plan with a set of measureable outcomes. The school-based wraparound process includes the following elements: (1) a school-based coordinator, (2) an individualized child-focused plan, (3) families who are full and active partners in the process, (4) a school team that includes support from community agencies, (5) access to flexible sources of financial support, (6) unconditional commitment of team members, and (7) outcomes that are transparent and measurable and written in a manner that provides accountability for completing the goal (Eber et al., 2002). A wraparound plan should assess strengths and areas of need as well as address problematic behaviors using a behavior intervention plan (BIP) that is based on existing functional classroom behavioral and academic performance data. If some of the problematic behaviors include aggression, the BIP should address emergency procedures for managing such behaviors.

# EVIDENCE-BASED PRACTICE SCHOOL SOCIAL WORKER STRATEGIES FOR EVALUATING SCHOOL, GROUP, AND STUDENT OUTCOMES

The screening and assessment data gathered as practice requirements for selecting EBTs in a tiered prevention model also serve as the baseline for school, group, and individual students. That is, these data produce a measure of functioning prior to the allocation of universal, selective, and indicated EBTs. However, to establish practice-based evidence, EBP SSWers must administer post-test measures at the end of the school year. Readministering screening instruments and brief assessments will allow SSWers to compare pre- and post-test scores at the universal school (i.e., average of all student scores), selective group (i.e., average scores of small groups of students), and indicated (i.e., scores of individual students) levels. Comparing post-test scores against baseline scores will assist SSWers and other staff to determine if the package of EBTs and prevention supports were successful in facilitating positive changes. There are several strategies to facilitate these types of data analysis, but primarily, SSWers can rely on average school and group scores and standard deviations to calculate what is known as an ES estimate:

$$d = (M_1 - M_2) / SD_{Pre}$$

This ES statistic, also known as Cohen's $d$, is estimated by taking the average of the pretest screening or assessment scores ($M_1$) for all students or small groups of students and subtracting the average post-test screening or assessment scores for that group ($M_2$). Last, the difference between baseline and post-test scores is divided by the standard deviation of pretest scores ($SD_{Pre}$; i.e., average variation in scores for all students at pretest). Effect size statistics are useful for communicating the degree of change within a group while also accounting for variation in pretest scores. In general, ES = 0.2 is considered mild, ES = 0.5 is considered moderate, and ES = 0.8 is considered strong (Rubin & Babbie, 2012).

In addition, the same process can be applied using the ongoing indicators of performance discussed previously (e.g., discipline referrals, attendance rates, truancy referrals, dropout rates, grades, and achievement scores) at the school, group, and student levels to determine if the tiered EBTs or prevention strategies were effective at reducing the number of office referrals or if rates of attendance increased from the prior school year to the current school year. Data for ongoing progress monitoring are important as a formative or process feedback tool to (1) monitor the gap between baseline and expected levels of functioning, (2) inform mid-course corrections, and (3) monitor the overall effectiveness of a package of tiered strategies (Shute, 2008). Data gathered as part of this process can be obtained through student and teacher report, direct observation, and using existing sources of data listed previously. The discussion now turns to the barriers that impede EBP and available resources to assist SSWers to overcome those barriers.

# BARRIERS FOR EVIDENCE-BASED PRACTICE SCHOOL SOCIAL WORKERS

Although SSWers are a valued asset in the educational system, several barriers may limit their effectiveness to engage in the EBP described here, including the following:

- Early prevention: Many schools do not hire elementary SSWers, which limits opportunities for early prevention and often results in early problems becoming exacerbated once students enter later grades.
- Lack of EBTs: Middle and high schools often require guidance counselors to provide classroom lessons regarding SEL, and the curriculum they access and provide to students may not be based on evidence-based models.

- Caseload: Often, the SSWer will be the only social work professional in his or her building. This may potentially affect the availability of services due to the size of the student population and the caseload assigned to the SSWer.
- Reactive versus proactive: Many SSWers find themselves to be in a reactive and crisis mode as opposed to a proactive or prevention planning role. This may be a result of insufficient time available to spend on developing programs and curriculum, as well as being viewed as the "go to" person when a crisis situation develops. Having the opportunity to tap into the expertise and wide array of problem-solving techniques that a SSWer can offer is an asset to school administrators.
- Support and collaboration—lack of opportunities for professional collaboration: Many districts have very few SSWers on staff, which may result in feelings of isolation.
- Lack of training: In states in which SSWers are not mandated, school districts may fill the "social work" role with unlicensed/noncredentialed individuals who do not have the education and/or background in social work. This can result in ineffective practice and can potentially cast a negative perspective on the skills and abilities of a SSWer.
- Limited planning time: SSWers in secondary schools are faced with the "bottom line" focus on graduation rates. There is often no time to spend doing literature reviews when there are pressures to focus primarily on grades, discipline, and attendance in developing interventions for serving those students at risk.
- Lack of investment: The scope of practice of school district employees is limited due to state and federal guidelines. Payment for services is not part of the equation, and therefore most interventions are brief, time-limited, and focused on crisis-based work.
- Contextual barriers: The work of SSWers must be performed within the context of the school day and calendar. This limits access to students on weekends, school breaks, and summer vacation.

In addition to daily practice barriers to the application of the EBP model, there are also barriers to selecting and applying evidence-based programs in school settings. First, the resource demands of many evidence-based programs make them unlikely options for implementation in school settings. Indeed, a cost analysis of 51 programs found that a majority of school-based programs cost between $1,001 and $10,000, and many programs require significant staff training or necessitate staff with specialized skill sets to implement those programs (Powers, Bowen, & Bowen, 2010). These requirements represent important barriers for SSWers seeking to adopt evidence-based strategies where budget shortages offer no discretionary time or funds to support the implementation of such supports. Interestingly, in a cost–benefit analysis of the most common school-based interventions, it was noted that the most expensive programs were not always the most effective (Powers & Thompson, 2013).

# RESOURCES FOR EVIDENCE-BASED PRACTICE SCHOOL SOCIAL WORKERS

To reduce the previously discussed barriers, many web-based resources are available to help social workers with each of the steps described in this chapter. This section discusses publically available resources to assist with each of the steps described previously.

## RESOURCES FOR SCREENING AND ASSESSMENT OF RISK FACTORS

Table 10.1 includes a range of screening and assessment instruments. Some of these instruments are publically available, and others cost money to access and use. In addition, SSWers should be aware of "compendiums" that address a range of tools tapping many different assessment needs on social emotional learning (http://www.isbe.net/learningsupports/pdfs/sel-compendium.pdf), mental health (http://www.schoolsocialwork.net/tools-for-screening-assessment-and-evaluating-pratice), and positive youth development outcomes (http://forumfyi.org/files/MeasuringYouthProgramQuality_2ndEd.pdf).

## RESOURCES FOR PLANNING FOR UNIVERSAL, SELECTIVE, AND INDICATED INTERVENTIONS

Resources for EBP abound. The following list presents some of the more common resources, but again, SSWers must be critical consumers of the content covered on these websites because

### Table 10.1:  Screening and Assessment Resources

| Developmental Domain | Risk Factors |
| --- | --- |
| Home and family | • Family management problems<br>• Coercive parenting practices<br>• Sibling dropped out of school<br>• Substance use<br>• Low education engagement |
| Neighborhood | • Availability of drugs or weapons<br>• High neighborhood crime and violence<br>• Community norms toward aggression/crime<br>• Low neighborhood collective efficacy<br>• High neighborhood social disorganization<br>• Saturation of low income |
| Peers | • Peer rejection/acceptance<br>• Friends with problem behavior<br>• Friends' acceptance of problem behavior |
| School | • Early academic failure<br>• Lack of behavioral, cognitive, and academic engagement<br>• Poor teacher–student relationship<br>• Large school/classroom |
| Individual/health | • High psychosomatic complaints<br>• Absences from school for illness<br>• Poor cognitive concentration |
| Individual/behavioral | • Early aggression<br>• Authority acceptance problems<br>• Poor social competency |

they use different criteria to determine if interventions are supported by evidence. The National Center for Education Evaluation and Regional Assistance's "Identifying and Implementing Educational Practices Supported by Rigorous Evidence: A User Friendly Guide" (http://ies.ed.gov/ncee/pubs/evidence_based/evidence_based.asp) may help determine if the interventions have "strong" evidence, "possible" evidence, or neither.

- What Works Clearinghouse: http://www.whatworks.ed.gov
- Blueprints for Healthy Youth Development: http://www.blueprintsprograms.com
- Promising Practices Network: http://www.promisingpractices.net
- Best Evidence Encyclopedia: http://www.bestevidence.org
- The Campbell Collaboration: http://www.campbellcollaboration.org
- Child Trends: http://www.childtrends.org
- The National Registry of Evidence-Based Programs and Practices: http://www.nrepp.samhsa.gov

## RESOURCES EVALUATING SCHOOL, GROUP, AND STUDENT OUTCOMES

Readers are encouraged to review the web center for Social Research Methods (http://www.socialresearchmethods.net), a free website dedicated to EBP professionals who seek to critically appraise findings from psychosocial and educational research studies to inform their practice.

# CONCLUSION

To become an EBP SSWer, one must cultivate an evolving awareness of existing and trending research in the areas of risk and protection, measurement, and EBTs that can be applied at the school, group, and individual student levels. However, simply applying strategies suggested in a handful of research studies is not enough to be an evidence-based school social work practitioner. That is, SSWers must also adapt the practice-based skills when applying evidence-based findings in practice settings to produce proof that those research findings are effective across multiple domains and levels. To guide SSWers to effectively cultivate positive and safe learning environments using the EBP framework in school settings, we must have a clear understanding of how to conceptualize and apply the EBP and EBTs within the MTSS response model (see Figure 10.1). We must also engage in practice-based evaluation to generate our own information communicating our effectiveness. As depicted in Figure 9.2, school EBP SSWers require a range of skills and knowledge that bridge or close the gap between research and practice. It requires a mindset that acknowledges the need to cultivate the skills, language, and concepts from both worlds—the research-driven evidence-informed world and the practice-based evidence world. When we are better able to accept the mindset that SSWers are responsible for closing the gap between research and practice, we will be better able to help all students develop the skills to be successful in school and life beyond.

# CASE STUDY

W. is a 16-year-old African American male who is a sophomore in high school. He lives with his biological mother and his stepfather. His biological father lives out of state, and W. has never had a relationship with him. His parents were never married. He has a severely handicapped older brother who requires 24-hour care and lives in their home. His mother attended post-secondary training and works in the health care field. She was recently diagnosed with colon cancer and is receiving chemotherapy treatments. His mother is still able to work, but the family income is much less due to her having to miss work more frequently. His stepfather does have a part-time job and contributes to the family income. W. is struggling with academics. He is failing multiple classes and is refusing to work during class time. He does have regular school attendance, but due to his insubordination, he is frequently removed from the classroom and sent to in-school suspension.

W. is an athletic individual and has aspirations to play football for the high school team. The one class that he is successful in is his weight training class, which is taught by the high school football coach. However, W. is aware that if he does not pass all his classes for the semester, he will be ineligible to play football in the fall. W. is well-liked by his peers and appears to have friends in school, but he does not generally socialize outside of school. He was recently referred to an after-school support program for high school boys who are involved in sports. This program is free and provides individualized tutoring, dinner, and mentoring. W. has attended a few times, but he often finds excuses not to attend. He offers reasons such as "My mom needed me at home" or "I didn't feel like going." During the previous school year, W. became unmotivated and exhibited some behavior problems in the classroom. He failed most of his classes, and because of the lack of credits, he was recommended for the Success Center for Grade 10. W. is currently enrolled in the Success Center for one class period every day, but even with the one-on-one assistance he is continuing to struggle. W.'s intelligence tests from elementary school were not of concern and showed above-average intelligence. W. has been referred to the student support team in order to seek recommendations to assist him in increasing academic performance and school success. The following questions may serve as a guide for the SSWer and multidisciplinary student support team as they respond to W.'s referral:

- Refer to Table 9.1. Where would you place W's most significant area(s) of concern?
- What types of interventions might you recommend that the school implement?
- Would this student benefit from wraparound? If so, what goals might the plan include?
- Could this student benefit from mental health counseling?
- How do the health concerns of W.'s mother potentially affect his school performance?
- What are the strengths that can be identified in both school and family settings?

## FOLLOW-UP

The SSWer's role in this case study was that of a facilitator with the multidisciplinary student support team, as well as coordinating wraparound services for the student and family. The student support team made the following recommendations:

Set up meeting with W.'s mother and stepfather to share school concerns.

Ask the football coach to talk to W. about classroom behaviors, academics, and the potential effect on eligibility to play for the high school football team.

Develop behavior plan for W. that outlines classroom expectations. Meet with W. to review plan. Meet with teachers to provide details of behavior plan, answer questions regarding teacher role/responsibilities, and provide support and encouragement.

Pursue referral for W. to receive counseling services from outside therapist to address anger issues.

The SSWer was able to meet with W. and his parents soon after the support team meeting. The parents were angry with W., but ultimately they were able to communicate their desire for his school success and agreed to work closely with the school to provide consistency with expectations for W. W. responded very well to the one-on-one discussion with the football coach as well as the clear behavior expectations that were developed. W. refused to meet with an outside therapist, but he was agreeable to meet on a regular basis with the SSWer to work on anger issues and develop strategies that would alleviate him being sent out of class. W.'s teachers reported that classroom behaviors were markedly improved, which resulted in W. remaining in class instead of being sent to in-school suspension. As a result of W. being able to focus in class, his grades began to improve. W. developed a close relationship with the SSWer and was able to share how the stress of his mother's illness had carried over to the classroom. With improved grades, W. became eligible to play football for the school team. This provided him with a consistent opportunity for physical activity, which ultimately helped to provide a healthy outlet for W.'s stress and suppressed anger.

## ACTIVITY AND DISCUSSION QUESTIONS

Using the previously presented case study, individuals will select characters to portray; these may include student, parent(s), classmates, teacher, administrator, coach, and counselor. Spend a few moments reviewing the important facts from the case study, and as a group determine a *situation* that the characters can re-enact—for example, an in-school meeting with W. to talk about what types of supports/services may be put in place to improve school success. After the scenario is presented, the group may then proceed to reflect on the situation. Discussion questions might include the following:

- What was W.'s demeanor?
- How did the parents react? Angry, defensive, understanding?
- What role will the parents assume following this intervention? Has anything changed?
- What types of wraparound services might be suggested?
- How is W.'s progress going to be measured/evaluated?
- How can the after-school program become more of an attractive option for W.?
- Was any type of mental health evaluation suggested? If so, what type(s)?
- Who is going to be responsible for coordination of the plan?

## REFERENCES

Briesch, A. M., & Chafouleas, S. M. (2009). Review and analysis of literature on self-management interventions to promote appropriate classroom behaviors (1988–2008). *School Psychology Quarterly, 24*(2), 106–118.

Carney, M. M., & Buttell, F. (2003). Reducing juvenile recidivism: Evaluating the wraparound services model. *Research on Social Work Practice, 13*(5), 551–568.

Cheney, D. A., Stage, S. A., Hawken, L. S., Lynass, L., Mielenz, C., & Waugh, M. (2009). A 2-year outcome study of the check, connect, and expect intervention for students at risk for severe behavior problems. *Journal of Emotional and Behavioral Disorders, 17*(4), 226–243.

Clark, H. B., & Clarke, R. T. (1996). Research on the wraparound process and individualized services for children with multi-system needs. *Journal of Child and Family Studies, 5*(1), 1–5.

Clark, H. B., Lee, B., Prange, M. E., & McDonald, B. A. (1996). Children lost within the foster care system: Can wraparound service strategies improve placement outcomes? *Journal of Child and Family Studies, 5*(1), 39–54.

Crone, D. A., Hawken, L. S., & Horner, R. H. (2010). *Responding to problem behavior in schools: The behavior education program.* New York, NY: Guilford.

Delpit, L. D. (2006). *Other people's children: Cultural conflict in the classroom.* New York, NY: The New Press.

Dishion, T. J., & Dodge, K. A. (2005). Peer contagion in interventions for children and adolescents: Moving towards an understanding of the ecology and dynamics of change. *Journal of Abnormal Child Psychology, 33*(3), 395–400.

Dishion, T. J., McCord, J., & Poulin, F. (1999). When interventions harm: Peer groups and problem behavior. *American Psychologist, 54*(9), 755.

Dishion, T. J., & Tipsord, J. M. (2011). Peer contagion in child and adolescent social and emotional development. *Annual Review of Psychology, 62*, 189.

Dweck, C. (2006). *Mindset: The new psychology of success.* New York, NY: Random House.

Eber, L., Sugai, G., Smith, C. R., & Scott, T. M. (2002). Wraparound and positive behavioral interventions and supports in the schools. *Journal of Emotional and Behavioral Disorders, 10*(3), 171–180.

Fantuzzo, J. W., Polite, K., Cook, D. M., & Quinn, G. (1988). An evaluation of the effectiveness of teacher- vs. student-management classroom interventions. *Psychology in the Schools, 25*(2), 154–163.

Fo, W. S., & O'Donnell, C. R. (1975). The buddy system: Effect of community intervention on delinquent offenses. *Behavior Therapy, 6*(4), 522–524.

Gifford-Smith, M., Dodge, K. A., Dishion, T. J., & McCord, J. (2005). Peer influence in children and adolescents: Crossing the bridge from developmental to intervention science. *Journal of Abnormal Child Psychology, 33*(3), 255–265.

Hawken, L. S., & Horner, R. H. (2003). Evaluation of a targeted intervention within a schoolwide system of behavior support. *Journal of Behavioral Education, 12*(3), 225–240.

Kelley, M. L., & Stokes, T. F. (1984). Student–teacher contracting with goal setting for maintenance. *Behavior Modification, 8*(2), 223–244.

Lochman, J. E., Barry, T., & Pardini, D. (2003). Anger control training for aggressive youth. *Evidence-Based Psychotherapies for Children and Adolescents, 2*, 263–281.

Lochman, J. E., Bierman, K. L., Coie, J. D., Dodge, K. A., Greenberg, M. T., McMahon, R. J., & Pinderhughes, E. E. (2010). The difficulty of maintaining positive intervention effects: A look at disruptive behavior, deviant peer relations, and social skills during the middle school years. *Journal of Early Adolescence, 30*(4), 593–624.

Lochman, J. E., & Wells, K. C. (2002). The Coping Power program at the middle-school transition: Universal and indicated prevention effects. *Psychology of Addictive Behaviors, 16*(4 Suppl.), S40–S54.

Magee, H. E. (2006). Teacher ratings of the perceived acceptability of school-based interventions (3252020 Ph.D.), The University of Alabama, Ann Arbor.

Mitchell, B. S., Stormont, M., & Gage, N. A. (2011). Tier two interventions implemented within the context of a tiered prevention framework. *Behavioral Disorders, 36*(4), 241–261.

Powers, J. D., Bowen, N. K., & Bowen, G. L. (2010). Evidence-based programs in school settings: Barriers and recent advances. *Journal of Evidence-Based Social Work, 7*(4), 313–331.

Powers, J. D., & Thompson, A. M. (2013). Evidence-based programs for schools: Relationships between effect sizes and resource requirements. *Journal of Evidence-Based Social Work, 10*(1), 299–307. doi:10.1080/15433714.2012.663664

Rubin, A., & Babbie, E. R. (2012). *Brooks/Cole empowerment series: Essential research methods for social work*. Pacific Grove, CA: Brooks/Cole.

Shute, V. J. (2008). Focus on formative feedback. *Review of Educational Research, 78*(1), 153–189.

Skiba, R. J., & Peterson, R. L. (2000). School discipline at a crossroads: From zero tolerance to early response. *Exceptional Children, 66*(3), 335–396.

Smith, S.-R. S. (2009). *Positive behavior support in schools—Universal intervention: Suspension rates and school climate in implementing middle schools*. PsyD dissertation, Fairleigh Dickinson University, Teaneck, NJ.

Stormont, M., Reinke, W., Herman, K., & Lembke, E. (2012). *Academic and behavior supports for children at risk for failure: Tier two interventions*. New York, NY: Guilford.

Thompson, A. M. (2010). A systematic review of evidence-based classroom interventions for students with challenging behaviors in school settings. *Journal of Evidence-Based Social Work, 8,* 304–322.

Thompson, A. M. (2012a). Improving classroom conflict management through positive behavior supports. In C. Franklin, M. B. Harris, & Paula Allen-Meares (Eds.), *The school services sourcebook: A guide for school-based professionals* (2nd ed., pp. 491–506). New York, NY: Oxford University Press.

Thompson, A. M. (2012b). *A randomized trial of the Self-Management Training and Regulation Strategy (STARS): A selective intervention for students with disruptive classroom behaviors*. Ann Arbor, MI: Proquest.

Thompson, A. M. (2014). A randomized trial of the Self-Management Training and Regulation Strategy for disruptive students. *Research on Social Work Practice, 24*(4), 414–427.

Thompson, A. M., Ruhr, L. R., Maynard, B. R., Pelts, M. D., & Bowen, N. K. (2013). *Self-monitoring interventions for reducing challenging behaviors among school-age students: A systematic review*. Retrieved from the Campbell Collaboration website at http://www.campbellcollaboration.org/lib/project/264.

Thompson, A. M., & Webber, K. C. (2010). Realigning student and teacher perceptions of school rules: A behavior management strategy for students with challenging behaviors. *Children & Schools, 32*(2), 71–79.

Webster-Stratton, C., Reid, M. J., & Hammond, M. (2004). Treating children with early-onset conduct problems: Intervention outcomes for parent, child, and teacher training. *Journal of Clinical Child and Adolescent Psychology, 33*(1), 105–124.

Weiss, B., Caron, A., Ball, S., Tapp, J., Johnson, M., & Weisz, J. R. (2005). Iatrogenic effects of group treatment for antisocial youths. *Journal of Consulting and Clinical Psychology, 73*(6), 1036.

White-Blackburn, G., Semb, S., & Semb, G. (1977). The effects of a good-behavior contract on the classroom behaviors of sixth-grade students. *Journal of Applied Behavior Analysis, 10*(2), 312–312.

# CHAPTER 11

# MENTAL HEALTH SERVICES IN THE SCHOOLS

*Collaboration in a Multi-tiered System*

KATERI PICARD RAY AND CHRIS AHLMAN

S chool social workers have had an important role in linking home, school, and community agencies in the delivery of services for children with emotional distress for more than 100 years (Rippey Massat, Constable, McDonald, & Flynn, 2008). The mental health needs of children and adolescents continue to demand that school social workers develop programs and provide mental health services supporting healthy social and emotional development of all children in 21st-century schools. This chapter provides an overview of the school in the provision of mental health services for children and prevention efforts. As a way to address the need for mental health services for children, this chapter discusses the importance of home, school, and community linkages as well as interdisciplinary collaboration. This chapter discusses the importance of the integration of prevention and intervention efforts in the delivery of mental health services that emphasize collaboration with school personnel, family, and community agencies. A multi-tiered model as outlined by the School Social Work Association of America (SSWAA; http://c.ymcdn.com/sites/www.sswaa.org/resource/resmgr/Res_Statements/Multi_Tiered_Systems_of_Supp.pdf) is used to demonstrate how evidence-based preventions and interventions can be modified to respond to developmental and cultural characteristics of the children and the school. Discussion includes how to develop the school–mental health community collaborations necessary for the model to be successful.

## CURRENT NEED FOR MENTAL HEALTH SERVICES IN SCHOOLS

The US Surgeon General's *Report on Mental Health* indicates that each year, 20% of children and adolescents in the United States experience symptoms of a mental health problem and 5%

experience "extreme functional impairment" (US Department of Health and Human Services, 1999). However, the Centers for Disease Control and Prevention (CDC) argues that an overall estimate of the prevalence of childhood mental disorders is not available from current data. A lack of consistency in survey methodology and definition as well as actual changes in prevalence rates prevents an accurate rate from being determined (CDC, 2013).

Although current prevalence rates differ by study, in general, attention deficit/hyperactivity disorder is most prevalent (7–9%), followed by depression (2–13%), behavioral or conduct problems (3.5–4.5%), substance use disorders (2.8–4.7%), anxiety (2–5%), autism spectrum disorders (1–2%), and Tourette syndrome (0.2–0.3%) (CDC, 2013). Some childhood mental disorders do not have regularly collected data, but available data report rates of between 0.3% (generalized anxiety disorder) and 19% (specific phobia) for a variety of anxiety disorders, 2.9% for Bipolar I or II disorder, and 0.1% for eating disorders (CDC, 2013).

Despite the CDC's reluctance to declare prevalence rates of mental disorders in childhood, the National Comorbidity Survey–Adolescent Supplement was undertaken with a nationally representative sample of US adolescents (10,123 adolescents aged 13–18 years) and reported the first prevalence data on a broad range of mental disorders (Merikangas et al., 2011). Researchers personally interviewed each participant using a modified version of the World Health Organization Composite International Diagnostic Interview to detect *Diagnostic and Statistical Manual of Mental Disorders* (DSM-IV) diagnoses. Their findings indicated that anxiety was the most common condition (31.9%), followed by behavioral disorders (19.1%), mood disorders (14.3%), and substance use disorders (11.4%).

Trauma is another pressing public health concern. In a recent study, 89.7% of adult respondents reported at least one exposure to a DSM-5 Criterion A (exposure to actual or threatened death, serious injury, or sexual violence) event (Kilpatrick et al., 2013). Specifically, 53.1% of respondents reported direct interpersonal violent victimization. Specific to children's experiences, a study conducted by the National Survey of Children's Exposure to Violence found that more than 60% of children surveyed were exposed to violence within the past year (Finkelhor, Turner, Ormrod, Hamby, & Kracke, 2009). Traumatic childhood experiences can lead to problems with academic performance, behavior, and relationships (Cole et al., 2009). Early identification, intervention, and continued follow-up can decrease the impact of exposure to violence (Finkelhor et al., 2009). A variety of community organizations share responsibility for responding to children exposed to trauma, including child welfare, juvenile justice, and mental health providers. Schools are a key partner to these organizations because they are the central community for most children (Cole et al., 2009). Schools implementing a trauma-informed or trauma-sensitive approach to school culture are experiencing significant reductions in school-related problems. Washington and Massachusetts are leading the way in developing trauma-sensitive approaches to school discipline. One school in Brockton, Massachusetts, experienced a 40% decrease in school suspensions, and in Walla Walla, Washington, school suspensions decreased by 85% following implementation of a trauma-sensitive approach (Stevens, 2012).

There is no denying that many US public school students have mental health needs, but of particular note are the most vulnerable students who experience poverty, immigrant or minority status, homelessness, LGBT orientations, the foster care system, high-crime/low-resource neighborhoods, homes with domestic violence, and/or characteristics likely to be bullied or harassed (Center for Mental Health in Schools at UCLA, 2014). For many of these students, mental health services must include collaboration with additional services that work to support the vulnerable areas of these student's lives.

# SERVICE DELIVERY FOR CHILDREN
# WITH MENTAL HEALTH NEEDS

Schools can be the location where teachers, administration, families, and mental health professionals work together to create a safe and mentally healthy school climate (Colorado Department of Education, 2007). The coordination of these stakeholders is often the job of the school social worker, whose role is to help all students benefit from the education offered them (Avant, 2014). This collaboration among the various stakeholders helps to break down social–emotional barriers using effective interventions aimed at helping students achieve academically and to go on to become productive citizens (Colorado Department of Education, 2007). School-based mental health services is one example of an effective intervention.

School-based mental health services (SBMH) is, by its nature, a combination of two systems: education and mental health. Effective collaboration has been difficult because the two systems have inherently different foci, language, and theoretical influences (Kutash, Duchnowski, & Lynn, 2006). Three major models of SBMH were identified by Kutash et al.: mental health spectrum, interconnected systems, and positive behavior support. The mental health spectrum approach provides traditional mental health interventions such as prevention strategies, psychotherapy, psychopharmacology, and maintenance/recovery interventions in the school setting (Kutash et al., 2006). The interconnected systems approach seeks to form an integrated continuum of services through collaboration of three systems: prevention systems, early intervention systems, and care for children with severe and chronic problems (Adelman & Taylor, 2012). The positive behavior support approach uses a functional behavioral assessment to understand problem behaviors and then decrease these behaviors by teaching new skills and changing a person's environment (Crone & Horner, 2003).

In addition to the models mentioned previously, many approaches to SBMH systems focus on identifying intervention levels as a way to distinguish interventions. A variety of classification systems for differing levels of prevention services currently exist. Most systems include the terms *universal, selective,* and *indicated* to describe increasingly focused prevention interventions. Generally, universal prevention targets the general public or a whole population. Selective prevention targets individuals or a subgroup at risk of developing mental health problems, and indicated prevention targets individuals with signs/symptoms foreshadowing mental health problems (Kutash et al., 2006).

An expanded model of prevention and treatment was offered by Weisz, Sandler, Durlak, and Anton (2005). Their model adds a less focused level of prevention termed *health promotion/ positive development*. This level targets entire populations with the goal of increasing strengths to reduce risk of problems later. They also included a more focused level of intervention termed *treatment*. This level targets those with high symptom levels or a diagnosed disorder.

Response to intervention (RTI) requires that progress toward student educational goals is monitored (US Department of Education, 2004). The tools offered by the government-funded website for the National Center for Response to Intervention focus on math, reading, and other academic goals. However, for monitoring progress of interventions or positive behavior supports that address behaviors specifically of children with mental health issues, school personnel need to find other sources (Ahlman, 2013).

The School Social Work Practice Model was developed by Frey et al. (2013) to address the social work professional's role in SBMH. This model is endorsed by the SSWAA. It consists of a framework of interacting components, including home–school–community linkages, ethical guidelines and educational policy, education rights and advocacy, and data-based decision-making. The practice model encourages school social work professionals to (1) provide evidence-based mental health services, (2) promote a school climate and culture conducive to learning, and (3) maximize access to school-based and community-based resources (Frey et al., 2013). Inherent in this model is the understanding of the individuality of each and every student and family. It is often the school social workers' responsibility to complete a comprehensive assessment including a social history that incorporates the concept of intersectionality of all characteristics and experiences to best explain the person-in-environment perspective of the social work profession (García & Ortiz, 2013). Often, it is the school social worker who recognizes the biological, cognitive, cultural, economic, and social diversity of students and is able to assess how these influence the student's identity and functioning (Alameda-Lawson, Lawson, & Lawson, 2010; Altshuler, 1997; Dunlap, 2014; Pagan-Rivera, 2014; Robles, Dettlaff, & Fong, 2013).

## CURRENT SCHOOL CLIMATE

The public school system in the United States has functioned for more than a decade under the mandates of Public Law 107–110 enacted January 8, 2002, better known as the "No Child Left Behind" Act (NCLB) (US Department of Education, 2010). The emphasis on academic achievement as defined by student performance on a set of standardized tests has forced schools to focus their educational efforts on preparing students to do well. This has marginalized the need to promote social and emotional development (Dollarhide & Lemberger, 2006). The Center for Mental Health in Schools at UCLA has proposed changes to be incorporated into the next reauthorization of the Elementary and Secondary Education Act (ESEA). Fortunately for students who experience barriers to learning such as mental health conditions, the current administration supports services that address the full range of student needs. This includes services for English learners and students with disabilities, Native American students, homeless students, migrant students, rural students, and neglected or delinquent students (US Department of Education, 2010).

The *Blueprint for Reform: Reauthorization of ESEA* includes provision of funds for "creating safe and disciplined school climates that promote student health and well-being" (US Department of Education, 2014). Understanding the person-in-environment perspective, the school social worker addresses school climate first through assessment (Birkenmaier, Berg-Weger, & Dewees, 2014). School climate measures such as the Comprehensive School Climate Inventory (http://www.schoolclimate.org) include assessment of safety, teaching and learning, interpersonal relationship, institutional environment, leadership, and professional relationships. The next steps are to implement programs and services that promote optimum school climate, which include supportive teaching practices and supportive development of social skills—effective listening, conflict resolution, self-reflection and emotional regulation, empathy, personal responsibility, and ethical decision-making (see http://www.schoolclimate.org). Finally, research indicates that these programs and services are only effective or are more effective when coordinated with the entire school curriculum to address the whole child and involve all the school staff (Elias, DeFini, & Bergmann, 2010). The school social worker is uniquely qualified to facilitate this coordination (School Social Work Association of America, 2013).

# COLLABORATION WITH MULTIDISCIPLINARY TEAMS

From as early as 1906–1907, the role of the school social worker has been the link between the school, the family, and the community (Franklin, Gerlach, & Chanmugam, 2012). Although school social workers in individual school settings may have very specified or limited roles to perform, the school social work profession remains committed to its historic liaison or linking role between the school setting, the student and his or her family, and the community. When delivering mental health services to children in the schools, this linkage provides the basis for the collaboration needed to ensure the participation of parents, the school's administration and staff, and the local mental health agency.

The SSWAA practice model emphasizes the role of school social workers in promoting interdisciplinary collaboration and identifies home–school–community linkages as a key construct for school social workers (Frey et al., 2013). As schools and community providers join forces to expand school-based mental health services, interagency collaboration is essential. In fact, Weist, Ambrose, and Lewis (2006) call the expanded school mental health framework "inherently collaborative." Although interdisciplinary collaboration is widely acknowledged as essential to school-based mental health, it is notoriously difficult to achieve in practice (Mellin, 2009). There are many reasons for this difficulty, including limited budgets and time, space, and personnel; lack of formalized training; and competing responsibilities (Powers, Edwards, Blackman, & Wegmann, 2013).

Because school social workers are the link between school, home, and community, they are in a distinctive position to promote cross-systems collaboration. Strategies for promoting collaboration are offered by Powers et al. (2013), who completed a study that evaluated the effectiveness of a school-based mental health project that developed a multisystem partnership between a school district, a public mental health agency, and a university. During the course of one school year, the program served more than 75 high-risk and vulnerable youth. Caregivers and teachers reported overwhelmingly that the project made a positive difference in academic and behavioral outcomes. Because the program was so successful despite a historical lack of mental health services in the school and a lack of systems collaboration, researchers examined how the administrators overcame barriers to collaboration. The researchers were able to identify four themes that impacted successful collaboration: (1) perceptions of the project (project significance, beneficial qualities, and importance of mental health), (2) barriers to collaboration (resistance to mental health, system silos, and lack of communication), (3) motivating factors (stakeholders, relationships, and timing), and (4) sustainability (expansion, funding, and need to show outcomes). Their evaluation showed a clear need for positive relationships and increased and open communication across systems for collaboration to be successful (Powers et al., 2013).

Successful collaboration requires effective communication between key stakeholders (Weist et al., 2006). School social workers can be instrumental in identifying and engaging with key stakeholders, including school leaders and administrators (school superintendent or principal), school mental health leaders (social workers, school psychologists, and school counselors), and the community mental health provider or agency director. School social workers can help these leaders acknowledge and address inherent agenda differences by integrating goals, contributing to each other's missions, and elevating the work to a high priority for all (Powers et al., 2013). Suggestions for improved communications and positive relationships include regularly scheduled meetings of leaders from both systems to discuss goals, status, and next steps (Powers et al., 2013).

Table 11.1:  Matrix for Assessing Supports in the School

| | | Subsystems for | | |
| --- | --- | --- | --- | --- |
| | | Promoting Healthy Development and Preventing Problems | Early Intervention | Intervention and Care |
| Areas of Intervention Content | In classroom | | | |
| | Support for transitions | | | |
| | Crisis response/prevention | | | |
| | Home involvement | | | |
| | Community engagement | | | |
| | Student and family assistance | | | |

*Source: Reproduced with permission from the Center for Mental Health in Schools at UCLA.*

# DEVELOPING A CONTINUUM OF SERVICES FOR INDIVIDUAL/GROUPS OF STUDENTS

According to the Center for Mental Health in Schools at UCLA, the matrix shown in Table 11.1 helps the school social worker assess the present state of supports for student learning and provides a plan for filling the gaps. The matrix is based on first acknowledging what an integrated full-service continuum of service might be.

Although a fully integrated continuum of services is the responsibility of the whole community, the school social worker is capable and competent to bring all stakeholders together to develop the full services necessary for all students to succeed academically. For further information on the matrix shown in Table 11.1, see Additional Resources at the end of this chapter.

# MENTAL HEALTH SERVICE DELIVERY USING MULTI-TIERED SYSTEMS OF SUPPORT

Pressure from a variety of sources for empirically based interventions for SBMH programs has led to a proliferation of programs that meet criteria as evidence based or empirically supported. Social work practitioners need to use available resources to keep up with the latest advancements in the field regarding evidence-based interventions. Resources include the Substance Abuse and Mental Health Services Administration's National Registry of Evidence-Based Programs and Practices, an online database of mental health and substance abuse interventions. For programs specific to school-based interventions, the School Services Sourcebook (Franklin, Harris, & Allen-Meares, 2013) covers a wide variety of evidence-based programs organized by problem area.

Evidence-based interventions are best categorized by the three tiers of the multi-tiered systems of support model. Prevention programs can be at the universal level addressing the needs of the general student population. Prevention programs at the selective level include interventions that are targeted to individuals or a subgroup at risk of developing mental disorders (Kutash et al., 2006). Prevention efforts at the indicated level are targeted to high-risk individuals who may have symptoms or signs of a mental disorder but do not meet criteria for a DSM diagnosis (Kutash et al., 2006). Interventions for students with serious mental health issues must be addressed by the school in collaboration with parents and community mental health agencies (Center for Mental Health in Schools at UCLA, 2011; Sheridan et al., 2012). For these cases, there must be collaboration and coordination with emergency and crisis treatment, long-term therapy, hospitalization, drug treatment, and other community services (Center for Mental Health in Schools at UCLA, 2011). This type of partnership can be difficult to achieve because these two systems—schools and community mental health—have their own policies about confidentiality and sharing information, payment for services, and goals for treatment (Garstka, Lieberman, Biggs, Thompson, & Levy, 2014). Because of the complexity in aligning systems and the importance of community knowledge, the role of the school social worker is integral in facilitating these types of services to students with severe mental health issues (D'Agostino, 2013).

Finally, the issue of funding must be addressed. To provide SBMH services, many schools fund some of the mental health services they provide to low-income students eligible for Early Periodic Screening, Diagnosis and Treatment (EPSDT) by billing Medicaid if the school has taken the steps to become a Medicaid provider (Bundy & Wegener, 2000). Due to the states' powerful discretion, this funding option varies greatly from state to state, even with an ambitious federal mandate. The Center for Health and Health Care in Schools (CHHCS) has been tracking the impact of the Affordable Care Act (2010) on SBMH services and has identified five states currently addressing issues of children's mental health services that have historically been lacking (see http://www.healthinschools.org/School-Based-Mental-Health.aspx). Although the Affordable Care Act expanded parity in mental health services, it is up to the state markets to respond (CHHCS, 2013). Illinois unanimously passed the Children's Mental Health Act (2003), which is an exemplar when adequately funded (see http://icmhp.org).

# PROCESS OF DEVELOPMENT
# OF MEASURABLE INTERVENTIONS

When providing a prevention or intervention strategy that is evidenced based, there must be ongoing evaluation of services provided whether working with individual students, small groups of students, or whole classrooms (Sabatino, Kelly, Moriarity, & Lean, 2013). First, it is important to identify the stakeholders involved in delivering programs and services, as well as establishing a system of accountability. How will they know when they have reached their goals? What process is in place to modify programs and services that are not meeting goals? The one constant in these interventions is that they are predicated on a set of goals developed, it is hoped, by the interventionist, the individual student, and the student's family taking all his or her unique characteristics and experiences into consideration while noting any vulnerabilities as listed previously in the chapter.

Whether addressing special education, 504 plans, whole classroom programs, or interventions for individual students, these goals are based on a problem-solving perspective that lends itself to collecting measureable data from a variety of specific criteria. Each goal needs a benchmark to be established. Once in place, a benchmark can be operationalized so that observation of it results in the ability to collect frequencies about it because interventions expect some behavior to increase or decrease. If at some point the intervention is not meeting the benchmark set collaboratively, then school, family, student, and community need to come together to problem solve the next steps. For example, a student with bipolar disorder is involved in Positive Behavior Supports at school, while her parents are receiving support and parenting classes in the community and while she sees her psychiatrist monthly for review of her medications and has weekly meetings with her therapist. The goal here is to stabilize her behavior so she can better function in the classroom and achieve passing grades. If she continues to achieve academically below passing standards, a meeting will be called to address whether she is in compliance with her interventions, whether there are barriers to her success, or whether there needs to be modification to the intervention or the benchmarks. This process of monitoring and evaluating is necessary at all levels of intervention to ensure the best outcome for students and the best use of resources for those involved in the prevention or intervention activities (Johnson et al., 2014).

## CONCLUSION

This chapter provided an overview of the need for school-based mental health services for students and included examples of evidence-based prevention and intervention efforts. The role of the school social worker in recognizing and facilitating important home, school, and community linkages was presented along with ways to develop and assess these linkages. A multi-tiered model as outlined by SSWAA was used to demonstrate how evidence-based preventions and interventions can be modified to respond to developmental and cultural characteristics of the children and the school through a comprehensive assessment that takes intersectionality into consideration to understand individuality. Issues related to school–community mental health collaborations were introduced so that practitioners understand that the differences in rules, protocols, and goals must be addressed up front. Finally, funding was introduced as a consideration for implementation of services and often a topic for advocacy.

---

## CASE STUDIES

### UNIVERSAL SCENARIO

Emily is a fifth grade teacher in an urban kindergarten through fifth grade school. She expresses her frustration to the school social worker because her class of 30 diverse students are in the habit of calling each other names as put-downs. The atmosphere in the classroom is somewhat hostile. She has tried to teach them the proper way to address each other, she has developed a zero tolerance policy in her classroom, and she has punished offenders. Still the problem occurs. The social worker and the teacher meet.

1. What level of intervention could be use?
2. Where could you find evidence-based programs that address name-calling?
3. If the school social worker chooses not to address this his- or herself, what other school or community programs or resources might be utilized?
4. Who would be responsible for the intervention?
5. What are some ways to measure the success of the intervention?

## TARGETED SCENARIO

Jan is a master's level school social worker in a small school district. She is responsible for providing social work services to several schools at the elementary and middle school levels. She has been concerned that a number of children in her schools have unidentified and unmet mental health needs. Tragically, two students have committed suicide at the district high school in the past year. Jan believes that early identification and treatment of mental health problems may reduce suicide risk in the future. She wants to approach school administrators to explore the idea of expanding school-based mental health services in her district.

1. Before she asks for a meeting, what elements does she need to consider?
2. Who are the key stakeholders?
3. How can Jan work to engage key stakeholders and reduce potential barriers?
4. Would Jan's approach be different if her school district was urban instead of rural?
5. Once you have helped Jan choose an intervention, how might she monitor its progress?

# ADDITIONAL RESOURCES

Center for Health and Health Care in Schools, mental health resources: http://www.healthinschools. org/School-Based-Mental-Health.aspx

Center for Mental Health in Schools at UCLA

The System Change Toolkit: http://smhp.psych.ucla.edu

*Mental Health in Schools: Moving in a New Direction*: http://smhp.psych.ucla.edu/pdfdocs/contschpsych. pdf

*School–Community Partnerships: A Guide*: http://smhp.psych.ucla.edu/qf/Commout_tt/School-Com2-8.pdf

Table 1. From Primary Prevention to Treatment of Serious Problems: A Continuum of Community–School Programs to Address Barriers to Learning and Enhance Healthy Development: http://smhp.psych.ucla.edu/pdfdocs/specialannouncements/table1.pdf

*Clarifying the Full Continuum: Risk, Protective Buffers, and Youth Development Factors*: http://smhp. psych.ucla.edu/pdfdocs/fullcontinuum.pdf

*Integrating Mental Health in Schools: Schools, School-Based Centers, and Community Programs Working Together*: http://smhp.psych.ucla.edu/pdfdocs/briefs/integratingbrief.pdf

Centers for Disease Control and Prevention: http://www.cdc.gov

Child Trauma Academy: This organization translates emerging findings about the human brain and child development into practical implications for the ways we nurture, protect, enrich, educate, and heal children: http://childtrauma.org

Collaborative for Academic, Social, and Emotional Learning (CASEL): This organization is the leader in the social–emotional development of children and they address what programs are effective in address this issue. http://www.casel.org

*Report of the Attorney General's Task Force on Children Exposed to Violence* (2012): http://www.justice. gov/defendingchildhood/cev-rpt-full.pdf

School Social Work Association of America: This organization is the national representative of school social workers and has developed many resources to enhance the productivity of the profession: http://www.sswaa.org

## SUCCESSFUL SCHOOL-BASED INTERVENTIONS

Jackson, T.: *Activities that teach* (a must in any school social worker's tool kit). The various books available give step-by-step instruction in how to engage youth in learning life skills: https://www.google. com/#q=tom+jackson+activities+that+teach

McCarthy, S. B., & Cummins Wunderlich, K. (2014). *Pre-referral intervention manual* (4th ed.). Columbia, MO: Hawthorne. This manual provides a direct response to state mandated pre-referral intervention activities.

Positive Behavioral Interventions & Support Technical Assistance Center: www.pbis.org

Substance Abuse and Mental Health Services Administration, *Trauma-Informed Approach and Trauma-Specific Interventions*: http://www.samhsa.gov/nctic/trauma-interventions

## EVALUATION TOOLS FOR IMPROVING STUDENT OUTCOMES

National School Climate Center, *The Comprehensive School Climate Inventory*: https://www.schoolcli-mate.org/climate/documents/How_CSCI_was_developed.pdf

# REFERENCES

Adelman, H. S., & Taylor, L. (2012). Mental health in schools: Moving in new directions. *Contemporary School Psychology, 16*, 9–18.

Ahlman, C. (2013). Positive behavior supports for children with major mental illness: Working with teachers and parents. In C. Franklin, M. B. Harris, & P. Allen-Mears (Eds.), *The school services sourcebook: A guide for school based professionals* (2nd ed.). New York, NY: Oxford University Press.

Alameda-Lawson, T., Lawson, M. A., & Lawson, H. A. (2010). Social workers' roles in facilitating the collective involvement of low-income, culturally diverse parents in an elementary school. *Children & Schools, 32*(3), 172–182.

Altshuler, S. J. (1997). A reveille for school social workers: Children in foster care need our help! *Social Work in Education, 19*(2), 121–127.

Avant, D. W. (2014). The role of school social workers in implementation of Response to Intervention. *School Social Work Journal, 38*(2),11–31.

Birkenmaier, J., Berg-Weger, M., & Dewees, M. (2014). *The practice of generalist social work* (3rd ed.). New York, NY: Routledge.

Bundy, A., & Wegener, V. (2000). Maximizing Medicaid funding to support health and mental health services for school age children and youth. *The Final Project, 1*(5), 1–20. Retrieved May 16, 2015, from http://www.communityschools.org/assets/1/AssetManager/Brief5_Maximizing_Medicaid.pdf

Center for Mental Health in School at UCLA. (1997). *Comprehensive school-based health centers and full service schools: Development of 6 enabling components to support student learning.* Retrieved from http://smhp.psych.ucla.edu/compapp2.htm

Center for Mental Health in Schools at UCLA. (2011). *Moving beyond the three tier intervention pyramid toward a comprehensive framework for student and learning supports.* Retrieved from http://smhp.psych.ucla.edu/pdfdocs/briefs/threetier.pdf

Center for Mental Health in Schools at UCLA. (2014). *Clarifying the full continuum: Risk, protective buffers, and youth development factors.* Retrieved from http://smhp.psych.ucla.edu/pdfdocs/fullcontinuum.pdf

Centers for Disease Control and Prevention. (2013). Mental health surveillance among children—United States, 2005–2011. *Morbidity and Mortality Weekly Report, 62*(Suppl. 2), 1–35.

Cole, S. F., O'Brien, J. G., Gadd, M. G., Ristuccia, J., Wallace, D. L., & Gregory, M. (2009). *Helping traumatized children learn.* Boston, MA: Massachusetts Advocates for Children.

Colorado Department of Education. (2007). *A guide to school mental health services,* Cooperative Services Handbook Series. Denver, CO: Author. Retreived from: https://www.cde.state.co.us/cdesped/guide_schoolmentalhealthservices

Crone, D. A., & Horner, R. H. (2003). *Building positive behavior support systems in Schools: Functional behavioral assessment.* New York, NY: Guilford.

D'Agostino, C. (2013). Collaboration as an essential school social work skill. *Children & Schools, 35*(4), 248–251.

Dollarhide, C., & Lemberger, M. (2006). No Child Left Behind: Implications for school counselors. *Professional School Counseling, 9,* 295–304.

Dunlap, A. (2014). Supporting youth in the coming-out process: Theory-based programming. *Smith College Studies in Social Work, 84*(1), 107–129. doi:10.1080/00377317.2014.861173

Elias, M., DeFini, J., & Bergmann, J. (2010). Coordinating social–emotional and character development (SECD) initiatives improves school climate and student learning. *Middle School Journal, 42*(1), 30–37.

Finkelhor, D., Turner, H., Ormrod, R., Hamby, S. & Kracke, K. (2009, October). *Children's exposure to violence: A comprehensive national survey.* Office of Juvenile Justice and Delinquency Prevention, Juvenile Justice Bulletin. Retrieved from https://www.ncjrs.gov/pdffiles1/ojjdp/227744.pdf

Franklin, C., Gerlach, B., & Chanmugam, A. (2012). School social work. In C. N. Dulmus & K. M. Sowers (Eds.), *Social work fields of practice: Historical trends, professional issues, and future opportunities* (pp. 81–111). Hoboken, NJ: Wiley.

Franklin, C., Harris, M. B., & Allen-Meares, P. (Eds.). (2013). *The school services sourcebook: A guide for school-based professionals* (2nd ed.). New York, NY: Oxford University Press.

Frey, A. J., Alvarez, M. E., Dupper, D. R., Sabatino, C. A., Lindsey, B. C., Raines, J. C., . . . Norris, M. A. (2013). *National school social work practice model.* London, KY: School Social Work Association of America. Retrieved from http://www.sswaa.org/general/custom.asp?page=459

García, S. B., & Ortiz, A. A. (2013). Intersectionality as a framework for transformative research in special education. *Multiple Voices for Ethnically Diverse Exceptional Learners, 13*(2), 32–47.

Garstka, T., Lieberman, A., Biggs, J., Thompson, B., & Levy, M. (2014). Barriers to cross-system collaboration in child welfare, education, and the courts: Supporting educational well-being of youth in care through systems change. *Journal of Public Child Welfare, 8*(2), 190–211.

Johnson, M., George, P., Armstrong, M., Lyman, D., Dougherty, R., Daniels, A., . . . Delphin-Rittmon, M. (2014). Behavioral assessment for children and adolescents: Assessing the evidence. *American Psychiatric Association, 65*(5), 580–590.

Kilpatrick, D. G., Resnick, H. S., Milanak, M. E., Miller, M. W., Keyes, K. R., & Friedman, M. J. (2013). National estimates of exposure to traumatic events and PTSD prevalence using DSM-IV and DSM-5 criteria. *Journal of Trauma Stress, 26*(5), 537–547. doi:10.1002/jts.21848

Kutash, K., Duchnowski, A. J., & Lynn, N. (2006). *School-based mental health: An empirical guide for decision-makers.* Tampa, FL: University of South Florida, The Louis de la Parte Florida Mental Health Institute, Department of Child & Family Studies., Research and Training Center for Children's Mental Health.

Mellin, E. A. (2009). Unpacking interdisciplinary collaboration in expanded school mental health: A conceptual model for developing the evidence base. *Advances in School Mental Health Promotion, 2*(3), 4–14.

Merikangas, K. R., He, J., Burstein, M., Swanson, S. A., Avenevoli, S., Cui, L., . . . Swendsen, J. (2011). Lifetime prevalence of mental disorders in US adolescents: Results from the National Comorbidity Study–Adolescent Supplement (NCS-A). *Journal of the American Academy of Child and Adolescent Psychiatry, 49*(10), 980–989.

Pagan-Rivera, M. S. (2014). Using integrative short-term treatment in addressing the social–emotional needs of immigrant students: Implications for school social work practice. *School Social Work Journal, 38*(2), 61–76.

Powers, J. D., Edwards, J. D., Blackman, K. F., & Wegmann, K. M. (2013). Key elements of a successful multi-system collaboration for school-based mental health: In-depth interviews with district and agency administrators. *Urban Review, 45,* 651–670. doi:10.1007/s11256-013-0239-4

Rippey Massat, C., Constable, R., McDonald, S., & Flynn, J. (2008). *School social work: Practice, policy, and research perspectives* (7th ed.). Chicago, IL: Lyceum.

Robles, E. H., Dettlaff, A., & Fong, R. (2013). Effectively working with Latino immigrant families in the schools. In C. Franklin, M. B. Harris, & P. Allen-Meares (Eds.), *The school services sourcebook: A guide for school-based professionals* (2nd ed., pp. 707–717). New York, NY: Oxford University Press.

Sabatino, C. A., Kelly, E. C., Moriarity, J., & Lean, E. (2013). Response to intervention: A guide to scientifically based research for school social work services. *Children and Schools, 35*(4), 213–223.

School Social Work Association of America. (2013). *School social workers' role in addressing students' mental health needs and increasing academic achievement.* London, KY: Author. Retrieved from http://www.sswaa.org/?page=600&hhSearchTerms=%22school+and+climate%22

Sheridan, S., Kim, E. M., Coutts, M., Sjuts, T., Homes, S., Shannon, R., . . . Garbacz S. A. (2012). *Clarifying parent involvement and family–school partnership intervention research: A preliminary synthesis.* CYFS Working Paper No. 2012–4.

Stevens, J. E. (2012). *Massachusetts, Washington State lead US trauma sensitive school movement.* Retrieved from http://acestoohigh.com/2012/05/31/massachusetts-washington-state-lead-u-s-trauma-sensitive-school-movement

US Department of Education. (2010). *ESEA blueprint for reform.* Washington, DC: Office of Planning, Evaluation and Policy Development.

US Department of Education. (2014). *Reauthorization of the Elementary and Secondary Education Act.* Retrieved from http://www2.ed.gov/about/overview/budget/budget14/justifications/a-eseaoverview.pdf

US Department of Health and Human Services. (1999). *Mental health: A report of the Surgeon General.* Rockville, MD: Substance Abuse and Mental Health Services Administration, Center for Mental Health Services.

Weist, M. D., Ambrose, M. G., & Lewis, C. P. (2006). Expanded school mental health: A collaborative community–school example. *Children and Schools, 28*(1), 45–50.

Weisz, J. R., Sandler, I., Durlak, J., & Anton, B. (2005). Promoting and protecting youth mental health through evidence-based prevention and treatment. *American Psychologist, 60*(6), 628–648.

# CHAPTER 12

# THE SCHOOL SOCIAL WORKER

*Supporting Academic Success Through Social and Emotional Learning*

## ANNETTE JOHNSON AND CASSANDRA MCKAY-JACKSON

The American educational landscape continually changes in ways that impact the context in which school social workers practice. The broad changes in education policy, such as increased emphasis on high-stakes testing (Weber, 2014) or privatization in education (Hill & Welsch, 2009), and the increasing mental health needs of children and families have greatly impacted the role of the school social worker. A relatively recent field of study, social and emotional learning (SEL), has considerably changed the way in which today's school social workers practice. SEL provides role-expansion opportunities of the school social worker and a mechanism to align school social work outcomes to academic outcomes directly.

The school social worker plays a critical role in addressing the social and emotional needs of students. It is equally important that school social workers and other school staff assess their own SEL competencies, particularly as they relate to issues of diversity and equity. Moreover, as social workers enhance their SEL skills, they will increase their capacity to consult and provide guidance to classroom teachers on the significance of the classroom context in the development of the student's social and emotional competencies.

This chapter expands this dialogue through the lens of SEL as a prevention and intervention approach. It discusses strategies that school social work practitioners can use at multiple levels, theoretical frameworks that reinforce SEL, the alignment of SEL and Common Core State Standards (CCSS), and the social–emotional competence of school social workers.

## SOCIAL AND EMOTIONAL LEARNING

Social and emotional learning is "the process through which children and adults acquire and effectively apply the knowledge, attitudes, and skills necessary to understand and manage emotions" (Elias et.al. 1997, p. 2). Students learn to set and achieve positive goals, feel and show empathy for others, establish and maintain positive relationships, and make responsible decisions with SEL training (Collaborative for Academic, Social, and Emotional Learning (CASEL), 2005). Social and emotional learning is an essential component of school social work practice—whether the focus addresses promoting, preventing, or intervening, with an emphasis on providing opportunities for young people to acquire the skills necessary for maintaining personal well-being and positive relationships across their life span. According to CASEL, the five SEL competency clusters for students are as follows:

- *Self-awareness*: The ability to accurately recognize one's emotions and thoughts and the influence on behavior. This includes assessing one's strengths and limitations and possessing a well-grounded sense of confidence and optimism.
- *Self-management*: The ability to regulate emotions, thoughts, and behaviors effectively in different situations. This includes managing stress, controlling impulses, motivating oneself, and setting and working toward achieving personal and academic goals.
- *Social awareness*: The ability to understand the perspective of others, particularly those of others from diverse backgrounds and cultures; to understand social and ethical norms for behavior; and to recognize family, school, and community resources and supports.
- *Relationship skills*: The ability to establish and maintain healthy and rewarding relationships with diverse individuals and groups. This includes communicating clearly, listening actively, cooperating, resisting inappropriate social pressure, negotiating conflict constructively, and seeking and offering help when needed.
- *Responsible decision-making*: The ability to make constructive and respectful choices about personal behavior and social interactions based on ethical standards, safety concerns, social norms, a realistic evaluation of the consequences of various actions, and the well-being of self and others.

A growing body of research shows that the mastery of these five SEL competencies improves interpersonal and intrapersonal skill development and also significantly impacts academic performance (Zins, Weissberg, Wang, & Walberg, 2004). Moreover, well-implemented SEL approaches can lead to student gains in social–emotional skill; improved attitude about self, others, and school; positive classroom behavior; and 10 percentile-point gains on standardized achievement tests (Durlak, Weissberg, Dymnicki, Taylor, & Schellinger, 2011; Elias, 2014). In addition, negative behaviors that compromise academic and life stressors such as conduct problems, aggressive behavior, and emotional distress were significantly reduced (Elias, 2014).

When students learn to manage emotions and care about others, they decrease unproductive behavior and poor academic performance in the school environment (Hawkins, Farrington, & Catalano, 1998). By the time students reach high school, 30% have multiple high-risk behaviors (e.g., substance use, sex, violence, and depression), which interfere with school performance (Centers for Disease Control and Prevention, 2008; Dryfoos, 1997). These risks are compounded by educational disengagement that has the potential to jeopardize students' later successes in life (Durlak et al., 2011). Social and emotional learning promotes engagement and focuses on the connection between social life and emotional life to encourage positive relationships, positive decision-making, and ethical and responsible behavior in society.

## THEORETICAL FRAMEWORK THAT SUPPORTS SEL

The strengths-based approach and positive youth development (PYD) represent two theoretical frameworks that support SEL. The strengths-based approach assumes that all individuals and communities have abilities and inner strengths (Saleeby, 1996). The approach veers from a pathological viewpoint of the individual to a focus on assets and capabilities. Within school social work, this perspective minimizes student resistance to change by capitalizing on the student's skills and talents and facilitating constructional behaviors instead of just eliminating negative behaviors (Constable, Thomas, Leyba, & 2009).

PYD also represents an asset-based conception of adolescence created from developmental systems theory (Lerner, Alberts, & Bobek, 2007). The goal of PYD involves facilitating a more adaptive development and increasing youths' awareness beyond self to extend outward toward valuing and contributing to family and community in meaningful ways. Deeply woven into the fabric of the PYD framework lays SEL. A basic conception of SEL details the development of self-awareness, social awareness, and decision-making skills (Illinois State Board of Education, n.d.). These competencies (self-awareness, social awareness, and decision-making skills) are actualized through the approach's coordinated and progressive series of activities and experiences that assist young people in developing social, moral, emotional, physical, and cognitive competence in their community (Barton, Watkins, & Jarjoura, 1997). PYD, considered a participatory approach, includes youth in all aspects of the program or project. As with the strengths-based perspective, practitioners employing the techniques of PYD seek to encourage the development of competence in youth, generate a sense of belonging, and empower youth to act on their own behalf.

The PYD model by Lerner consists of the following: (1) cognitive and behavioral competence, (2) confidence, (3) positive social connections, (4) character, and (5) caring (Lerner & Benson, 2003). According to Lerner et al. (2007), students who possess these traits can thrive and, as a result, achieve the sixth C—contribution to society—if developed and practiced. This sixth C aligns with the expectation of behavioral skill progression, which is the generalization and application of social–emotional competence in real-world events.

An example of how these theoretical frameworks come together can be seen through the use of critical service learning as a school social work intervention (McKay, 2010; McKay & Johnson, 2010). Critical service learning (CSL) represents a therapeutic strategy that encompasses a philosophy of youth empowerment. CSL emphasizes youths becoming empowered to view themselves as partners to others in order to bring about change in their environments. Mitchell (2008) defines CSL as an approach that challenges youth to become self-aware in how their own situations influence their relationship with community partners. When these relationships are built based on the concerns of the community, they can facilitate CSL through the examination of issues of power, privilege, and oppression—and disparaging assumptions of class, gender, and race—and then taking action to address unjust and inequitable social and economic systems (Cipolle, 2010). In addition, CSL integrates the student's academic and social and emotional curriculum to enhance real-life applications and engages youths in active construction and integration of problem-solving and conflict resolution. Heavily integrating SEL, this intervention requires youth to assert an ability to generate alternative solutions to problems, anticipate consequences of each, and evaluate and learn from one's decision-making—all protective factors for youth successes (Nelson & Eckstein, 2008). A service project that simply supports charitable giving can reify stereotypes and does not necessarily create such positive youth outcomes.

However, CSL that elevates service to mutual support, problem-solving, relationship building, and deliberate integration of developmentally appropriate reflection activities produces the most positive results (Billig, 2000). Moreover, service learning engages students in meaningful service activities in their schools and communities, which helps them to develop a sense of civic responsibility, caring, and concern for others. In addition, it develops a feeling of self-worth (Stukas, Clary, & Snyder, 1999),

CSL is integrated into the social work or academic curriculum where students are empowered to brainstorm, plan, and implement activities that have a direct impact on their school, community, and their own personal development (McKay & Johnson, 2010). By supporting critical thinking, CSL helps to bolster the student's perspective regarding societal change (Argenal & Jacquez, 2015; McKay, 2010). A school social worker may also collaborate with the classroom teacher in engaging the students in a service-learning project that provides an opportunity for youth to demonstrate skills in prosocial interactions and responsible decision-making. Such an activity may decrease social isolation and withdrawal and increase empathy and perspective-taking (Fredericks, 2009; McKay & Johnson, 2010). The benefits of service-learning projects among the high-risk youth population may provide these youths with a way to build many of the developmental assets that help, such as positive experiences, resources, and other healthy characteristics. A case study of CSL is provided later in this chapter.

## ALIGNMENT OF SEL AND COMMON CORE STATE STANDARDS

Common Core State Standards provide a consistent and clear understanding of the knowledge and skill that young people need to achieve success in college and their careers (National Governors Association, 2010). Standards designed to be robust and relevant to the real world have been adopted by 43 states and the District of Columbia. Although an agreement on how to implement and test these standards does not exist and it is unclear if these standards will stand the test of time, they do provide uniformity in the expected academic preparation of students and attempt to address the disproportionality seen in schools in the United States.

Education can enable children to be lifelong learners and effective citizens. Just as students come to school with different levels of academic skills, they also come to school with different social and emotional skill levels. Thus, it is necessary to promote social, emotional literacy, as well as the three R's. Furthermore, as youth are encouraged to become "college, career, and contribution ready" (Elias, 2014, p. 58), SEL is a critical catalyst in achieving this goal. For example, CCCS requires that youth are able to engage more deeply with complex text; hence, youth must acquire a nuanced understanding of emotions—theirs and those of others (Elias, 2014). SEL supports this necessary emotional maturation.

Historically, elementary school educators have been particularly attuned to the fact that SEL provides the platform for learning and the development of self-reflection, responsibility, caring, cooperation, and effective problem-solving. The growing research has deepened the understanding of how essential these competencies are and how they can effectively be integrated into the academic setting (Cohen, 2001). Although this new focus on SEL benefits all students, it is especially critical for low-income students, marginalized students, and students of color (Hamedani & Darling-Hammond, 2015).

Social and emotional competence refers to the capacity to understand, process, and express the social and emotional aspects of our lives. These competencies represent a mode of intelligence, which Gardner (1983) defines as follows:

> Skills of problem-solving—enabling the individual to resolve genuine problems or difficulties that he or she encounters; and when appropriate, to create an effective product that entails the potential for finding or creating problems, thereby laying the foundation for the acquisition of new knowledge. (p. 60)

Cohen (2001) purports that social–emotional intelligence involves the *decoding* of others (social awareness) and ourselves (self-awareness). This ability provides the foundation for problem-solving and enables one to grapple with a wide variety of learning challenges. Social–emotional capacities powerfully affect and even determine the ability to do the following:

- Listen and communicate
- Concentrate
- Recognize and modulate emotional state
- Understand and solve problems
- Generate creative solutions
- Form friendships and working relationships
- Cooperate
- Become self-motivating
- Resolve conflicts adaptively

Because of the rigor of CCSS, students will need self-control to persist with the expanded text and self-management to stay motivated and engaged over time (Elias, 2014). Students will be asked to work frequently with peers to engage in academic discourse and problem-solve around a text. In this case, students will need to use their social awareness competency to take others' points of view, as well as their relationship skills competency to work collaboratively (Chicago Public Schools, 2014). For example, in the Language Arts Standard (RL 3.3), students are asked to describe characters in a story (e.g., their traits, motivations, or feeling) and explain how their actions contribute to the sequence of events. These directly align with the SEL goals of self-awareness and social awareness skills where students learn to label and recognize their own and the emotions of others, analyze emotions and how they affect others, and evaluate others' emotional reactions. The story becomes a tool for drawing parallels to student behavior, individually and as a group, thus promoting SEL goals. Students will not only learn how to understand the motivations and feelings of the characters but also learn to understand their own feelings; to evaluate these emotions, the immediate behavioral impact, and the future outcomes; and, ultimately, to improve their ability to make good choices.

In mathematics, one of the practices highlighted in the CCSS is *modeling with mathematics*. Students will need to analyze problems in real contexts that require them to use social awareness to understand the needs of the individual and groups involved in the problem. In addition, students will need to engage in reflective and improvement processes. In this case, students need to use decision-making skills to solve problems responsibly, as well as to use self-management skills to persevere in the process and monitor progress toward final completion (Chicago Public Schools, 2014). Problem-solving, particularly word problems, remains the most challenging part of math for many students. Often, students will take one look at a problem and decide that it is too difficult without even trying—especially those students with *math phobia*. This is where the social emotional skills of self-efficacy and perseverance are helpful.

Students need first to trust in their ability to solve a problem (self-efficacy) and then work toward that goal. Students must be able to focus on the problem rather than become distracted by what a peer on the other side of the room is doing. If students get stuck, they must manage their stress levels by regulating their emotions and, if necessary, asking for help (Brackett, Rivers, Reyes, & Salovey, 2012). Another example of the alignment of CCSS and SEL can be seen in the Math Standards MP3, construct viable arguments and critique the reasoning of others (Illinois State Board of Education, 2015). Here, students must justify their conclusions and communicate and respond to the arguments of others, which support the competency of social awareness, relationship, and management skills. It becomes important to understand the perspective or divergent points of views, identify social cues (verbal and physical), and express one's own feelings appropriately (Yoder, 2013).

For students to be successful with CCSS, they need strong skills in academics and SEL (Elias, 2014). Therefore, school social workers, teachers, and other staff need to work collaboratively to intentionally introduce these SEL skills by proactively infusing SEL skills in school social work practice and classroom instruction. For the school-based practitioner, it is critically important to address these skills in both prevention and intervention activities (Zakrzewski, 2014).

## SCHOOL SOCIAL WORK PRACTICE STRATEGIES

The multi-tiered systems of support framework discussed in Chapters 9 and 10 enables the school social worker to organize SEL prevention and intervention supports by proactively intervening at every tier level (universal, targeted, and tertiary) within a school. In most schools, approximately 80% of the student population remains resilient and experiences adequate supports within the home, school, and community. This population of student is often served by universal schoolwide supports and is generally successful without needing additional supports. However, the remaining students in a school population will likely need support at the tier 2 or tier 3 level. Tier 2 interventions play a key role in supporting students at risk of academic or social problems and may prevent the need for more intensive interventions (Hawken, O'Neil, & MacLeod, 2011). Tier 3 interventions are intensive supports needed for approximately 5–10% of the student population.

SEL directly aligns with school social work practices, and in many instances the school social worker may believe this work represents what many view as traditional school social work practices. However, the difference here is that the SEL standards provide a framework to link the school social workers' interventions to academic achievements, and the SEL practices are clearly understood and accepted by school leaders as important and necessary (Kelly, 2008).

The school social worker can integrate SEL in clinical work with students in individual, group, or classroom settings.

## SEL INTERVENTIONS ACROSS TIERS

Increasing empirical evidence shows that schoolwide approaches that introduce SEL programming have positive impacts on students' academic and emotional successes (Dulak et al, 2011). Increasingly, researchers recognize that schools cannot focus solely on students' academic learning to improve academics. Current research has shown that schoolwide SEL implementation positively impacts school climate and students' relationships with adults, as well as builds greater engagement in school and social supports and stronger feelings of self-efficacy (Hamedani & Darling-Hammond, 2015).

Schoolwide SEL programing offers an excellent way for school social workers to use their skills in system theory by participating as members of the school leadership team helping to design and implement schoolwide SEL programing. CASEL's (2013) *CASEL Guide* is a resource that provides schoolwide (universal), evidence-based, social and emotional programs. The guide introduces well-designed, evidence-based programs from preschool to high school that, based on research, have shown positive impacts on student behavior and/or academic success.

In both tier 2 and tier 3, individual and group counseling are viable modalities. Classroom-based, push-in supports are appropriate at the tier 1 and tier 2 levels. The school social work practitioner can integrate SEL into clinical work with students in individual counseling for both regular and special education students. The SEL core competencies outline the skills that students need to be successful in school and life. If a state does not have state standards, the School Social Work Association of America (SSWAA) provides national standards for social and emotional learning based on the five core competencies (SSWAA, n.d.).

## EVIDENCE-BASED PROGRAM EXAMPLES

A growing body of literature exists that documents the effectiveness of treatments for students at risk or in need of intensive supports (tier 2 and tier 3 interventions). Cognitive–behavioral therapy has proven to be a dominant approach in evidence-informed, school-based interventions. Table 12.1 presents a nonexhaustive list of examples.

## SEL AND EQUITY: THE SCHOOL SOCIAL
## WORKER AS EQUITY CONSULTANT

Our education system is becoming increasingly diverse while barriers for marginalized students such as students of color, undocumented students, and low-income students continue to mount. We know that education plays a critical role in determining how youth will spend their adult life; for instance, a higher level of education can mean higher earnings, better health, and

Table 12.1: Examples of Evidence-Based Programs (Empirical Support)

| Program | Participants | Description/Objective | Intervention Strategies | Intervention Outcome |
|---|---|---|---|---|
| Tier 1 Prevention<br><br>I Can Problem Solve | Preschool through sixth grade | Teaches students how to generate alternative solutions, anticipate consequences, and effectively solve problems. The scripted lessons focus on both pre-problem-solving skills and problem-solving skills. | Divided into three sets of lessons for pre-kindergarten (59 lessons), kindergarten and primary grades (83 lessons), and intermediate elementary grades (77 lessons). | Increased positive social behavior, reduced conduct problem, and improved social and emotional skills performance (Substance Abuse and Mental Health Services Administration, 2006) |
| Tier 1 Prevention<br><br>Second Step | Ages 6–12 years | Classroom-based, social skills program that teaches socioemotional skills aimed at reducing impulsive and aggressive behavior while increasing social competence. | Consists of in-school curricula, parent training, and skill development. Curriculum addresses all five SEL competencies. | Improved social competence and prosocial behavior (Substance Abuse and Mental Health Services Administration, 2006) |
| Tier 1<br><br>Promoting Alternative Thinking Strategies (PATHS) | Kindergarten through sixth grade | Promotes peaceful conflict resolution, emotion regulation, empathy, and responsible decision-making skills. Designed to facilitate the development of self-control, emotional awareness, and interpersonal problem-solving skill. | Instructional manuals and lessons intended to enhance the social competence and social understanding of children. | Improved academic performance, increased positive social behavior, reduced conduct problem, and reduced emotional distress (CASEL, 2013) |
| Tiers 1 and 2 Prevention and Intervention<br><br>Check-In, Check-Out (CICO) | Elementary and middle school students | Students are presented with daily/weekly goals and receive frequent feedback on meeting the goals throughout the day. | Daily check-in with an adult at the start of school and end of the day. Teacher provides feedback on the monitoring logs throughout the day. Parent is engaged. | Significant reduction in problem behavior, increase in academic engagement, and reduction in office discipline referral (Anderson, Christenson, Sinclair, & Lehr, 2004) |

| | | | | |
|---|---|---|---|---|
| Tier 2 Intervention Anger Coping Power | Late-elementary through middle school students and also parents | 15- to 18-month program that addresses substance abuse, social competence, self-regulation, and parental involvement. | Thirty-four structured cognitive–behavioral group sessions for the selected children and periodic individual sessions. Sixteen behavioral parent-training groups, periodic home visits, and individual contacts. | Reduced substance abuse and delinquent behavior, improved behavior at home and school, increased home-related self-esteem, and increased parental involvement (Lochman, 1992) |
| Tiers 2 and 3 Coping Cat | Ages 8–14 years with anxiety disorders | Goal entails teaching children to recognize signs of anxious arousal and use these signs as cues to apply anxiety management strategies. | Individual or group therapy sessions that cover the following: Education Coping skills training Graded exposure activities | Decrease in child-reported anxiety symptoms (Kendall, Safford, Flannery-Schroeder, & Webb, 2004) |
| Tiers 2 and 3 Intervention Cognitive Behavioral Intervention for Trauma in Schools | Ages 3–12 years who experienced events including violence, natural or man-made disasters, accidents, or abuse | Reduce symptoms of post-traumatic stress disorder, reduce depression and behavioral problems, improve peer and parent support, and enhance coping skills. | Teaches the following cognitive behavioral techniques: Education about reaction to trauma Relaxation training Cognitive therapy Real-life exposure Stress or trauma exposure Social problem-solving | Improvement in post-traumatic stress disorder and depressive (Kataoka et al., 2003) |

a longer life. On the other hand, the long-term social and financial costs of educational failure are high. Those without the skills to participate socially and economically generate higher costs for health, welfare, and criminal justice systems (Levin & Rouse, 2012). Some ethnic groups have not fared well historically currently in the US education system. It is widely documented that disparities exist for African Americans, Latinos, Native Americans, and several Asian American subgroups where these individuals underperformed relative to their Caucasian counterparts (American Psychological Association, 2012). These groups are underrepresented in high schools' graduation rates (National Center for Education Sciences, 2015), placement in gifted and talented programs (Michael-Chadwell, 2011), and admission rates to postsecondary education (National Center for Education Sciences, 2012), whereas they are overrepresented in disciplinary referrals (Anyon et al., 2014), expulsions (Mendez, Knoff, & Ferron, 2002; Vavrus & Cole, 2002), and special education. A fair and inclusive system that makes the advantages of education available to all is one of the most powerful levers to make society more equitable (Kuczera, 2007).

More attention must be given in teaching to learning, discerning, and building on the social, cultural, linguistic, experiential, and intellectual assets that students from diverse backgrounds bring with them into classrooms (American Psychological Association, 2012). The school social worker must lead the charge in advocating against educational disparities. Furthermore, according to Germain (2006), school mental health professionals, such as school social workers, should engage "the progressive forces in people and situational assets, and [effect] the removal of environmental obstacles to growth and adaptive functioning" (p. 30). Therefore, the school social worker must eliminate disparities by changing social structures where feasible, help students negotiate problematic situations (Payne, 2005; Wood & Tully, 2006), and further explore the sociopolitical and economic context of individual difficulties to help collectivize personal troubles (Weinberg, 2008).

The application of structural social work interrogates institutions, which inherently disempower some while unfairly privileging others based on distinctions of class, race, gender, ability, sexual orientation, age, religion, and other social identities (Weinberg, 2008). Using the structural social work principles, it is necessary to unpack an assumption of faulty socialization of individual students who lack self-management and self-awareness skills. Instead, the social worker further explores ways in which youth can develop voice through decision-making skills and social capital through social awareness and positive relationships. Social capital, in this vein, is not identified as an SEL goal but may be a by-product of an individual's ability to interact and manage relationships with others, glean the resources embedded within the social structures available, meaningfully participate in opportunities afforded by those networks, and gain social currency (Lin, Cook, & Burt, 2008).

The authors, however, are not naive to simply externalizing structures that contribute to a discriminatory social order. Social workers themselves can also be complicit with discriminatory practices within school settings (Weinberg, 2008). In order to control for this tendency, practitioners must be self-reflective about their advantages accrued through their positioning (Mullaly, 1997) and must always question the purpose of their interventions—whether they are intended to comply with a corrupt system or challenge oppressive social structures (McKay, 2010). Furthermore, school social workers must be keenly aware of their emotions and unconscious bias and how they impact others. It is necessary that reflection and introspection be utilized to be in touch with underlying or unconscious bias regarding race and culture. This can help the school social worker be effective as a consultant to teachers and others. School social workers can also facilitate professional development in this area, helping teachers and staff explore their own views about race, ethnicity, gender, etc. The book *Emotional Intelligence 2.0*, by Travis Bradberry and Jean Greaves (2009), represents a useful tool for adults that succinctly helps them review, reflect, and enhance their SEL skills.

---

# CASE STUDY

The following case study exemplifies critical SEL in application. It depicts how students' involvement in social justice issues can create a stronger connection to school and the community.

The development of the critical service learning project occurred in a high school in which African American students comprised more than 90% of the student population. A student reported to a school social work intern that he felt deeply disturbed by the recent events of police brutality plaguing the United States, particularly with the 2015 deaths of Michael Brown and Eric Garner. Michael Brown was an unarmed African American teen who was shot and killed by police in Ferguson, Missouri. Eric Garner was an unarmed African American man who died after a New York City police officer arrested and put Garner in an illegal chokehold. Furthermore, the student stated that he felt that the school provided an insufficient means of learning about and addressing these social issues to the point that the student felt compelled to leave school and join the protests occurring in major cities throughout the nation, which he viewed as a direct method of addressing police brutality. However, after careful discussion, the social work intern was able to redirect the student toward school engagement and engage other invested students in using the project as a platform to address these major concerns. The intern rallied a core group of five students who decided to create a student video discussing racism and police brutality in the United States. The project's aim was to enable students in viewing themselves as agents of social change through the promotion of teamwork and group participation. Through this process, students would learn how to develop healthy interpersonal relationships with their peers through mutual collaboration. In that, the SEL goal (2C.5b) was utilized: "Use communication and social skills to interact effectively with others in order to plan, implement, and evaluate participation in a group project" (Illinois State Board of Education, n.d.). To assess the acquisition of these skills, the Social Consciousness instrument was used as a pre-/post-measure in order to assess the students' awareness of how individual behaviors affect others (Flewelling, Paschall, & Ringwalt, 1993, as cited in Dahlberg, Toal, Swahn, & Behrens, 2005). Through student coordination, audiovisual acumen, and sheer perseverance, the student video was completed and posted to YouTube and other social media outlets. The video chronicled the statistics of racial disparities regarding police brutality and legal outcomes, student views of their future outcomes regarding racial profiling, and their call for solidarity to non-African American youth in addressing this tragic phenomenon.

As measured by the Social Consciousness instrument, the students demonstrated an increase in social consciousness by the end of the project. Using a Likert scale, five items assessed the level of agreement with statements such as "the problems of other people don't really bother me" to "telling a lie makes me feel uncomfortable." At the beginning of the project, a prominent attitude among the students stemmed from feeling apathetic about tackling any issues involving racism. However, by the end of the project, the students viewed social change as something within their reach. The average pretest score for the entire group was

3.2; the average post-test score for the entire group was 3.8. The results indicated a slight increase in social consciousness as well as social awareness of the measured students.

---

# CONCLUSION: EXPANDING THE HORIZON FOR THE SCHOOL SOCIAL WORKER

In our global society, students need to be competitive. America's educational system places great emphasis on student achievement, learning standards, and the correlation between academic achievement and social and emotional development. Vitally important is the need for school social work services to clearly demonstrate the relationship in supporting the academic achievement of students. Social and emotional learning provides the opportunity for the school social worker to intervene in the educational process at multiple levels, align social work practices with academics by utilizing the systems approach, and offer prevention and intervention supports at every level (Johnson, 2012). The school social worker should consider incorporating the following strategies into his or her practice:

- Actively participate as a member of the school leadership team that helps to design schoolwide SEL programming. Utilizing systems and leadership and facilitation skills, lead the change process by engaging all aspects of the school community and developing a team of people who can help lead the charge, such as school administrators, grade-level teachers, parents, pupil personnel staff, and other support staff (e.g., lunchroom staff and custodians).
- Align school social work interventions with the SEL learning standard in your state. If standards do not exist, then advocate with other education partners to develop SEL standards for the state or district or use the *National School Social Work Standards for Social Emotional Learning* (SSWAA, n.d.).
- Utilize data to assess the need for prevention and intervention services across all tiers.
- Continue to expand your adult SEL skills. Utilize this consultant expertise to expand the discussion on SEL and equity to school staff. The collaborative efforts of all school staff, school leaders, teachers, school social workers, and other staff can infuse SEL in education, making it a reality for every child in every school.

# DISCUSSION QUESTIONS

1. What schoolwide SEL prevention approaches currently exist in your school or district? How broad or narrow is the scope of your school's work? How is the school social worker involved?
2. It has come to the attention of the school principal that several students in the fourth grade classroom have been bullying other students on the playground. Using the SEL competencies, develop a tier 2 intervention. Will the intervention be a group counseling intervention or a classroom-based push-in intervention? What is your rationale for your choice of intervention?

3. When implementing the PYD approach, what strategy could you use to encourage the sixth C (contribution to society) with your assigned student caseload? How will this strategy support student strengths and empowerment, as well as skill development?

4. Based on the needs of your group of students exposed to trauma, what intervention strategy and empirically supported program would promote positive youth emotional outcomes? Give your rationale for your choice supported by available literature.

## ACKNOWLEDGMENT

The authors acknowledge graduate student N. Sethupathi, JACSW MSW 2015, for his invaluable contribution of the case study provided in this chapter.

## REFERENCES

Anderson, A. R., Christenson, S. L., Sinclair, M. F., & Lehr, C. A. (2004). Check & Connect: The importance of relationships for promoting engagement with school. *Journal of School Psychology, 42*(2), 95–113.

Anyon, Y., Jenson, J. M., Alschul, I., Farrar, J., McQueen, J., Greer, E., . . . Simmons, J. (2014). The persistence effect of race and the promise of alternatives to suspension in school discipline outcomes. *Children and Youth Services Review, 44*, 379–386.

American Psychological Association, Presidential Task Force on Educational Disparities. (2012). *Ethnic and racial disparities in education: Psychology's contributions to understanding and reducing disparities.* Retrieved from http://www.apa.org/ed/resources/racial-disparities.aspx

Argenal, A., & Jacquez, T. (2015). Critical service-learning and social justice. In O. Delano-Oriaran, M. W. Penick-Parks, & S. Fondrie (Eds.), *The Sage sourcebook of service-learning and civic engagement* (pp. 61–65). Thousand Oaks, CA: Sage.

Barton, W. H., Watkins, M., & Jarjoura, R. (1997). Youth and communities: Toward comprehensive strategies for youth development. *Social Work, 42*, 483–493.

Billig, S. (2000, August). The effects of service learning. *School Administrator.* Retrieved from http://www.aasa.org/SchoolAdministratorArticle.aspx?id=14436

Brackett, M. A., Rivers, S. E., Reyes, M. R., & Salovey, P. (2012). Enhancing academic performance and social and emotional competence with the RULER Feeling Words curriculum. *Learning and Individual Differences, 22*, 218–224.

Bradberry, T., & Greaves, J. (2009). *Emotional intelligence 2.0.* San Diego, CA: TalentSmart.

CASEL: Collaborative for Academic, Social, and Emotional Learning. (2005). *What is social and emotional learning?* Retrieved from http://www.casel.org/social-and-emotional-learning

CASEL: Collaborative for Academic, Social, and Emotional Learning. (2013). *Explore the CASEL library.* Retrieved from http://www.casel.org/library/2013-casel-guide

Centers for Disease Control and Prevention. (2008). Youth risk behavior surveillance—United States, 2007. *MMWR, 57*(No. SS-4).

Chicago Public Schools. (2014). *Raising the bar: The Common Core State Standards (CCSS).* Retrieved from http://cps.edu/commoncore/Pages/commoncore.aspx

Cipolle, S. B. (2010). *Service-learning and social justice: Engaging students in social change.* Lanham, MD: Rowman & Littlefield.

Cohen, J. (Ed.). (2001). Social and emotional education: Core concepts and practices. In *Classrooms/ intelligent schools: The social–emotional education of young children.* New York, NY: Teachers College Press.

Constable, R., Thomas, G., & Leyba, E. G. (2009). Planning and setting goals: Behavioral intervention plans and individualized education program and the individualized family service plan. In C. R. Massat, R. Constable, S. McDonald, & J. P. Flynn (Eds.), *School social work: Practice, policy and research* (7th ed., pp. 494–521). Chicago, IL: Lyceum.

Dahlberg, L. L., Toal, S. B., Swahn, M. H., & Behrens, C. B. (2005). *Measuring violence-related attitudes, behaviors, and influences among youths: A compendium of assessment tools.* Atlanta, GA: Centers for Disease Control and Prevention.

Dryfoos, J. G. (1997). The prevalence of problem behaviors: Implications for programs. In R. P. Weissberg, T. P. Gullotta, R. L. Hampton, B. A. Ryan, & G. R. Adams (Eds.), *Healthy Children 2010: Enhancing children's wellness* (pp. 17–46). Thousand Oaks, CA: Sage.

Durlak, J. A., Weissberg, R. P., Dymnicki, A. B., Taylor, R. D., & Schellinger, K. B. (2011). The impact of enhancing students' social and emotional learning: A meta-analysis of school-based universal interventions. *Child Development, 82,* 405–432. doi:10.1111/j.1467-8624.2010.01564

Durlak, J. A., Weissberg, R. P., Dymnicki, A. B., Taylor, R. D. & Schellinger, K. B. (2011). The impact of (enhancing students' social and emotional learning: A meta-analysis of school-based universal interventions. *Child Development, 82*(1): 405–432.

Elias, M. (2014). Social–emotional skills can boost Common Core implementation. *Phi Delta Kappan, 96*(3), 58–62.

Elias, M., & Zins, L. (1997). *Promoting social and emotional learning: Guidelines for educators.* Alexandria, VA: Association for Supervision and Curriculum Development.

Flewelling, R. L, Pashcall, M. J., & Ringwalt, C. L. (1993). Sage baseline survey. Research Triangle Park, NC: Research Triangle Institute.

Gardner, H. (1983). *Frames of mind: The theory of multiple intelligences.* New York, NY: Basic Books.

Germain, C. (2006). An ecological perspective on social work in the schools. In R. Constable, C. R. Massat, S. McDonald, & J. P. Flynn (Eds.), *School social work practice, policy and research* (6th ed., pp. 28–39). Chicago, IL: Lyceum.

Hamedani, M. G., & Darling-Hammond, L. (2015). *Social emotional learning in high school: How three urban high schools engage, educate, and empower youth.* Retrieved from https://edpolicy.stanford.edu/sites/default/files/publications/scope-pub-social-emotional-learning-research-brief.pdf

Hawken, L. S., O'Neil, R. E., & McLeod, K. S. (2011). An investigation of the impact of function of problem behavior on effectiveness of the behavior education program (BEP). *Education & Treatment of Children, 34,* 551–574. doi:org/10.1353/etc.2011.0031

Hawkins, J. D., Farrington, D. P., & Catalano, R. F. (1998). Reducing violence through the schools. In D. S. Eliot, B. A. Hamburg, & K. R. Williams (Eds.), *Violence in American schools: A new perspective* (pp. 188–216). Cambridge, England: Cambridge University Press.

Hill, C. D., & Welsch, D. M. (2009). For-profit versus not-for-profit charter schools: An examination of Michigan student test scores. *Education Economics, 17*(2), 147–166.

Illinois State Board of Education. (n.d.). *Illinois learning standards: Social/emotional learning, performance descriptors.* Retrieved from http://www.isbe.net/ils/social_emotional/descriptors.htm

Illinois State Board of Education (2015) *The new Illinois learning standards for mathematics incorporating the Common Core.* Retrieved from http://www.isbe.net/common_core/pdf/Math_common_core_standards.pdf

Johnson, A. (2012). *For school social workers: The changing role of the school social worker.* Chicago, IL: NASW Illinois. Retrieved from http://naswil.org/news/chapter-news/featured/for-school-social-workers-the-changing-role-of-the-school-social-worker/

Kataoka, S. H., Stein, B. D., Jaycox, L. H., Wong, M., Escudero, P., Tu, W., . . . Fink, A. (2003, March). A school-based mental health program for traumatized Latino immigrant children. *Journal of the American Academy of Psychiatry, 42*(3), 311–318.

Kelly, M. (2008). *The domains and demands of school social work practice: A guide to working effectively with students, families and schools.* Oxford, England: Oxford.

Kendall, P. C., Safford, S., Flannery-Schroeder, E., & Webb, A. (2004). Child Anxiety Treatment: Outcomes in Adolescence and Impact on Substance Use and Depression at 7.4-Year Follow-Up. *Journal of Consulting and Clinical Psychology, 72*(2), 276–287.

Lerner, R. M., Alberts, A. E., & Bobek, D. (2007). *Thriving youth, flourishing civil society: How positive youth development strengthens democracy and social justice. Civic engagement as an educational goal* (pp. 21–35). Gutersloh, Germany: Verlag Bertelsmann Stiftung.

Lerner, R. M., & Benson, P. I. (2003). *Developmental assets and asset-building communities: Implications for research, policy, and practice.* New York, NY: Kluwer/Plenum.

Levin, H. M., & Rouse, C. E. (2012, January 25). The true cost of high school dropouts. *The New York Times*, A31.

Lin, N., Cook, K. S., & Burt, R. S. (2008). *Social capital: Theory and research.* New Brunswick, NJ: Transaction Publishers.

Lochman, J. E. (1992). Cognitive–behavioral intervention with aggressive boys: Three-year follow-up and preventive effects. *Journal of Consulting & Clinical Psychology, 60*(3), 426–432.

McKay, C. (2010). Critical service learning: A school social work intervention. *Children and Schools, 32*(1), 5–13.

McKay, C., & Johnson, A. (2010). Service learning: An example of multilevel school social work practice. *School Social Work Journal, 35*(1), 21–36.

Mendez, L. M. R., Knoff, H. M., & Ferron, J. M. (2002). School demographic variables and out-of-school suspension rates: A quantitative and qualitative analysis of a large, ethnically diverse school district. *Psychology in the Schools, 39*(3), 259–277.

Michael-Chadwell, S. (2011). Examining the underrepresentation of the underserved students in gifted program from a transformational leadership vantage point. *Journal for the Education of the Gifted, 34*, 99–130.

Mitchell, T. (2008). Traditional vs. critical services learning: Engaging the literature to differentiate two models. *Michigan Journal of Service Learning, 14*(2), 50–65.

Mullaly, R. (1997). *Structural social work* (2nd ed.). Toronto, Ontario, Canada: Oxford University Press.

NationNational Center for Education Sciences. (2012, August). *Higher education: Gaps in access and persistence study: Statistical analysis report.* Retrieved from https://nces.ed.gov/pubs2012/2012046.pdf

National Center for Education Sciences. (2015, May). *The condition of education: Public high school graduation rates.* Retrieved from http://nces.ed.gov/programs/coe/indicator_coi.asp

National Governors Association Center for Best Practices & Council of Chief State School Officers. (2010). *Common Core State Standards.* Retrieved from http://www.corestandards.org/other-resources

Nelson, J. A., & Eckstein, D. E. (2008). A service learning model for at-risk adolescents. *Education and Treatment of Children, 31*, 223–237.

Payne, M. (2005). *Modern social work theory* (3rd ed.). Chicago, IL: Lyceum.

Saleeby, D. (1996). The strengths perspective in social work practice: Extensions and cautions. *Social Work, 41*, 296–305.

School Social Work Association of America. (n.d.). *National school social work standards for social emotional learning.* Retrieved from http://c.ymcdn.com/sites/www.sswaa.org/resource/resmgr/SSWAA_Documents/School_Social_Work_SEL_Stand.pdf

Stukas, A. A., Clary, E. G., & Snyder, M. (1999). Service learning: Who benefits and why. *Social Policy Report, 13*(4), 1–19.

Substance Abuse and Mental Health Services Administration. (2006). *National Registry of Evidence-Based Practice, Second Step.* Retrieved from http://www.samhsa.gov/nrepp

Vavrus, F., & Cole, K. (2002). "I didn't do nothin": The discursive construction of school suspension. *Urban Review, 34,* 87–111.

Weber, A. (2014). The misdirection of modern American education. *Education Digest, 79*(9), 43–48.

Weinberg, M. (2008). Structural social work: A moral compass for ethics in practice. *Critical Social Work, 9*(1). Retrieved from http://www1.uwindsor.ca/criticalsocialwork/structural-social-work-a-moral-compass-for-ethics-in-practice

Wood, G. G., & Tully, C. T. (2006). *The structural approach to direct practice in social work.* New York, NY: Columbia University Press.

Yoder, N. (2013). *Linking social–emotional learning to instructional practices in an urban context: A mixed methods study.* Unpublished manuscript.

Zakrzewski, V. (2014, January 22). *How to integrate social–emotional learning into Common Core.* Berkeley, CA: The Greater Good Science Foundation. Retrieved from http://greatergood.berkeley.edu/article/item/how_to_integrate_social_emotional_learning_into_common_core

Zins, J., Weissberg, R., Wang, M., & Walberg, H. J. (2004). *Building academic success on social and emotional learning: What does the research say?* New York, NY: Teachers College Press.

# CHAPTER 13

# PROGRESS MONITORING AND DATA-BASED DECISION-MAKING

## KIMBERLY ISRAEL AND JULIE O'DONNELL

S chool social workers make significant contributions to children's academic and life success, but in an age of educational accountability, these efforts may be undervalued unless the profession increases its monitoring and data-based decision-making. This chapter covers the reasons why monitoring, evaluation, and dissemination are important; discusses strategies and tools for evaluation; and provides a case study of a district that used evaluation data to develop, sustain, and greatly expand school social work services.

## RATIONALE FOR SCHOOL SOCIAL WORK PROGRESS MONITORING AND EVALUATION

Schools influence multiple domains in the lives of children; however, their primary mission is the education of children. Under federal legislation, such as No Child Left Behind (NCLB) and the Individuals with Disabilities Education Act (IDEA), schools have become increasingly accountable for achieving this mission with even the most vulnerable of children and publicizing their results (Bye, Shepard, Partridge, & Alvarez, 2009; Hopson & Lawson, 2011). Given this accountability mandate, combined with education budget cuts that have recently plagued many school districts throughout the country (Bye et al., 2009; Harrison & Harrison, 2014; Raines, 2006), it is critical that school social workers are able to document and clearly demonstrate the contributions they make toward improving children's academic achievement. Since there is limited literature that demonstrates a clear link between school social work practice and educational outcomes (Alvarez, Bye, Bryant, & Mumm, 2013; Newsome, Anderson-Butcher, Fink, Hall, & Huffer; 2008), this increased level of accountability demands that school social workers and researchers consistently evaluate practices and produce better studies (Franklin, 2005).

If school social workers do not evaluate and demonstrate how their interventions contribute to the core educational mission of schools, it is unlikely that the profession will continue to grow (Franke & Lynch, 2006; Franklin, Kim, & Tripodi, 2009; Newsome, et al.; 2008).

There has been clear movement, in the fields of both education and social work, toward the use of evidence-based or evidence-informed approaches (Franklin & Kelly, 2009). Evidence-based practice is the consistent use of interventions that have a research base to support their potential effectiveness (Drisko, 2014). According to the National Association of Social Workers (NASW) *Code of Ethics*, social workers must remain current on, understand, and use evidence-informed practice to meet their ethical obligations to vulnerable populations (NASW, 2012). The social work profession also recognizes that ethical practice requires social workers to evaluate the impact of their work, both to show that interventions are effective or understand when they must be modified with diverse populations or locations, and to ensure no unanticipated consequences occur (Franklin & Kelly, 2009). To successfully implement evidence-based practice, one must ensure fidelity or that the model was implemented as designed. This can be done only by monitoring the process to ensure the intervention was provided as planned (Cawood, 2013). The careful monitoring of interventions has the added benefit of providing school social workers with information to determine when and, possibly, how to modify interventions if needed. This is important because, in addition to the research base, evidence-based practice must consider practitioner expertise, the setting, demands, and politics of the school, as well as the cultural diversity of the community (Cawood, 2013; Drisko, 2014).

## COMMON CORE STATE STANDARDS

In 2009, state leaders from 48 states, two territories, and the District of Columbia met to develop a set of consistent learning goals that would ensure all students, regardless of the state in which they attended school, would exit high school prepared for college, career, and life (National Governors Association, 2010). This set of goals became what is now known as the Common Core State Standards. As of 2015, 44 states, the District of Columbia, four territories, and the Department of Defense Education Activities had implemented the Common Core State Standards for use as a consistent measurement of student achievement (National Governors Association, 2010).

At the foundation of the Common Core State Standards is the assumption that students enter the classroom with the ability to problem solve, empathize with the perspectives of others, tolerate ambiguity, think creatively, dialogue respectfully, and collaboratively work with others. Unfortunately, schools often fail to teach these critical strategies that vulnerable students may need to be successful (Elias, 2014). As teachers transition from educational pedagogy focusing on memorizing and repetition to pedagogical structures that encourage students to think, to apply their knowledge to different situations, to learn deeply about a subject, and to work with other students in more relevant, real-life exercises, struggles in learning may become even more apparent among those students who experience social, emotional, and behavioral barriers to learning (Elias, 2014; Gubi & Bocanegra, 2015). According to the Collaborative for Academic, Social, and Emotional Learning (CASEL), the five competencies that contribute to the success of all students are the development of self-awareness, self-management, social awareness, relationship management, and responsible decision-making (Weissberg & Cascarino, 2013).

Unfortunately, despite the expectation that students will engage in these higher order tasks in the classroom due to Common Core instruction, only three states have adopted free-standing standards that keep schools accountable for proactively teaching these socioemotional skills comprehensively to students in grades kindergarten through 12 (Dusenbury, Weissberg, Goren, & Domitrovich, 2014).

There does appear to be some movement in the integration of social–emotional learning into school classrooms because throughout the country, federal and state initiatives are encouraging or requiring schools to take a lead role in providing interventions to build students' behavioral and social–emotional skills (Bezinque, Darling-Churchill, Start-Cassel, Schmitz, & Ryberg, 2014). In 2011, the US Department of Education, in conjunction with the US Department of Justice, launched the Supportive School Discipline Initiative (SSDI). In January 2014, guidelines and strategies for school districts to enhance school climate and discipline were released (US Department of Education, 2014). These guidelines set forth action steps that schools should take to proactively encourage positive behavior and to ensure students have the social and emotional skills needed to promote learning in the classroom, including implementing a range of social–emotional interventions to meet diverse student challenges. These guidelines also recommend the establishment of partnerships with mental health agencies to expand on-site services to students and families. Data collection and evaluation are key components of SSDI and are critical to not only confirming the effectiveness of interventions but also seeing the impact of interventions on disciplinary outcomes such as suspensions and expulsions (US Department of Education, 2014).

As of March 2010, 14 states had adopted legislation to partially or completely require the use of the Response to Intervention (RTI) framework to qualify students as having a specific learning disability for special education services, Other states are currently recommending the implementation of a multi-tiered system of support (MTSS) such as RTI or Positive Behavior Interventions and Supports (PBIS) (Zirkel & Thomas, 2010). With the advent of MTSS, school social workers are now also required to collect and analyze data as part of the assessment phase to guide intervention, during the intervention phase to monitor implementation and adjust as necessary, and after the intervention to evaluation outcomes (Sabatino, Kelly, Moriarity, & Lean, 2013). Given the three-tier RTI and PBIS approaches and their emphasis on prevention, school social workers must have the skills to gather, analyze, and interpret data on diverse systems, such as individuals, groups, families, schools, and possibly communities, so they can effectively intervene (Bowen & Swick, 2013; Frey & Dupper, 2005; Garrett, 2009; Hopson & Lawson, 2011). These evaluation processes should allow school social workers to better match interventions to needs and, with evidence of their effectiveness, potentially expand their services on all tier levels, especially if they are able to align their outcomes with those of the district.

One example of state legislation focused on student engagement and climate was introduced in California in 2013. The program, called the Local Control Funding Formula (LCFF), provides local communities with the opportunity to determine educational priorities and accountability for student success (California Department of Education, 2015). Through this funding formula, all California public school districts receive base funding, and those districts serving vulnerable students—identified as English learners, youth in foster care, and students receiving free and reduced price lunch—receive additional supplemental and concentration grant support. As a requirement of the funding process, school districts are required to create a Local Control and Accountability Plan (LCAP) to align state and local priorities to programs, budget, and outcomes equally in the areas of academic achievement, administration of basic services, course access for all students, implementation of Common Core standards, parental involvement, student engagement, school climate, and other student outcomes (California Department of Education, 2015).

In addition to setting goals, school districts in California are now required to document regular progress toward goals in areas traditionally addressed by school social workers and other student support providers (school climate, student engagement, and parental involvement). In response to this legislation and the changes in funding structure, California public schools are now held accountable for developing, implementing, and monitoring services and supports that have an impact on more than the traditional focus on academic outcomes. Student success is now examined through a multidimensional lens that includes a number of student indicators and a much stronger emphasis on student and family engagement and school climate. Thus, California school districts are more accountable for the creation of school environments that are welcoming to all and help students, staff, and families feel connected, safe, and supported.

Finally, practice monitoring is essential because some school social workers are hired on grants, particularly during economic downturns (Raines & Alvarez, 2006). Most grants require an evaluation plan to document that the objectives and outcomes promised in the grant have been accomplished. To accomplish these tasks and, it is hoped, retain and attract additional funding, school social workers must understand how to select appropriate data collection and analytic methods to address their specific research questions. In most instances, this means both process—information on whether the activities promised were actually completed—and outcome data that measure the extent to which the proposed changes occurred (Raines & Alvarez, 2006).

## SCHOOL SOCIAL WORK PRACTICE RELATED TO MONITORING AND EVALUATING

Clearly, it is important for school social workers to monitor and evaluate their practices, particularly those related to academic achievement and other school performance measures such as attendance and disciplinary referrals. Unfortunately, there is evidence that these practices may not regularly occur in schools. Meta-analyses and reviews on school social work practice outcomes indicate that there is still a limited number of well-designed school social work research studies, and unfortunately, few of the quality studies included in these reviews actually focused on academic and school performance outcomes (Allen-Meares, Montgomery, & Kim, 2013; Early & Vonk, 2001; Franklin et al., 2009). Of the 21 controlled school social work outcome studies on risk and resilience reviewed by Early and Vonk, none focused on changes in school attendance or academic performance even though both have been shown to be risk factors for adolescent problem behaviors (Hawkins, Catalano, & Miller, 1992). In Franklin et al.'s meta-analysis of 21 school social work studies, only 4 (19%) used attendance as an outcome, whereas 5 (24%) investigated the impact of school social work services on academic achievement (grades and credits earned). They concluded that school social work services were not predictive of changes in school attendance; however, there were medium to large effect sizes for the majority of studies that focused on academic achievement. They suggested that more social work research should include academic performance measures, particularly using proximal measures such as school engagement and homework completion (Franklin et al., 2009).

It also appears that school social workers may infrequently track or report practice outcomes linked to academic performance in the field. Using data from four school districts in

Minnesota, Bye et al. (2009) found that both school social workers and administrators believed that increased attendance, decreased discipline problems, and improved school climate and achievement were the top four expected outcomes for school social work services. However, less than half (48%) of the same school social workers reported on program outcomes related to discipline problems, and only 26% collected data on student achievement. Almost one-third (29%) did not present any outcome data at all.

In a study of school social workers in New Mexico, Whittlesey-Jerome (2013) found that although many social workers engaged in monitoring and evaluation, less than half (47%) "usually" used school performance as an outcome measure or "used data whenever possible" (46%), whereas only one-third used evaluation information to improve services (p. 84). Using a sample of school social workers from Iowa, Peckover, Vasquez, Van Housen, Saunders, and Allen (2013) reported that only about 5% of school social work time was spent on academic assessment and screening, and 42% of social workers did not feel very confident in this area. Indeed, it was the second highest area identified as needing professional development. It is possible that the lack of social work studies and district-level outcome reporting may be influenced by the micro approach most school social workers continue to adopt, lack of training and knowledge of evaluation methods, the difficulties associated with school-based intervention research, and limited resources for evaluation (Berzin & O'Connor, 2010; Kelly et al., 2010a; Mishna, Muskat, & Cook, 2012). Regardless of the reasons for the lack of documentation of the link between school social work services and educational outcomes, the new trends in education underscore the need for school social workers to strengthen this aspect of their practice so they can enlarge their area of practice and underscore the importance of ecological school social work practice (Farwell & Sohng, 2009).

Beauchemin and Kelly (2009) also suggested that school social workers must actively market their services to teachers, administrators, and school boards by showing how their work contributes to district priorities, especially during economic downturns when funding decisions become competitive. Franklin (2005) indicated the need for school social workers to show their accountability by developing performance measures and sharing them with key stakeholders. However, it has been found that one-third of school social workers never share their evaluation outcomes with school boards or administrators (Whittlsey-Jerome, 2013). A second study indicated that school social workers were significantly more likely than school administrators to report that school social work outcomes were shared informally. Based on this finding, the authors suggested that program outcomes should be disseminated to district leaders and decision-makers through a more formal process (Bye et al., 2009). These findings are cause for concern, as the effective dissemination of outcomes have been directly related to increases in school social work services in some districts.

## EVALUATING SCHOOL SOCIAL WORK PROGRAMS

Because school social workers often have multiple and competing demands (Kelly, Berzin, Frey, Alvarez, Shaffer, & O'Brien, 2010a, 2010b), the best evaluation approaches are those closely tied to practice that could, in addition to providing data for key stakeholders, be used to monitor and strengthen school social work services. School social work services benefit from gathering and analyzing assessment data prior to intervention. Assessment data are an important component in evidence-based planning because they identify students' strengths and needs and ecological circumstances (Bowen & Swick, 2013). Assessment data can be used to determine the systems (individual, peer, family, school, and community) most in need of intervention as well as provide baseline data that can be used to determine whether changes have occurred as a result of intervention. Bowen and Swick (2013) developed the School Success Profile, a survey that can be used with middle and high school youth to better understand their perceptions of both their own individual capabilities (physical and mental health and academic achievement) and the larger social environment (community, family, school, and peers). The information gathered through the profile can be analyzed and used at the individual, school, or even district level (Bowen & Swick, 2013).

The Communities That Care (CTC) Youth Survey is an evidence-based, prevention survey that measures risk and protective factors in the community, family, school, and individual/peer domains related to adolescent problem behaviors, including school dropout. The CTC Youth Survey has been shown to be a valid measure across ethnic and gender groups and has established cut points that can be used to identify cumulative risk (Briney, Brown, Hawkins, & Arthur, 2012; Glaser, Van Horn, Arthur, Hawkins, & Catalano, 2005). Both instruments have been used nationwide, and the factors they measure are predictive of important school goals. One of the major benefits of these surveys is the fact that they link each of the dimensions of risk and protective factors measured to evidence-based approaches (Bowen & Swick, 2013; *CTC Prevention Strategies Guide*, n.d.). This can make it easier for school social workers to ensure that the approaches they select, on each of the three RTI levels, reflect best practices.

# PROCESS EVALUATION OF SCHOOL SOCIAL WORK SERVICES

School social workers need to collect process data to document their interventions, ensure their interventions were implemented as designed, and identify ways in which services can be improved. Process or formative evaluation is often conceptualized as the "who," "what," and "how" of the intervention (Kettner, Moroney, & Martin, 2008; Rubin & Babbie, 2014). School social workers might demonstrate the "who" through the collection of demographics on the youth they serve. In addition to providing the total number of youth and families served, this also helps school social workers understand the characteristics of the population they are serving and, potentially, determine if different interventions are warranted. For example, if African American students constitute 20% of the school population but 80% of the school social work caseload, it would be important for school social workers to explore the reasons for this disproportionate rate, including the possibility of training staff on cultural differences. Likewise, if Cambodian students make up a substantial proportion of the school population but family members never come to school events, this might suggest the need to provide Khmer translation or to modify outreach approaches to make the events more culturally relevant.

School social work practice is multidimensional, but most evaluations of school social work practice have typically focused on interventions with specific problems (Alvarez et al., 2012). However, evaluating the multifaceted aspects of school social work is critical to showing how the ability to intervene on multiple levels is particularly helpful in promoting attendance and academic achievement. To document the "what" and "how" of the intervention process, school social workers must develop mechanisms to collect all of the multi-systemic interventions they provide on behalf of each referral as well as document progress made toward goals (Garrett, 2012).

Unfortunately, when studying record-keeping practices, Garret found that less than half of her sample of school social workers in the United States and Canada consistently documented assessment and service information or progress toward goals, including data from before and after their interventions. This lack of basic information on implementation and outcomes makes it difficult for school social workers to provide reports on their services, reflect on their practice, and link their services to important district outcomes (Garret, 2012; Kagel & Kopels, 2008).

To evaluate the effectiveness of school social work services on school attendance, Newsome et al. (2008) created the School Social Work Intervention Checklist. The checklist was designed to collect information on both the type and the amount of social work services received by each youth, including interventions with youth, family members, school staff, and representatives from community agencies. Using this same type of form to document interventions (Table 13.1) can prove beneficial for school social workers in reviewing and reflecting on their practice. For example, if it becomes apparent when analyzing this process data that the primary or overwhelming service modality is individual work, school social workers might be encouraged to consider if their interventions are actually tailored to the circumstances of the child or why they are not working more with school staff, families, and the community as consistently suggested in the literature (Frey & Dupper, 2005; Kelly et al., 2010a, 2010b).

Attendance should also be kept for all groups, classroom interventions, and other meetings or events facilitated by school social workers. When implementing interventions, particularly those that are evidence based, it is important to know the extent to which participants actually receive the services (Kettner et al., 2008). For example, if a school social worker implemented an 8-week evidence-based family education program and the data show that only 30% of the parents or caregivers attended all the sessions, it is unlikely that the expected outcomes will be obtained. Collecting and reviewing attendance may also help school social workers to recognize when there might be a challenge in service retention and allow them to follow up with people who drop out of programs. Attendance keeping is also important because the amount of exposure to an intervention can be important. One study of a school-based family involvement program investigated the impact of the program on Latino children's academic achievement. After 2 years, it was found that the level of program participation significantly predicted improvements in student effort, social skills, work habits, grades, and standardized English Language Arts test scores (O'Donnell & Kirkner, 2014). However, these results would not have been evident if attendance had not been systematically collected.

Process evaluation approaches might also include the use of satisfaction surveys completed by students, family members, and school staff. Knowing what people like and do not

Table 13.1: Documentation of Social Work Interventions

| Student Name | Individual Contact | Family Contact | Teacher Consult | School Staff Contact | Classroom Observation or Education | Agency Referral | Agency Contact | Group | Other |
|---|---|---|---|---|---|---|---|---|---|
| Javier | 1 | Home visit | | Nurse | Observe | Food bank | | Social skills | |
| Lisa | 2 | Phone | 3 | Principal | Bullying prevention curriculum | | After-school program | | |

like can be helpful in strengthening school social work practice. Focus groups may also prove beneficial to understanding the implementation process, particularly for new programs, because data can be gathered on what participants preferred or want from the program (Berg & Lune, 2012).

# OUTCOME EVALUATION OF SCHOOL SOCIAL WORK SERVICES

Outcome evaluation focuses on the changes that occurred as a result of an intervention and should be guided by measurable goals (Rubin & Babbie, 2014). According to Raines (2002), school social workers can evaluate student progress using school records, interviews, logs, standardized measures, or observation. Outcome evaluation can be more challenging because statistical tests may need to be run to analyze quantitative data, which may prove difficult for some school social workers because they are not researchers (Garrett, 2009). It may be beneficial for school social workers to develop relationships with district research staff or local universities to collect and analyze outcome data. It is critical that school social workers choose outcome measures that match the goals of their interventions and are reliable and valid (Monette, Sullivan, & DeJong, 2008; Rubin & Babbie, 2014). School social workers might also want to use single-subject designs (Garrett, 2009; Raines, 2004) because they may provide some evidence of change.

## DESIGNING EVALUATION TO MATCH LOCAL GOALS AND PRIORITIES

Effective evaluation plans match the priorities of local decision-makers and reflect the scope of services of the individual school social work practitioner. Priorities most often will include academic achievement but may also focus on attendance, discipline, parental involvement, or school climate measures. Evaluation plans should be created on a local level by asking questions similar to those posed by Dibble (1999):

- Who are you trying to influence with results from your evaluation (i.e., who are the main stakeholders)?
- What are the priorities of the stakeholders (i.e., school board focus goals or district goals, single plan for student achievement, or Individualized Education Plan goals)?
- What data may already be available at the school, such as attendance, grade-point average, and discipline data, and what might need to be gathered from students, parents, school staff, and/or community members (i.e., surveys and individual behavior plan data collection)?
- What data would be most connected to the intervention provided (i.e., one would not collect discipline data for a student who has no history of behavior issues and is participating in a grief group)?
- Which data are most connected to your intervention and most relevant to stakeholders?

By following this five-step planning process, school social workers can ensure their interventions address the most pressing priorities of the local community.

Fortunately, given the aforementioned need for school social workers to evaluate the relationship between their services and educational outcomes, there is a wealth of readily available information for school social workers to access (Farwell & Sohng, 2009). Because schools are mandated to keep attendance data and state funding is typically dependent on attendance (Teasley, 2004), it is critical that school social workers access and analyze these data. This is particularly important because attendance increases can be directly linked to increased district funding, which can then be used to support school social work services (Raines, 2006). School social workers can calculate the estimated value gained through of their services by multiplying the decrease in absences by the amount of money the school receives daily per student. Because there is not much published evidence of the ability of school social work services to improve school attendance, it may also be important to gather information on factors that have been shown to impact attendance. Newsome et al. (2008) used the School Success Profile to assess truancy risk factors within the individual, family, school, and neighborhood before and after intervention. Although, in their study, school social work practice did not significantly increase attendance, there were significant improvements in school satisfaction, home academic environment, self-esteem, and academic performance, all of which have been linked to absenteeism. Thus, it is possible, in the long term, these reductions in truancy risk factors will result in improved attendance (Newsome et al., 2008).

Other objective secondary measures that are readily available at the individual, school, and district level are disciplinary referrals including suspensions and expulsions, grades, and test scores (Garret, 2009). Changes in these variables can be explored by comparing the data points prior to and after school social work intervention. This can be done using statistical analyses or even by counts and percentage changes. For example, if youth referred by school social worker services were suspended 20 days prior to intervention and 5 days after intervention, this would represent a 75% decrease in the number of days suspended. Given that grades and test scores may be less amenable to change due to school social work intervention or the fact that so many other factors may influence these measures, in the short term it can be advantageous to use other data that might be available (Franklin et al., 2009). For example, some report cards may contain effort, social skills, or homework completion grades that can also be used as measures related to academic performance.

School social workers may also provide services that have been shown to positively influence academic performance. Both family involvement in their children's education and participation in school-based family education have been linked to better academic achievement, particularly for urban, low-income youth of color (Jeynes, 2007, 2012). Engaging families in their children's education is a consistent expectation of school social work practice (Randolph, Teasley, & Arrington, 2006). Thus, school social workers should use standardized measures or existing surveys (Kohl, Lengua, & McMahon, 2000; Westmoreland, Bouffard, O'Carroll, & Rosenberg, 2009) to monitor whether their efforts with family members result in changes in actual educational involvement or help to build factors related to involvement such as a sense of self-efficacy or motivation or beliefs for involvement (Walker, Wilkins, Dallaire, Sandler, & Hoover-Dempsey, 2005). To complete this evaluation, family members participating in school social work programs would need to complete surveys prior to and at the completion of services or at the end of the school year that could then be analyzed statistically. The School Success Profile and the CTC student surveys, as well as the school climate measures identified in the resources section of this chapter, can be used in the same way to investigate whether schoolwide school social work initiatives result in positive changes.

---

# CASE STUDY

## THE ESCONDIDO UNION SCHOOL DISTRICT

The Escondido Union School District's (EUSD) expansion of school social work services from a single school social worker to 27 school social workers was a direct result of a well-designed strategic program and an evaluation plan that strongly supported the effectiveness of school social work services in meeting local, state, and federal goals. Before the development of the comprehensive districtwide plan for school social work, school social workers were funded on an hourly basis through school-site categorical funding to provide individual or group counseling services. At that time, process or outcome evaluation measures were not collected to determine service efficacy. Rather than a formal evaluation plan, principal and school staff satisfaction (based on positive relationships made by the school social worker and completion of principal-assigned tasks, not on formal survey mechanisms) was the sole determinant of the continuation of school social work services throughout the district.

In an effort to ensure ongoing placement of school social workers at schools, the district identified the federal Safe Schools/Healthy Students (SS/HS) initiative as a potential funding source for helping develop systematic structures around the use of school social work services in EUSD. For 2 years, a pupil services administrator (the district's first school social worker) used an array of data collection mechanisms to determine the needs of the district and begin planning for the best use of funding for the community of Escondido. Through qualitative (key informant interviews, focus groups, and facilitation of a grant development committee) and quantitative data collection (attendance, discipline, and student and staff perception data), the school social worker and grant development team developed a comprehensive plan and a vision for the development of the CARE (Collaborative Agency Resources for Education) Youth Project.

The CARE Youth Project grant proposal was designed to support the placement of school social workers at 13 (8 elementary and 5 middle) schools throughout the district to provide linkages for students to supports at school and in the community; with the ultimate goal to enhance and support their academic and personal success. The school social work services were comprehensive in nature and included the following key components: application of the MTSS, adoption of evidenced-informed practices such as coordinating Comprehensive Student Assistance Teams at school sites, implementing Positive Behavioral Interventions and Supports, developing supportive and consistent attendance intervention practices, building a system of support that included school-based and community-linked agency partners, and offering consultative and direct clinical services. The EUSD was awarded the federal SS/HS grant between June 2009 and July 2013, with a 1-year extension to expend unused funds.

The key to the ultimate success of the CARE Youth Project and the sustainability of program services was the development of an evaluation plan that provided meaningful outcomes to the individuals who would ultimately be responsible for continuing to fund school social workers at the end of the grant period. Although the SS/HS initiative required all projects to collect student self-report data on missing school due to perception of safety at school or on their way to and from school, being in a fight on campus, using alcohol and marijuana during the past 30 days, receiving mental health services, and receiving referrals to mental health providers, the CARE Youth Project administrative team (inclusive of a contracted program evaluator) determined the need to collect more robust local data to ensure outcomes resonated with the priorities of local funders, most notably the district's board of education. For this reason, the evaluation plan for EUSD's SS/HS grant included a plan for regularly examining attendance, discipline, school climate, and parent involvement data. When the evaluation plan was developed in 2010, the administrative team did not know how important these measures would truly be by the end of the grant period. The end of the SS/HS grant period aligned with the inception of Local Control Funding, where school districts throughout California were required to begin implementing programs and services to address school climate and student and parent engagement.

In addition to a regular review of data outcomes from the project, at the end of the 5 years of program implementation, 2,925 of students had received services by a school social worker, 504 teachers had participated in a PBIS workshop provided by a school social worker, and approximately 2,100 unduplicated parents had attended a Parent University workshop coordinated by a school social worker (with a district parent liaison). During the 5-year period, there was a 31.5% decrease in days of absence at the 13 project school sites, a 75% decrease in days of suspension due to violence at EUSD middle schools, a 84% decrease in days of suspension due to violence at EUSD project elementary schools, a 37% decrease in seventh grade students reporting being in a fight at school, a 16% increase in seventh grade students reporting feeling connected to school, and a 29% increase in seventh grade students reporting having opportunities for meaningful participation in school as measured through the annual California Healthy Kids Survey.

In 2010, the EUSD CARE Youth Project was awarded a California School Board Association Golden Bell Award and the California Cities, Counties, Schools Award for "Community Schools Through Partnership and Collaboration." In 2012, the project was awarded a "Public Health Champion" award from the County of San Diego's Health and Human Services Agency. The positive program outcomes and recognition were presented to the district's board of education, along with a video of qualitative reports from key stakeholders including students, teachers, school administrators, and community members. As a result of highlighting the success of school social work interventions funded through the SS/HS grant to stakeholders (both process and outcome data) and showing a clear link between the interventions used and interventions suggested for school districts through the new California local control funding and accountability model, school social workers were funded to support each of EUSD's 23 schools during the following school year. At the start of the 2016–2017 school year, 25 school social workers were employees of EUSD through local funding. In addition, 2 school social workers remained in their administrative positions after the grant ended to ensure the continuation of districtwide support in the area of positive school discipline, student health and mental health support, and family/community outreach.

## CONCLUSION

School social workers must strengthen their monitoring and evaluation practices not only to ensure that their interventions are effective, but also to comply with reporting and accountability requirements set forth on local, state, and federal levels. As demonstrated in the example of the Escondido Union School District, linking school social work services to children's academic success and/or state and local district priorities, and providing evidence of service effectiveness, will help the school social work profession grow and expand. Thus, it is important that schools of social work prepare school social workers to engage in these tasks and/or for school social workers to partner with others (district evaluators or university professors) to develop and implement strong monitoring and evaluation systems. Once data have been collected and analyzed, school social workers should use this information to improve their practice and to disseminate their social work to key stakeholders, such as legislators, school administrators, teachers and other school staff, and parents.

## DISCUSSION QUESTIONS

1. How has the implementation of Common Core State Standards, Response to Intervention, and Positive Behavioral Interventions and Supports fundamentally changed the role of data in school social work practice?
2. What is the difference between process and outcome data?
3. What are two process measures and two outcome measures that you might collect to show the efficacy of your group intervention for students experiencing chronic poor attendance?
4. What are five steps that school social workers can follow in designing a relevant evaluation plan for interventions conducted at their school site?
5. How can you use these five steps to implement progress monitoring and data-based decision-making at your specific school site?

## ADDITIONAL RESOURCES

California Healthy Kids Survey–West Ed: https://chks.wested.org

Centers for Disease Control and Prevention, *Youth Risk Behavior Surveillance System*: http://www.cdc.gov/healthyyouth/data/yrbs/index.htm

Common Core State Standards Initiative: http://www.corestandards.org

Family involvement measures can be accessed at the Harvard Family Research Project: http://www.hfrp.org/family-involvement/publications-resources/data-collection-instruments-for-evaluating-family-involvement

Model or promising program lists can be found on the Blueprints for Violence Prevention website at http://www.colorado.edu/cspv/blueprints and the Substance Abuse and Mental Health Services Administration's National Registry for Evidence-Based Programs and Practices at http://www.nrepp.samhsa.gov.

National Education Association, *Common Core Toolkit*: http://www.nea.org/assets/docs/17456-CommonCare_Tolkit_INTtabs4NEW.pdf

School climate measures can be accessed at the following websites:

http://www.schoolclimate.org/climate/practice.php

http://safesupportivelearning.ed.gov/topic-research/school-climate-measurement

School Success Profile and evidence-based approaches: https://www.schoolsuccessonline.com/

Socioemotional measures for youth can be accessed at the following websites:

  http://www.casel.org/library/2013/12/9/social-emotional-learning-assessment-measures-for-middle-school-youth

  http://www.uwheartmo.org/sites/uwheartmo.org/files/Compendium_SELTools.

  http://www.search-institute.org/sites/default/files/a/DAP-Raikes-Foundation-Review.pdf

  http://www.schoolclimate.org/climate/documents/RaikesReportFinalOct.pdf

Substance Abuse and Mental Health Services Administration, *Communities That Care Youth Survey*: http://store.samhsa.gov/product/Communities-That-Care-Youth-Survey/CTC020

# REFERENCES

Allen-Meares, P., Montgomery, K., & Kim, J. (2013). School-based social work interventions: A cross-national systematic review. *Social Work, 58*(3), 253–262.

Alvarez, M., Bye, L., Bryant, R., & Mumm, A. (2013). School social workers and educational outcomes. *Children & Schools, 35*(4), 235–243. Not sure why deleted as is cited in the text

Alvarez, M., Sabatino, C., Frey, A., Dupper, D., Lindsey, B., et al. (2012). Implications of Race to the Top grants on evaluation of school social workers. *Children & Schools, 34*(4), 195–199.

Beauchemin, P., & Kelly, M. (2009). Adopting a social marketing mind-set in school social work practice. *School Social Work Journal, 34*(1), 61–73.

Berg, B. L., & Lune, H. (2012). *Qualitative research methods for the social sciences* (8th ed.). New York, NY: Pearson.

Berzin, S., & O'Connor, S. (2010). Educating today's school social workers: Are school social work courses responding to the changing context? *Children & Schools, 32*(4), 237–249.

Bezinque, A., Darling-Churchill, K., Stuart-Cassel, V., Schmitz, H., & Ryberg, R. (2014). *Compendium of school discipline laws and regulations for the 50 states*. Washington, DC: National Center on Safe Supportive Learning Environments.

Bowen, G. L., & Swick, D. C. (2013). Using the school success profile to assess outcomes. In C. Franklin, M. B. Harris, & P. Allen-Meares (Eds.), *The school services source book: A guide for school-based professionals* (pp. 915–924). New York, NY: Oxford University Press.

Bye, L., Shepard, M., Partridge, J., & Alvarez, M. (2009). School social work outcomes: Perspectives of school social workers and school administrators. *Children & Schools, 31*(2), 97–108.

California Department of Education. (2015). *Local control funding formula*. Retrieved from http://www.cde.ca.gov/fg/aa/lc

Cawood, N. (2013). Addressing interpersonal violence in the school context: Awareness and use of evidence-supported programs. *Children & Schools, 35*(1), 41–52.

Communities that Care Prevention Strategies Guide (n.d.) http://www.sdrg.org/ctcresource/Prevention%20Strategies%20Guide/introduction.pdf

Dibble, N. (1999). *Outcome evaluation of school social work services*. Madison, WI: Wisconsin Department of Education.

Drisko, J. (2014). Research evidence and social work practice: The place of evidence-based practice. *Clinical Social Work Journal, 42*(2), 123–133.

Dusenbury, L., Weissberg, R., Goren, P., & Domitrovich, C. (2014). *Findings from the CASEL's state scan of social emotional learning standards, preschool through high school, 2014*. State Standards to Advance Social and Emotional Learning, Collaboration for Academic, Social, and Emotional

Learning. Retrieved from http://static1.squarespace.com/static/513f79f9e4b05ce7b70e9673/t/52f95691e4b0a41caba778b8/1392072337661/casel-brief-on-state-standards-january-2014.pdf

Early, T., & Vonk, M. (2001). Effectiveness of school social work from a risk and resilience perspective. *Children & Schools, 23*(1), 9–31.

Elias, M. J. (2014). Social–emotional skills can boost Common Core implementation. *Kappan, 96*(3), 58–62.

Farwell, N., & Sohng, S. (2009). Conducting and using research in the schools: Practitioners as agents for change. In C. R. Massat, R. Constable, S. McDonald, & J. P. Flynn (Eds.), *School social work: Practice, policy, and research* (7th ed., pp. 233–253). Chicago, IL: Lyceum.

Franke, T., & Lynch, S. (2006). Linking school social work interventions to educational outcomes for schools. In C. Frankly, M. Harris, & P. Allen-Meares (Eds.), *The school services sourcebook: A guide for school-based professionals* (pp. 1021–1030). New York, NY: Oxford University Press.

Franklin, C. (2005). The future of school social work practice: Current trends and opportunities. *Advances in Social Work, 6*(1), 167–181.

Franklin, C., & Kelly, M. (2009). Becoming evidence-informed in the real world of school social work practice. *Children & Schools, 31*(1), 46–56.

Franklin, C., Kim, J., & Tripodi, S. (2009). A meta-analysis of published school social work practice studies: 1980–2007. *Research on Social Work Practice, 19*(6), 667–677.

Frey, A., & Dupper, D. (2005). A broader conceptual approach to clinical practice for the 21st century. *Children & Schools, 27*(1), 33–44.

Garrett, K. J. (2009). Working with groups in schools: Monitoring of process and evaluation of outcomes. In C. R. Massat, R. Constable, S. McDonald, & J. P. Flynn (Eds.), *School social work: Practice, policy, and research* (7th ed., pp. 610–620). Chicago, IL: Lyceum.

Garrett, K. J. (2012). Managing school social work records. *Children & Schools, 34*(4), 239–248.

Gubi, A. A., & Bocanegra, J. O. (2015). Impact of the Common Core on social–emotional learning initiatives of diverse students. *Contemporary School Psychology, 19*, 98–102.

Harrison, K., & Harrison, R. (2014). Utilizing direct observation methods to measure social–emotional behaviors in school social work practice. *School Social Work Journal, 39*(1), 17–34.

Hawkins, D., Catalano, R., & Miller, J. (1992). Risk and protective factors for alcohol and other drug problems in adolescence and early adulthood: Implications for substance abuse program. *Psychological Bulletin, 112*(1), 64–105.

Hopson, L., & Lawson, H. (2011). Social workers' leadership for positive school climates via data informed planning and decision making. *Children & Schools, 33*(2), 106–118.

Jeynes, W. H. (2007). The relationship between parental involvement and urban secondary school student academic achievement: A meta-analysis. *Urban Education, 42*(1), 82–110.

Jeynes, W. H. (2012). A meta-analysis of the efficacy of different types of parental involvement programs for urban students. *Urban Education, 47*(4), 706–742.

Kagel, J. D., & Kopels, S. (2008). *Social work records* (3rd ed.). Long Grove, IL: Waveland Press.

Kelly, M., Frey, A., Alvarez, M., Berzin, S., Shaffer, G., & O'Brien, K. (2010a). School social work practice and response to intervention. *Children & Schools, 32*(4), 201–209.

Kelly, M., Frey, A., Alvarez, M., Berzin, S., Shaffer, G., & O'Brien, K. (2010b). The state of school social work: Findings from the National School Social Work Survey. *School Mental Health, 2*(1), 132–141.

Kettner, P. M., Moroney, R. M., & Martin, L. L. (2008). *Designing and managing programs: An effectiveness-based approach* (3rd ed.). Thousand Oaks, CA: Sage.

Kohl, G. O., Lengua, L. J., & McMahon, R. J. (2000). Parent involvement in school conceptualizing multiple dimensions and their relations with family and demographic risk factors. *Journal of School Psychology, 38*, 501–523.

Mishna, F., Muskat, B., & Cook, C. (2012). Anticipating challenges: School-based social work intervention research. *Children & Schools, 34*(3), 135–144.

Monette, D. R., Sullivan, T. J., & DeJong, C. R. (2008). *Applied social research: A tool for the human services* (7th ed.). Belmont CA: Thomson Wadsworth.

National Association of Social Workers. (2012). *NASW standards for school social work services.* Retrieved from http://www.naswdc.org/practice/standards/naswschoolsocialworkstandards.pdf

National Governors Association, Center for Best Practices, Council of Chief State School Officers. (2010). *Common Core State Standards.* Washington, DC: Author. Retrieved from http://www.corestandards.org

Newsome, W., Anderson-Butcher, D., Fink, J., Hall, L., & Huffer, J. (2008). The impact of school social work services on student absenteeism and risk factors related to school truancy. *School Social Work Journal, 32*(2), 21–38.

O'Donnell, J., & Kirkner, S. L. (2014). The impact of a collaborative family involvement program on Latino families and children's educational performance. *School Community Journal, 24,* 211–234.

Peckover, C., Vasquez, M., Van Housen, S., Saunders, J., & Allen, L. (2013). Preparing school social work for the future: An update of school social workers' tasks in Iowa. *Children & Schools, 35*(1), 9–17.

Raines, J. (2002). Present levels of performance, goals, and objectives: A best practice guide. *School Social Work Journal, 27*(1), 58–72.

Raines, J. (2004). Evidence-based practice in school social work: A process in perspective. *Children & Schools, 26*(2), 71.

Raines, J. (2006). SWOT! A strategic plan for school social work in the twenty-first century. *School Social Work Journal, 31,* 132–150.

Raines, J. C., & Alvarez, M. (2006). Cash through collaboration: A relational approach to grant writing for social workers in schools. *School Social Work Journal, 30*(2), 45–63.

Randolph, K. A., Teasley, M. L., & Arrington, J. (2006). School social workers' perceptions of parent involvement in education. *School Social Work Journal, 31*(1), 76–89.

Rubin, A., & Babbie, E. (2014). *Research methods for social work.* Belmont, CA: Brooks/Cole.

Sabatino, C., Kelly, E., Moriarity, J., & Lean, E. (2013). Response to intervention: A guide to scientifically based research for school social work services. *Children & Schools, 35*(4), 213–223.

Teasley, M. L. (2004). Absenteeism and truancy: Risk, protection and best practice implications for school social workers. *Children and Schools, 26*(2), 117–128.

US Department of Education. (2014) *Guiding principles: A resource guide for improving school climate and discipline.* Washington, DC: Author.

Walker, J. T., Wilkins, A. S., Dallaire, J. R., Sandler, H. M., & Hoover-Dempsey, K. V. (2005). Parental involvement: Model revision through scale development. *Elementary School Journal, 106*(2), 85.

Weissberg, R. P., & Cascarino, J. (2003). Academic learning + social emotional learning = national priority. *Kappan Magazine, 95*(2), 8–13.

Westmoreland, H., Bouffard, S., O'Carroll, K., & Rosenberg, H. (2009). *Data collection instruments for evaluating family involvement.* Cambridge, MA: Harvard Family Research Project. Retrieved from http://www.hfrp.org/family-involvement/publications-resources/data-collection-instruments-for-evaluating-family-involvement

Whittlesey-Jerome, W. (2013). Results of the 2010 statewide New Mexico school social work survey: Implications for evaluating the effectiveness of school social work. *School Social Work Journal, 37*(2), 76–87.

Zirkel, P. A., & Thomas, L. B. (2010). State laws and guidelines for implementing RtI. *Teaching Exceptional Children, 43*(1), 60–73.

C H A P T E R   1 4

# EVALUATION

## BRENDA LINDSEY, CHRISTINE ANLAUF SABATINO, KARI SMITH, AND REBECCA KUNKEL

The No Child Left Behind Act of 2001 (NCLB; P.L. 107-110) created sweeping educational reforms that are intended to ensure student academic achievement. The law requires each state to implement a statewide evaluation system to document that all schools and school districts are achieving Adequate Yearly Progress (AYP) as defined by NCLB.

Some of the main principles of the legislation include an emphasis on scientifically based instructional curriculum and teaching methods, accountability through assessments that verify students are meeting or exceeding academic performance goals, and state authority to set academic standards (Allen-Meares, 2010). In other words, this law proposes to move American education toward outcome-based education measures.

In addition, NCLB requires schools to place a "highly qualified teacher" in the classroom for all core academic subjects. The federal definition of a highly qualified teacher is one who holds at least a bachelor's degree from a 4-year university (education), demonstrates proficiency in core subject areas taught (competency), and is fully endorsed by the state (certification) (20 U.S.C. § 6319, No Child Left Behind Act of 2001).

To meet the challenges of newly emerging federal reforms, the National Governors Association Center for Best Practices and the Council of Chief State School Officers sponsored a state-led process to develop a common set of academic subject matter competencies and benchmarks for grades kindergarten through twelve (K–12), commonly known as the Common Core State Standards (CCSS). The goal of the CCSS is to provide a clear, consistent statement for teachers and parents of what students are expected to learn, reflecting the knowledge and skills they need to have upon graduation for success in college and careers. As of 2014, CCSS had been adopted by 43 states and the District of Columbia (CCSS, 2015; NEA, 2014).

Current research indicates that there is an additional critical element necessary for academic achievement. Findings suggest that educational success is fostered within the context of social and emotional processes. The Collaborative for Social and Emotional Learning (CASEL) has identified five interrelated sets of competencies that studies indicate are crucial to the learning experience: self-awareness, self-management, social awareness, relationship skills, and responsible decision-making (CASEL, 2015).

American education is currently driven by federal initiatives on accountability and teacher qualifications; state standards on grade-level academic benchmarks; and social and emotional competencies that promote academic achievement, positive behaviors, and students' connection to school. How do these factors impact school social work practice? They set the stage for school systems to place a demand on school social workers to demonstrate that they promote academic and behavioral achievements through their practice and to validate their knowledge and skills through employee performance evaluation measures for these responsibilities.

How do we establish accountability for our practice? How should that be measured through employee performance evaluations? How do school social work services reinforce CCSS or other state learning standards? How do school social work methods address social and emotional learning competencies?

# PERFORMANCE EVALUATION OF SCHOOL SOCIAL WORK PRACTICE

To answer the previous questions, a task force of school social work practitioners and school social work researchers developed the National School Social Work Practice Model (Frey et al., 2013) and the National Evaluation Framework for School Social Work Practice (Sabatino et al., 2013) under the auspices of our professional organization, the School Social Work Association America (SSWAA), with a grant from Minnesota State University, Mankato.

The process began by reviewing the practice model definitions of our fellow non-classroom specialist colleagues, school psychologists and school counselors, as well as reviewing teacher evaluation frameworks in keeping with the context of the host setting—the school system. The aim was to examine official policy statements from educational professionals about proper delivery and evaluation of their services.

The National Association of School Psychologists (NASP) practice standard is titled the *Model for Comprehensive and Integrated School Psychological Services* (NASP, 2010), and its evaluation framework is titled *A Framework for the Personnel Evaluation of School Psychologists Utilizing the NASP Practice Model* (NASP, 2012). The American School Counselor Association (ASCA) practice standard is the *ASCA National Model: A Framework for School Counseling Programs* (ASCA, 2005), and its performance is evaluated "on basic standards of practice expected of school counselors implementing a comprehensive school counseling program" (ASCA, 2015, p. 1). Furthermore, accountability is measured by analyzing school data, including achievement scores, attendance, and behavior.

Between 2011 and 2013, the school social work national task force began the work of drafting a school social work practice model. Working drafts were presented at the annual program meetings for the Society of Social Work Research and the SSWAA. The draft document also was posted on the SSWAA website for public comment. In each instance, important feedback was obtained that strengthened successive drafts of the practice model. The SSWAA Delegate Assembly approved the final document, and the National School Social Work Practice Model became the official standard for the profession in 2013 (see Chapter 2).

It is a significant achievement to have developed a practice model tailored for school social workers and endorsed by the professional organization. However, the advent of outcome-based education measures requires a companion piece that reflects the profession's recommendations on how to evaluate employee performance of the practice model, demonstrating accountability for school social work knowledge and skills. The task force understood the necessity of creating a framework that succinctly conveyed critical competencies unique to school social work and how they differ from competencies for teachers. Ultimately, the task force's goal was to dovetail a desire to strengthen the profession by developing a practice model and evaluation framework that recognizes school social work as a specialized and much needed area of expertise within education.

The task force looked to the professional education literature on teacher performance evaluations and chose to adapt Charlotte Danielson's (2013) *The Framework for Teaching Evaluation Framework* because its structure is similar to those of the teacher performance evaluation frameworks used by many school systems. It was thought that this framework would make the performance evaluation of school social workers more user-friendly to school administrators. Furthermore, a strength of this latest edition of the teacher evaluation framework is that it has incorporated the underlying philosophy of CCSS, specifically the notion of "engagement" in which, in this case, school social workers are expected to take an active rather than passive role in implementing their work responsibilities. Thus, the National Evaluation Framework for School Social Work Practice uses observable behaviors and tangible artifacts to measure performance.

The draft performance evaluation model was presented at the Annual Program Meeting for the SSWAA and placed on its website for public comment. Feedback from SSWAA members greatly strengthened the document, and their recommendations were incorporated into the final version. The SSWAA Delegate Assembly adopted it in 2013, and the National Evaluation Framework for School Social Work Practice became the official standard for school social work performance evaluations.

The evaluation framework consists of four practice Domains that are viewed as the basic competencies required for school social work practice: (1) Planning and Preparation, (2) the School Environment, (3) Service Delivery and Resources, and (4) Professional Responsibilities.

Each domain is guided by a descriptive "Element" that articulates the practice focus for the domain. The substance of each practice domain, however, consists of a set of "Components" that define the major duties to be performed as part of the domain with "Examples" that illustrates the responsibilities. The components have been cross-walked and labeled with school social work practice standards found in the National Association of Social Workers' (NASW) *National Standards for School Social Work Services* (2012) and the SSWAA's National School Social Work Practice Model and the *National School Social Work Standards for Social Emotional Learning* (Lindsey et al., 2014).

The evaluation model also includes a discussion of levels of performance and defines four levels of ratings: unsatisfactory, basic, proficient, and distinguished. Using best practices in research, documentation from multiple sources is to be used to measure performance. Likewise, school administrators should use best practices and are invited to add components to domains that meet specific needs for evaluating professional social work programs and services in their district.

For example, the first domain is Planning and Preparation. Its guiding element is "The school social worker identifies school needs and organizes responses consistent with professional social work." The first component is the classic micro, mezzo, macro needs approach and states that the school social worker "conducts multi-tiered needs assessments." This component reflects the SSWAA Model Practice 1—Provide evidence-based education, behavior, and mental health services; Model Practice 2—Promote a school climate and culture conducive to student learning and teaching excellence; Key Construct 4—Data-based decision-making; as well as NASW Standard 3—Assessment. Multi-tiered assessments conducted by school social workers are focused on social and emotional learning knowledge and skills described in the *National School Social Work Standards for Social Emotional Learning*. Together, the *National Evaluation Framework for School Social Work Practice*, the National School Social Work Practice Model, and the *National School Social Work Standards for Social Emotional Learning* provide a comprehensive approach for establishing priorities for the evaluation of school social work practice. Examples cited are (1) assessing individual student needs, (2) assessing classroom and small group needs, and (3) assessing schoolwide or universal needs. Using multiple data sources, observable behaviors, and documentation, school social workers' performance may be viewed as (1) "unacceptable," requiring an improvement plan; (2) "developing," with partial or inconsistent performance but without need for an action plan; (3) "expected," demonstrating practice excellence; and (4) "exemplary," exceeding performance expectations. A complete copy of the *National Evaluation Framework for School Social Work Practice* is available on SSWAA's website (http://www.sswaa.org/?page=408).

# EVALUATION MODEL AND THE NATIONAL SCHOOL SOCIAL WORK STANDARDS FOR SOCIAL AND EMOTIONAL LEARNING

Development of social and emotional competencies is just as important as development of academic skills (Greenberg et al., 2003). It is an important component of students' schooling experience and is linked to improved behavioral and academic performance for students (CASEL, n.d.; Cohen, 2006; Durlak, Weissberg, Dymnicki, Taylor, & Schellinger, 2011; Jones & Buoffard, 2012; Zins, Weissberg, Wang, & Walberg, 2004). Research has shown positive outcomes for students who demonstrate social–emotional competency, including being connected to school, having positive relationships, and improved academic performance (Bonny, Britto, Klostermann, Hornung, & Slap, 2000; CASEL, n.d.; Cohen, 2006; Durlak et al., 2011; Jones & Buoffard, 2012; Zins et al., 2004).

With the growing push for national standards in education, social–emotional learning standards for children from early childhood through 12th grade should not be excluded. Board members of SSWAA recognized a need to create common standards to guide school social work practice for students' social–emotional development that were consistent K–12. The standards were written in order to identify the specific skills that students need to be able to demonstrate by the end of a particular point in their school careers. The standards become increasingly more complex and build on previous standards as students matriculate through the grade levels. As described previously, the *National School Social Work Standards for Social Emotional Learning* are aligned with the *National Evaluation Framework for School Social Work Practice* and the National School Social Work Practice Model. The process used to create the *National School Social Work Standards for Social Emotional Learning* began in 2013 and is outlined next.

# PROCESS USED TO DEVELOP NATIONAL SCHOOL SOCIAL STANDARDS FOR SOCIAL EMOTIONAL LEARNING

The development of the *National School Social Work Standards for Social Emotional Learning* began with a review of states' social–emotional learning standards and included the Illinois State Board of Education's (ISBE) social–emotional learning standards (see http://isbe.net/ils/social_ emotional/standards.htm), the Association of Alaska School Boards' Initiative for Community Engagement (see http://alaskaice.org/school-climate/sel), and CASEL (see http://www.casel. org). The ISBE's (2013) social–emotional learning standards were used as the framework for deciding on the specific skills students need to master at each point in their educational career. Members of the SSWAA board then identified the critical social–emotional skills that students must gain at each point in their schooling career. Following this process, a draft document was created and presented at a workshop at the SSWAA conference in March 2014. Workshop participants reviewed the document, shared feedback, and helped to further clarify the standards. Feedback from this workshop was incorporated into a second draft of the document and shared with the Association's Delegate Assembly in July 2014. Responses from the Delegate Assembly were incorporated into a subsequent version that was posted for public comment on the SSWAA website and vetted by the membership. The final version was adopted by the SSWAA board in 2015 and is available at http://www.sswaa.org/?page=2.

# APPLICATION OF SOCIAL–EMOTIONAL LEARNING IN ALL THREE TIERS

In addition to a need for consistent national social–emotional learning standards, social–emotional learning and development are important aspects of a multi-tiered framework of support, also referred to as multi-tiered systems of support (MTSS). The universal supports at tier 1 are the practices that are a part of the school community's beliefs and expectations with which all students are knowledgeable (Jones & Buoffard, 2012). These routines and expectations are reiterated and reinforced on a consistent basis with the entire school community, including students, parents/guardians, and staff (Jones & Bouffard, 2012). Supports at the secondary level of MTSS are identified for a smaller group of students, usually 10–15% of the student population, and include time-limited, small group, intensive instruction of skills (Lewis-Palmer, Bounds, & Sugai, 2004; Walker et al., 1996). This may include cognitive–behavioral therapy, individual and/ or group counseling, social skills training, and differentiated instructional approaches to meet students' individual needs (Pearce, 2009). Targeted supports at the tertiary level of MTSS are for the smallest 3–5% of the student population and may be longer term, are intensive, and may include additional resources outside of the school such as wraparound support (Lewis-Palmer et al., 2004.) All three tiers work together to provide a continuum of schoolwide services for students.

Competency in social–emotional skills is critical for social–emotional development (CASEL, n.d.; Durlak et al., 2011; Greenberg et al., 2003). SSWAA recognized the need to lay out the most critical skills that students need to develop at each stage of their educational career based on the current trends in social–emotional learning (CASEL, n.d.; ISBE, 2013). School social workers serve a critical role in assisting students to develop these skills through classroom, group, and individualized instruction. School social workers support the development of a positive school climate in which students are aware of the behavioral expectations. They play an important role within an MTSS model by developing plans for students who require additional support; monitoring students' progress; developing and implementing interventions; collecting data on the interventions; communicating progress with students, staff, and families; and linking families to outside resources when necessary. This type of integration between academics and behavior is critical for student success (.; Bohanon, McIntosh, & Goodman, n.d.; Bohanon & Wu, 2012; Goodman, McIntosh, & Bohanon, n.d.; Greenberg et al., 2003; McIntosh, Bohanon, & Goodman, n.d.). The *National School Social Work Standards for Social Emotional Learning*, the *National Evaluation Framework for School Social Work Practice*, and the National School Social Work Practice Model underscore the importance of this as the cornerstone of school social work practice.

# CULTURAL COMPETENCY AND SCHOOL SOCIAL WORK PRACTICE

A hallmark of school social work acknowledges the intersectionality of cultural and social diversity and the importance of demonstrating cultural competency in practice. Domain 2 of the *National Evaluation Framework for School Social Work Practice* specifically addresses this by the expectation that school social workers will demonstrate cultural competency by advancing student-centered school environments that are conducive to learning and show respect for differences in culture, background, and learning needs. Components within Domain 2 further delineate the various aspects to include contributing to a safe and healthy school environment; advocating for policies, programs, and services that respect diversity; addressing individual needs; supporting the inherent dignity and worth of all students, families, and school personnel; identifying historical and current political, social, cultural, and economic conditions that impact the context for learning; and promoting change.

Cultural competence is also reflected in the National School Social Work Practice Model, specifically Practices 1 and 2—Provide evidence-based education, behavior, and mental health services and promote a school climate and culture conducive to student learning and teaching excellence. All four key constructs of the model emphasize cultural competency as a foundation of school social work practice. The key constructs are (1) home–school–community linkages, (2) ethical guidelines and educational policy, (3) education rights and advocacy, and (4) data-based decision-making. Cultural competency is also a significant part of the *National School Social Work Standards for Social Emotional Learning*. SEL Goal 3 is Social Awareness: Recognize and express acceptance of the thoughts, feelings, and perspectives of others in a variety of social and cultural settings, with the subgoal of identifying individual and group similarities and differences.

The *National Evaluation Framework for School Social Work Practice* includes examples of ways to demonstrate cultural competency, such as implementing interventions that address risk factors affecting school performance, providing services in a manner that shows respect for diverse populations, and establishing school–community partnerships to expand resources for low-performing students. Table 14.1 illustrates examples of how to align school

**Table 14.1:** Aligning School Social Work Practice with the *National School Social Work Practice Model*, the *National School Social Work Standards for Social Emotional Learning*, and the *National Evaluation Framework for School Social Work Practice*

| Intervention Example | National School Social Work Practice Model—Alignment | National School Social Work Standards for Social Emotional Learning—Alignment with Academic Standards | National Evaluation Framework for School Social Work Practice—Domains and Components | Sample Artifacts to Demonstrate Competencies |
|---|---|---|---|---|
| **Tier 1**<br>Creating a Peaceful School Learning Environment (CAPSLE) is a tier 1 intervention that uses weekly classroom lessons to promote a positive school climate for K–12 students. See http://www.backoffbully.com/PDF%20files/PeacefulSchools/manual.pdf | Practice 1: Provide evidence-based education, behavior, and mental health services.<br><br>Practice 2: Promote a school climate conducive to student learning and teaching excellence.<br><br>Practice 3: Maximize access to school-based and community-based resources.<br><br>Key construct 1: Home–school–community linkages<br><br>Key construct 2: Ethical guidelines and educational policy<br><br>Key construct 3: Education rights and advocacy<br><br>Key construct 4: Data-based decision-making | SEL Goal 3: Recognize and express acceptance of the thoughts, feelings, and perspectives of others in a variety of social and cultural settings.<br><br>CC Speaking and Listening<br>1a. Engage effectively in collaborative discussions.<br>1a. Come prepared.<br>1b. Follow agreed upon rules.<br>1c. Ask and answer questions.<br>1d. Explain own ideas.<br>2. Determine main ideas and supporting details.<br>3. Ask and answer questions.<br>4. Report on a topic or tell a story.<br>5. Include multimedia in presentations.<br>6. Adapt speech to variety of contexts and tasks.<br><br>Depending on lesson, additional academic standards can be met. | 1a Identifies scientifically supported educational, behavioral, and mental health services to address school needs.<br><br>2a Contributes to a safe and healthy school environment.<br><br>2b Advocates for policies, programs, and services that respect dignity, address individual needs, and support the inherent dignity and worth of all students, families, and school personnel.<br><br>3a Implements and monitors multi-tiered empirically-supported interventions that improve academic and behavioral performance.<br><br>3b Provides programs and services that foster social and emotional competencies.<br><br>3d Provides programs and services in a culturally sensitive manner. | **Tier 1**<br>Sample CAPSLE lesson plan<br><br>**Tier 2**<br>Sample BEP Daily Progress Report<br><br>**Tier 3**<br>RENEW goals worksheet<br>Pre-/post-assessments<br>Developing school–community partnerships to provide additional resources to students<br>Advocating for changes in school policies to enhance student learning |
| **Tier 2**<br>Behavior Education Program (BEP) is a targeted group intervention for students who exhibit externalizing problem behaviors (Crone, Hawkins, & Horner, 2010). | | | | |
| **Tier 3**<br>Rehabilitation, Empowerment, Natural Supports, Education, and Work (RENEW) comprises individualized school and community-based services and supports (Eber, Malloy, Rose, & Flamini, 2013). | | | | |

social work practice with the National School Social Work Practice Model and the *National School Social Work Standards for Social Emotional Learning*, and it suggests artifacts that can be used to demonstrate competency with the *National Evaluation Framework for School Social Work Practice*.

---

## CASE STUDY: IMPLICATIONS FOR PRACTICE

A school social worker, employed by a large school district in the Midwest, reflected on her personal experience after having undergone a performance evaluation using the Danielson Framework.

I recently completed my first year after having had my performance evaluated under the Danielson Framework. My school district piloted the evaluation system for the first time a year ago. I was evaluated by an instrument that is used to evaluate school social workers, school psychologists, and speech therapists. The process began with a meeting with my principal at the beginning of the school year. She clearly communicated to me what her expectations were and what she hoped to see with respect to observations and artifacts. We went through the Danielson Evaluation in detail and she provided specific examples for 1a, 1b, etc. For example, when we discussed my role at IEP meetings, she told me that she wanted to see me provide information to parents in multiple ways. This meant that I was expected to orally explain BASC2 results to parents as well as visually present information in a graph and also give them a written summary of the results.

I work at a school that uses RTI for academics and behavior. As a school social worker, I am involved at all three tiers. I was observed presenting Second Step lessons to classrooms [http://www.secondstep.org], interacting with families at IEP meetings, and conducting therapeutic sessions with students. I was required to submit artifacts for every indicator and domain. Some of the artifacts included things such as the actual Second Step lesson that I presented in a class-room. In that case, I took a picture of the storyboard and uploaded it to Teachscape [https://www.teachscape.com], which is an online evaluation management tool.

I learned a great deal from the evaluation experience. My principal expects that everything I do must link back to academic learning goals. For example, she observed my work with students on appropriate ways to take turns. Using vocabulary words they were learning in class, I created a game for them to play that helped them practice taking turns while reinforcing vocabulary words at the same time. My principal gave me helpful feedback that I used to fine-tune what I needed to do during the next observation.

I believe that my experience was positive and I received a very positive evaluation. However, I think my experience was specific to my principal, and I am not sure it would have been the same if I were assigned to a different building. Administrators appear to have a great deal of freedom in how they interpret and use the Danielson Evaluation. I was lucky in that my principal understands and values school social workers. If a principal that expected school social workers to perform the responsibilities of an assistant principal had evaluated me, my evaluation could have looked differently. In my case, my principal encouraged dialogue and invited me to explain why I did things a certain way. She took that into consideration when she completed my evaluation.

---

# CONCLUSION

This chapter discussed the influence of outcome-based assessments and their impact on school social work practice. NCLB educational policy reforms led to increased emphasis on evidence-based practices and programs that align with K–12 learning standards. Social–emotional competencies are correlated with improved behavioral and academic outcomes for students (CASEL, n.d.; Cohen, 2006; Durlak et al., 2011; Jones & Buoffard, 2012; Zins et al. 2004). School social workers have a clear role in providing programs and services that enhance social–emotional competencies and improve student learning. The educational reforms also promoted new performance evaluation frameworks to assess teachers and specialized school support personnel, including school social workers, that rely on evidence to demonstrate mastery of professional competencies. In response, SSWAA developed the *National Evaluation Framework for School Social Work Practice*, the National School Social Work Practice Model, and the *National School Social Work Standards for Social Emotional Learning*. Each of these is aligned with the others and linked to K–12 learning outcomes. They represent a collection of resources that define what school social work practice should be and how to evaluate professional competencies.

# DISCUSSION QUESTIONS

1.  If your school system adopted the *National Evaluation Framework for School Social Work Practice*, what artifacts could you use to demonstrate competency?
2.  SSWAA invites school systems to adapt the *National Evaluation Framework for School Social Work Practice* to meet specific needs of their school social work programs and services. What changes would you recommend to reflect the programs and services implemented in your school system?
3.  Classroom activity: Host a guest speaker panel discussion that includes representatives from school systems that use a Danielson-based performance evaluation system. Suggested speakers could include principals, teachers, and school social workers. Panelists share personal experience with the performance evaluation system and their recommendations to improve the process.

# ADDITIONAL RESOURCES

The Danielson Group: https://danielsongroup.org/framework

School Social Work Association of America, *National Evaluation Framework for School Social Work Practice*: http://www.sswaa.org/?page=408P&hhSearchTerms=%22national+and+evaluation+and+framework%22

School Social Work Association of America, *National School Social Work Practice Model*: http://www.sswaa.org/?page=459&hhSearchTerms=%22national+and+model%22

School Social Work Association of America, *National School Social Work Standards for Social Emotional Learning*: http://www.sswaa.org/?page=2

Teachscape: https://www.teachscape.com

# REFERENCES

American School Counselor Association. (2005). *The ASCA national model: A framework for school counseling programs* (2nd ed.). Alexandria, VA: Author.

American School Counselor Association. (2015). *Accountability*. Retrieved from https://www.school-counselor.org/school-counselors-members/asca-national-model/accountability

Bohanon, H., Goodman, S., & McIntosh, K. (n.d.). *Integrating academic and behavior supports within an RtI framework: Part 1. General overview*. Retrieved from http://www.rtinetwork.org/learn/behavior-supports

Bohanon, H., McIntosh, K., & Goodman, S. (n.d.). *Integrating academic and behavior supports within an RtI framework: Part 4. Tertiary supports*. Retrieved from http://www.rtinetwork.org/learn/behavior-supports

Bohanon, H., & Wu, M. (2012). Integration of social, behavioral, and academic initiatives: Part 1. *Communiqué, 41*(2), 4–6.

Bonny, A. E., Britto, M. T., Klostermann, B. K., Hornung, R. W., & Slap, G. B. (2000). School disconnectedness: Identifying adolescents at risk. *Pediatrics, 106*(5), 1017–1021.

CASEL: Collaborative for Academic, Social, and Emotional Learning. (n.d.). *The CASEL Forum: Educating all children for social, emotional, and academic excellence: From knowledge to action*. Chicago, IL: Author. Retrieved from https://casel.squarespace.com/s/the-casel-forum.pdf

CASEL: Collaborative for Academic, Social, and Emotional Learning. (2015). Retrieved from http://www.casel.org

Center on Positive Behavioral Interventions and Supports. (2009). *Is school-wide positive behavior support an evidence-based practice?* Washington, DC: Office of Special Education Programs, US Department of Education. Retrieved from https://www.pbis.org/.../pbisresources/Evidence%20base%20for%20SWPBS.Doc

Cohen, J. (2006). Social, emotional, ethical, and academic education: Creating a climate for learning, participation in democracy, and well-being. *Harvard Educational Review, 76*(2), 201–237.

Common Core State Standards. (2015). Retrieved from http://www.corestandards.org

Crone, D., Hawkins, L., & Horner, R. (2010). *Responding to problem behavior in schools: The Behavior Education Program* (2nd ed.). New York, NY: Guilford.

Danielson, C. (2013). *The framework for teaching evaluation instrument*. Princeton, NJ: The Danielson Group.

Durlak, J. A., Weissberg, R. P., Dymnicki, A. B., Taylor, R. D., & Schellinger, K. B. (2011). The impact of enhancing students' social and emotional learning: A meta-analysis of school-based universal interventions. *Child Development, 82*(1), 405–432.

Eber, L., Malloy, J. M., Rose, J., & Flamini, A. (2013). School-based wraparound for adolescents: The RENEW model for transition-aged youth with or at-risk of EBD. In H. Walker & F. Gresham (Eds.), *Handbook of evidence-based practices for emotional and behavioral disorders: Applications in schools* (pp. 378–393). New York, NY: Guilford.

Frey, A. J., Alvarez, M. E., Dupper, D. R., Sabatino, C. A., Lindsey, B. C., Raines, J. C., . . . Norris, M. A. (2013). *National school social work practice model*. London, KY: School Social Work Association of America. Retrieved from http://sswaa.org/displaycommon.cfm?an=1&subarticlenbr=459

Goodman, S., McIntosh, K., & Bohanon, H. (n.d.). *Integrating academic and behavior supports within an RtI framework: Part 2. Universal supports*. Retrieved from http://www.rtinetwork.org/learn/behavior-supports

Greenberg, M. T., Weissberg, R. P., Utne O'Brien, M., Zins, J. E., Fredericks, L., Resnik, H., & Elias, M. J. (2003). Enhancing school-based prevention and youth development through coordinated social, emotional, and academic learning. *American Psychologist, 58*(6–7), 466–474. doi:10.1037/0003-66X.58.6-7.466

Illinois State Board of Education. (2013). *Illinois learning standards: Social/emotional learning (SEL).* Retrieved January 5, 2014, from http://www.isbe.net/ils/social_emotional/standards.htm

Jones, S. M., & Bouffard, S. M. (2012). Social and emotional learning in schools: From programs to strategies. *Social Policy Report, 26*(4), 3–22.

Lewis-Palmer, T., Bounds, M., & Sugai, G. (2004). Districtwide system for providing individual student support. *Assessment for Effective Intervention, 30*(1), 53–65.

Lindsey, B., Smith, K., Cox, T., James, M., Alvarez, M., & Kunkel, R. (2014). *National school social work standards for social emotional learning.* London, KY: School Social Work Association of America. Retrieved from http://www.sswaa.org/?page=2

McIntosh, K., Bohanon, H., & Goodman, S. (n.d.). *Integrating academic and behavior supports within an RtI framework: Part 3. Secondary supports.* Retrieved from http://www.rtinetwork.org/learn/behavior-supports

National Association of School Psychologists. (2010). *Model for comprehensive and integrated school psychological services.* Retrieved from http://www.nasponline.org/standards/2010standards/2_PracticeModel.pdf

National Association of School Psychologists. (2012). *A framework for the personnel evaluation psychologists using the NASP Practice Model.* Retrieved from https://www.nasponline.org/Documents/Standards%20and%20Certification/Standards/V41N3_AframeworkforthepersonnelEvaluation.pdf

National Association of Social Workers. (2012). *National standards for school social work services.* Retrieved from http:// http://www.naswdc.org/practice/standards/NASWSchoolSocialWorkStandards.pdf

National Education Association. (2014). *Common Core State Standards toolkit.* Retrieved from http://www.nea.org/home/ccss-toolkit.htm

Pearce, L. R. (2009). Helping children with emotional difficulties: A response to intervention investigation. *The Rural Educator, 30*(2), 34–46.

Sabatino, C. A., Alvarez, M., Frey, A., Dupper, D., Lindsey, B., Raines, J., . . . Norris, M. (2013). *National evaluation framework for school social work practice.* Retrieved from http://www.sswaa.org/?page=408&hhSearchTerms=%22evaluation+and+framework%22

Twemlow, S., Sacco, F., & Twemlow, S. (2000). *Implementation manual for "Creating the Peaceable School Learning Environment" program and philosophy.* Retrieved from http://www.backoffbully.com/PDF%20files/PeacefulSchools/manual.pdf

Walker, H. M., Horner, R. H., Sugai, G., Bullis, M., Sprague, J. R., Bricker, D., & Kaufman, M. J. (1996). Integrated approaches to preventing antisocial behavior patterns among school-age children and youth. *Journal of Emotional and Behavioral Disorders, 4*(4), 194–209.

Zins, J. E., Weissberg, R. P., Wang, M. C., & Walberg, H., J. (Eds.). (2004). *Building academic success on social and emotional learning: What does the research say?* New York, NY: Teachers College Press.

# CHAPTER 15

# SCHOOL SOCIAL WORK IN A GLOBAL CONTEXT

LETICIA VILLARREAL SOSA, SACHIKO BAMBA,
GUNAY ISMAYILOVA, AND MEI LING TAN-WU

Globalization, or the removal of barriers to free trade and the movement of capital, has the potential to enrich everyone throughout the world, reduce isolation, and increase access to knowledge (Stiglitz, 2003). However, the way in which globalization has been managed has had devastating consequences for the Global South, increasing the numbers of individuals living in poverty (Stiglitz, 2003). Globalization not only can have a negative impact on well-being but also disadvantages some more than others. As a response to the heightened awareness of globalization and its impact, there is a growing interest in global or international social work (Healy & Link, 2012).

Definitions of international social work are varied and are both practice and value based. We define international social work consistent with the definition proposed by Healy and Link (2012). International social work is a way of viewing the world that appreciates diversity and understands the global issues facing the profession and those we serve. This understanding comes with a responsibility to act, with special attention to differences in privilege and access to resources as a result of that privilege. As social workers, our practice is informed by international knowledge while also considering how local contexts inform social work roles and practice. Practicing from a global social work perspective means participation in international organizations and a focus on development and human rights. Thus, regardless of where one lives and practices, we can all be "global" social workers by understanding how global issues impact our students, understanding our own identities as global citizens, and acting in ways that promote human rights locally and across international borders.

The growing emphasis on international social work has also been paralleled in the specific practice area of school social work. School social work is now established in approximately 50 countries (Huxtable, 2014). Countries such as the United States and England trace the beginning of school social work to the early 1900s with the development of compulsory education

(Jarolmen, 2014; see Chapter 1, this volume). Since in the 1980s, social workers throughout the world have been engaged in successful advocacy for school social work practice (Huxtable & Blyth, 2002). In countries such as Singapore and China, school social workers are now developing standards and have a professional organization. At the other end of the spectrum, countries such as Azerbaijan and Guatemala are in the early stages of development of social work more generally. Even in countries such as these, where school social work is nonexistent, social workers and educators acknowledge the importance of providing social services in the schools and are making efforts to coordinate existing services through the schools (Villarreal Sosa, 2013). In this chapter, we discuss the development of the specialization in various national contexts, emerging challenges, and opportunities for growth. With an emphasis on children's rights, school social work internationally can contribute to the continued development of the School Social Work Association of America's (SSWAA) Practice Model, which includes educational rights and advocacy, an area of practice underemphasized in the United States (see Chapter 2).

## CHILDREN'S RIGHTS

In 1989, the United Nations signed and ratified the United Nations Convention on the Rights of the Child (UNCRC). The UNCRC[1] addresses issues such as the rights of unaccompanied minors, the right to alternative placement if a child cannot be with his or her parents, the rights of children with disabilities, the right to physical and mental health care, and the right to an adequate standard of living. Most countries, if not all, have much work to do in order to come close to attaining the goals and objectives as outlined in the UNCRC. School social workers can play a significant role in advancing these rights. The UNCRC specifically mentions access to higher education, encouraging school attendance, and reducing dropout rates. School discipline is also a focus in the document, noting that the State has a responsibility to "ensure that school discipline is administered in a manner consistent with the child's human dignity" (Article 28, #2). Using the case studies presented in this chapter, we discuss how school social workers in various global contexts can address children's rights, with a particular emphasis on educational rights.

## THE NEED FOR SCHOOL SOCIAL WORK IN AZERBAIJAN

Azerbaijan, with a population of approximately 9,686,000, is a post-Soviet country situated on the coast of the Caspian Sea, bordered by Russia, Iran, Turkey, Georgia, and Armenia. The country first gained its independence from the Russian Empire from 1918 to 1920 and then again in 1991 after the Soviet Union collapsed. At approximately that time, Azerbaijan experienced an undeclared war by neighboring country Armenia in 1988, and despite a 1994 ceasefire, the conflict with Armenia over Nagorno-Karabakh that resulted in the occupation of 20% of

---

1. Only two countries, the United States and Somalia, have not ratified the UNCRC.

Azerbaijan's territory remains unresolved. Due to the occupation, 1 million people have scattered throughout the country as internally displaced people and refugees (Central Intelligence Agency, 2014).

## BRIEF HISTORY OF SOCIAL WORK IN AZERBAIJAN

Social work in Azerbaijan is a new profession, and it was only recently legally recognized by the government. Soviet governance left an unclear perception of the role of social workers in society. The profession sowed its first seeds through the Social Work Fellowship Program established by the Open Society Institute in 1999. The program aimed to send national applicants to pursue 2-year master's degrees at top US universities. Approximately 30 graduates of the program have paved the path toward the development of the social work profession in the country through developing and teaching the first social work master's degree in 2005 and the first bachelor's degree in 2008 at Baku State University. All of these efforts resulted in the National Parliament of Azerbaijan adopting the Law of the Republic of Azerbaijan on Social Services in 2011, which defines roles and responsibilities for the social work profession.

## EDUCATIONAL RIGHTS OF CHILDREN IN AZERBAIJAN

In Azerbaijan, the education system is co-educational, with girls accessing education at similar rates as boys. The overall enrollment rate at the primary education level is 98%, and the literacy rate is 100% (Education Policy and Data Center, 2014). Compulsory education includes children ages 6–16 years, with noncompulsory preschool education available for children from birth to age 6 years. The education system in Azerbaijan continues to be teacher centered. Despite the powerful role of teachers in the classroom, teacher training is weak and teachers tend to be unqualified or underqualified (Asian Development Bank, 2004). Like many post-Soviet societies, the educational system overall is highly centralized in both funding and administration (Baimova, 2003).

In 1992, Azerbaijan ratified the UNCRC, which was a significant step toward creating an educational system consistent with international norms and standards. Nonetheless, the education system continues to face unrecognized problems. For example, despite high enrollment rates, non-attendance and dropouts are among the underreported educational challenges. There are also inequities in school dropout rates based on socioeconomic status, region (urban or rural), and for children who are among the internally displacement population as a result of war (Baimova, 2003).

One of the most significant challenges in Azerbaijan is the grim reality for children with disabilities, of which only 15.8% receive education in inclusive settings, only 25.8% receive any kind of special services, and the majority are educated in the home (Mikailova et al., 2009). Due to strong stigma and discrimination against children with disabilities, including the lack of accessible school settings, they are not fully integrated into the education system (Mikailova et al., 2009). Current policies support separating children with disabilities from the rest of society by presenting them with only two options—receiving an education in separate special education institutions or "at home."

Services for children with disabilities were first pioneered and provided by a nongovernmental sector without much government support. From 2006 to 2009, the government of Azerbaijan ran the National Program on Development of Inclusive Education with support from UNICEF. The program focused on including children with mild and moderate disabilities in mainstream education at the preschool and primary school level. Despite positive results of this pilot program, inclusive education was not reflected in the revised "Law on Education" that was adopted by Parliament in 2009.

## DEVELOPING SCHOOL SOCIAL WORKERS

In Azerbaijan, schools have psychologists, but their role is unclear, they have limited training, and they are without legal acts or regulations ("There Is Need," 2013). However, the presence of school psychologists alone would not be sufficient to address the increasing social problems faced by schools and students. The multifunctional role of social workers working in collaboration with school psychologists can better address the emerging issues in a school environment. Social workers in school settings are effective in terms of holistically addressing problem and mobilizing multiple resources from school, family, and community (Jonson-Reid, 2008). In the Azerbaijani context, one can argue that without the presence of social workers in school settings, it can be difficult to adequately address issues such as school dropouts; delinquency; truancy; early marriages; lack of child-centered services; and weak school, parent, and community collaboration.

Because schools in Azerbaijan already have psychologists as well as teachers in need of retraining due to reforms such as the deinstitutionalization of children from boarding schools to small group homes and foster care (Villarreal Sosa, 2013) and because there are few trained social workers in the country, existing school psychologists and teachers can be retrained to serve in the role of school social workers. In addition, recent social work graduates from local universities can be introduced to educational settings at the national level. Qualified social workers with master's degrees can provide the training and education with a view to expanding their skills and knowledge in order to provide the following services to students and their families: (1) identifying and addressing systemic barriers to academic performance; (2) acting as change agents to bring stakeholders together in collaborative efforts to solve problems; (3) conducting needs assessments and progress monitoring; (4) assisting administrators and staff to understand the familial, cultural, and community components of students' responses to instruction, learning, and academic success; (5) serving as the liaison to families, the community, and other stakeholders; and (6) facilitating and coordinating the delivery of educational and community services with and by community agencies and other service providers. With continued evaluation of the outcomes and impact of school social work services, these services can be introduced to national decision-makers for inclusion in governmental legislation.

Major stakeholders in this process are the Ministry of Education, social work faculty at public and private universities, local and international agencies, school administration, teachers, students, families/parents, and communities. The government of Azerbaijan is currently considering implementing internationally recognized best practices and, therefore, open to ideas for reform. In order to accomplish this purpose, the Azerbaijani government adopted a new education strategy in 2013, with some reforms addressing the needs of children with disabilities with a focus on inclusion ("National Strategy," 2013). In order to achieve these strategic and nationwide goals, school social workers should be key players in the provision of the services in school settings. As such, the role of school social workers is invaluable in providing children with opportunities to exercise their educational rights and facilitate the process of inclusion not only into the education system but also into society as a whole.

# SCHOOL SOCIAL WORK IN JAPAN: CREATING LINKAGES FOR CHILDREN IN POVERTY

Maximizing access to school-based and community-based resources as well as home–school–community linkages are critical roles stipulated in SSWAA's Practice Model. Regardless of whether in Japan, the United States, or other countries, such a role is vital for school social workers to support students who face additional challenges due to poverty and less access to resources at home and in the community.

## SCHOOL SOCIAL WORK IN JAPAN

Social work in Japan has more than a 60-year history: The Japanese Society for the Study of Social Welfare was established in 1954, the Japanese Association of Social Workers was established in 1959, the national certification for social workers began in 1987, and the national certification for psychiatric social workers began in 1997 (Iwama, 2009; Japanese Association of Social Workers, n.d.; Japanese National Committee of the International Council of Social Welfare, n.d.; Japanese Society for the Study of Social Welfare, n.d.).

Since the national certification systems were established in 1987, an increasing number of social workers have been working in many public and private organizations such as those for children and families, older adults, people with disabilities, people needing public financial assistance, and people with health/mental health problems. By 2007, there were 95,216 certified social workers and 34,600 certified psychiatric social workers registered (Ministry of Health, Labor, and Welfare (MHLW), 2011). However, social workers in education were not widely introduced until 2008.

School social work as a national program started in 2008 in Japan. That year, 141 municipalities in 46 prefectures[2] employed school social workers. The national government introduced social work in school settings explaining as follows (Ministry of Education, Culture, Sports, Science, and Technology (MECSST), 2008):

> Issues around student guidance such as bullying and attendance problems, as well as emotional/ mental problems experienced by students, are becoming more complicated and diverse. Thus, collaboration with families and with professionals outside of school is critical. Professionals who actively collaborate with school, family, and community agencies, who improve children's surrounding environments while sharing tasks and collaborating with people involved, who nurture

2. There are 47 prefectures in Japan. Prefectures form the country's first jurisdiction and administrative division levels. Each prefecture is subdivided into cities and districts, and each district is subdivided into towns and villages.

students' competences to cope with their own difficulties, and who develop support system—namely, school social workers—are needed. By allocating school social workers, schools' student guidance systems will become more open and schools' functions as places where children learn and grow will be promoted.

At the inception of the program, the national government (MECSST, 2008) set forth five roles for school social workers:

1. Working on environments of students with problems
2. Establishing networks, collaborating, and coordinating with related agencies
3. Establishing and supporting a team system within school
4. Providing support, consultation, and information for parents and school staff
5. Providing training for school staff

As described previously, a major role for school social workers in Japan is consultation with and referrals to professionals within and outside of schools, such as teachers, school counselors (clinical psychologists at school), and social welfare agency professionals. In addition, facilitating collaboration and establishing support systems within schools as well as with people outside of the schools is considered a critical role. Unlike in the United States, counseling or child-focused therapy is usually considered as the role of school counselors, not that of school social workers. School counselors were introduced nationwide in the mid-1990s (MECSST, 2007) and are well known as support staff professionals at school. The national government's budget for school counselors was 3,892 million yen during fiscal year 2013, whereas its budget for school social workers was 355 million yen that year (MECSST, 2013a, 2013b).

School social workers are relatively new in school settings, and they are not allocated in all school districts. Currently, there are only approximately 1,500 school social workers in Japan, and most school social workers are part-time workers (MECSST, 2015; Yamano, 2013). Employed by a city or by a prefecture, the majority of school social workers visit schools only when they are called by the schools, although some municipalities allocate school social workers at specific school sites. Thus, school social workers are not yet well recognized. They often are asked, "What are the differences between school counselors and school social workers?" In most schools, therefore, school social workers often must first explain the role difference between the two professionals and establish work relations with teachers and administrative staff in the school district.

Establishing work relations and collaborating with staff within the school are vital for school social workers to support children in need. In collaborating with the school, school social workers may work closely with teachers who serve as a "support coordinator." Because school social workers visit schools for limited times and hours, they often ask nurse-teachers to become members of the support teams and to work closely with the students. Nurse-teachers work full-time at schools and as such can serve different roles from classroom teachers; students often talk more freely with them than to other teachers. School social workers may also ask school counselors, who in many municipalities work at the school site, to provide therapy to the students.

Five major issues that school social workers deal with in Japan are family environment issues (excluding child maltreatment), attendance problems, "developmental disabilities" (learning disabilities, attention deficit/hyperactivity disorder, Autism spectrum etc., not including mental retardation), physical and mental health problems, and child maltreatment issues. Family environment issues may include poverty, parental physical/mental health problems, and single parenthood. Family environment issues and child's attendance problems are often related (MECSST, 2015).

Often by the time school social workers are asked for help, the problem has already become very serious and not easy to handle. In such situations, teachers are often overwhelmed and expect school social workers to solve the problem for them. The teachers may view the students as "problem kids" and the parents as "problem parents." Thus, one of school social workers' important roles is to provide an ecological perspective that allows teachers to see the students and their families as those "who are facing a lot of life challenges" rather than as "problem kids" or "problem parents." This perspective helps teachers understand environmental factors of the problem situation, and it allows teachers to become more supportive to the students and to develop support systems around the students and their families.

## CASE EXAMPLES

At a Japanese Society for the Study of Social Welfare symposium in 2011, Kadota, a professor and a school social work supervisor, discussed "issues around support systems to counter child poverty." In his discussion, Kadota provided the following case example:

> A boy at a junior high lives with his mother, receiving public assistance. His mother divorced because of violence from his father, and is suffering from depression. Having an erratic lifestyle, she does not prepare meals for her son, and does not clean the house. The home is roach infested and is overflowing with garbage from hoarding. The boy wears dirty clothes and smells, which triggered bullying from his peers. Gradually, his attendance became irregular and he became absent from school for months. Even when his teacher visited his home, no one responded and they did not see him or his mother for a year. His school asked for help from the local child guidance center, however, the child guidance center does not respond to such neglect cases very well because of their heavy caseloads. After experiencing difficulty receiving help from the center, his school asked the school social worker for help.

This is not an atypical case for Japanese school social workers. Although the previously described family received public assistance, there are many families living in poverty that do not. In such cases, it is more difficult to obtain information about the families because community agencies frequently do not know about their situations.

As demonstrated by the previous case, parents of children in poverty often have multiple challenges. Without supporting their parents, it is difficult to meet the educational needs of children experiencing poverty. Thus, linking the family to community agencies is necessary to secure children's schooling. By holding case conferences with teachers and with staff from social welfare agencies in the community, school social workers share information and collaboratively work with them to support students and their families.

During the previously mentioned symposium held in 2011, a school social worker, Toyama, reported an equally complex case. Toyama discussed a case of a child who attended special education classes and whose mother was diagnosed with mental retardation. The mother earned a living from part-time work, and the father did not provide money for the family. The child had challenges with regulating their emotions. The school social worker took the mother to visit a women's support center, police office, and city hall. Collaborating with the school, and with support from district welfare commissioners (volunteers in the community), the school social worker tried to alleviate the mother's anxiety/uneasiness and to foster the child's emotional stability. The father was also assisted by the school social worker. The father was diagnosed as having physical disabilities, which allowed him to receive a disability pension. In addition, both the child and the mother received disability certificates, which allowed them to access public services for people with mental disabilities. These economic supports eased the family's financial hardship, improving the parental relationship and increasing their sense of hope for their child's future. This case demonstrates how financial difficulties can contribute to stress and rupture family relationships, impacting a child's behavior at school. Thus, helping families alleviate financial problems by linking them to proper services is critical to support children's school success.

## EMERGING POVERTY ISSUES IN JAPAN AND EXPECTATIONS FOR SCHOOL SOCIAL WORKERS

Japan experienced major economic growth after World War II, and the economy in Japan was the second largest in the world based on gross domestic product between 1968 and 2009 (it is currently third largest) ("Chugoku, Nihon nuki niikakutei," 2011). Thus, until recently, it was widely believed that Japan had solved the poverty problem. It was once said, "All 100 million people [approximately the total Japanese population at that time] are middle class." The notion that Japan had achieved economic growth and an egalitarian society had sunk deep into the Japanese public consciousness—so much so that it had become a source of national pride and identity (National Institute of Population and Social Security Research, 2014). According to Goodman (2000), until the late 1990s,

> full employment was a main plank of post-war social policy. In many ways, therefore, Japanese policy-makers' emphasis on preventing people from falling into poverty through investment in education, health, employment, and a set of universal benefits could be termed a success. (p. 25)

However, holes in these preventive measures have become increasingly apparent. The worldwide economic crises of the first decade of the 21st century significantly impacted Japan's economy, causing financial problems for many families. The economy in Japan has not yet fully recovered.

According to a 2008 report by the Organization for Economic Cooperation and Development, Japan's relative poverty rate[3] in 2004 was 14.9%, the fourth highest among the 30 member countries after Mexico, Turkey, and the United States ("Hinkon ritsu," 2009). The relative poverty rate in Japan in 2012 was 16.1% (MHLW, 2014).

Japan's child poverty rate reached an all-time high of 16.3% in 2012, meaning that roughly one in six children lived in poverty. In addition, single, female-headed families experienced a poverty rate of 54.6% in 2012. Although 80% of single mothers are currently employed, many work in low-paying part-time and non-regular jobs (MHLW, 2014).

---

3. Relative poverty rate is determined by the percentage of households with an annual income of less than half of the median income. A high relative poverty rate means that there are large income gaps between rich and poor.

Recognizing the problem, the government established "A Law on Measures to Counter Child Poverty" in 2014, with a particular policy emphasis on educational assistance for children living in poverty. School social workers are described as a key in implementing the policy. Describing school social workers as "those who take an important role of linking education and welfare," the policy calls for an enormous increase in the number of school social workers who liaise with social welfare organizations (from 1,500 school social workers to 10,000 in 5 years) (Cabinet Office Government of Japan, 2014).

## GOVERNMENT DEFINITIONS AND MANDATES
## FOR SCHOOL SOCIAL WORK

The government's expectations for school social workers can also be seen in some other policy changes. For example, the national government changed the guidelines of the national school social work program in April 2015. Previously, it stated, "For employment screening, *it is desirable* [emphasis added] to choose ones who have professional certifications such as certifications for social workers or psychiatric social workers," whereas it currently states, "*As a general rule* [emphasis added], school social workers ought to be chosen from people who have professional certifications such as certifications for social workers or psychiatric social workers" (MECSST, 2015). Among school social workers in the national school social work program in 2015, 43.7% were certified social workers and 24.7% were certified psychiatric social workers (some had both certificates) (MECSST, 2015). Many school social workers did not have any educational background in social work; for example, many were retired school teachers or retired police officers. This policy change may reflect the government's expectations about the increased professionalization of school social workers in order to better support children.

In addition, according to a 2015 newspaper report, the government plans to clarify school social workers' roles and to have them employed as full-time workers (Takahama, 2015). Currently, the vast majority of school social workers are part-time workers. Although an increasing number of local governments employ school social workers 4 days a week and provide social security, the majority of local governments employ school social workers only 1–3 days a week and do not provide social security. School social workers cannot function fully when, for example, they are in charge of 10 schools and work only 2 days a week. More school social workers who work full-time are in urgent need.

Japanese school social work is still its infancy, but it is rapidly and steadily expanding. As one way to address child poverty, the Japanese government expects social workers to take major roles in supporting children in schools. Indeed, school social workers can create home–school–community linkages and support children's success and well-being.

# ADVOCACY FOR CHILDREN'S EDUCATIONAL
# RIGHTS IN THE UNITED STATES

A key construct within the SSWAA's model of school social work practice is the expectation that school social workers address issues of structural inequality and social and economic injustice that can lead to school failure or educational inequity (see Chapter 2). Within the US context, there have been two populations of youth within the schools that face significant barriers and challenges: (1) Latino and African American boys and (2) undocumented youth. The UNCRC specifically addresses the issue of school discipline, which is particularly relevant to youth of color in the United States, who experience disproportionate suspensions and exclusionary discipline.

For Black and Latino youth, particularly boys, schools are often where they experience failure, negative stereotypes, and exclusion through suspensions from school or by being labeled special education students (Noguera, 2008). This failure is so pervasive that it has become "normalized." This marginalization of Black and Latino youth is not just in the form of physical exclusion from school; it also has a psychological impact from being labeled as "troublemakers" or "underachievers." These labels not only become internalized among the youth but also lead to lowered expectations by their teachers and other adults in the school (Noguera, 2008, Villarreal Sosa, 2011).

For these youth, instead of experiencing a school context of loving, nurturing, and supportive discipline to help them cope with the often challenging and hostile context they must navigate on a daily basis (from racial profiling by police to navigating a gang context), they face assumptions by the school staff that they are all potentially violent and are treated as potential threats. Andres' case is one such example:

> Andres reported having such an experience, leaving him feeling humiliated in front of his peers. When his teacher discovered that he was hiding something during class in his backpack, she suspected he was carrying a weapon and called security. As the contents of his backpack were poured out in front of his peers and the hidden content revealed, Andres felt the double humiliation of being overweight and being caught with a candy bar during class in addition to being treated as though he was a violent, weapon-carrying student. The teacher wrote the following regarding the incident:

> "Andres was looking inside his school bag. I ask to see what was inside and he said—no. I thought that it might be something else (a gun, a knife, spray paint, etc.) that could hurt or destroy property. I asked the security guard to search his bag— (Teacher discipline referral, 9th grade)

> Andres was not gang-involved and did not have any discipline reports for fighting or disrespecting teachers. Yet, the teacher's first assumption was that Andres could be carrying a concealed weapon rather than stolen hall passes or food that should not be brought into the classroom, which would be the likely assumption in a different school context or with a student belonging to a different social group.

Ultimately, these experiences leave youth feeling powerless and frustrated. Social workers can respond to the needs of Latino and African American boys by focusing on various levels of intervention. Social workers can help students address individual-level issues such as the trauma they may have experienced living in communities with high rates of gang violence. They can also impact the school climate overall by advocating for, developing, and supporting interventions such as alternatives to suspension, restorative justice practices, and positive behavioral interventions. It is critical that school social workers engage in interventions at various levels that address the needs and the rights of Latino and African American boys and work to promote environments that support their development rather than increased criminalization and marginalization.

A second and arguably the most marginalized group of children in US schools are undocumented children. Migration is a global phenomenon occurring in the United States and many other countries. In the Unites States, many undocumented youth face not only challenges due to issues of poverty or racism, task as 78% of undocumented youth are Latino (Passel, 2006), but also another level of oppression and exclusion due to their undocumented status. They face barriers to college attendance because they do not qualify for financial assistance, in most states they are not eligible for a driver's license, they are legally barred from employment, and they experience the social and psychological consequences of "living in the shadows" with a constant threat of deportation or being separated from their parents and siblings. Not surprisingly, undocumented students report having significant psychological distress and experiences of depression, suicidal ideation, and anxiety (Gonzalez, Súarez-Orozco, & Dedios-Sanguineti, 2013).

Although there is limited research on best practices with undocumented youth in the school social work literature, school social workers throughout the country are working to advocate for undocumented students in a variety of ways. In a suburban school district in which one of the authors of this chapter (Villarreal Sosa) worked as a school social worker, advocacy and accompaniment of undocumented youth began the moment they attempted to enroll in school. Often, undocumented youth faced barriers at the first encounter with registering for school due to the fact that they were not able to provide proof of address or the proper documentation from employers to qualify for school fee waivers or reduced lunch. My first was to ensure they had access to school and to resources they and their families needed. Later, as a school social worker, interventions included creating a safe space for undocumented youth by providing staff development, making sure students had a way to identify "safe" people in the school to whom they could go for help, and forming networks of other informal and formal support services and allies for undocumented youth. For example, if a youth wanted to apply to the community college but did not have a Social Security number, I could refer him or her to an ally in the college who could help the undocumented student navigate the system.

Our work as allies in the schools extended beyond direct services to students and also involved advocacy in support of the Illinois Dream Act, which would allow in-state tuition for undocumented students. It is critical that school social workers understand any current legislation that impacts undocumented youth (see Chapter 6) and assess their own school environment to ensure they are creating a safe space (i.e., pamphlets that outline the rights of undocumented students or resources, "safe zone" posters for undocumented students, etc.). In promoting resilience, undocumented students often state that a key adult in the school provided them with the hope and support to continue their education or plan for their future. Unfortunately, many undocumented students continue to report that they had to remain "in the shadows" with school staff, including counselors. Social workers are in a key position to assist with not only providing the "safe space" to individual students but also supporting larger schoolwide efforts to make school a safe place for undocumented students.

# ADDRESSING EMERGING NEEDS OF CHILDREN: A CASE STUDY OF SINGAPORE

Singapore is a city-state and island country in Southeast Asia. Its land area is 718 square kilometers, and its population is approximately 5.5 million (Department of Statistics,, 2015).

Singapore's lack of natural resources makes people its most precious asset. In a 1991 publication, "Singapore: The Next Lap," the Government of Singapore stated,

> People are, and will always be, our most precious resource. More than anything else, it is the effort of Singaporeans, with their drive and talent, that has made the country what it is today. Overcoming great odds, as a newly independent state without natural resources, we have turned our city-state into a thriving and modern economy. (p. 19)

The development of its people is thus an important priority in the governance of the country. Education is one of the ways in which Singapore develops its people.

## THE SINGAPORE EDUCATION JOURNEY

Singapore's Ministry of Education (MOE) states the aim of the education system as one that "helps our students to discover their own talents, to make the best use of these talents and realise their potential, and develop a passion for learning that lasts through life." (MOE, 2016) Structurally, the education system extends from preschool into primary, secondary, post-secondary, and finally university or work, with continuing education and training. The Compulsory Education Act implemented in 2003 is applicable only to the primary school years and for children who are "above the age of 6 years and who have not yet attained the age of 15 years" (MOE, 2016). From secondary school years onward, students are provided with flexible and diverse options that focus on both academic and non-academic areas (MOE, 2016). The flexibility and diversity are characterized by the wide range of options made available to students—from specialized independent schools (e.g., Singapore Sports School and the School of the Arts) to different examination systems (e.g., Singapore–Cambridge General Certificate of Education Ordinary Level and the International Baccalaureate) and the various elective modules within a school's curriculum.

Apart from flexibility and diversity, Singapore's education system also strives toward a student-centric and values-driven holistic approach. This approach is enacted in four main ways: instilling deep values; building deep foundation for learning; learning for life; and providing broad, inclusive, and holistic education (MOE, 2013). Various programs and activities have been implemented across schools in Singapore along these four main thrusts.

## THE NEEDS OF CHILDREN IN SCHOOLS AND
## THE ROLE OF SCHOOL SOCIAL WORKERS

Although the evolution of a flexible, diverse, and holistic education is conceived to take into account the diversity of needs and interests among the student population, it is inevitable that not all students can be sufficiently engaged nor all developmental needs adequately addressed. From an ecological perspective, misfit can occur between a student's needs, rights, goals, and capacities and the qualities and operations of his or her physical and social environment, which in this case is the school (Germain & Gitterman, 1995, as cited in Allen-Meares, 2007). On the occasions when this results in underachievement, misbehaviors or emotional disturbances, the role of school social workers in Singapore is to partner with schools in reaching out to the affected students and their families. The end goal is to, together with schools and families, create a goodness-of-fit that will enable students to "obtain maximum benefits from their schooling experience" (National Council of Social Service, 2007).

## ROLE OF SCHOOL SOCIAL WORKERS IN SINGAPORE

School social work in Singapore was introduced in 1965 with a Pilot Scheme for School Social Work (Schooling, 1965). Through the years, the mission and role of school social workers remained partnering with schools in order to enable students to obtain maximum benefits from their schooling experience. However, actualizing this mission has been shaped by a confluence of funding opportunities, policy changes, and emerging needs of children.

Subsequent to the pilot scheme in 1965, school social work was officially established through the setting up of a school counseling service staffed by social workers in Anglican schools and the setting up of a Social Work Unit in the MOE in the 1970s. At that time, Singapore had just recently become an independent nation. Its pertinent tasks as a young nation were to unite its people and build its trade and economy for survival. Education was key because it was a means to develop human capital and unite people through a common language—English (Tan, 2001). The role of school social workers, then, was to facilitate children's access to education, help them be ready to learn in school, and help them complete their education.

As Singapore's economy grew in the late 1970s through the 1990s on the back of industrial development, survival needs were well taken care of. Consequently, social concerns with regard to children began to shift toward a higher level on Maslow's hierarchy of needs—that of love, belonging, and self-esteem. Thus, the Pastoral Care Unit of the MOE provided funding to schools to engage social services to provide interventions to address the needs of students in the aforementioned areas. During this period, a proliferation of school social work services took place. The role of school social workers was expanded to include not just facilitating children's access to education but also examining child-related socioemotional issues such as juvenile delinquency, stress, and lack of self-confidence.

Since then, the needs of children have continued to grow in complexity as the advent of the Internet and globalization brings with it new challenges, such as cyber-bullying, easy access to pornography, and greater awareness of children-related issues. In response, support services to students in school settings have also grown. In 2005, the full-time school counselor scheme was established by MOE, placing at least one school counselor in every school by 2008. Special needs officers (now known as allied educators—learning and behavioral support) were also placed in every mainstream primary school in 2005 to support children with mild special educational needs.

As the support services for children in school settings grow, there is an increasing need for school social workers to redefine their role in relation to those of other professionals alongside the evolving needs of children. This shift emphasizes the importance of a collaborative role that a school social worker in Singapore needs to play. Apart from partnering with schools to reach out to students and their families, the school social worker's role is to forge trusting, respectful, and interdependent professional relationships based on shared outcomes with other student support service professionals (Dupper, 2003).

## AN ASPIRATION OF ROLE AND PRACTICE

From its beginnings to the present, the role of school social workers in Singapore has been shaped by the socioeconomic context, funding, policy changes, and the emerging needs of children. Despite these external factors that shape school social work, school social workers aspire toward a day when their role is also defined by the contributions that their specialized body of skills and knowledge can offer to engage, enable, and empower children in school settings.

For this aspiration to become reality, the training of school social workers needs to be formalized and take place in institutes/centers of social work training. Currently, school social workers in Singapore are largely untrained in this specialization. The handful who have been trained received their training overseas. Second, school social workers need to definitively articulate their professional role and identity. The drawing up of the "Core Competencies for the Practice of School Social Work in Singapore" was completed in 2007. However, application of and reference to the document have been rare. Other than stating that a school social worker is first and foremost a social worker, the set of competencies neither derive nor define school social workers. Moving forward, a role definition based on the body of school social work knowledge and skills will enable the appropriate and effective deployment of school social workers to address child-related social issues in school settings, a clearer understanding of school social workers' contributions on interprofessional collaborative teams, and eventually a more focused development of this field of practice for the betterment of children in Singapore.

# EMERGING CHALLENGES AND A UNIFIED RESPONSE

The various case examples of school social work discussed in this chapter demonstrate that there are very universal struggles for children throughout the world, such as various forms of social exclusion, social–emotional challenges, and issues of access to education. Consequently, the role of advocacy and a focus on children's rights are an essential component of practice. Just as social workers involved in child welfare in the United States have called on the National Association of Social Workers to use the UNCRC as a basis for all child welfare statements (Scherrer, 2012), organizations of school social workers, including SSWAA, should consider how to incorporate the UNCRC into practice and policy statements and recommendations. UNCRC provides a framework for social and cultural shifts regarding how children are viewed and can provide a foundation for advocating for the rights of children encountered by school social workers, such as those mentioned in the country case examples in this chapter—children experiencing poverty, children with disabilities, immigrant children, and ethnic/racial minority children—within the educational context.

Another challenge facing school social workers regardless of whether one is a school social worker in the United States, Singapore, or another nation is that, as a profession, school social workers must continue to work toward defining their role and advocating for school social work services. It seems that in all countries, school social workers face external pressures due to funding issues or a lack of understanding of the skills and knowledge base that school social workers contribute to the educational environment. Therefore, as a profession, school social workers need to continue to establish and develop international networks in order to exchange information. As a result of globalization, social work has become an international profession, with interventions and policies going across national borders (Buzducea, 2010). Therefore, school social workers should develop their own identities as global citizens and consider the implications for their practice and professional development. Global citizenship is considered to have various dimensions: (1) social responsibility, which includes global justice, altruism and empathy, and global interconnectedness; (2) global competence, which includes self-awareness, intercultural communication, and global knowledge; and (3) global civic engagement, which includes participation in civic organizations, political voice, and global civic activism (Morais & Ogden, 2011). Thus, as global citizens and school social workers, we can continue to advance the profession, collaborating across national borders, and, according to the mission of the International Committee on School Social Work Collaborations (n.d.), meet

the needs of children in schools globally by ensuring quality school social work services through school social work training and credentialing as well as promoting the exchange of expertise, experience and resources with a view to strengthen the international presence of school social workers.

## ADDITIONAL RESOURCES

Facebook group for the International Committee on Schools Social Work Collaboration: https://www.facebook.com/groups/international.school.social.work.collaboration/?ref=bookmarks

*Fact Sheet: A Summary of the Rights Under the Convention on the Rights of the Child*: http://www.unicef.org/crc/files/Rights_overview.pdf

Global Institute of Social Work: http://www.thegisw.org

International Network for School Social Work: http://internationalnetwork-schoolsocialwork.html-planet.com

## REFERENCES

Allen-Meares, P. (2007). *Social work services in school* (5th ed.). Boston, MA: Pearson Education.

Asian Development Bank. (2004). *Education reforms in countries in transition: Policies and processes. Six country case studies commissioned by the ADB*. Retrieved from http://www.pitt.edu/~weidman/2004-educ-reforms-countries.pdf

Baimova, N. (2003). *Issues of equity, increased drop-out rate in education system in Azerbaijan*. Budapest, Hungary: Central European University, Center for Policy Studies.

Buzducea, D. (2010). Social work in the new millennium: A global perspective. *Revista de Asistenta Sociala, 1*, 31–42.

Cabinet Office Government of Japan. (2014, August 29). *Kodomono hinkon taisaku kaigi* [*A meeting on the measures to counter child poverty*]. Retrieved June 20, 2015, from http://www8.cao.go.jp/kodo-monohinkon/pdf/taikou.pdf

Central Intelligence Agency. (2014). *Azerbaijan: The world factbook*. Retrieved from https://www.cia.gov/library/publications/the-world-factbook/geos/aj.html

Chugoku, Nihon nuki niikakutei. (2011, February 14). *Nihon Keizai Shinbun*. Retrieved June 20, 2015, from http://www.nikkei.com/article/DGXNASFS1400K_U1A210C1MM0000

Department of Statiscs, Ministry of Trade and Industry, Republic of Singapore (2015). *Population trends 2015*. Retrieved from http://www.singstat.gov.sg/docs/default-source/default-document-library/publications/publications_and_papers/population_and_population_structure/population2015.pdf

Dupper, D. (2003). *School social work: Skills and interventions for effective practice*. Hoboken, NJ: Wiley.

Education Policy and Data Center. (2014). *Azerbaijan*. Retrieved from http://www.epdc.org/country/azerbaijan

Germain, C., & Gitterman, A. (1995). Ecological perspective. In R. Edwards (Ed.), Encyclopedia of social work (19th ed., pp. 817-825). Washington, DC: NASW>

Gonzales, R. G., Suárez-Orozco, C., & Dedios-Sanguineti, M.C. (2013). No place to belong: Contextualizing concepts of mental health among undocumented immigrant youth in the United States. *American Behavioral Scientist*, 57(8), p. 1174-1199. doi: 10.1177/0002764213487349.

Goodman, R. (2000). *Children of the Japanese state: The changing role of child protection institutions in contemporary Japan*. New York, NY: Oxford University Press.

Government of Singapore. (1991). *Singapore: The next lap*. Singapore: Author.

Healy, L. M., & Link, R. (2012). *Handbook of international social work: Human rights, development, and the global profession*. New York, NY: Oxford University Press.

Hinkon ritsu: 07 nendo wa 15.7% [Poverty rates: 15.7% in 2007]. (2009, October 20). *Asahi Shinbun*, p. 1.

Huxtable, M. (2014, March). *A snapshot of school social work in 2014*. International Network for School Social Work. (For newsletter, contact mhuxtable@olympus.net)

Huxtable, M., & Blyth, E. (Eds.). (2002). *School social work worldwide*. Washington, DC: NASW Press.

International Committee on School Social Work Collaborations. (n.d.). *Name, vision, and mission*. Retrieved from https://www.facebook.com/groups/international.school.social.work.collaboration/files

Iwama, N. (2009). Roles and significance of certified social workers [in Japanese]. *Soudanenjo no kibanto senmolnshoku*, pp. 2–6. Tokyo, Japan: Chuohoki.

Japanese Association of Social Workers. (n.d.). *History of JASW*. Retrieved June 20, 2015, from http://www.jasw.jp/enkaku/enkaku.html

Japanese National Committee of the International Council of Social Welfare. (n.d.). *History of the National Committee* [in Japanese]. Retrieved June 20, 2015, from http://www.icsw-japan.or.jp/japan/index3.html

Japanese Society for the Study of Social Welfare. (n.d.). *History of JSSW* [in Japanese]. Retrieved June 20, 2015, from http://www.jssw.jp/society/history.html

Jonson-Reid, M. (2008). School social work: Engaging the community. *Children & Schools, 30*(3), 131–133.

Kadota, K. (2011, February 27). *Comments at the symposium "Issues Around Child Poverty Support System." The 6th Forum of the JSSW* [in Japanese]. Retrieved from http://www.jssw.jp/event/doc/forum/forum_2011_05.pdf

Mikailova, U., Ismayilova, A., Karimova, Y., Isazde, U., Behbudov, R., Agayev, Y., et al. (2009). Education of children with disabilities in Azerbaijan: Barriers and opportunities. *Human Rights Education in Asian Schools, 12*, 107–128.

Ministry of Education. (2005). *Greater support for teachers and school leaders*. Singapore: Author. Retrieved March 22, 2015, from http://www.moe.gov.sg/media/press/2005/pr20050922b.htm

Ministry of Education. (2013). *Students-centric and values-driven holistic education*. Singapore: Author. Retrieved June 5, 2016, from https://www.moe.gov.sg/docs/default-source/document/education/files/student-centric-values-driven-poster.pdf

Ministry of Education. (2014). *Support for children with special needs*. Singapore: Author. Retrieved March 22, 2015, from http://www.moe.gov.sg/education/programmes/support-for-children-special-needs

Ministry of Education. (2016). *Education system*. Singapore: Author Retrieved June 5, 2016, from https://www.moe.gov.sg/education/education-system

Ministry of Education. (2016). *Compulsory education*. Singapore: Author Retrieved June 5, 2016, from https://www.moe.gov.sg/education/education-system/compulsory-education

Ministry of Education, Culture, Sports, Science, and Technology. (2007, July). *About school counselors*. Retrieved June 20, 2015, from http://www.mext.go.jp/a_menu/shotou/seitoshidou/kyouiku/hou-koku/07082308/002.htm

Ministry of Education, Culture, Sports, Science, and Technology. (2008, March). *School social work program*. Retrieved June 20, 2015, from http://www.mext.go.jp/b_menu/shingi/chousa/shotou/046/shiryo/08032502/003/010.htm

Ministry of Education, Culture, Sports, Science, and Technology. (2013a). *School counseling program*. Retrieved from http://www.mext.go.jp/component/a_menu/education/detail/__icsFiles/afieldfile/2013/07/09/1337584_2.pdf

Ministry of Education, Culture, Sports, Science, and Technology. (2013b). *School social work program*. Retrieved from http://www.mext.go.jp/a_menu/shotou/seitoshidou/__icsFiles/afieldfile/2013/10/21/1340480_05.pdf

Ministry of Education, Culture, Sports, Science, and Technology. (2015). *A trend of the School Social Work Program, Year 2015* [in Japanese]. Handouts distributed at a school social workers' study group (2014 Kanto-ken School Social Workers rengo-kenshukai) on March 29, 2015.

Ministry of Health, Labor, and Welfare. (2011, August). *About Center of Social Welfare Promotion and National Examination* [in Japanese]. Retrieved June 20, 2015, from http://www.mhlw.go.jp/stf/shingi/2r9852000001lbxv-att/2r9852000001lc9q.pdf

Ministry of Health, Labor, and Welfare. (2014). Poverty rates [in Japanese]. In *Kokumin seikatsu kiso chosa no gaikyo* (p. 18). Retrieved June 20, 2015, from http://www.mhlw.go.jp/toukei/saikin/hw/k-tyosa/k-tyosa13/dl/03.pdf

Morais, D. B., & Ogden, A. C. (2011). Initial development and validation of the global citizenship scale. *Journal of Studies in International Education, 15*(5), 445–466.

National Council of Social Service. (2007). *A guide to school social work*. Singapore: Author.

National Institute of Population and Social Security Research. (2014). 6–1: Re-emergence of poverty in Japan. *Social Security in Japan 2014*. Retrieved from http://www.ipss.go.jp/s-info/e/ssj2014/006.html

National Strategy on the development of education in the Republic of Azerbaijan. (2013, October 24). Retrieved from http://www.president.az/articles/9779

Passel, J.S. (2006, March 7). *The size and characteristics of the unauthorized migrant population in the U.S.: Estimates based on the current population survey*. Pew Hispanic Center. Retrieved from http://www.pewhispanic.org/files/reports/61.pdf

Scherrer, J. (2012). The United Nations Convention on the Rights of the Child as a policy and strategy for social work action in child welfare in the United States. *Social Work, 57*(1), 11–22.

Schooling, N. (1965). Report on the school social work project. Singapore: The Singapore Children's Society and The Singpaore Association of Professional Social Workers.

Stiglitz, J. E. (2003). *Globalization and its discontents*. New York, NY: Norton.

Takahama, Y. (2015, June 13). Bukatsudo shienin no haichi kentou "Team Gakkou" kosshian [in Japanese]. *Asahi Shinbun*. Retrieved June 20, 2015, from http://www.asahi.com/articles/ASH6C4PPJH6CUTIL02H.html

Tan, L. (2001). The development of education in Singapore since independence: A 40-year perspective. Singapore: National Institute of Education. Retrieved 5 June, 2016, from http://siteresources.

worldbank.org/INTAFRREGTOPEDUCATION/Resources/444659-1204656846740/4734984-1204738243676/Session15-ProfLeoTan-OverviewofSingaporesMilestoneReforms.pdf

Tan, W. S. (2009). *Education in Singapore: Special needs*. Singapore: Singapore Infopedia, Singapore Government. Retrieved March 22, 2015, from http://eresources.nlb.gov.sg/infopedia/articles/SIP_1600_2009-10-31.html

*There is need for psychologists at schools: An interview with a school psychologist*. (2013, July 31). Retrieved from http://news.day.az/society/419673.html

Toyama, H. (2011, February 27). *Poverty experienced by children and their families and support for them: What is seen in school social work practice*. Paper presented at the symposium "Issues Around Child Poverty Support System": The 6th Forum of the JSSW [in Japanese]. Retrieved from http://www.jssw.jp/event/doc/forum/forum_2011_02.pdf

United Nations Educational, Scientific, and Cultural Organization. (2011). *World data on education 2010–2011* (7th ed.). Retrieved from: http://www.ibe.unesco.org/fileadmin/user_upload/Publications/WDE/2010/pdf-versions/Azerbaijan.pdf

United Nations Office of the High Commissioner for Human Rights. (2008). *Convention on the Rights of the Child*. Retrieved from http://www.ohchr.org/en/professionalinterest/pages/crc.aspx

Villarreal Sosa, L. (2011). *Mexican origin students in the borderlands: The construction of social identity in the school context*. Doctoral dissertation. Available from ProQuest Dissertations and Theses database (UMI no. 3472970).

Villarreal Sosa, L. (2013). *Evaluation of the project: Developing a model for cooperation between LA and NSA in introducing foster care and family support services*. Unpublished report.

## CHAPTER 16

# CONCLUSION

*The Future of the Profession*

## LAURA HOPSON, CYNTHIA FRANKLIN, AND MARY BETH HARRIS

School social workers are operating in a landscape that is rapidly evolving. New standards for accountability and evidence-based practice are creating new roles for social workers and challenging them to be more diligent about their effectiveness. Changes in special education, technological advances, new policies that guide educational practice, and shifting trends in health and mental health care are constantly impacting the work of school social workers (Hopson, Franklin, & Harris, 2015; Kelly, Raines, Stone, & Frey, 2010). Schools are also undergoing important changes to their norms and values, which profoundly impact school social work. New policies, heightened expectations for accountability, and changing demographics have driven many of these changes. Schools are microcosms of broader societal issues (e.g., racism, political ideologies, and religious diversity). As a result, today's school professionals have to be prepared to respond to the complexities and differences in our society and to stay abreast of the changes in educational policy and practice (Kelly et al., 2010). In addition to summarizing key themes and issues discussed in the preceding chapters, this chapter helps guide current school social workers to prepare themselves for their future and to advocate for the specialization of school social work.

## EVIDENCE-BASED PRACTICE

Evidence-based practice (EBP) as a process that integrates the use of research evidence with clinical expertise has become the standard for the provision of school social work services and, especially, for mental health interventions in school. As the EBP process is used more in education, it becomes important for school social workers to understand how to improve their work using the best scientific knowledge and clinical decision-making protocols (Franklin & Hopson, 2004). In addition, school social workers' skills are needed to assist school personnel in identifying research-based practices, especially those related to behavioral and mental health, and facilitating their implementation.

Unfortunately, as Thompson and Piester explain in Chapter 10, research-based interventions have often been applied inconsistently in schools. A host of challenges get in the way of EBP, including time constraints, inadequate training and other resources, and competing priorities (Franklin & Hopson, 2004). Frey and associates (2013) propose that social workers employ a Motivational Interviewing Navigation Guide (MING), which consists of a five-step process to motivate teachers to implement research-based interventions. Through the use of motivational interviewing techniques, social workers can serve as coaches to build motivation among teachers and other school personnel for adopting new interventions and to guide them through implementation (Frey et al., 2013).

It will also be increasingly important for social workers to demonstrate that they are using research-based practices and that the practices and programs they select fit the culture, values, and needs of the school and the community (Franklin & Hopson, 2004). This means that social workers need to continue to educate themselves about research on interventions relevant for working with children in schools. They will need to seek professional development opportunities to learn to implement research-based practices. They will, then, need to be skilled in evaluating the effectiveness of their interventions and demonstrating their outcomes in terms that are valued by the school community (Bowen, 2013).

## DATA-INFORMED DECISION-MAKING AND ACCOUNTABILITY

As discussed previously, an EBP process requires that social workers document their effectiveness. In addition, current policies such as No Child Left Behind (NCLB) require schools to provide data demonstrating students' academic success. Schools are threatened with a loss of federal funding when they are unable to show evidence of progress. At the same time, schools must provide data on student needs and academic outcomes in order to compete for private grants and foundation funds to provide services to students. In this climate, school social workers must demonstrate how their services clearly lead to improved educational achievement (Bowen, 2013). Toward this end, school social workers will need to provide meaningful data demonstrating the effectiveness of their services to school administrators. This means connecting social work services to educational outcomes, such as attendance, grades, behavior, and retention. A framework for evaluating school social work services and connecting those services to educational outcomes—such as that provided in Chapter 14 by Lindsey, Sabatino, Smith, and Kunkel—will be important for promoting the role of school social workers as integral to the mission of the school.

School social workers will need to help school stakeholders understand the importance of their role by periodically providing data-informed reports to administrators, school personnel, parents, and community stakeholders, including civic organizations, service providers, and the media. These reports need to explain the outcomes of social work services and their linkages to academic success. In addition to creating a variety of formats that are receivable by a wide diversity of audiences, they will need to explain clearly how these results will improve academic outcomes as well as have other beneficial outcomes for the students, the school, and the community (Bowen, 2013).

## PROVISION OF MENTAL HEALTH SERVICES

Social workers will continue to serve a central role in the provision of school mental health services, although the context in which those services are provided has changed considerably (Atkins, Hoagwood, Kutash, & Seidman, 2010). Recent efforts to improve mental health service provision, including the President's New Freedom Commission on Mental Health (2003), propose the expansion of mental health services for children in schools. Similarly, NCLB calls for linking school systems with mental health systems in order to provide students with better access to mental health services (Atkins et al., 2010; No Child Left Behind Act of 2001, 2002). These reform efforts open up additional opportunities for school social workers to increase their leadership in providing school mental health services as well as developing innovative ways to link families with mental health services in the community.

As Ray and Ahlman explain in Chapter 11, mental health services will often need to be delivered in the context of multidisciplinary teams. The wide range of mental health services models includes community schools, student assistance programs, school-based health centers, and comprehensive school mental health programs (Kelly et al., 2010). All of these models require collaboration among several service providers (Kelly et al., 2010). The trend toward greater use of integrative health care models in the community also emphasizes the importance of transdisciplinary teamwork between school social workers and other health care professionals, with school mental health services often serving as a hub for these services.

Despite mounting evidence that providing mental health services to students is a foundation for success in school, barriers to mental health service delivery that persist in the school include an insufficient number of school-based social workers or other mental health professionals, inadequate training and funding, stigma associated with mental health services, and competing priorities such as improving test scores (Reinke, Stormont, Herman, Puri, & Goel, 2011). School social workers will need to advocate for school-based and school-linked mental health services by providing evidence linking the need for these services with the educational mission of the school.

School social workers will need to continue to work closely with professionals within and outside the school as partners in the delivery of school mental health interventions. In doing so, school social workers will need to define their roles explicitly with other professionals whose roles also involve the provision of mental health services (Streeter & Franklin, 2002). For example, school social workers can articulate their unique contribution to supporting students by fostering linkages with families and resources in the community. School social workers are well-equipped to conduct outreach to families, including visits to families in their homes. Given the complex needs of many students and families, school social workers' skills in finding resources and connecting families with those resources provide critical support that can enhance the services of any mental health professional. These are tasks that other school personnel are not trained to engage in. Because of school social workers' unique knowledge of the influence of environment on development, these resources will have tangible benefits for students (Franklin & Streeter, 2002). School social workers need to continue to clearly articulate the unique supports they bring to the table. This role clarification may help other student support professionals understand how school social work services complement, rather than duplicate, other services provided to students and families.

## INTERPROFESSIONAL PRACTICE

As discussed previously and also by Teasley and Richard in Chapter 3, collaborative skills will remain essential to the future of school social workers. A prerequisite for success in a school setting is the ability to work with groups of people toward goal-setting, problem-solving, and accountability (Kelly et al., 2010). For example, school social workers often operate as members of interprofessional teams that work together to formulate plans for prevention of behavioral and academic problems, as is often the case for teams overseeing the implementation of schoolwide interventions such as Positive Behavioral Interventions and Supports (PBIS), which is discussed in more depth later. Interprofessional teams also develop intervention plans for students who are already experiencing difficulty. One example is a team working to develop an Individual Education Program (IEP), which often includes the student's parent or guardian, a school administrator, a school social worker, and other relevant school personnel. The IEP team is responsible for developing a plan of services for the student based on a functional behavioral assessment (FBA) of the student and participating in IEP meetings (Geltner & Leibforth, 2008).

Although social workers have always been relationship specialists, the future of the profession will be firmly grounded in relationship management that requires social workers to maintain a network of diverse constituencies both within the school and in the community (Hopson & Lawson, 2011). Linkages are increasingly important to schools as educators struggle to meet the complex needs of students that may stretch the available resources. More than ever, schools rely on the active involvement of families, businesses, and community-based service providers to create the conditions for academic success (Hopson & Lawson, 2011). For example, school data may suggest that it is important to create schoolwide tier 1 approaches to prevent problems such as bullying, violence, and self-harming behaviors (Hopson, MacNeil, & Stewart, 2015). The school social worker may be called on to engage the family and other professionals in the community to create approaches that will prevent these problems as well as intervene in individual cases in which the problems have occurred. Today's school social workers may also be called on to consult with teachers and community professionals and to develop and foster the professional and personal relationships necessary to directly influence others to support a student's academic success (Franklin & Hopson, 2004). Relationship management, communication skills, and networking are the essential abilities that each professional needs to foster linkages between the school, home, and community (Streeter & Franklin, 2002).

## SOCIAL WORK ETHICS AND
## THE SCHOOL ENVIRONMENT

School social workers are in a unique position to provide ethical leadership to the school because of the shifting norms in society and ideological conflicts that may occur between the school's constituencies (Powell, Harris, & Franklin, 2015). The National Association of Social Workers' (NASW, 2008) code of ethics continues to shape the future roles of school social workers, as discussed in Chapter 8 by Raines and Dibble. Guided by the code of ethics, social workers have responsibilities that are unique among other professionals in the school regarding client rights to confidentiality; consent issues of cultural, racial, and economic diversity; notification; and a commitment to respect different values, preferences, and lifestyles (Powell et al., 2015). Such a commitment requires the ability to mediate between groups of people and a resolve to advocate for the best interests of students and families, even if that is not the prevailing popular perspective. School social workers need to be committed to the essential practice skill of advocacy derived from the code of ethics in order to create schools with shared respect for all students and families.

## SPECIAL EDUCATION

Although many school social workers spend a large percentage of their time with students who are enrolled in special education, their role with these children has evolved. In addition to being part of the interdisciplinary team formulating a student's IEP and FBA, school social workers often carry an important advocacy role with students and families involved in special education (Allen-Meares, 2008). In this regard, they serve a critical function in advocating for parents to be involved in co-planning service delivery. In Chapter 7, Powers, Swick, and Cherry emphasize the continued disparities by race and socioeconomic status in special education. Thus, a vital role for school social workers will be to voice with increasing volume their concerns when students of color are placed disproportionately into special education (Allen-Meares, 2008). This advocacy aligns with social work's code of ethics on cultural and social diversity, which requires that social workers act to prevent discrimination on the basis of race, ethnicity, national origin, color, sex, sexual orientation, gender identity or expression, age, marital status, political belief, religion, immigration status, or mental or physical disability (NASW, 2008). This definition of advocacy requires that school social workers examine whether school norms and values create or reinforce inequities in access to educational opportunities. Allen-Meares proposes that school social workers can lead schools in integrating culturally grounded assessments in the schools by choosing assessment instruments that have demonstrated cultural sensitivity. School social workers will also need to integrate the culture and values of students and their families into discussions about resources and supports that may be helpful (Powell et al., 2015).

As a member of the school-based IEP team who will advocate for additional services, the school social worker needs to be well-versed in the policies guiding special education services. A school social worker's ability to advocate effectively for students and families hinges on the ability to use a strengths-oriented perspective, thereby avoiding stigma and potentially harmful labels while helping parents and teachers find hope for change even in the bleakest of situations.

## DEMOGRAPHIC SHIFTS IN SCHOOLS AND WORKING WITH DIVERSE GROUPS

The 2010 Census indicated that the US population is becoming increasingly diverse in terms of race and ethnicity (Grieco et al., 2012). During the past decade, the percentage of White students enrolled in public schools decreased from 59% to 51%. In contrast, the percentage of Hispanic students enrolled in public schools increased from 18% to 24%, and these trends are expected to continue during the next decade (Kena et al., 2015). More than 12% of the population in the United States in 2010 were not US citizens at birth, and approximately 25% of children have a parent who was born in another country. These numbers have increased steadily since the 1970s (Grieco et al., 2012). In response, social workers will need to constantly update their knowledge of diverse cultures in order to support these students, and there will be an increasing need for social workers who are bilingual (Engstrom, Piedra, & Min, 2009). Thus, school social workers will need to be competent in working with an increasingly diverse student population (Powell et al., 2015).

Children of color are more vulnerable to school failure and punitive disciplinary actions (e.g., suspensions) than White children (Planty et al., 2008; Skiba et al., 2011). Stone and Moragne-Patterson discuss the racialization of achievement gaps and discipline in Chapter 5. With a strong social justice perspective, school social workers must be a critical voice in the effort to reduce these disparities. Instead of attributing these disparities to characteristics of students, social workers are trained to determine when the school and larger environment reinforce these inequities (Blanchett, Mumford, & Beachum, 2005; Shealey, 2006). In Chapter 4, Teasley and Richard discuss strategies for school social workers to promote educational equity.

In addressing social inequities in schools, school social workers can intervene by modeling culturally grounded strategies to school staff, students, and families (Hecht & Krieger, 2006). They will need to advocate for instructional methods, communication strategies, and disciplinary approaches that are sensitive to the needs and values of students and their families (Banks & Banks, 2010). Social workers should advocate for making a curriculum more culturally competent by integrating the observable characteristics (e.g., language) and deeper influences, such as values and norms, of a given culture (Hecht & Krieger, 2006). In Chapter 15, Sosa and colleagues extend this discussion to social work practice internationally.

# WHOLE SCHOOL/SCHOOL ENVIRONMENT INTERVENTIONS

In order to create a school environment that provides students with equal access to educational opportunities, it will be increasingly important that school social workers intervene at the school level. Response to Intervention and PBIS are interventions categorized as multi-tiered systems of support (MTSS) that are being widely implemented to improve the whole school environment. In fact, many states now require that school-based interventions be implemented within an MTSS framework that provides data-driven feedback in real time for the purpose of improving academic performance and behavior. As discussed by Thompson and Cox in Chapter 9, MTSS addresses the unique needs of students through a tiered framework consisting of three levels of intervention: universal programs that involve teaching skills to all students; selective programs that provide more intensive services for children identified as at-risk for academic and behavioral problems; and indicated programs for students with identified behavioral, academic, or mental health needs that cannot be addressed by universal or selective interventions (Cohen, McCabe, Michelli, & Pickeral, 2009).

Implementing interventions that aim to improve the whole school environment can be resource intensive. If schools do not have the capacity to implement these interventions, there are interventions that target improving key relationships within the school, including school-based mentoring programs that aim to strengthen relationships between teachers and students.

Restorative justice is increasingly being promoted as an alternative to punitive disciplinary practices that may have a disproportionately negative impact on students of color. In addition, traditional discipline practices have been blamed to some extent for criminalizing disciplinary problems in school and resulting in involvement in the criminal justice system for students (González, 2012). Restorative justice presents an alternative through which school social workers could begin to work more collaboratively with students to promote positive behavior and a safe school environment. The approach aims to repair the impact of wrongdoing while reducing risk for further harm and empowering the community to be actively involved in the process of repairing harm (Pavelka, 2013). Techniques commonly employed include peer mediation, through which students mediate conflicts between other students; peer accountability boards, in which a board of other students, the victim, and the perpetrator process the impact of an incident on the victim, determine accountability, and develop a plan for the perpetrator; conferencing, which typically involves a larger group of individuals (e.g., families and friends) who are also affected by the incident and a facilitator who helps the group formulate a plan; and circles, which typically involve an even larger group of constituents by including community members as well (Pavelka, 2013).

School social workers should become involved, if they are not already, in implementation of comprehensive school reform efforts, which will require clear and consistent expectations for students, parents, and teachers. Close collaboration among school support personnel and strong partnerships between schools and families are the foundation for this work and match the skill set of school social workers. Thus, they will have an important role to play in creating the conditions for these large-scale interventions by establishing the necessary linkages within and outside the school building (Hopson & Lawson, 2011).

## TECHNOLOGY IN EDUCATION AND ITS IMPACT ON SCHOOL SOCIAL WORK SERVICES

So far, many of the school social worker roles that have been discussed have focused on providing "high touch" skills to human encounters. Along with these encounters, technology will continue to play a growing role in schools and in the provision of school social work services (Lindsey & White, 2007). It is increasingly essential for social workers to understand and be able to use technological resources and advances while at the same time maintaining their investment in human capital. A valuable example of this is using technology as an efficient and effective tool to collect and report program information. Another example is the use of interactive software as part of direct service and clinical intervention. An increasing number of interventions are being offered online in platforms that allow social workers to provide services to students and families who would have difficulty accessing these services in person. Although the research on these online interventions is somewhat new, they are demonstrating promising results and will likely play a larger role for social work practice in the future (Hopson, Wodarski, & Tang, 2015).

Perhaps most notably, school social workers must stay current on how students are using technology, both at school and at home. Facebook and other social media are increasingly important to students, as are devices such as smartphones and iPads. The use of instant messaging, for example, is a means for students to spontaneously communicate and socialize with peers (Lindsey & White, 2007). Although these media are also used in teaching, they enable students to be perpetually in contact with one another. In the same way, it is also important for school social workers and other professionals to harness the possibilities that social media provides instead of maintaining resistance to new technology. Technology can be used to stay in contact with students and to respond immediately to concerns through emergency alert systems in which student can report issues that need to be addressed. For example, SOS (Signs of Suicide) is a school-based suicide prevention program that relies on communication among students to identify those in need of intervention. The program is innovative in its focus on peer intervention in which youths are taught to intervene when a friend is exhibiting signs of depression and suicide and to alert adults in the school about the friend's need of help (Aseltine & DeMartino, 2004). Because students will likely use their cellular phones to alert others, school personnel should establish criteria for the appropriate and timely use of these types of communications.

Technology can be used to help students, but it can also be a source of problems, as is noted in the trend toward cyberbullying. Incidents of cyberbullying have included hurtful and/or private information being posted on the Internet, harassing text or instant messages and e-mails, and being excluded online (US Department of Education, 2013). Because cyberbullying is not limited to the school building or the school day, it can be particularly harmful. Students may feel that they have no way to escape the harassment. As a result, students victimized by cyberbullying are more likely to report skipping school and carrying a weapon to school than are students who have not been bullied online (Ybarra, Diener-West, & Leaf, 2007). Other issues with social media include Internet sexual solicitation of children and youth and unwanted exposure to sexual material online, which was reported by 25% of youth aged 10–17 years in a nationwide survey (Mitchell, Finkelhor, & Wolak, 2003).

There is little research on the effectiveness of approaches to prevent cyberbullying or online harassment. However, the prevalence of cyberbullying indicates that it should be an important part of schoolwide bullying prevention programs. Recommendations for school social workers include helping districts develop clear policies prohibiting the use of computers or other technologies at school to harass or bully others (Kowalski, Limber, & Agatston, 2008).

## ADVOCACY AND POLICY INTERVENTIONS

School social workers tend to spend less of their time on advocacy and policy interventions than they do on micro-level interventions. However, political advocacy can be essential for effective social work practice because federal and state policies may determine whether social work interventions are likely to have any meaningful impact on youth outcomes.

The Individuals with Disabilities in Education Act (IDEA) and NCLB are policies that have shaped the way services are provided to students. IDEA requires schools to provide any supports needed to ensure that a child with special needs has the same educational opportunities as any other child. These supports may include counseling services, speech therapy, psychiatric services, school health services, and school social work services (Kataoka, Rowan, & Hoagwood, 2009; US Department of Education, 2004).

The NCLB Act of 2001 aims to improve student outcomes through consistent standards across schools, districts, and state departments of education. It calls for results-oriented accountability (as driven by standardized achievement tests) and the use of effective, research-based teaching strategies (NCLB, 2002).

A key shortcoming of IDEA and NCLB is that they focus only on improving dynamics within the school building. These strategies are unlikely to be sufficient for affecting meaningful improvement for students facing complex, multisystemic problems, including poverty-related stressors (Hopson & Lawson, 2011). For these students, policies will need to acknowledge and address the dynamics in students' homes and neighborhoods, as well as in their schools, to create the conditions for academic success. School social workers should have influence when districts formulate these policies for the next reauthorization of the Elementary and Secondary Education Act, the formal name for NCLB.

In Chapter 6 on education policy, Brake and Roth highlight four additional education policies that impact school social work practice: (1) the 2010 Common Core Standards and the integration of social–emotional learning; (2) the federal 2014 School Discipline Guidance Package and the challenges of violence, trauma, and the school-to-prison pipeline; (3) the 2012 Deferred Action for Childhood Arrivals (DACA) and increasing access to higher education for undocumented youth; and (4) the 2013 Safe Schools and Improvement Act and the potential antidiscrimination protections for transgender youth. Knowledge of these policies is essential to the future of school social work, and social workers will need to stay attuned to the changing landscape of educational policy.

School social workers have an important role to play in the implementation of new policies, such as those outlined previously. Parents may need support in navigating these new policies and understanding their rights. School personnel may also need assistance in understanding the implications of these new policies for their work with students. For example, social workers can provide leadership in integrating social–emotional learning into the curriculum, as Johnson and McKay-Jackson discuss in Chapter 12. Addressing the many non-academic barriers to learning, including the need for mental health services, poverty-related stressors, and unsafe neighborhoods, is a critical foundation for the success of any new educational policy. School social workers can advocate for policies that convey a more holistic understanding of children such that students' social and emotional health could be emphasized alongside academic outcomes. School social workers will also be important in ensuring educational policies are implemented in ways that involve the family and attend to the child's overall health and well-being, in addition to improving academic outcomes.

## CONCLUSION

The themes in this book transverse changes in society, the educational system, and the roles of the professional school social worker. Social workers are tasked with meeting people where they are in their environment with the aim of improving their social functioning. For this reason, the work of the school social worker is interconnected with people and their social contexts. The knowledge, values, and practice skills of school social workers continue to evolve within the changing landscape of public education. Educational institutions are going through mass restructuring and are constantly impacted by the shifting norms, political movements, and changes in society. This book provides a preparation for key changes and emphasizes the essential skills of the school social worker, including the ethical decision-making required for successful practice.

Among the important changes are the new standards for accountability and evidence-based practice that are creating new roles for social workers and challenging us to be more diligent about our effectiveness. In addition, there are significant changes in special education, technological advances, new policies that guide educational practice, and shifting trends in health and mental health care that shape school social work practice, along with increasingly diverse populations and complex social problems. The success of the school social work profession hinges on school social workers' understanding of human change processes and the nature of systems that constantly change and shape the future.

## REFERENCES

Allen-Meares, P. (2008). Assessing the adaptive behaviors of youths: Multicultural responsibility. *Social Work, 13*(4), 307–316.

Aseltine, R. H., & DeMartino, R. (2004). An outcome evaluation of the SOS suicide prevention program. *American Journal of Public Health, 94,* 446–451.

Atkins, M. S., Hoagwood, K. E., Kutash, K., & Seidman, E. (2010). Toward the integration of education and mental health in schools. *Administration and Policy in Mental Health, 37*(1–2), 40–47. doi:10.1007/s10488-010-0299-7

Banks, J. A., & Banks, C. A. M. (2010). *Multicultural education: Issues and perspectives* (7th ed.). Hoboken, NJ: Wiley.

Blanchett, W. J., Mumford, V., & Beachum, F. (2005). Urban school failure and disproportionality in a post-Brown era: Benign neglect of the constitutional rights of students of color. *Remedial and Special Education, 26*(2), 70–81.

Bowen, N. K. (2013). Using data to communicate with school stakeholders. In C. Franklin, M. B. Harris, & P. Allen-Meares (Eds.), *The school services sourcebook* (2nd ed., pp. 889- 902). New York, NY: Oxford University Press.

Cohen, J., McCabe, L., Michelli, N. M., & Pickeral, T. (2009). School climate: Research, policy, practice, and teacher education. *Teachers College Record, 111,* 180–193.

Engstrom, D. W., Piedra, L. M., & Min, J. W. (2009). Bilingual social workers: Language and service complexities. *Administration in Social Work, 33,* 1–19.

Franklin, C., & Hopson, L. M. (2004). Into the schools with evidence-based practice. *Children & Schools, 26*(2), 67–70.

Frey, A. J., Lee, J., Small, J. W., Seeley, J. R., Walker, H. M., & Feil, E. G. (2013). The Motivational Interviewing Navigation Guide: A process for enhancing teachers' motivation to adopt and implement school-based interventions. *Advances in School Mental Health Promotion, 6*(3), 158–173.

Geltner, J. A., & Leibforth, T. N. (2008). Advocacy in the IEP process: Strengths-based school counseling in action. *Professional School Counseling, 12*(2), 162–165.

González, T. (2012). Keeping kids in schools: Restorative justice, punitive discipline, and the school to prison pipeline. *Journal of Law & Education, 41*(2), 281–335.

Grieco, E. M., Acosta, Y. D., de la Cruz, G. P., Gambino, T., Larsen, L. J., Trevelyan, E. N., & Walters, N. P. (2012). The foreign-born population of the United States. Washington, DC: US Census Bureau.

Hecht, M. L., & Krieger, J. K. (2006). The principle of cultural grounding in school-based substance use prevention: The Drug Resistance Strategies Project. *Journal of Language and Social Psychology, 25,* 301–319.

Hopson, L. M., Franklin, C., & Harris, M. B. (2015). Social work in schools. In E. Schott & E. Weiss (Eds.), *Social work practice in health, mental health and communities: A meta-framework for micro, mezzo, macro and global action.* Thousand Oaks, CA: Sage.

Hopson, L. M., & Lawson, H. (2011). Social workers' leadership for positive school climates via data-informed planning and decision-making. *Children & Schools, 33*(2), 106–118.

Hopson, L. M., Wodarski, J., & Tang, N. (2015). The effectiveness of electronic approaches to substance abuse prevention for adolescents. *Journal of Evidence-Based Social Work, 12*(3), 310–322. doi:10.1080/15433714.2013.857178

Kataoka, S. H., Rowan, B., & Hoagwood, K. E. (2009). Bridging the divide: In search of common ground in mental health and education research and policy. *Psychiatric services, 60*(11), 1510–1515.

Kelly, M. S., Raines, J. C., Stone, S., & Frey, A. (2010). *School social work: An evidence-informed framework for practice.* New York, NY: Oxford University Press.

Kena, G., Musu-Gillette, L., Robinson, J., Wang, X., Rathbun, A., Zhang, J., . . . Dunlop Velez, E. (2015). *The condition of education 2015* (NCES 2015–144). Washington, DC: US Department of Education, National Center for Education Statistics. Retrieved July 14, 2015, from http://nces.ed.gov/pubsearch

Kowalski, R. M., Limber, S. P., & Agatston, P. W. (2008). *Cyberbullying: Bullying in the digital age.* Malden, MA: Blackwell.

Mitchell, K.J., Finkelhor, D., & Wolak, J. (2003). Victimization of youth on the internet. *Journal of Aggression, Maltreatment & Trauma, 8*(1/2), 1-39.

National Association of Social Workers. (2008). *Code of ethics of the National Association of Social Workers.* Retrieved from https://www.socialworkers.org/pubs/code/code.asp

New Freedom Commission on Mental Health. (2003). *Achieving the promise: Transforming mental health care in America. Final report* (DHHS Publication No. SMA-03-3832). Rockville, MD: US Department of Health and Human Services.

No Child Left Behind (NCLB) Act of 2001, Pub. L. No. 107–110, § 115, Stat. 1425 (2002).

Pavelka, S. (2013). Practices and policies for implementing restorative justice within schools. *Prevention Researcher, 20*(1), 15–17.

Planty, M., Hussar, W., Snyder, T., Provasnik, S., Kena, G., Dinkes, R., . . . Kemp, J. (2008). *The condition of education 2008* (NCES 2008-031). Washington, DC: US Department of Education, Institute of Education Sciences, National Center for Education Statistics.

Powell, T., Harris, M. B., & Franklin, C. (2015). The design of social work services: Responding to needs of culture, race, gender, language, and sexual orientation. In P. Allen-Meares (Ed.), *Social work services in schools* (7th ed.). Boston, MA: Pearson.

Reinke, W. M., Stormont, M., Herman, K. C., Puri, R., & Goel, N. (2011). Supporting children's mental health in schools: Teacher perceptions of needs, roles, and barriers. *School Psychology Quarterly, 26*, 1–13.

Shealey, M. W. (2006). The promise and perils of "scientifically-based" research for urban schools. *Urban Education, 41*(1), 5–19.

Skiba, R. J., Horner, R. H., Chung, C.-G., Rausch, M. K., May, S. L., & Tobin, T. (2011). Race is not neutral: A national investigation of African American and Latino disproportionality in school discipline. *School Psychology Review, 40*(1), 85–107.

Streeter, C. L. & Franklin, C. (2002). The changing environment of social work practice in schools. In Roberts, A. R. and Greene, G. J. (Eds.) *Social Worker's Desk Reference.* NY: Oxford University Press.

US Department of Education. (2004). *Individuals with Disabilities Education Improvement Act of 2004.* Retrieved September 15, 2011, from www2.ed.gov/policy/speced/guid/idea/idea2004.html

Ybarra, M. L., Diener-West, M., & Leaf, P. J. (2007). Examining the overlap in internet harassment and school bullying: Implications for school intervention. *Journal of Adolscent Health, 41*, S42-50.

# Supplemental Ethical Standards for School Social Work Practice[1]

## INTRODUCTION

School social workers use a wide range of evidence-based strategies to ensure that students are in the classroom physically and mentally ready to learn. They utilize a strength-based approach that views students and organizations as parts of systems. The functioning of and relationships within and between systems are enhanced to improve student learning. School social workers go into the greater community to engage families and community organizations to create better outcomes for students (e.g., increased academic achievement, safety, attendance, and social–emotional–behavioral functioning).

The National Association of Social Workers (NASW) *Code of Ethics* is the primary ethical guidance for social workers, including school social workers, but social workers may use ethical standards from other related professions for ethical guidance (NASW *Code of Ethics*, p. 3). Additional guidance is provided in the NASW *Standards for School Social Work Services*.

The School Social Work Association of America (SSWAA) developed an *Ethical Guidelines Series* that addresses issues related to school social work practice in host settings, group work, and the privacy of minor students.

Other sources that informed the development of these supplemental ethical standards include federal law (Family Educational Rights and Privacy Act, Individuals with Disabilities Education Act, Protection of Pupil Rights Amendment), *Principles for Professional Ethics* (National Association of School Psychologists, 2010), *Ethical Standards for School Counselors*

---

1. This appendix is reproduced with permission from the Midwest School Social Work Council. (2015). *Supplemental ethical standards for school social work practice*. Lexington, KY: Author.

(American School Counselor Association, 2010), and *Ethical Decision Making in School Mental Health* (Raines & Dibble, 2011).

These supplemental ethical standards build on the values, principles, and ethical standards articulated in the NASW *Code of Ethics*. They (1) specifically address issues critical to school social work practice but not addressed in the NASW *Code of Ethics* and (2) are in addition to and do not in any way supplant the NASW *Code of Ethics*. Issues addressed include responsibilities to clients and stakeholders, parent rights and participation, collaborative decision-making, sharing and protecting confidential information, differential treatment of minor students, consent for services, advocacy, knowledge of laws and school district policies, assessment for school-based services, contributions to the profession, and ethical decision-making.

Definitions are included to provide a common understanding of terms used (page 4).

Special gratitude is extended to the hundreds of school social workers who reviewed these beliefs and supplemental ethical standards in small groups and offered consensus feedback to shape them to reflect the reality of school social work practice. In addition, feedback from the School Social Work Association of America (SSWAA) and the American Council for School Social Work (ACSSW) helped shape the final version.

## BELIEFS

1. When children are young, their parents exercise control over decisions that affect their lives. As they grow older, youth begin to exercise more independent judgment and to make choices and decisions separate from their parents.

2. Parents have rights, roles and responsibilities in relationship to their children. Their ability to exercise and fulfill these rights, roles and responsibilities are [sic] enhanced by knowledge and understanding of their children's activities and needs. School social workers, absent information to the contrary, believe parents seek to act in the best interests of their children.

3. Minor students have the right to indicate assent or dissent to specific school-based services and activities, consistent with their respective age, development, decision-making ability, and understanding of the proposed services and activities.

4. Children and adolescents vary widely in their maturity and skills related to decision-making, coping, and problem-solving. Some may be affected by substance abuse or disabilities or may struggle with challenges to their mental health. Mindful consideration of these and other factors is necessary to achieve outcomes that are in the best interests of students and other stakeholders.

5. School district employees and officials have a responsibility to act in the best interests of students (both individually and collectively) while they are entrusted into their care.

6. A fundamental responsibility of schools and other educational programs is to help prepare children and youth for their adult lives following graduation. Schools are structured and protected environments in which students gradually develop more autonomy as they move through preschool, elementary, middle, and high school. A student's developing autonomy is supported and enhanced in the social worker–client relationship

when the NASW Ethical Standards of Self-Determination (1.02), Informed Consent (1.03), and Privacy and Confidentiality (1.07) are honored by the school social worker.

7. School social workers are educators, as well as social workers. School social work interventions provide both social–emotional–behavioral and educational benefits to students.

# SUPPLEMENTAL ETHICAL STANDARDS FOR SCHOOL SOCIAL WORK

## ETHICAL RESPONSIBILITIES

1. School social workers have a primary ethical responsibility to students and secondary ethical responsibilities to other stakeholders.

## STUDENT AUTONOMY AND PARENT INVOLVEMENT

2. School social workers encourage the participation of parents in decisions that affect their children and strive to empower parents with the knowledge and skills to act in the best interests of their children.

3. School social workers support the developing autonomy of students as they mature from childhood to adolescence to adulthood and utilize a collaborative decision-making process, consistent with students' age, development and mental health.

4. School social workers seek to balance (1) the legal and ethical rights of students to privacy, confidentiality and self-determination; (2) school social workers' primary responsibility to promote the well-being of clients; and (3) the rights of parents to be informed of and provide consent for activities in which their minor children are involved. School social workers share the limits of privacy, confidentiality, and self-determination with students and parents initially and, as needed, throughout the social worker–client relationship.

## CONFIDENTIALITY

5. School social workers take appropriate and necessary proactive and reactive measures to protect the confidentiality of students and families, including, but not limited to, in individual and student group social–emotional–behavioral interventions.

6. School social workers share information about students and families only with professional colleagues who need this information to provide instruction or services, consistent with state and federal statutes and local school district policy. See definition of "legitimate educational interest" (page 4).

## CONSENT FOR SERVICES

7.  School social workers obtain active or passive consent to provide services to students consistent with state and federal statutes and local school district policy and practice. However, some services may not require prior consent, including, but not limited to, building team services (e.g., consultation, progress monitoring, and classroom observations) and immediate interventions to address health and safety emergencies. School social workers may provide services to mature minor students without active consent from parents where legally permissible and consistent with local school district policy and practice. Age, development, mental health, disabilities and the presenting issue(s) are all considered when determining if a student has the capacity to assent to services without prior active consent from a parent.

## ADVOCACY

8.  School social workers advocate for the rights of students and families in school and community settings.

## KNOWLEDGE OF LAWS AND POLICY

9.  School social workers are knowledgeable about (1) state and federal laws and local school district policies related to the delivery of school social work services and (2) authoritative sources from which to obtain additional information when questions arise.

## EVIDENCE-BASED PRACTICE

10. School social workers utilize reliable and valid screening and assessment instruments and strategies that (1) they are competent to utilize, (2) are appropriate for the student(s), and (3) achieve the purpose(s) of the screening or assessment.
11. School social workers (1) utilize available evidence-based strategies and programs, (2) analyze available data to guide their practice, and (3) regularly evaluate their practice to improve services.

## CONTRIBUTIONS TO THE PROFESSION

12. School social workers contribute to the profession in a variety of ways. Examples include (1) educating others about how school social work services contribute to student success, (2) mentoring practicum students and school social workers new to the profession, and (3) joining and actively supporting state and national school social work professional associations.

## ETHICAL DECISION-MAKING

13. School social workers utilize ethical decision-making processes to help manage ethical predicaments in the best interests of clients and stakeholders, such as proposed by Raines and Dibble (2011).
    1. Know yourself and your professional responsibilities.
    2. Analyze the predicament.
    3. Seek consultation.
    4. Identify courses of action.
    5. Manage clinical concerns.
    6. Implement the decision.
    7. Reflect on the process.

# DEFINITIONS

Definitions designated with an asterisk below are in whole or part from *Ethical Decision Making in School Mental Health* by Raines and Dibble (2011) published by Oxford University Press.

Assent *—A minor's affirmative agreement to participate in an activity or service. This is usually accompanied by the express permission of parents.

Autonomy—The ability and freedom to select and take responsibility for one's own actions.

Active consent (school context)—The practice of providing a school-based program, service, or activity only after parents have been notified and given prior written consent.

Belief—Something one accepts as true or real; a firmly held opinion or conviction (Oxford Dictionary).

Client *—The person who knowingly enters into a fiduciary relationship with a professional. Clients may be voluntary or involuntary, but they should normally be aware that they are the recipients of professional services unless they have some type of cognitive disability resulting in loss of awareness (e.g., traumatic brain injury).

Confidentiality *—Information that is communicated to another with the understanding that the disclosure is not meant to be shared with others.

Legitimate educational interest—Public school districts and other educational agencies receiving funds from the US Department of Education are to ensure that only employees and other school officials with a legitimate educational interest obtain information from a student's education records (34 CFR 99.31(a)(1)(ii)). While this term is not defined in statute or regulation, a common standard applied to determine if a school district employee or other official has a legitimate educational interest in information from a student's education records is: Does the person need the information in order to fulfill her or his professional responsibilities? In conjunction with NASW Ethical Standard 1.07 Privacy and Confidentiality, the same standard can be applied to information school social workers possess that is not part of a student's education records.

Mature minor—A young person who has not reached majority age but whose maturity is such that he/she demonstrates the ability to interact on an adult level for the purposes of understanding and consenting to services that do not necessarily require parental consent.

Minor *—Someone who has not yet reached legal maturity, either through the age of majority or emancipation.

Parent—A parent of a student and includes a natural parent, a guardian, or an individual acting as a parent in the absence of a parent or a guardian (34 CFR 99.3).

Passive consent (school context)—The practice of notifying parents of the availability of a school-based program, service, or activity that is available to students with direction to parents regarding whom to contact at school if they have any questions or wish to opt their children out of the program, service, or activity.

Privacy *—The right or value to maintain personal control of one's belongings, body, decisions, information, and thoughts against unauthorized intrusions by others.

School district official—A contractor, consultant, volunteer, or other party to whom an agency or institution has outsourced institutional services or functions (34 CFR 99.31(a) (1)(i)(B)).

Self-determination *—The autonomy to make decisions and choose a course of action so long as there is no infringement on the rights of others to do the same.

Stakeholders *—Parties with a vested interest in a decision because they are affected by the outcome. The client is the primary stakeholder, but there are many others that have a stake in the conclusion (e.g., parents and other family members, school administrators, teachers and other professional colleagues, and community-based professionals, including child welfare or juvenile justice workers and community-based mental health therapists).

# REFERENCES

American School Counselor Association. (2010). *Ethical Standards for School Counselors.* Alexandria, VA: Author.

Belief [Def. 1]. (n.d.). In *Oxford Dictionary Online.* Retrieved December 12, 2013, from http://www.oxforddictionaries.com/us/definition/american_english/belief

Dibble, N. (2011). Minor students' rights to confidentiality, self-determination, and informed consent in Wisconsin. In N. Dibble (Ed.). *Wisconsin School Social Work Practice Guide.* Madison: Wisconsin Department of Public Instruction.

Frey, A., & Lankster, F. (2008). *School Social Work in Host Settings.* Columbia, SC: School Social Work Association of America.

National Association of School Psychologists. (2010). *Principles for Professional Ethics.* Bethesda, MD: Author.

National Association of Social Workers. (2008). *Code of Ethics.* Silver Spring, MD: Author.

National Association of Social Workers. (2011). *The Legal Rights of Students.* Washington, DC: Author.

National Association of Social Workers. (2011). *NASW Standards for School Social Work Services.* Washington, DC: Author.

Olson, A. (1998). *Authoring a Code of Ethics: Observations on Process and Organization.* Retrieved August 9, 2012, from the Illinois Institute of Technology Center for the Study of Ethics in the Professions website: http://ethics.iit.edu/research/authoring-code-ethics

Raines, J. (2008). *School Social Work and Group Work*. Columbia, SC: School Social Work Association of America.

Raines, J., & Dibble, N. (2011). *Ethical Decision Making in School Mental Health*. New York: Oxford University Press.

Strom-Gottfried, K. (2008). *The Ethics of Practice with Minors: High Stakes, Hard Choices*. Chicago: Lyceum Books.

US Government Printing Office. (2010, July 1). Family Educational Rights and Privacy, 34 CFR Part 99. Retrieved July 31, 2012, from http://www.gpo.gov/fdsys/pkg/CFR-2010-title34-vol1/pdf/CFR-2010-title34-vol1-part99.pdf

US Government Printing Office. (2010, July 1). Student Rights in Research, Experimental Programs and Testing, 34 CFR Part 98. Retrieved August 13, 2012, from http://www.gpo.gov/fdsys/pkg/CFR-2010-title34-vol1/pdf/CFR-2010-title34-vol1-part98.pdf

Wisconsin Department of Public Instruction. (2013). *Consent and Notification in a Multilevel System of Support (Response to Intervention): Frequently Asked Questions & Definitions*. Madison, WI: Author.

Wisconsin Department of Public Instruction. (2012). *Pupil Services Professions Ethical Standards Cross-Reference*. Madison, WI: Author.

# Supplemental Ethical Standards for School Social Work Practice: Background Information

## WHY WERE THE *SUPPLEMENTAL ETHICAL STANDARDS FOR SCHOOL SOCIAL WORK PRACTICE* DEVELOPED?

There are two primary reasons why the *Supplemental Ethical Standards for School Social Work Practice* were developed:

1.  Although the NASW *Code of Ethics* is the primary source of ethical guidance for all social workers, it has long been recognized that the *Code* does not address some issues of significant importance to school social workers. The SSWAA *Ethical Guidelines Series* (2008) was created to address issues related to practice with minors, group work, and practice in a host setting. The NASW *Standards for School Social Work Services* (2012) provide additional guidance that goes beyond the NASW *Code of Ethics*. Although both of these resources are informative, they do not carry the weight and authority of ethical standards endorsed by the profession. Furthermore, the *Supplemental Ethical Standards for School Social Work Practice* provide critical new direction not addressed in any of these documents.

2.  Response to Intervention (RTI) is fast becoming the norm in public schools, and school social workers must be full participants in its provision. RTI involves a variety of activities and practices to support students' academic and behavioral success, including (1) high-quality, evidence-based instruction and practices; (2) screening and progress monitoring; (3) brief to intensive interventions; and (4) data-based decision-making. The result is a wide range of different kinds of instruction and services for many, if not most, students designed to match their respective learning needs within the general education classroom, small groups, and individualized programs.

The RTI process cannot function well if active consent is sought from parents for every instructional modification or different activity for each and every student. Inherent in the RTI process is the necessary capacity to respond quickly and efficiently when students fail to make adequate progress, regardless of whether they qualify for a formal program or services (e.g., special education). The National Association of School Psychologists (NASP) recognized this in its 2010 revision to the NASP *Principles for Professional Ethics* that sought to ensure that school psychologists were full participants in the RTI process by specifically describing circumstances when school psychological services may be provided without parental consent. The American School Counselor Association's (ASCA) *Ethical Standards for School Counselors* are silent on the need for active parent consent for services. Specifically, use of passive consent is the norm because the student's right to school counseling services is considered to take precedence over the parent's right to provide active consent to services.

School social workers must be able to participate in the RTI process within their respective schools and districts on a level playing field with school psychologists, school counselors, and other educators. The school social work profession simply cannot afford to have school administrators favor other professions over school social work because the latter has greater restrictions on its ability to work with students.

Parents both explicitly and implicitly authorize their children to be involved in a wide range of school activities when they enroll their children in school. Some instruction and services are provided to all students (or all students in particular grades or groups), whereas other instruction and services are available based on student needs or student and parent preferences. A review by the Wisconsin Department of Public Instruction (2013) found few federal requirements for active parental consent when alternative instruction and services are provided to students. They are summarized in *Consent and Notification in a Multilevel System of Support (Response to Intervention): Frequently Asked Questions & Definitions*, which can be accessed at http://rti.dpi.wi.gov/files/sped/pdf/rti-consent.pdf.

*Merricken v. Cressman* (1973) is commonly used to caution against the use of passive consent as a method of ensuring parents are fully informed of and agree to their children's participation in different school services. The federal Protection of Pupil Rights Amendment (PPRA, 1978) specifically addressed the concerns raised in this court case and controls in this area because of its later passage date. Importantly, the PPRA does not require active consent for behavioral health screening or social–emotional–behavioral counseling, unless students are required to participate.

# HOW WERE THE *SUPPLEMENTAL ETHICAL STANDARDS FOR SCHOOL SOCIAL WORK PRACTICE* DEVELOPED?

An initial draft of the *Supplemental Ethical Standards for School Social Work Practice* was created in summer 2012 using the following resources as guidance:

- NASW *Code of Ethics*
- NASW *Standards for School Social Work Services*
- SSWAA *Ethical Guidelines*
- Family Educational Rights and Privacy Act (FERPA)

- Protection of Pupil Rights Amendment (PPRA)
- Individuals with Disabilities Education Act (IDEA)
- NASP *Principles for Professional Ethics*
- ASCA *Ethical Standards for School Counselors*
- *Ethical Decision Making in School Mental Health* (Raines & Dibble, 2011)

During the next 2 years, this working draft was shared with many groups of school social workers who reviewed the beliefs and ethical standards in small groups and provided highly specific, written consensus feedback. Participants indicated their level of agreement or disagreement with each item on a 5-point Likert scale and provided specific suggestions for revisions. Feedback was reviewed after each session for themes, and indicated changes were made in the working draft. Each subsequent group then reviewed a version that was a successively closer approximation to the eventual current document, resulting in a truly practitioner-driven product.

The Midwest School Social Work Council adopted the *Supplemental Ethical Standards for School Social Work Practice* in March 2014 but solicited feedback from SSWAA, ACSSW, and NASW to further refine and improve the document.

# INDEX

Note: Page numbers followed by italicized letters indicate *figures*, *tables*, or *notes*.

CPSIA information can be obtained
at www.ICGtesting.com
Printed in the USA
BVHW050340241220
596413BV00002B/14

9 780190 273842